# NERVOUS SYSTEMS

Edited by Anselm Franke,
Stephanie Hankey, Marek Tuszynski

Haus der Kulturen der Welt
and Tactical Technology Collective
Spector Books

# NERVOUS SYSTEMS

Quantified Life
and the Social Question

## THE PARADOXES OF NERVOUS SYSTEMS

In the past we had problems understanding the world, today we have problems living in the world that we have created. The paradoxes of knowledge have been transformed into the paradoxes of life, or more precisely: we have made them such.

How could this happen? The Haus der Kulturen der Welt's long-term projects, *Anthropocene* and *100 Years of Now*—of which *Nervous Systems* is a part—can be understood as an answer to this question.

With the classic paradoxes, contradictions in thought arise when we attempt to understand reality. This is the case with Zeno's paradox, who theoretically demonstrated that the fleet-footed Achilles was not even capable of overtaking a tortoise. Inviting his listeners to participate in a thought experiment in which the Greek hero gives his opponent a ten-meter head start, Zeno asks what happens when Achilles passes the tortoise's starting point. At this instant the tortoise will have already traveled a certain distance. And so it continues. Accordingly, Achilles can close the gap until it is infinitely small, but can never catch up with his opponent. However, at the same time, all the participants know from experience that Achilles effortlessly overtakes the tortoise.

In today's world we encounter paradoxes both in our thought and in our living environment, which is increasingly permeated by technologies which are themselves a product of our thought. Our environment is progressively shaped by materialized consciousness. This is especially the case with the mechanisms of the digital world, which have begun to fundamentally change our understanding of subject and society.

Initially, the recording of data and its algorithmic processing was designed to improve the lives of individuals and societies, making them easier to organize.

However, by feeding back into every area of life, these systems are now *de facto* shaping life itself. From a means designed to achieve a certain end, namely a better life, the means itself has now begun to dictate what the good life is.

A further transformation has occurred in the factual objectification of subjects. The system records past behavior as objectified data, which is reflected back to the subjects via algorithms to constitute their need worlds. However, because these objectified need worlds influence, in a complex manner, the decision-making processes of subjects, they determine their choices and thus increasingly limit their freedom. The objectified world of data replaces subjective decisions, which in the past were always defined by a certain degree of freedom.

The exhibition and publication project *Nervous Systems* aims to expose the categorical shifts of the digital world and the concomitant interventions into our self-understanding as subject and society by addressing the aforementioned paradoxes. It understands itself as a disruptive factor, scratching the aestheticized surfaces of the brave new digital world, whose role it is to mask the de-humanizing processes of the new world of technology. The goal is to unlearn the learnt in order to make our resocialization as subjects possible.

I would like to warmly thank the project curators: Stephanie Hankey, and Marek Tuszynski from the Tactical Technology Collective, and Anselm Franke, who through this exhibition have succeeded in critically illuminating and questioning the effects of the technological transformations on both our individual and social world by placing them in a broader historical context.

Bernd Scherer,
Director of the Haus der Kulturen der Welt

# NERVOUS SYSTEMS: AN INTRODUCTION

Anselm Franke, Stephanie Hankey, Marek Tuszynski

Can our inner thoughts be transmitted by our eye movements? Can our future actions be predicted by our current behavior? These are the kind of questions explored in Julien Prévieux's film *Patterns of Life*, in which dancers enact the history of human-movement tracking, from early experiments in chronophotography, through activity-based intelligence in today's "war on terror." The answer to these questions is indeed that our movements are tracked, along with our habits, interests, and intentions, which can be measured, calculated, and predicted.

Data transmitted by our everyday communications and movements are captured endlessly by billions of sensors and then stored. Data that we willingly emit in return for efficiency and gain, and yet for what purpose we may not even question, as increasingly it becomes the raw material of a new "social physics."[1] The representative of a major firm of data-brokers prides himself with statements such as, "We know what your propensity is to buy a handbag. We know what your propensity is to go on vacation or use a loyalty card."[2] This vast business of behavioral forecasting means that whatever it is we are likely to do someone has already predicted, and placed a financial bet or a

1 Charged with the promise to reveal the natural laws of social behaviour, the term "social physics" was initially coined by Belgian sociologist and mathematician Adolphe Jacques Quetelet, who first introduced statistical methods to the social sciences in the early nineteenth century. Reviving the promise to reveal the iron laws of society, the new social physics as promoted by Alex Pentland at the Massachusetts Institute of Technology (MIT) or Dirk Helbing at the Swiss Federal Institute of Technology (ETH) Zurich, relies on big data "to build a predictive, computational theory of human behaviour [so that] we can hope to engineer better social systems." See online http://socialphysics.media.mit.edu (accessed 02/20/2016). See also: Alex Pentland, *Social Physics: How Good Ideas Spread—The Lessons from a New Science*, New York 2014; and Dirk Helbing, *Thinking Ahead-Essays on Big Data, Digital Revolution, and Participatory Market Society*, Berlin 2015.

2 See online, https://www.democraticmedia.org/acxiom-every-consumer-we-have-more-5000-attributes-customer-data (accessed 02/20/2016).

categorized heading over our future actions. We are predictable insofar as we conform to the "rational-choice" consumer—the very model on which Cold War economics was built: engineered milieus, in which it is our nerves that act as extensions of data networks, not the other way around.[3] The same technologies are in use by the police and the military in an effort to predict crime and locate the proverbial "needle in the haystack." In the process, new statistical normativity is emerging, flattening and smoothing out our lifeworlds, and singling out any form of dissent. To anticipate and preempt become the guiding cultural logic.

The public debate and discourse on the rise of the data society and digital technologies tends to shift between the utopian and the dystopian, where either vision seems held as a tool of inevitable democratization and de-hierarchization,[4] or as a means for expanding the use of surveillance and deepening relations of exploitation. Nevertheless, shrouded in false myths, both the utopian and dystopian positions provide little by way of orientation. Either they naïvely position technologies and cybernetic thinking outside architectures of power or they are based on false and romantic assumptions of the integrity of the autonomous individual, as if there ever was a *human* that was not shaped, and even brought into being, through *inhuman* tools and machines. In creating the exhibition *Nervous Systems*, we attempt to capture a different and somewhat difficult, "third" ground, but not the one that sees technology as a "neutral" apparatus. Rather, it seems to us that our models of social-ness, and hence the principles on which our societies are built, may be fundamentally at odds with current technological developments. What happens if, the experience of in-

3 Philip Mirowski, *Machine Dreams: Economics Becomes a Cyborg Science*, Cambridge 2002.
4 Nicolas Negroponte from MIT's Media Lab predicted in 1999 that the internet will inevitably "flatten organisations, globalise society, decentralise control, and help harmonise people."

habiting the graph is jarring, or the algorithm is unable to live within the chaos?

We wanted this exhibition to distinguish itself from the wave of recent "Big Data" shows. *Nervous Systems* intends to bring to the foreground the tension between the ideologies and worldviews that are the basis for the current faith in data, and to contrast these with the sense of unease and unrest that emanates from the lived experience. We decided to focus less on quantification as a spectacle of the current information-based technological era and focus more on tracing the histories of certain ways of seeing: grand schemes of bureaucratization, governance of the masses, of the self, bound up with ideas of efficiency, insight, and progress. Our intention has been to acknowledge what has driven the evolution of directing, or piloting, through data. We seek to show how data-processing has not been motivated by advances in technology alone, but how political ideologies, moments in history, and desires for greater control also drove it; and that its realization, at different points during the last hundred years, holds up a mirror to the hopes and fears of that particular time. It is our hope that by reflecting on these grand schemes from different vantage points—the meeting room and the living room, the spreadsheet and the street—there lies the potential to reflect upon what happens when they collide. There is potential to move beyond the current coordinates of the field and to shift the kinds of choices and positions available for reflection.

In the shadow of the Edward Snowden revelations over the past few years, we have seen the rise of data corporations to positions of power previously inconceivable. Along with this, the egalitarian vision of the Information Age and the allure of its alleged ability to empower the individual have come into question, yet with astonishingly limited consequences. That the focus of contemporary public critical debate has been firmly on privacy and state surveillance is partially down to a symptom of the absence of a reflexive language for these other dimensions, where the empowered subject may appear simultaneously as a disempowered object. For what does "privacy" really mean in a context where subjectivity itself occurs in a data-processing environment, where the infamous distinction between personal data and seemingly anonymous metadata is rendered increasingly obsolete? What does privacy mean as it becomes possible to identify someone as easily from "anonymous" data as from a fingerprint or identity card?[5] Through artworks, artifacts, and objects combined in specific constellations, we have tried to move beyond the somewhat restrictive narratives and illuminate aspects that often go unnoticed: the paradoxes and inversions that are part of the current reorganization of society through data-technologies.

*Nervous Systems* illuminates the degree to which we, as selves, as users, as a bundle of technology-aided identity-effects, come to embody the very paradoxes that the new data economies yield. The continuous recording of our "self," social life, and the issues that confront us in daily life are subjected to scrutiny and filtered into patterns, along with the glitches and the anomalies. In targeting potential threats and "unknowns," a process of far-reaching consequences is set in motion, generating effects we have only begun to grasp. In the process, both subjectivity and social relations change fundamentally, while concurrently existing normative patterns and dispositions are reinforced by big-data feedback and personalized "filter bubbles."[6] In targeting users, the system tends to

5 See for example, online http://bits.blogs.nytimes.com/2015/01/29/with-a-few-bits-of-data-researchers-identify-anonymous-people/?_r=0 (accessed 02/20/2016).

6 Eli Pariser, *The Filter Bubble: What the Internet Is Hiding from You*, New York 2011.

mirror existing preferences, while simultaneously and increasingly these identities become effects of technological assemblages. Individuals use these technologies to gain greater personal control and efficiency in their lives, and paradoxically, in the same moment, lose control. As a result, this self-empowerment contributes to a system in which every individual becomes a digit, a dot, a self-entered data point.

The most obvious paradox is that while the personalization of technology makes the world seemingly revolve around the self more and more, the self gets mediated back to us through entirely de-subjectified calculations and statistical medians. Today, individuals are less and less separated from the cumulative data that can be extrapolated from their existence. Thus, as subjects, we find ourselves pulled in two directions at once, both equally unlivable: either, both subjectivity and identity are liquefied and flexible, as in the consumer-producer of neo-liberalism, or identity becomes fixed and disambiguated. We might find ourselves forced to enact both illusions; of self-identity and integrity as well as the prospect that we can transform into anything we want (or that market forces demand of us).

This situates the "self" at a critical junction of conceptual nervosity: the "human" aspect of an increasingly interconnected world enabled by an inhuman communication matrix, and the aesthetics of humanization and animation, which persists on the commercial surfaces of user–machine interfaces, appearing as distractions from this gap. What appear as technologies of recognition, in fact, are technologies of what Kodwo Eshun termed "de-cognition," technologies that are able to frame our cognitive operations without having to engage in the labor of understanding and interpreting, or in engaging with causes, for that matter.

In creating *Nervous Systems*, we also wanted to include explicit aesthetic investigations in order to trace the increasing opacity of authority and ideology, which puts social awareness and the possibility of lasting social mobilization and commitments into enduring crisis. The aesthetic dimension introduces not only the problematic of the type of experience and under what conditions it can be shared, but also tests discourses against sensuous experience in order to produce a mutual challenge, adding ambiguity, complexity, and resistance to the levels of form and language. This helps us to extrapolate alienation and incommensurability from an ideology of accessibility and availability. Furthermore, it is the aesthetic dimension, and sometimes the particulars of art history, that allow us a sort of archaeology of past experience, and hence an understanding of nonlinear historical developments, the vectorial inversions in human–machine interaction and the vast apparatus of quantification, identification, mapping, and standardization, which are at the core of both industrial capitalism and modern statecraft.

We chose to work with the metaphor of the *Nervous System* to give historical, vertical depth to the picture we have of the present. The advantage of this metaphor is that it can always be read in at least two ways, and hence never pretends to offer a stable object or set of facts. This is of great importance for exhibitions in particular, because only when the matter-of-factness of a subject, theme, or thing is *disputed* and *destabilized* can the exhibition become a space of thought that allows art/artifacts to enter into a thematic dialogue, without reducing the former to illustration. The metaphor of the nervous system, because of its ambiguity, forces us to think and seek a position, in order to engage actively in the processes that construct the currently dominant rationality and its evidences.

On the one hand, "nervousness" relates to the insecurity, perhaps even panic, at the heart of the current control framework, of today's "system," the totality of institutions and ideologies that make up the modern nation-state and market. It is a pervasive nervousness: will our systems remain stable? Will they allow us to come to terms with, to control, to contain the forces of chaos, disorder, and the unknown, the ubiquitous real, or imagined, threats? The consequence: paranoia, where "in the eyes of authority—and maybe rightly so—nothing looks more like a terrorist than the ordinary man."[7] "Nervousness" also invokes the possible resistance—of individual bodies, material, and collective realities—to the systems of registration and capture they are subject to, and also signifies any situation in which signifier and signified are out of joint.[8] From within the centered rationality of systems of order, it is the possibility of "re-volution"—the turning-upside-down of relations—that permanently feeds both the nervousness and the often-paranoid logic that these systems employ at their borders—internal and external. The concept also extrapolates the nervousness at the heart of modern classificatory, disciplinary knowledge, the non-identity of social order and practice, of social power and the body, the hysterical epistemic blindness produced by systems of oppression—a nervousness about systemic questions, legitimacy, rationality, that the neoliberal ideology of "smartness" has sought hard to exorcise. Today, this nervousness is most visible in relation to key themes of our time: national security and terrorism, migration and sovereignty, the economy and the financial sector, and food-, energy-, and climate-related security. *Nervous Systems* examines this sense of nervousness and

7 Giorgio Agamben, *What is an Apparatus? And Other Essays*, Stanford, CA 2009.

8 See: Franco Berardi, *The Soul at Work: From Alienation to Autonomy*, tr. Francesca Cadel and Giuseppina Mecchia, Los Angeles, CA 2009.

its relationship to data collection, analysis, and its use, illuminating aspects of its historical development through the past hundred years. Many of these significant developments can be counted together with moments of violence: warfare and the fear of war; or can be bound together with times of crisis and catastrophe, with change sometimes visibly groundbreaking or minute yet accumulative.

On the other hand, the metaphor of the nervous system has been a leitmotiv of progress in the technological era, tracing a genealogy of entanglement between humans and machines. The emergence of a ubiquitous control-framework, which we are seeing today with the "nervous nets" of big data, has its roots, ultimately, in the years during and immediately following World War Two. While the dominant paradigm before then was energy and electricity, after, it was the flow of information in bodies, systems, and circuits. This concept allowed for the creation of analogies between technological networks and biological systems, and implied that biological life and thought were computable and translatable into the same binary operations found in neural networks. It also raised the key problem of control and the nature of the organs of social control, questioning how to separate noise from signal and chaos from order. At the heart of this, was the fundamental belief that uncertainty is an informational problem, that prediction and anticipation could enable the process of governing. While the rhetoric has changed significantly since the era of nuclear stand-offs, the rationalities offered in response to the same challenges have not. When large tech-corporations (i.e. IBM, Hewlett-Packard, and Microsoft) propagate a "smart" future built on their next-generation big-data solutions and networks, projected on a planetary scale, then this is done explicitly to suggest that analysis of networked and real-time data will help to keep chaos, upheaval, and unrest under control, while also sustaining increased corporate profit margins.

"Nervous systems," promising the management of life on both a global and ecological scale, is a solution being built and propagated everywhere, by corporations and public bodies alike.[9] To connect, to communicate, and to make complex networks "smart": there seems to be an overwhelming consensus in the established culture and industry that this is where "progress" lies today. Behind the "smart" slogan lies the integration of humans and machines; the vision of the organic and the technological in mutually enhancing circuits, stabilized by adaptive algorithms. This is the continuation of capitalist modernity's project of "unlimited rationalization," now transformed into a vast project built on seeing our societies and their citizens as systems with feedback loops; worlds that "just need to be better organized," according to Google founder Larry Page. There is a renewed and widespread belief that big data will eventually, finally(!), reveal the laws of human behavior, make political crisis, revolutions, and other forms of political and economic instability predictable, exactly as physics and chemistry predict natural processes. There is a particular rationality at work here, one that operates through correlations and patterns, rather than through cause-and-effect and semantic interpretation.

Today, the framework of control amounts to a vast program designed to redesign our lifeworlds—from the shopping mall to entire cities to our private lives. In a loosening embrace with neoliberal ideology, this framework has transformed economic life and sovereignty, and this changes how, both collectively and individually, we navigate and make sense of the world,

9 See for example online: https://en.wikipedia.org/wiki/Watson_%28computer%29; https://en.wikipedia.org/wiki/CeNSE; http://www.coss.ethz.ch/research/nervousnet.html (all accessed 02/20/2016).

how we experience others and ourselves. In a certain sense, it does bring the world it is modeling into being. Yet, the prophesy is seldom self-fulfilling: the internet-driven "Long Boom," propagated prominently on the cover of *Wired* magazine in 1997,[10] did not bring about global prosperity in the techno-utopistic and libertarian image of Silicon Valley, any more than the "harmonious society" envisaged by Singapore and China,[11] aided by "smart" data-collecting technologies and "total information awareness," is likely to do. Instead, when China announces that it assigns every citizen with a real-time "citizen credit score,"[12] which drops when people or their friends post unauthorized political comments or buy certain goods, the government as caring management (Big Mama) turns straight back into the Orwellian universe.

The data-driven predictions of today are different from the modernist future that was conceived as a planned utopia. These planning utopias were simulations haunted by the specters of authoritarianism and unilateral action, operating on too rough a resolution, and failing to provide the possibility of replying to the structures of which one is part, which is so crucial to self-empowerment and the ecology of social practice. It is as if the perceived enormous currency held by concepts such as "feedback" in the age of cybernetics, and still held for some today, had designs to heal the ills of modernity. As Orit Halpern has pointed out, there is a "strange irony" that in "the martial environments of the World War II laboratory, the critique of modernity—and its horrors—became literally realized as a technical possibility."[13] Today, we increasingly re-

10 Peter Schwartz and Peter Leyden, "The Long Boom: A History of the Future, 1980–2020," *Wired*, 07/01/1997, online http://www.wired. com/1997/07/longboom/ (accessed 02/20/2016).
11 Shane Harris, "The Social Laboratory," *Foreign Policy*, 07/29/2014, online http://foreignpolicy.com/2014/07/29/the-social-laboratory/ (accessed 02/20/2016).
12 See online http://www.computerworld.com/article/2990203/security/aclu-orwellian-citizen-score-chinas-credit-score-system-is-a-warning-for-americans.html (accessed 02/20/2016).
13 Orit Halpern, *Beautiful Data: A History of Vision and Reason since 1945*, Durham, NC 2015, 59.

alize that the "smart" networks, too, are haunted, not by the "old" disciplinary reductionism but also by their own de-politized nature, which allows them to grow unobstructed. In doing so, they create a vast integrated web of technologies designed to integrate humans and machines more and more, and to extract wealth from the most innocuous activity, even, or especially, the "free" time of today's users. We realize that the reduction of democracy to markets, conceived as a permanent referendum, is undermining the public sphere, the nation-state and, in the end, democracy.

The exhibition assembles works by over twenty-five artists, displaying both contemporary and historical pieces. Installed in an architectural "grid," a system of squares is generated by use of metal poles. The reference here is both to today's data-centers, or computer architectures, and to their historical template—the Cartesian grid as an image for the rationalization, abstraction, and reorganization of modern life. Perhaps, in the vein of geographer Derek Gregory, one could perceive the "grid" as the quintessential modern ontological battlefield, as the template for abstraction and factorization, leading to the "weaponized time-geography" of the present day.[14] The "grid" in the exhibition invokes the vast technological "apparatus" in the modern quantified society. According to the philosopher Giorgio Agamben, "subjectivity" is the result of an encounter between "living beings" and the "apparatus"—which he defines, following Michel Foucault, as technologies that possess the power "to capture, orient, determine, intercept, model, control, or secure the gestures, behaviours, opinions, or discourses of living beings."[15] Art, according to the approach of *Nervous Systems*, possesses in turn the power to *release*

14 Derek Gregory, "From a View to a Kill: Drones and Late Modern War," *Theory, Culture & Society*, 28 (2011): 188–215.

15 Agamben, *What is an Apparatus?*, 14.

life from these apparatuses of capture—even if only for moments and in the imagination—thus undoing the current drift toward ever-greater systemic closure. It is in this realm that we can begin to assemble the fragments of lived experience historically, in order to observe the transformations of "the social" in the present, and the frontiers of its subsumption.

By focusing on the entangled construction of bodies, machines, and subjectivities, we looked for artworks that explore the processes of embodiment and the history of the senses and sensemaking; artwork that engages us with what it means and feels like to be a subject within certain systemic parameters. We sought works that employ a stereoscopic view of technology and the human subject, that trace and allegorize the relationship between humans and machines in the production process of capital, and map the advances of capitalism into ever-deeper strata of our social existences. The works in the "grid" oscillate between embodiment and abstraction, between system and subject, between the individual and the "dividual," moving back and forth from systemic backgrounds to human figures. It is in this movement that our understanding opens up to the dimensions of a social, bodily, technological, and political unconscious—exposing yet other dimensions of "nervousness" by strategically displacing signs from what they signify, destabilizing the fiction of a world submerged in the *datum*.

In order to break out of the prevailing, fear-induced sense of systemic closure, it seems to us crucial to posit the body and subjectivity as objects of construction and design, inscribed into emerging socio-technical super-systems. At the same time, however, it seems critical to insist that the language of these super-systems themselves is the product of a dialectics of power and of social struggles. In a constellation of intentionally fragmentary historical narratives and works of art that resist certain desires for representation, we tried to imagine and project a consciousness able to contest the frameworks that condition our choices, and hence our processes of identity-formation today, and instead open up a series of questions. How does the terror of abstraction and quintessentially inhuman quantifications take on visible form again in today's economy of visible selves?[16] How are we to understand the effects of inversions, such as when "abstraction" has transformed the "nature of concretion itself"?[17] What if it is no longer a case of machines built in the image of humans, but rather humans self-adapting to machines; what if humans give in to the mimicry of the normative and the framework that promises recognition?

The exhibition begins with historical references that seek to invoke this crisis within the history of the modern canon: Paul Klee's studies of "individuals" and "dividuals," his leveling of figure into ground and ground into figure, which anticipates the individual as statistical aggregate, less and less separable from cumulative behavioral data; Douglas Huebler's installation, which invited exhibition visitors to trade highly personal secrets with other visitors, made for the 1970's *Software* exhibition; or On Kawara's self-quantifications, in the form of the telegrams he sent to friends stating when he got up, or simply that he was still alive. In the "grid," the legacy of Conceptualism is tested and perhaps re-signified: for was Conceptualism's concern with pure and a-subjective, non-signifying systems of ordering and quantification not an act of critical mimicry of the "totally administered" world and its inhuman quantifications?[18] The collection of historical works hence calls

16 See also: Sven Lütticken, "Inside Abstraction," *e-flux*, 38, 20 (2012), online http://www.e-flux.com/journal/inside-abstraction/ (accessed 02/20/2016).

17 Idem.

18 Benjamin H. D. Buchloh, "Conceptual Art 1962–1969: From the Aesthetic of Administration to the Critique of Institutions," *October*, 55 (Winter, 1990): 105–43.

for a reinterpretation of early Conceptual art's concern with quantification, its "aesthetics of bureaucracy," and the deconstruction of the self in light of current data collection and self-quantification. It also reflects on the ambiguous use of the grid that is common to both high Modernism and Conceptual art: the grid as the ultimate a-subjective, depersonalized "system." Charles Gaines' experiments with the grid at the limits of representation, on the paradoxes of signification and the *impossibility* of a non-subjective, non-expressive aesthetics, today, seems equally to invoke the shifting frontiers between human interpretation and "objective systems." But how does history itself re-signify works of art? Could it be that in retrospect, these works could be seen to *uphold* the very difference between the "known" of the data-map in relation to the "unknown" of an always-contingent reality?

In our selection of contemporary artworks, we avoided *representing* "data," by refraining from *visualizing* its abstract operations as if it were an "object" that one could observe objectively from a safe, external, vantage point. Instead, we wanted to ask how it is possible to grasp the transformations of lived experience in the shifting terrain of human–machine interaction, and its processing of the "known" and the "unknown." We have tried to avoid what we perceived as the *flatness* of the usual representations and visualizations of data; the positivist matter-of-factness that they impose on us. In doing so, we sought artworks that may serve to *re-socialize* these "post-social" rationalities.

Julien Prévieux's film *Patterns of Life* is a central piece in the exhibition: a literal (perhaps "mediumistic") re-translation of abstractions into embodied, concrete, lived, and always-imperfect form. It is a choreographed experiment in embodying the history of quantifying and tracking human movement, extracting objectified patterns that can be recycled to reorganize everything from factory work to shopping malls to counter-terrorism. A choreographic enactment of history such as this brings into view the degree to which, today, the social and the subjective are mapped out as "patterned interaction," rather than through processes of negotiated symbolic meaning. This shift is reflected in the ideology of corporations like Google/Alphabet, which never tire of emphasizing that they are not interested in the content of any online search, but merely in the abstract statistical patterns and the correlations that the searches reveal. *Resocializing*, in this case, means to make the patterns and scripts that we enact and to which we adhere in our everyday lives, explicit—to expose and narrate them so that we may even begin to imagine what resisting subjection might look like.

Like *Patterns of Life*, various other artworks arranged in the "grid" engage with the way the quantification of behavior re-creates our sense of social-ness and transforms our environment, increasingly transforming these into echo chambers. It is by enacting such displacements—as when filmmaker Deborah Stratman superimposes two scenes of paranoiac enactment in *Hacked Circuit*, bringing together psychosis, cinematic construction, and government surveillance—that the works themselves can be seen to perform or represent shifts and glitches in today's cognitive maps. Circumventing the reconciliatory language of "smartness," "real-time feedback," and "sustainability," this insistence on a crisis of cognition brought on by capitalist globalization is, at the same time, an insistence on the non-identity of "map" and "territory," pointing to the ideological character of this reconciliatory rhetoric. As Harun Farocki made painfully clear in his Brechtian depiction of the neoliberal turn in a post-traumatic German society, *How to Live in the FRG*, it is no longer possible to articulate a critique based on a "life" that lies (or is imagined to lie) as-of-yet outside capture. Today, it is no longer possible to speak of "a core of resistance to cultural domestication"[19] or of the body and the senses, somehow, outside acculturation and historical modulation.

Is it even possible to imagine resistance, when the very system that is to be resisted is enacted and embodied by ourselves? This question is at the center of Melanie Gilligan's sci-fi mini-series *The Common Sense*, which takes us into a near future where people wear a prosthesis attached to the roof of the mouth through which emotions and sensations can be felt and monitored by others. This technological enhancement of the "self" amounts to a cybernetic realization of the critique of a (Cartesian) modernity. It exploits the fact that we are constituted, as subjects, through inter-subjective relations and processes of symbolic and emotional "feedback." But the technology development imagined in the film does not lead to emancipation; rather it results in a different form of labor, one that displaces the "social question" while intensifying relations of (self)exploitation. Yet in this imagined future, as in today and yesterday, the social question refers to the system's production of an artificial scarcity and its reliance on disenfranchisement.

In the attempt to account for these inversions, and in order to re-narrate the shifting terrain of quantification and humans and machines, we have added to the artworks on display a further layer of what we called "triangulations"; contributions by media historians and writers. These authors, in response to our invitation to develop a historical sketch from three or more disparate exhibits, have provided us with annotated narra-

19 Susan Buck-Morss, "Aesthetics and Anaesthetics: Walter Benjamin's Artwork Essay Reconsidered," *October*, 62 (Autumn, 1992): 3–41.

tives illuminating a particular aspect of today's "nervous systems," addressing issues such as pattern recognition, the genealogy of quantification, anomaly detection, cartography, and the epistemology of the "nervous" network. These "triangulations," of historical and contemporary documents and reference materials, enter into a direct dialogue with both the contemporary and historical artworks in the "grid." The "triangulations" stage historical and contemporary reference points such that they add up to a scenography of entangled frontiers. Their contributions are reproduced in this publication in full.

Next to "the grid," the exhibition features a second section that brings to life many of these core themes, placing them in the everyday and the recognizable within a live installation by the Tactical Technology Collective, entitled *The White Room*. *The White Room* is an inversion of a major company's sales and training facility, and just as one encounters experts there, equally in the *The White Room* trained experts are on hand. Yet what they have "in store" is not the polished, corporate image that seeks to seduce customers into an Aquarian universe of self-design. Rather, it is a practical yet excavation-based encounter with our everyday devices, with our digital shadows and data aggregates. It is a space in which we learn to de-familiarize ourselves with our familiar technological environment, in which we learn to look beyond the "black mirror" and the way it reflects our "self." The objects, books, artifacts, gadgets, and artworks gathered here offer a rather awkward contemplation on the void of "autonomy" as a disappearing *modus operandi* of political action. It recognizes the autonomous subject within a series of entangled processes of mediation, of "programs" of action, which are as much anticipated as scripted. It is in this realm of mediation and its "programming" in the form of technology, then, where we can also discern the outlines of a crisis of consciousness brought about by capitalist globalization, "algorithmic governmentality," and our participation within it. Ultimately, *The White Room*'s aim is to act as a platform for a discussion on the technology-enhanced "political body," where the way that "faith in data" is currently transforming power and our very understanding of the "political," can be explored. The last section of this publication is devoted to the contents of *The White Room*.

As a collection, the artworks, artifacts, and objects across the "grid" and *The White Room* touch upon a collection of interrelated themes, together reflecting a certain nervosity of both the system and the lived experience within it. The exhibition proposes that there is a certain need for *re-socializing*; meaning, here, the need to work against a blind "faith in data" in favor of a more complex understanding of social mediation and the historical forces that shape subjectivity. The objective is to reflect on the historical role of mass media as phantasmatic screens that paradoxically show what they suppress and hide, as several works in the exhibition make manifest. It means to trace how, according to Jean Baudrillard, "the social" itself, in the transition to a consumer society has disappeared, and "imploded into media."[20] *Re-socialization* could also mean that we have to attempt to undo this disappearance, to insist on bringing the "social question" back into the field of vision, to reflect on the radical forms of exclusion that underpin global capitalism, and the mechanisms by which its symptoms are being imputed and objectified. Cast against the post-social relations generated by data-interfaces, *re-socialization* brings us to a point of re-narration, or re-embodiment. Above

20 See http://networkcultures.org/geert/2015/09/17/interview-with-geert-lovink-on-social-media-the arts/?utm_content=buffer940c1&utm_medium=social&utm_source=facebook.com&utm_campaign=buffer (accessed 02/20/2016).

all, it invites us to undo the paradoxical eclipse of mediation that occurs in data-evidence and its hallucinatory facticity; it allows us to insist on the mediated nature of reality, and question the absence of transparency in mediation, its asymmetries, and the role of power in keeping its anarchic dimensions in check. *Re-socializing* can then assume the form of an archaeology of lived experience, of the transformative encounter with technology. It can force us to test and probe these abstractions for their livability, by engaging in an act of reflexive mimicry.

# ARTWORKS

# LAWRENCE ABU HAMDAN
# *CONTRA DICTION (SPEECH AGAINST ITSELF)*, 2015

Video installation with teleprompter

"Speech is what makes us into political animals": for several years the work of Lawrence Abu Hamdan has focused on the relationship between the voice and the technologies of its capture and assessment, and the ways in which the law increasingly penetrates our bodies by making speech a subject of technoscientific inquiry. In *Contra Diction (Speech Against Itself)*, Abu Hamdan asks what telling the truth might be exactly in times of algorithmic truth-production and mass surveillance. He looks at the contemporary implementation of voice recognition and lie detection technologies and how the self "gives itself away" through speech.

The installation investigates the Islamic practice of *Taqiyya* (ةىقت, literally "fear" or "caution"), portrayed here in a way similar to a glitch or spike in the systems of speech capture. Abu Hamdan studies how *Taqiyya*—a form of religious dissimulation whereby a believer may deny their faith or otherwise commit illegal or blasphemous acts under duress—is used by the Syrian Druze minority under ISIS. As a religious doctrine, the practice began in ninth-century Shi'a communities, then undergoing persecution by the Sunni Islam majority. Syria's Druze community—who practice a syncretistic brand of monotheism based on the teachings of Plato, Aristotle, Socrates, and Middle Eastern mystics and scholars—has undergone forced mass conversion by ISIS. Abu Hamdan suggests that *Taqiyya* may be the one act of barely perceptible resistance the Druze community can offer to Islamic fundamentalism. For him it is an admission that free speech is not about speaking freely, but reclaiming control over the very conditions under which one is being heard.

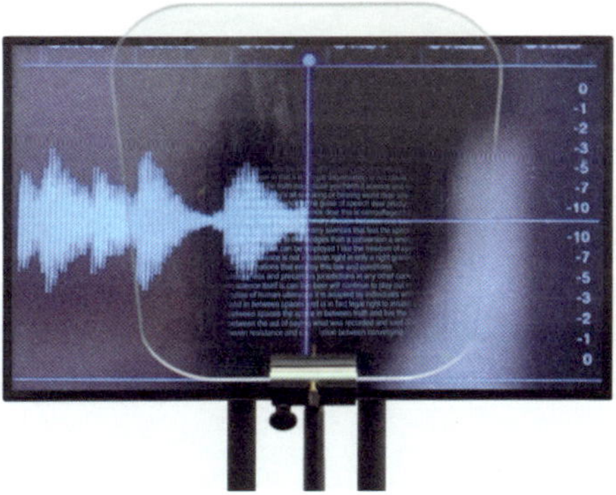

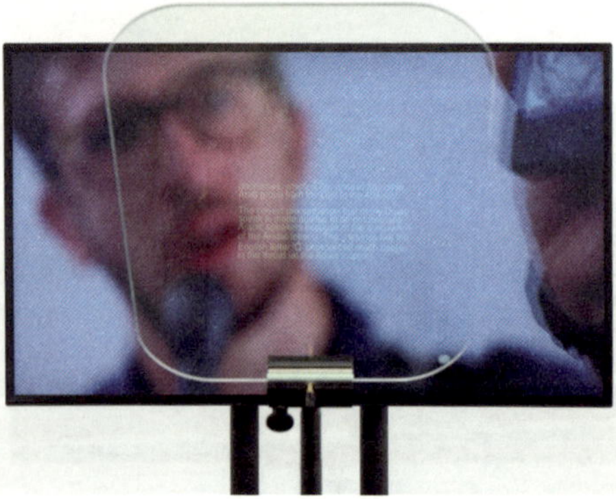

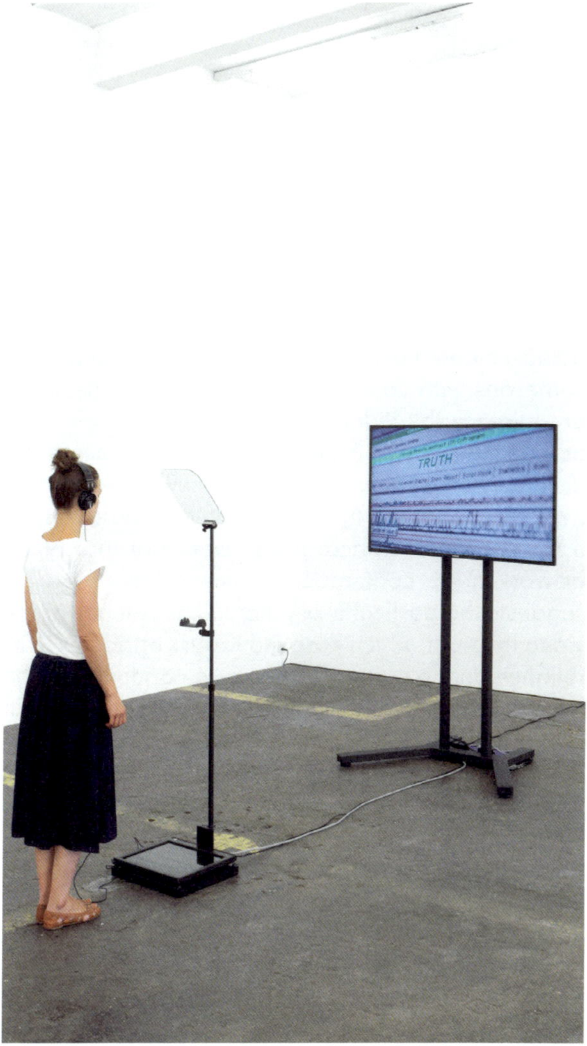
TRUTH

# VITO ACCONCI
# *THEME SONG*, 1973

Video, black and white, sound; 33′15″

Vito Acconci uses video to establish an absurdly intimate relation with his prospective viewer, performing a mediated attempt at seduction. Lying on his apartment floor, his head close to the video camera recording him, Acconci plays a succession of popular rock "theme" songs by the Doors, Bob Dylan, Van Morrison, and others, using their alternately romantic or melancholic lyrics as prompt for an ongoing commentary which mixes blatantly seductive come-ons with confessions about his dire need for an intimacy the video medium is in no position to assuage. Acconci's prattle serves to underscore the distance between himself and the viewer, yet this fact (which Acconci overtly and repeatedly addresses, as if his chosen rhetorical mode were not that of an artwork but a contemporary video-dating service) suggests the particular psychological potency of the video medium, which Rosalind Krauss attributes to its reliance on the human psyche as a conduit, with the body "as it were centered between two machines that are the opening and closing of a parenthesis."

From our contemporary perspective, the aesthetics of Acconci's primitive video set-up appears quaint, even homey, yet this work prefigures the use of digital media as a tool for finding romance and, at a level approaching absurdist theater, engaging the same cognitive logic of mirror neurons that pornography relies on for its titillating effect.

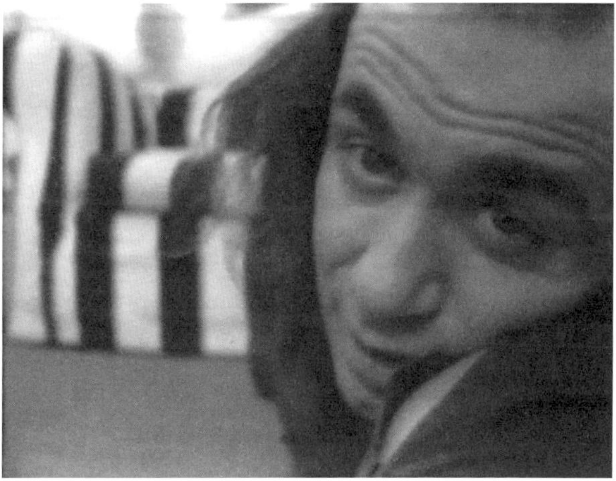

## TIMO ARNALL
## *ROBOT READABLE WORLD*, 2012

Video, color, sound; 5′09″

As the field of robotics and artificial intelligence moves from infancy into early childhood, we begin to confront a basic question: how do robots "see" the world? Timo Arnall's short film is an exploration of precisely this topic, an inquiry into how machines make sense of the world around them. Arnall, a designer, photographer, and filmmaker who is both a developer of emerging technologies while also taking them as subject matter in his creative work, is an internationally recognized researcher with a doctorate in interaction design. Struck by the incidental beauty of the machine-vision experiments he encountered in his professional work, Arnall composed the film as an ode of sorts to this nascent sensorial intelligence, mixing together footage excerpted from thirty-six separate studies.

The visuals are initially mesmerizing, presenting a view of the world imposed on computers by humans—cars moving, people walking, signs passing, and eyes and mouths talking—each shrinking the organic to a single moving data point. The video images, reduced to their simplest form, create an aesthetic that highlights the limitations of the code. What emerges is a world quantified and analyzed through perpetual motion, one where action counts and where the program registers anything it does not recognize as invalid. Throughout the film, we see the machines that we have designed to increase our understanding of the world, reducing what is valid to a pre-defined and primitive form, creating accurate traces and trails, yet stripped of context, nuance, and subtlety.

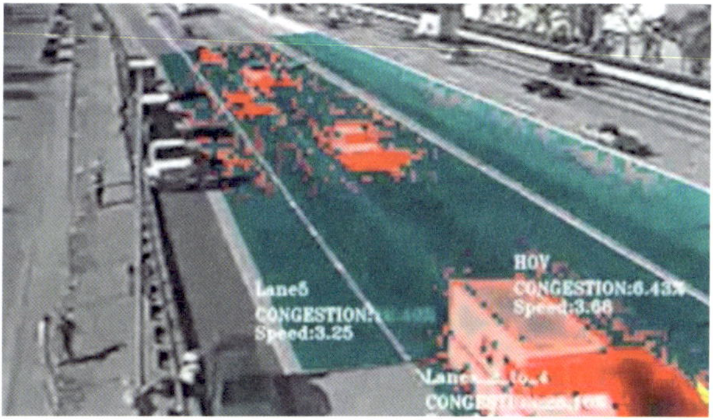
HOV
Lane5
Speed:3.25

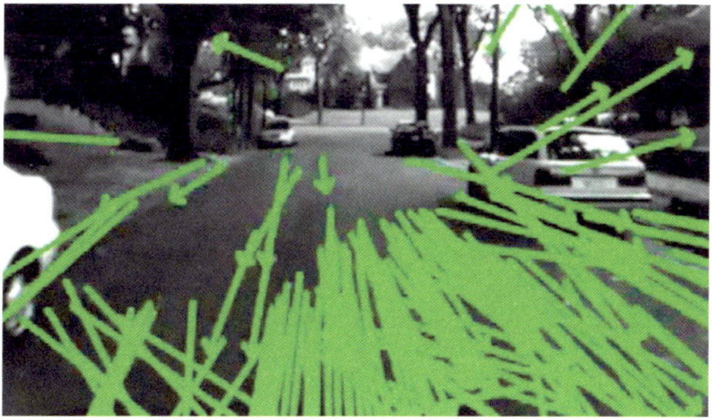

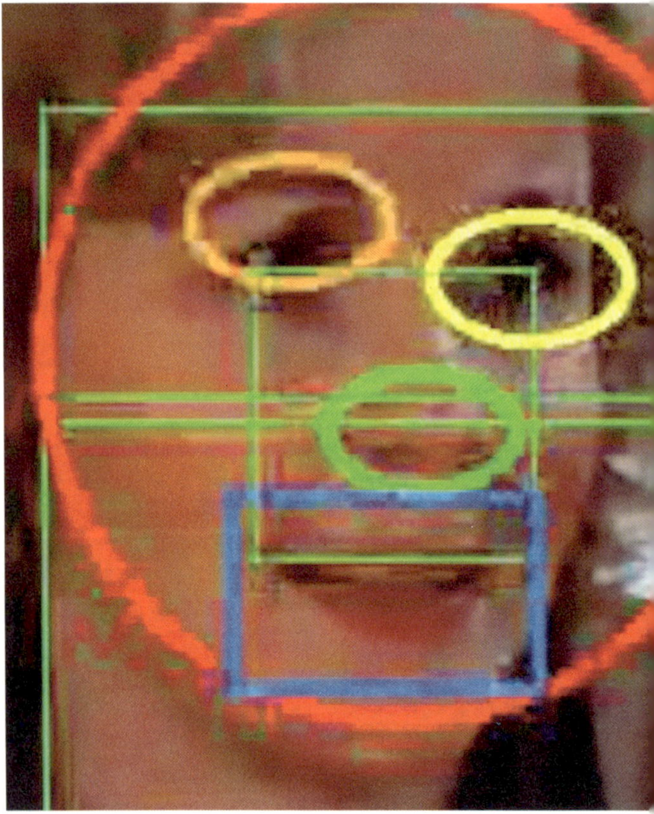

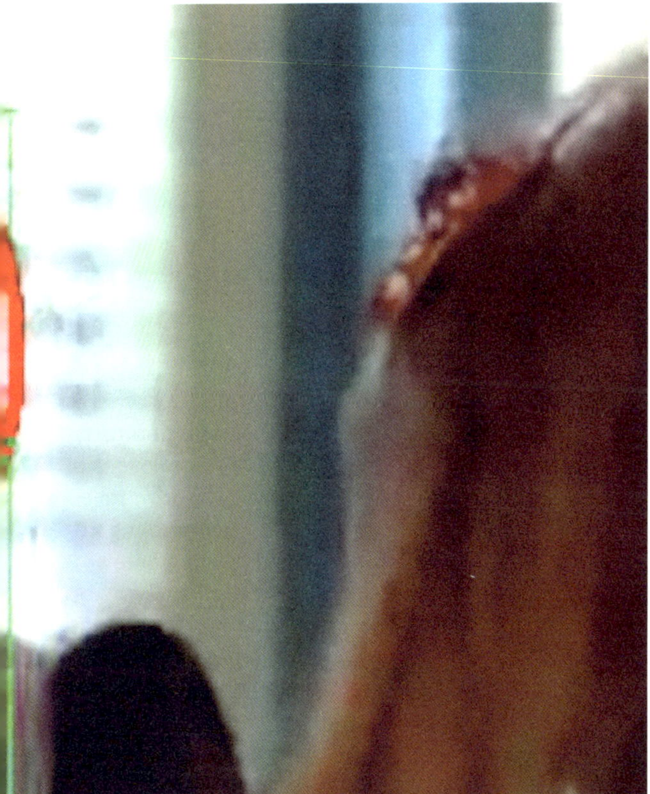

## MARI BASTASHEVSKI
## *SHREDS OF ACCOUNTABILITY*, 2014

16 ready-mades, paper; each 29.7 × 21 cm

*Shreds of Accountability* is the concluding chapter in a four-part series entitled *Empty with a Whiff of Blood and Fumes*. Mari Bastashevski, whose works blur boundaries between investigative journalism and art, is concerned here with the rampant corruption between economic and political elites in the Ukraine, revealed in shredded documents left behind by oligarch Serhiy Kurchenko, a close associate of Ukrainian President Viktor Yanukovych when he fled the country in February 2014, following months of popular protests.

*Shreds of Accountability* documents partial reconstructions of material selected from two caches of documents discovered shortly after Yanukovych's downfall—a large collection of state documents found on the grounds of his private estate, and forty-five large garbage bags recovered after employees of a business center, owned by Yanukovych's ally, failed in their attempts to dispose of the incriminating records. While the first document cache revealed the embezzlement practices of at least ten major Ukrainian corporations managed by state officials, the second contained a mixture of correspondence, transaction details, and photographs of luxury properties and goods—an unintended and unflattering portrait of the Ukraine's ruling elite. Bastashevski's ready-mades, collected by her from these incriminating finds, do not engage in an attempt to fully decipher individual documents, but rather fix them in a partially reconstructed state on monochrome backgrounds of varying colors, thus referring to the activists who labored to reassemble this material in order to make coherent the web of mendacity and deceit characterizing a ruling oligarchy's governance of modern-day Ukraine. The physicality of the activist's labor stands as testament to the challenge of making power accountable—bringing to mind similar processes of digital reconstruction, such as the efforts of the Fraunhofer Institute, through a technology called the ePuzzler, to reconstruct shredded Stasi documents. Bastashevski's visual reflections bring us back to the process of reconstruction, its real dimensions, and the poetics of corrupted information.

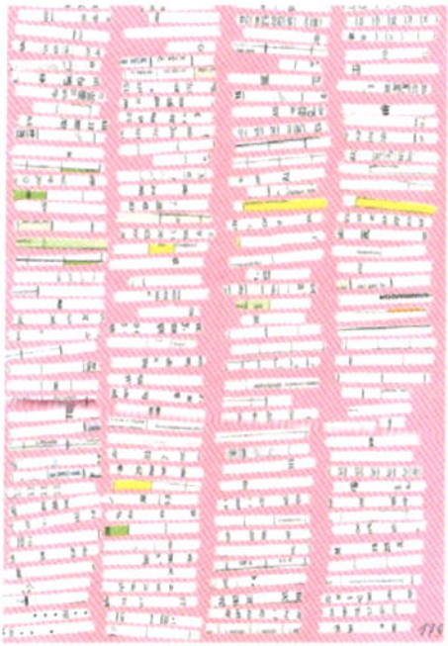

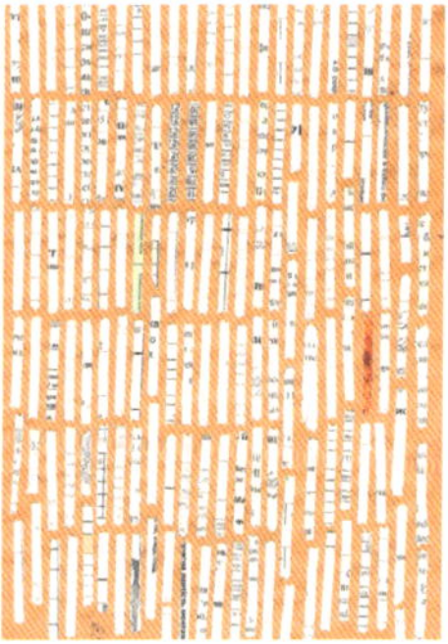

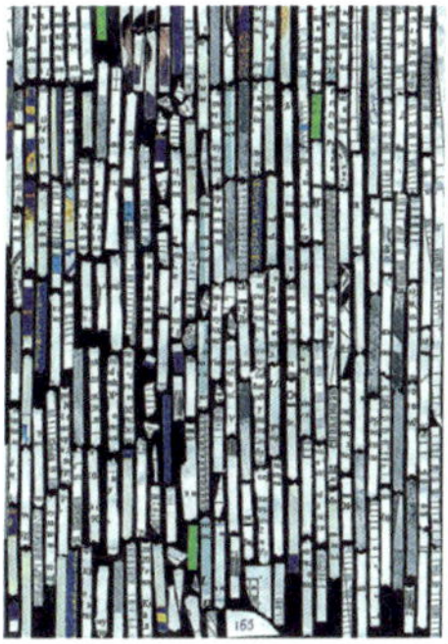

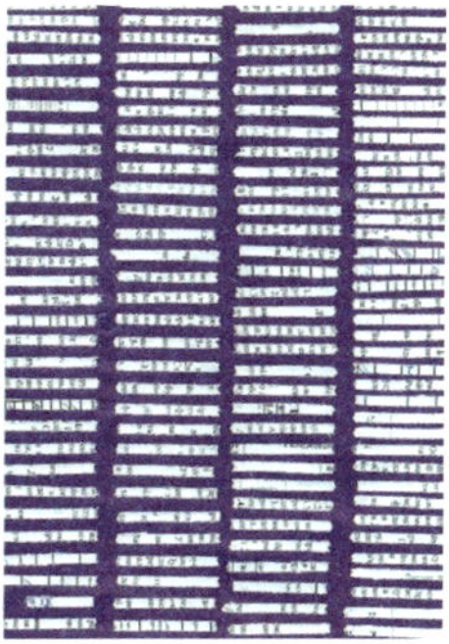

# EMMA CHARLES
# *FRAGMENTS ON MACHINES*, 2013

HD video, color, sound; 17'10"

> *"The economic system of capital, acting as general semiotic cage, forbids the possibility of emancipation from labor, while it simultaneously expands the capability of the general intellect to replace human work with technology."*
> —Franco "Bifo" Berardi[1]

The title of this video references a text by Karl Marx in which he seeks to trace the inversions that mark the relationship between man and machine in the production process of capital. Starting from the division of labor and moving toward greater automation and ever-greater integration of the machine, the text illustrates how the machine ends up no longer as a tool at the hands of the workers, but as an increasingly dominant power that envelops humans, leaving workers increasingly "scattered," and confronting scholars as a condition of "objectified knowledge."

In her video of the same title, Emma Charles portrays the continued logic of these inversions by moving beyond the façades of Lower Manhattan, where it is not humans at work, but computer servers. Indeed, these vast urban computer farms provide the technological infrastructure of much of today's global economy and internet traffic. Charles' camera examines in minute detail the installation processes of server farms within the nineteenth-century infrastructure of Lower Manhattan. As in many cities, entire floors in office towers where white-collar workers once congregated are now inhabited by banks of computers arrayed

1 Franco Berardi, *And: Phenomenology of the End*, Cambridge, MA 2015, 181.

along long corridors, connected to one another by miles of cable. Charles' camera focuses on the contrast between the highly controlled environment server farms require and the antiquated and decaying architectural infrastructure within which they are installed, and on the contrast between the "scattered," marginal human workers that deliver the basic maintenance services to these machines, but are barely noticeable in relation to its scale.

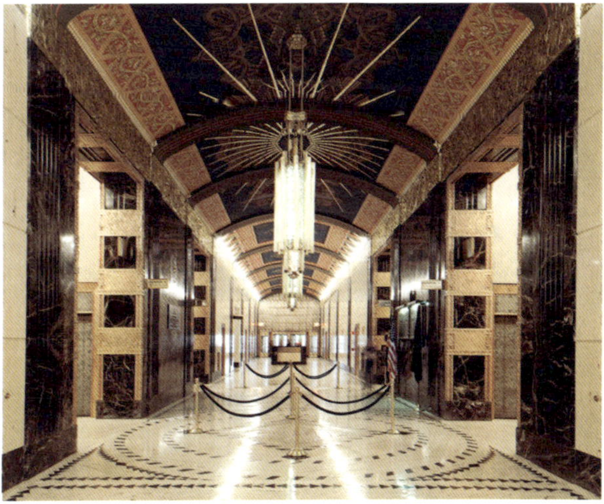

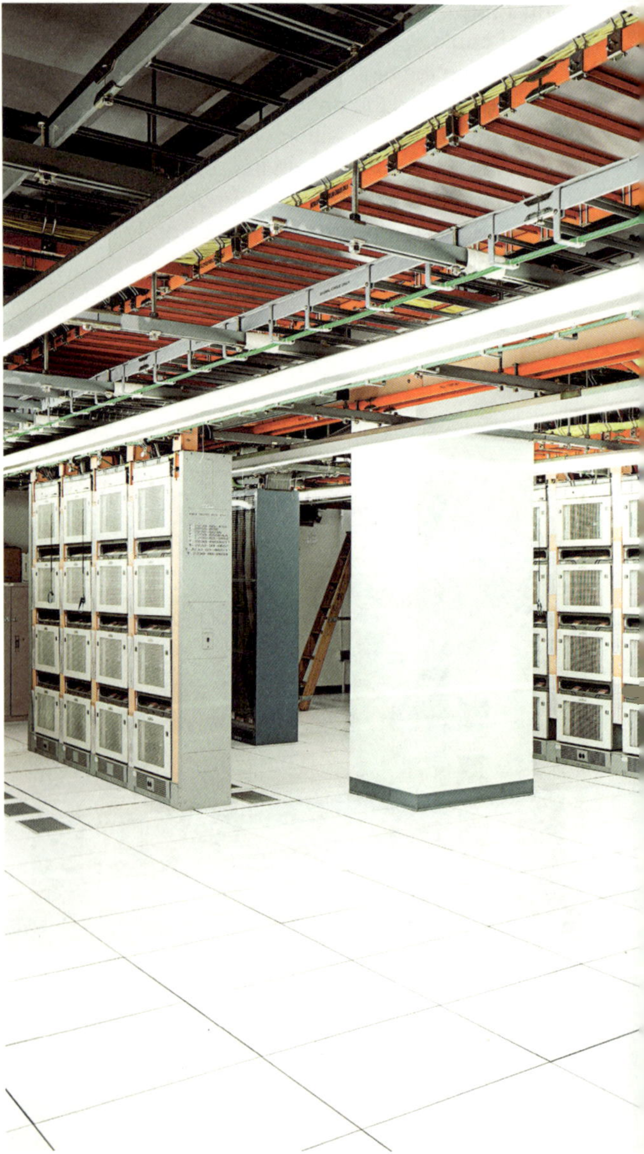

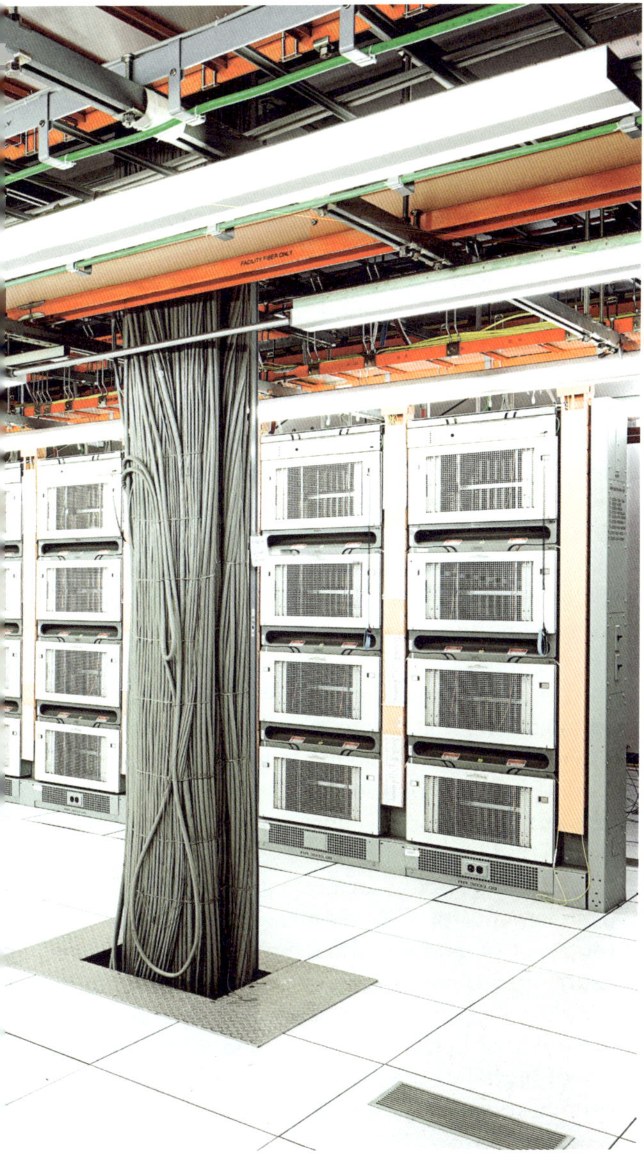
FACILITY FIBER ONLY

# MIKE CRANE
# *CHOICE MODELING*, 2015

Mixed-media installation: video, color, sound; 18′50″, plaster sculpture; 17.7 × 11.3 × 12.7 cm

In his video-work Mike Crane stages a dialogue of sorts between the character of a neuroscientist, performed by an actual neuroscientist, Dr. Aaron Bornstein, and one of his favorite test subjects, who appears both in his actual studies and in the staged variations performed by the actor and musician Beth Griffith. Each character narrates their experience from complimentary subject-positions—the neuroscientist as a researcher and his subject as a professional actor well-versed in the intricacies of human memory and emotion. The neuroscientist for his part is filmed delivering a scripted lecture on neuroeconomics, which uses functional magnetic resonance imagining (FMRI) to study the circulation of blood in the brain while test-subjects are engaged in a variety of decision-making processes. His research is an explicit critique of a premise common in mainstream economics —the assumption that an internal rational economic actor guides human beings to make decisions based on rational choice. He suggests to the contrary that decision-making processes are determined by context and emotional response, and are thus inherently associative and irrational.

These complex ideas are presented not only through the statements of Crane's actors, but in his use throughout of cutaway shots that interfere with the straightforward progression of a discourse, while also grounding the video in the fragmented, associative temporality of human existence; one inimical to the rational model of thought under which economists presume we operate.

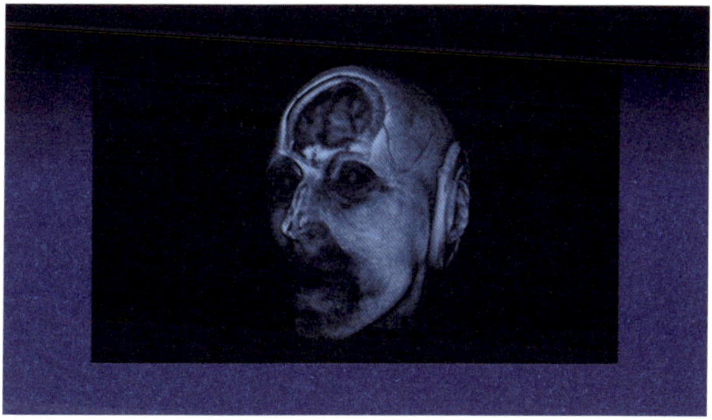

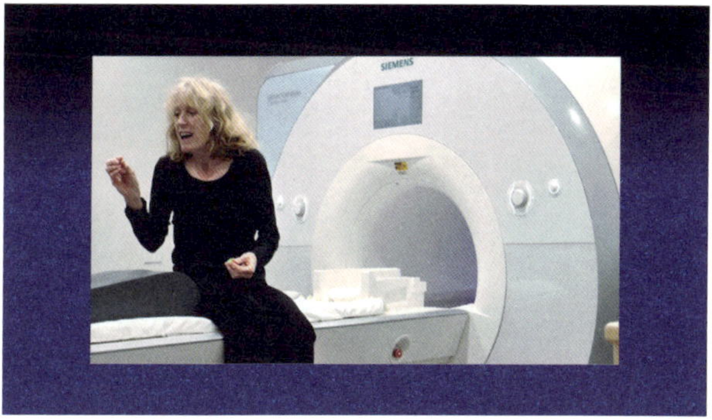
SIEMENS

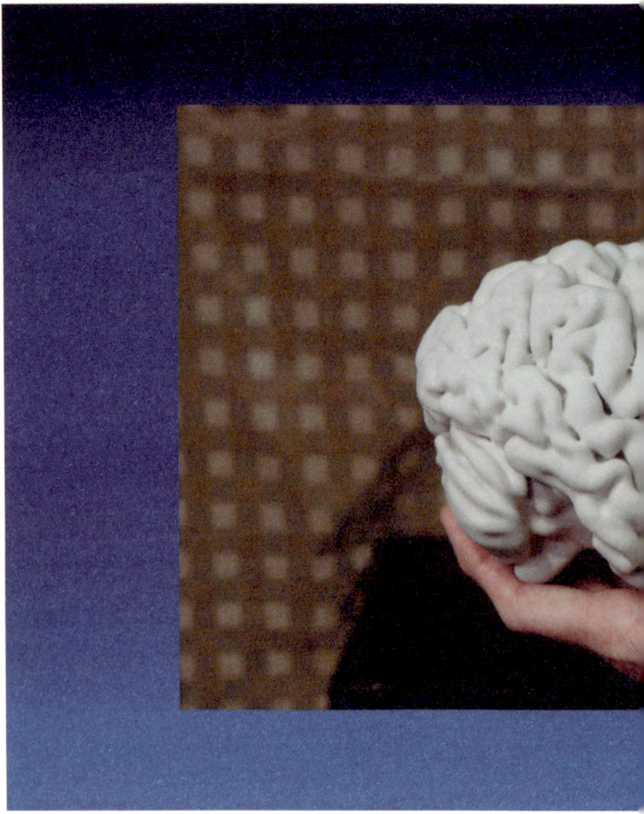

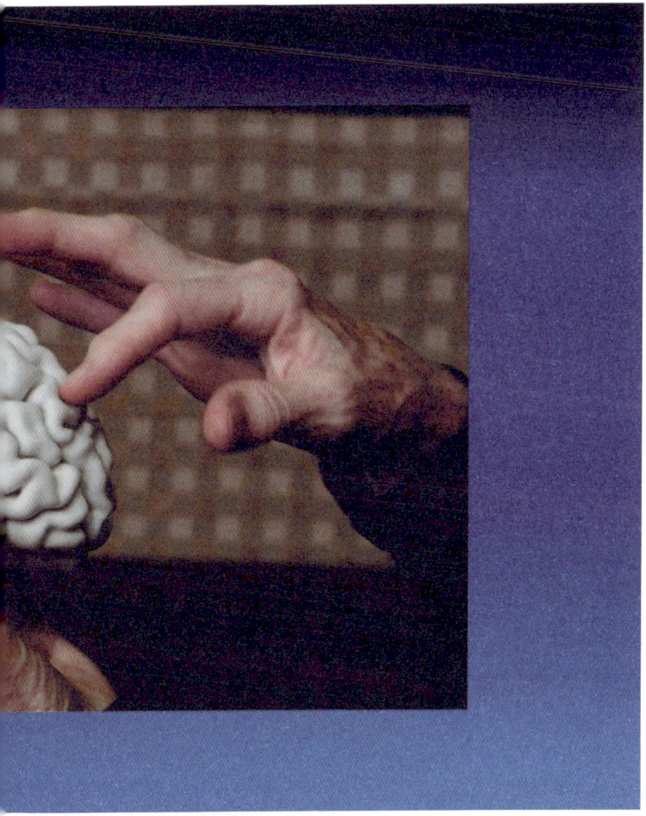

# STÉPHANE DEGOUTIN AND GWENOLA WAGON *WORLD BRAIN*, 2015

Film excerpt: *Automation*; 3'11"

*World Brain* by Stéphane Degoutin and Gwenola Wagon is a seventy-minute essay-film with an accompanying interactive website consisting of video clips and texts, arranged according to a rhizomatic structure. A work of monumental digression, the film follows a group of researchers who have set out to practice a peculiar form of techno-primitivism deep in a French forest. Using a solar-powered Linux laptop and precious little else, the group must figure out how to survive, using Wikipedia as a guide—one manifestation of the global brain concept that has inspired New Age techno-futuristic ideologies from the 1960s onward. But these researchers are themselves encrusted within a vast topical network, and the action shifts between their Arcadian exploits and thematic nodes entitled "Universal Fluid," "Between Animal and Crystal," and "Automation."

The work poses an essential question: In order to escape from an "automated society" that has increasingly turned humankind into production's spectator, how can the human being be reinvented? The somewhat paradoxical answer given by Degoutin and Wagon in this film is to recover basic survival skills, once practiced in almost every tribal context, with the aid of a computer, relying on the vast bank of human ingenuity now stored on the internet.

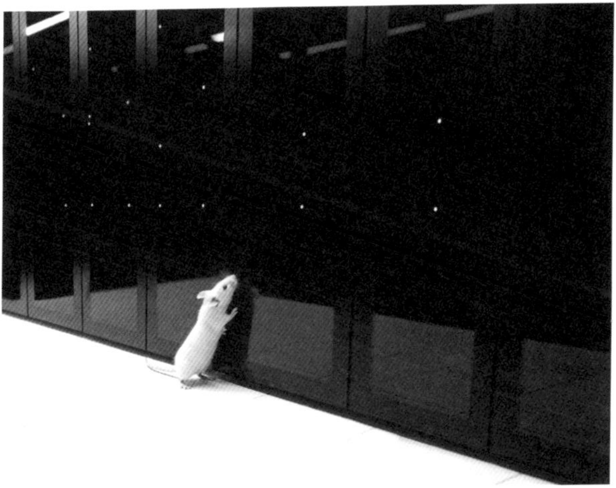

## ARTHUR M. EISENSON
## *ELLIS D. KROPOTECHEV AND ZEUS, A MARVELOUS TIME-SHARING DEVICE,* 1967

Digital transfer of 16 mm film, color, sound; 9′

The monetized "freeware" culture of today's internet economy, in which it is the user's data that produces value, has not developed from an innocent, originary gift economy later captured by large corporations. Rather, computer "users" have been conceptualized as a unit of economic value from the moment sharing-systems were first introduced.

Time-sharing systems implemented the idea of parallel computing, a significant revolution in the early development of computers which replaced the initial sequential program operated by a central processor and operator/middle-person. In parallel computing, a huge number of computing processes take place simultaneously. This idea drew directly from observations of the nervous system and the design of neural networks: the fact that while each single nerve is relatively slow, within the network these single operations add up to complex and fast operations due to their simultaneity. Early cyberneticians Warren McCulloch and Heinz von Foerster recount that observations of the compound eye of the praying mantis, a curious insect that earlier in the century had been at the center of the Surrealist's debate on mimicry, led to their invention of parallel computing—the template for the design of "machine learning" and neural networks in artificial intelligence.

*Ellis D. Kropotechev and Zeus, A Marvelous Time-Sharing Device* is a humorous, slapstick-like student film that documents the reverberations of this larger switch from linear to parallel computing. In the time-sharing system, each user is given a name in order to determine and document who is using the system. The film thus documents that this transition, simultaneously, amounted historically to the invention of the "user"—a traceable person with a name, address, and password, and a person whose use of the computer produces a new kind of data, a new kind of trace—that which later became the user "profile" in the era of "personal" computing.

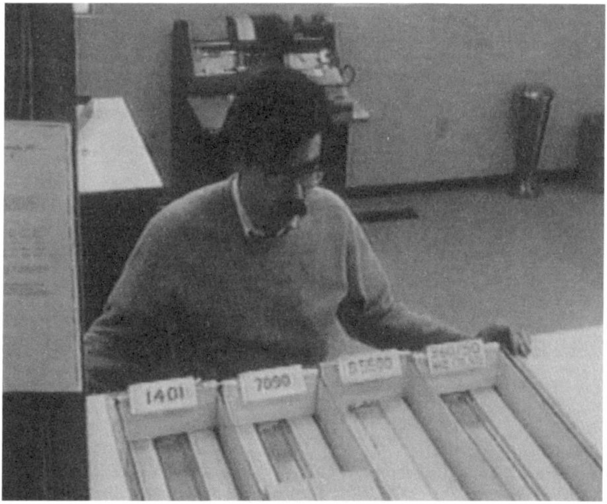

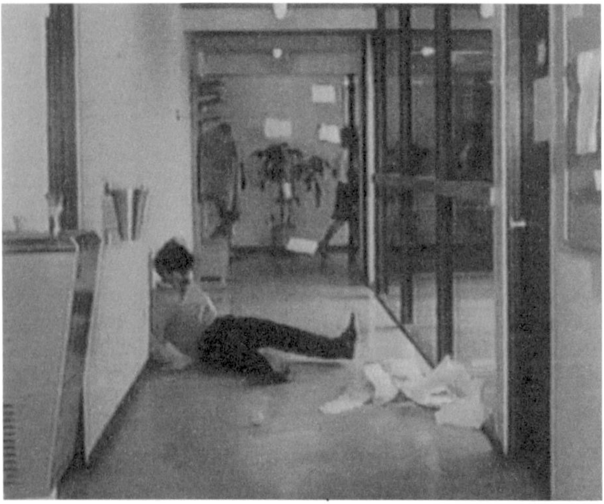

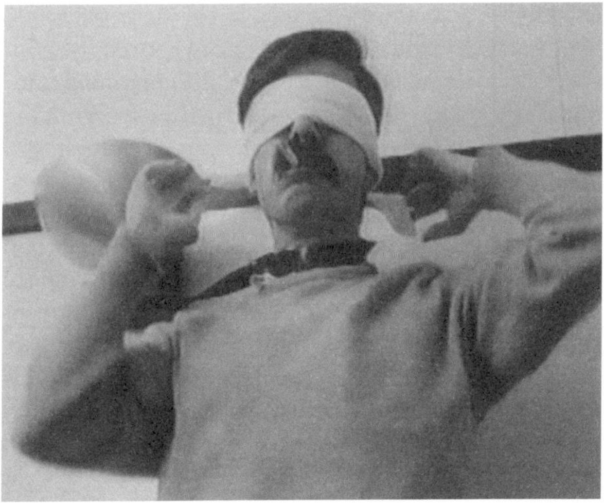

## HARUN FAROCKI
## *HOW TO LIVE IN THE FRG*, 1990

Film, color, sound; 83′

In a commentary Harun Farocki published after the release of this film, he wrote: "For a long time, I have been thinking of films in which the dismissed workers sing their dismissal, the development workers make rhymes of their adventures, the intermediate persons of contemporary history dance their experiences.... Here they document the conception of the world made by the military, the church, the social services, the insurance companies" (catalogue, *20. internationales forum des jungen films,* Berlin 1990). *How to Live in the FRG* does just this, assembling a near-comprehensive picture of a society where everything, from childbirth to death, mourning to maternal care, crossing the street to interdicting criminals, has become subject to institutionalized pedagogical procedures. It is the portrayal of a society that has unlearned all confidence in group instinct as well as individual instincts after World War Two.

The scenes of *How to Live in the FRG* appear, quite literally, to document the transition of disciplinary societies and their logic of normative suppression and containment, to the era of neoliberalism and its principles of self-motivation and modulated control along a median statistical norm. The training seminars for the neoliberal era take place at a time when old bureaucratic structures and systems of capture and productivity are being further developed into massive increasingly real-time data operations that promise to be able to "calculate" all human society. In such a relentless scripting of social interaction, the human world and the world of commodity take on a kind of equivalence, to which Farocki alluded in interspersing footage depicting automated quality-control procedures among the scenes of human instruction that make up the majority of the film. Man has become another kind of object, machined to ensure maximum dependability.

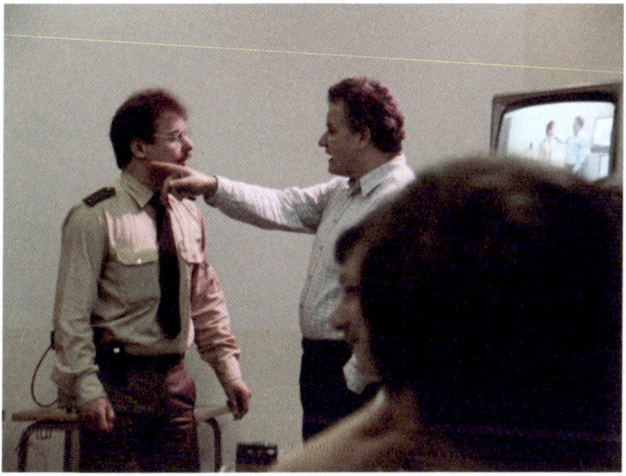

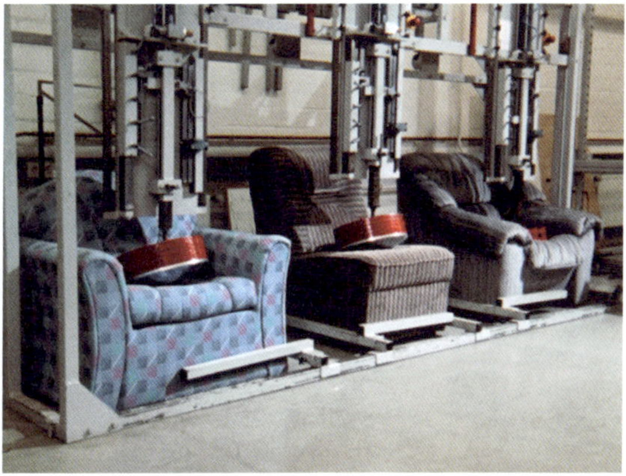

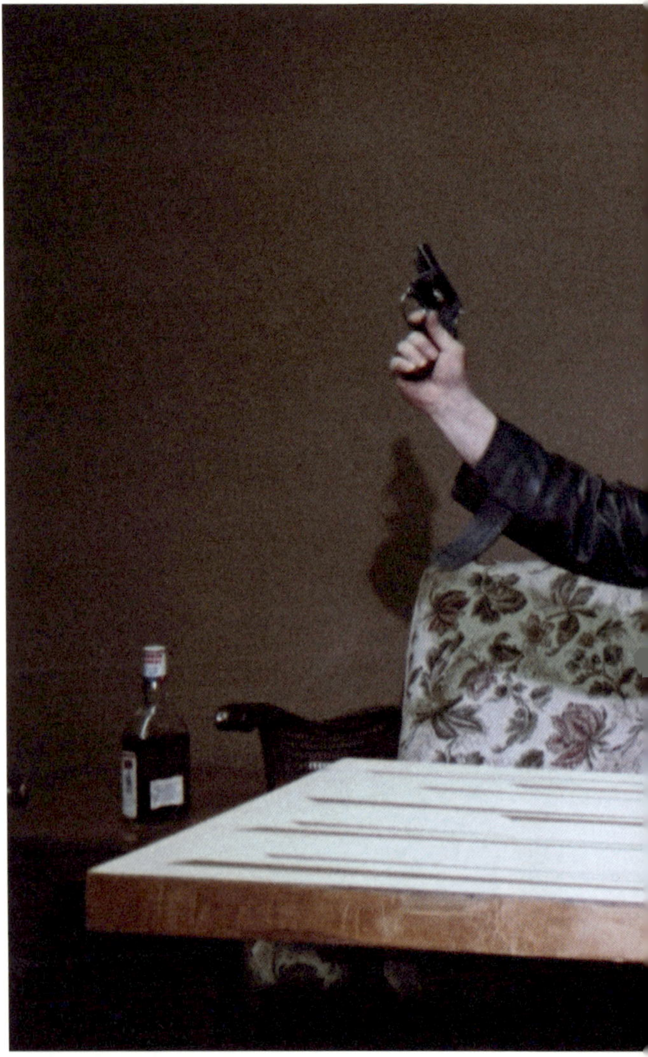

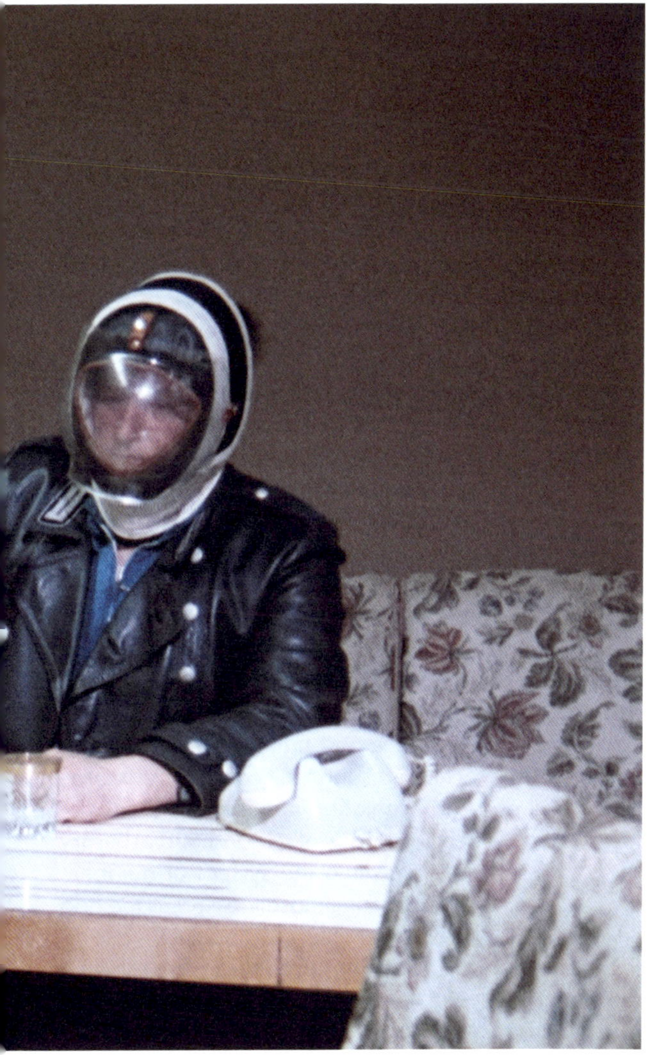

# CHARLES GAINES
# *WALNUT TREE ORCHARD, SET 3 AND 4,*
# 1975–2012

Photograph, ink on paper; two Triptychs: 73.66 × 58.42 cm (paper size); each 80.01 × 64.77 × 3.81 cm (framed)

Is the radical depersonalization in Conceptual art simultaneously a form of critique or a liberating enactment, or sometimes even a surrender to the very logic that they seek to expose, a representation of the "totally administered world"?

These questions point to crucial concerns at the heart of first-generation Conceptual artist Charles Gaines, who spent his formative years under the dictates of an arbitrary, rule-based system of oppression in the then-segregated Southern United States. Gaines' work certainly points to the constitutive, often unconscious role prejudice plays in judgment and discrimination as such, but he also tackles the paradoxes of all seemingly objective systems, and the impossibility of non-subjective experience. In decades of experimentation in multiple series of photos, drawings, and systematized applications of formulas, Gaines explored the metonymic quality of the grid and its ability to measure space and time. A recurring motif in Gaines' explorations of the limits of both representation and non-representation in the series *Gridwork* (1974–89) are trees—objects of a found and arbitrary "expressivity," translated into the system of numbers and squares. If for art theorist Rosalind Krauss the grid is what "art looks like when it turns its back on nature," then Gaines' grids invert this paradigm, subverting the difference between (rational) system and (irrational) expressivity.

Seen today and in the context of the exhibition *Nervous Systems*, the work of Charles Gaines may also bear witness to what happens when the grid turns its face toward nature to capture everything dynamic, contingent, and subjective, once loosely described as "reality." Thus, the works testify to a time when abstraction is about to transform the nature of concretion itself. It is perhaps not by chance that roughly at the same time Gaines produces *Numbers and Trees*, the globe is undergoing restless translation to "digital terrain models."

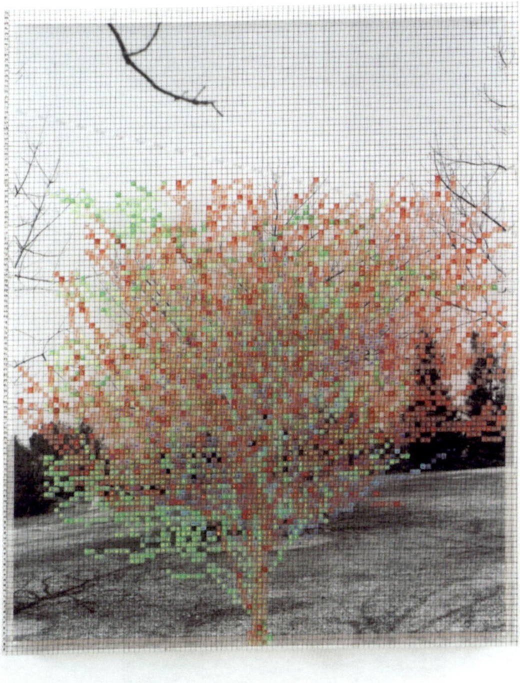

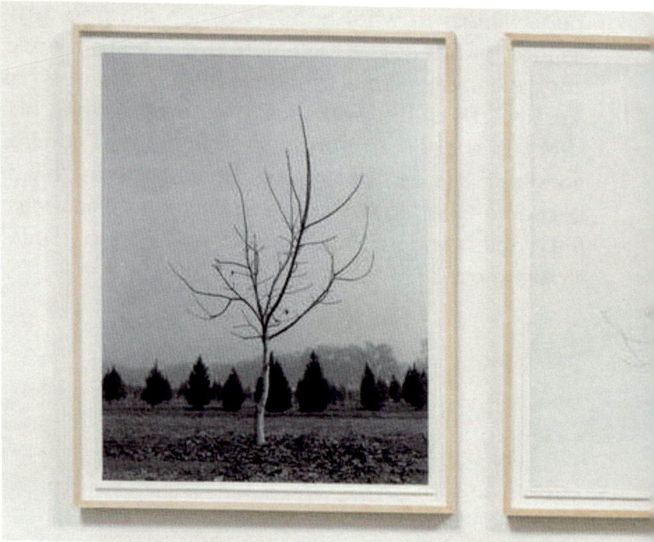

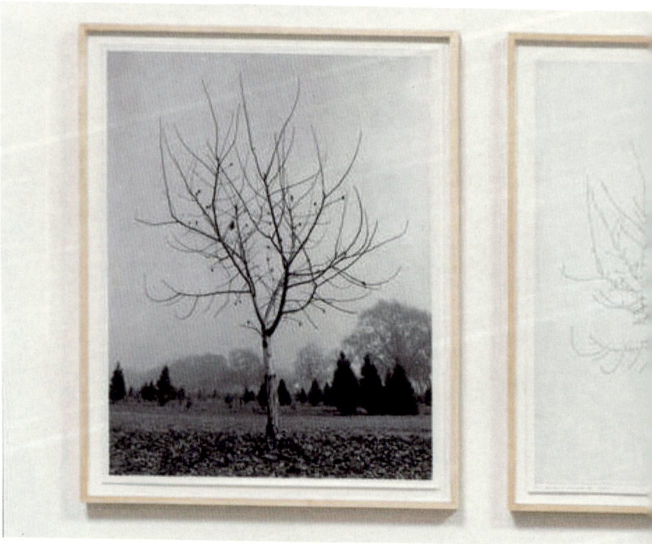

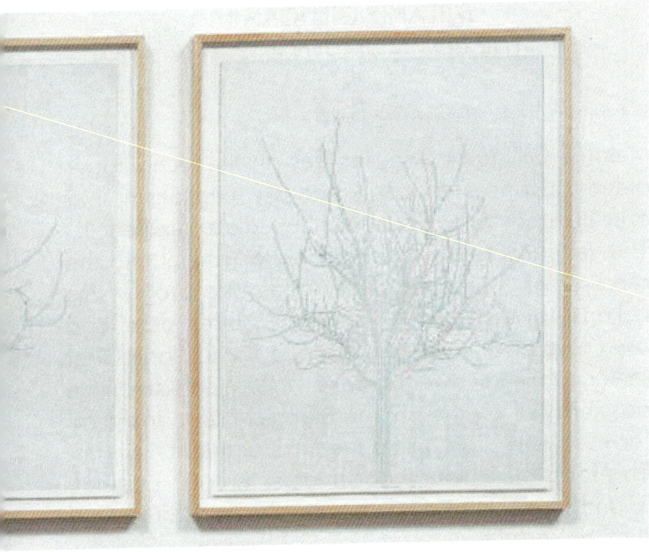

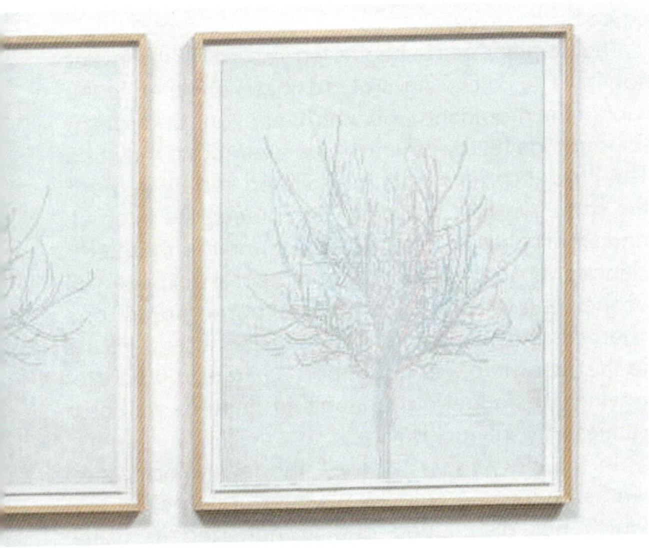

# MELANIE GILLIGAN
# *THE COMMON SENSE*, 2014

15-channel video installation (3 chapters); 15 × 6′50″; Edition of 5

Melanie Gilligan's work focuses on the technology-aided advances of contemporary capitalism into ever-deeper strata of our social, mediated existences. The very progress of the frontiers of capital into the recesses of "human capital" leads to a progressive collapse of distinctions—a process often described as a loss of an "outside." It is to this collapse that Melanie Gilligan's work speaks, while she insists on the possibility of a different, pedagogical and analytical form of "television" using the form of the mini-series. This form meticulously documents, through cinematic and theatrical dramatizations, the transformations that the social is undergoing in its inscription into networked technologies, and the way that abstract laws of the market and finance capitalism translate into embodied activity.

*The Common Sense* begins ten years after the invention of "The Patch," an oral prosthesis attached to the roof of the mouth through which emotions and sensations can be felt by others in one's computer network. The Patch has fundamentally altered society in much the same way as, presently, computers, the internet, and smart phones together, and combines these efficiencies with aspects of our contemporary experiential economy. It is a form of emotional pornography (one character has chosen to allow network users' access to the experiences of her unborn child as a means of paying off staggering amounts of debt) as well as a ruthless disciplinary device.

In the story's first "phase," the technology's networks undergo a cataclysmic interruption of service which has disoriented and immobilized its users.

After the network is restored, some of its users continue as before while a second group comes together to work toward resisting the technology's exploitative elements. In the end, however, the line between emancipation and ever-greater entrapment remain indissolubly blurred.

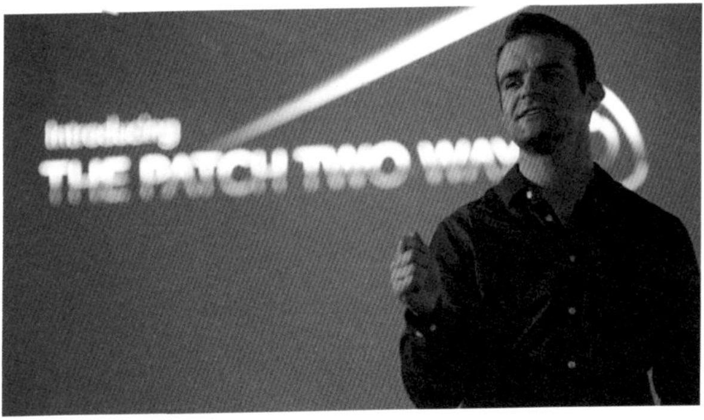

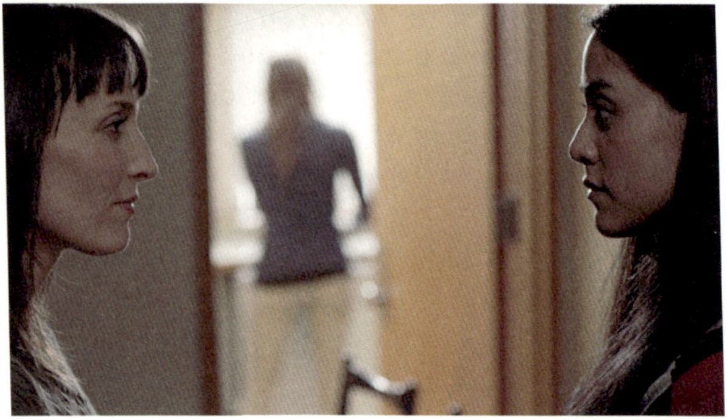

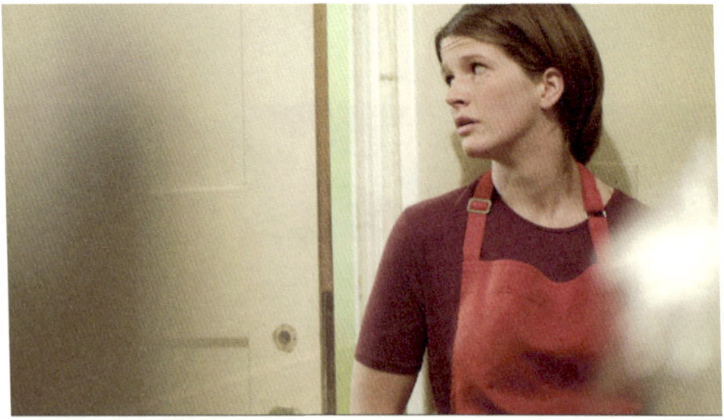

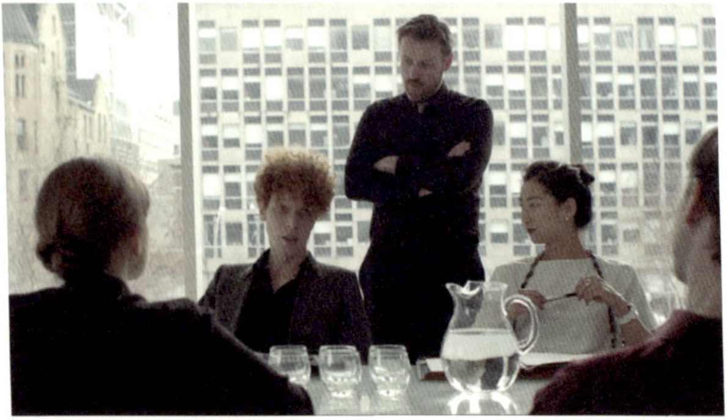

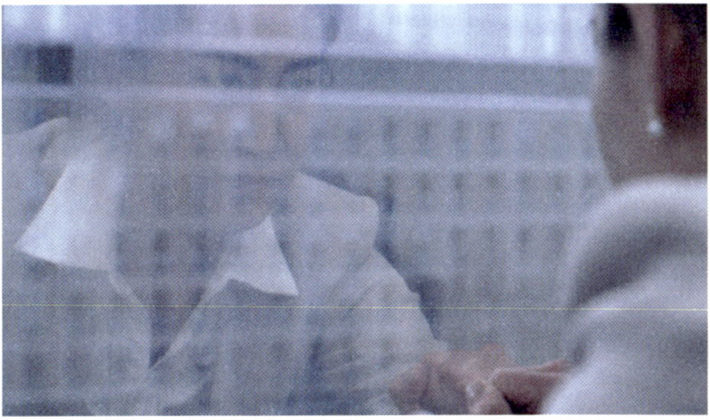

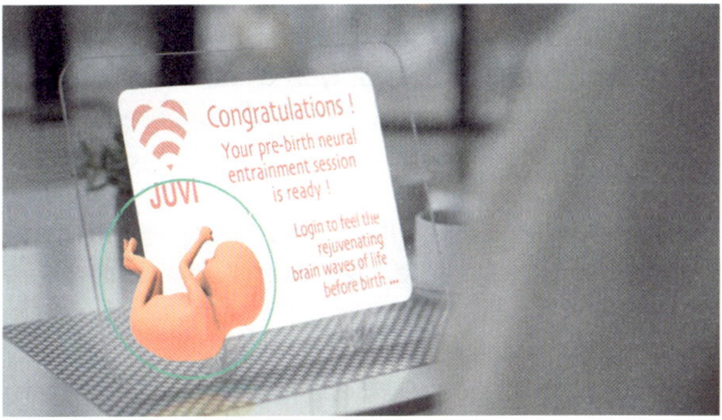
Congratulations !
Your pre-birth neural entrainment session is ready !
JUVI
Login to feel the rejuvenating brain waves of life before birth ...

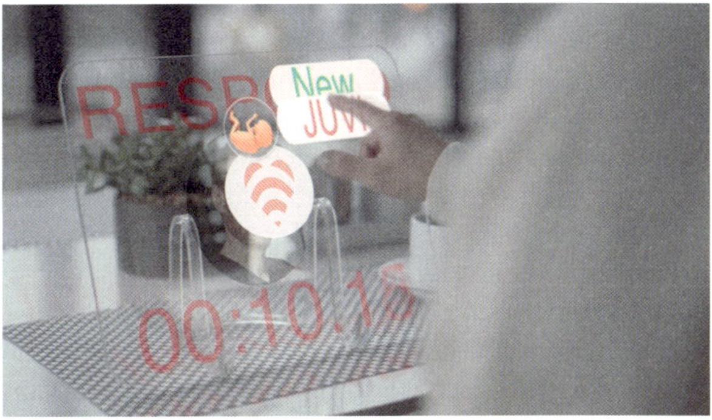
New
JUV

# GOLDIN+SENNEBY
# *NASSAU 6AM*,
# WITH JOHAN HJERPE (GRAPHIC DESIGN),
# 2008

Reproduction ink-jet print; 50 × 70 cm

In their work, artist duo Goldin+Senneby employ several layers of fictionalization, as a means of coming to terms with the deliberately obscure aspects of today's global economic and financial practices. Part of their long-term engagement with the functions of offshore centers is the blurring of subject matter and artistic method: in acts of performative mimicry, they assume the character of the object under investigation at one instance, only in order to reveal such mimicry in the next, as a means of documenting the practices of evasion and camouflage in the world of global offshore centers.

For their project *Headless*, the artists turn into characters of a novel where they investigate an offshore company in the Bahamas called Headless Ltd., and in which furthermore they hire the fictional British author of mystery novels, John Barlow, to ghostwrite a commercial thriller, also titled *Headless*, whose plot revolves around its own literary production. Underlying these weavings of fictions are allusions to a historical, obscure secret society founded by renegade Surrealist Georges Bataille, named *Acephale* (Headless).

The novel *Headless* produced a range of ancillary artworks, of which the etching *Nassau 6am* is just one. With this etching, the artists claim to have entered and been shortlisted for the competition of the Sovereign European Art Prize in 2008 (sponsored by the asset-management company of the same name). The etching is reminiscent of the work of André Masson, suggesting a graphic representation of the ecstatic condition of "headlessness" that Bataille sought, but acting simultaneously as an advertisement for the wealth-management firm Headless Ltd. In this sense, the work is a prime example of how the artists are employing the same outsourcing structure endemic in modern-day capitalism, an act of revelatory mimicry that hits the systemic and yet irrational nerve of contemporary global finance and its many masks.

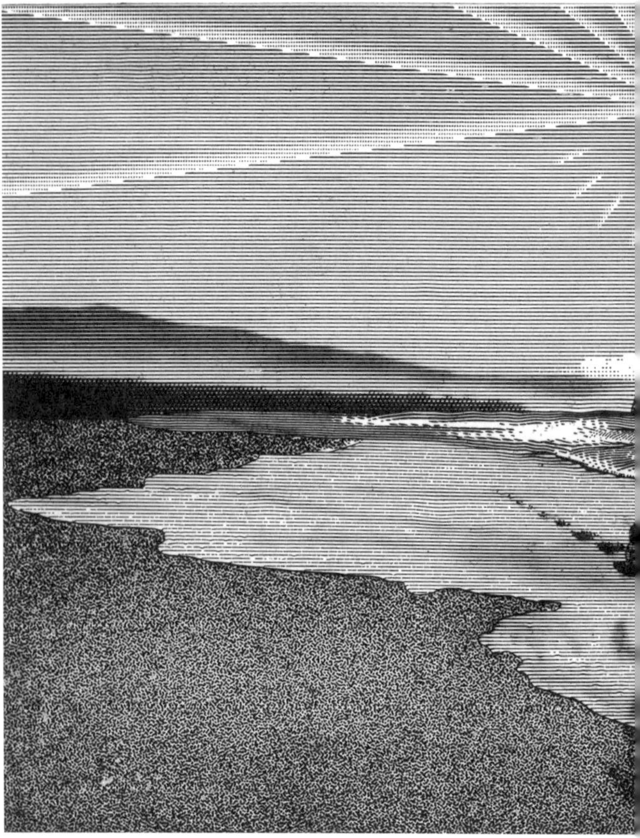

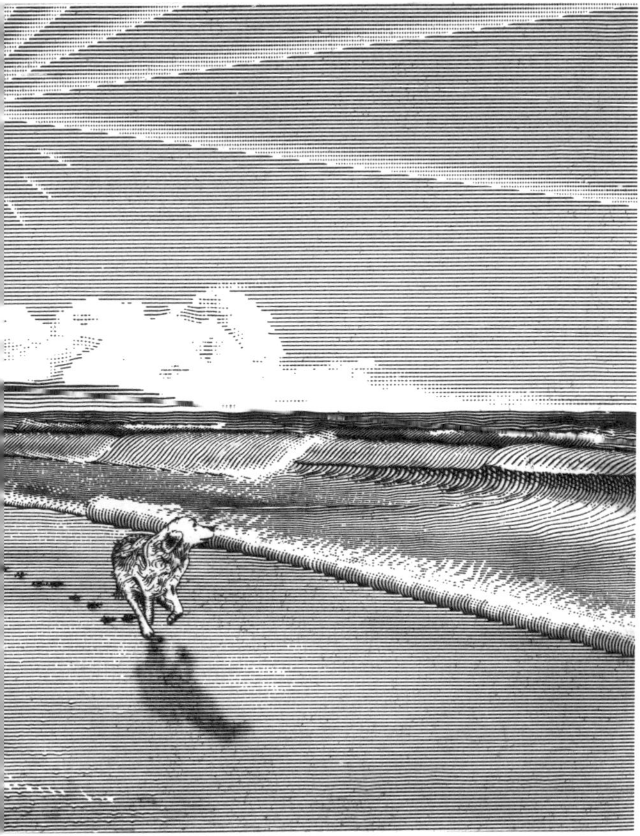

## LAURENT GRASSO
## *ON AIR*, 2009

Film 35 mm transferred onto DVD Pro HD, color, sound; 17'30"

In the constantly evolving game of cat and mouse that has come to characterize today's "war on terror," Western nations and their allies tend to rely increasingly on high-tech fixes, which their adversaries confound by resorting, at least in part, to older methods of communication. This is the situation to which Laurent Grasso alludes in his film, *On Air*, in which the artist releases a trained falcon, fitted with a video camera, above the mountainous landscape of the United Arab Emirates—a low-tech sort of animal-drone. The film oscillates between the frenetic perspective of the bird's-eye view and that of the earthbound tracker following the falcon's movements from the ground with an antenna.

As in Grasso's other films, the artist is interested in offering a reflection on the camera's perspective, but in this work he complicates the range of signifiers in play through situating this interplay between the human and avian in the context of the Middle East, where Falconry has long been an important part of heritage and culture. In the region, resorting to pre-technological modes of communication such as homing pigeons, apparently, has become one way for groups finding themselves in opposition to Western powers to evade omnipresent surveillance networks like ECHELON—the global system of electronic eavesdropping installations administered by the United States, the United Kingdom, and other British Commonwealth states—which monitors electronic communication. Asymmetrical warfare, it would seem, does not refer to weapons systems alone, but also to the ways one might exploit the blind spots of a technologically superior opponent.

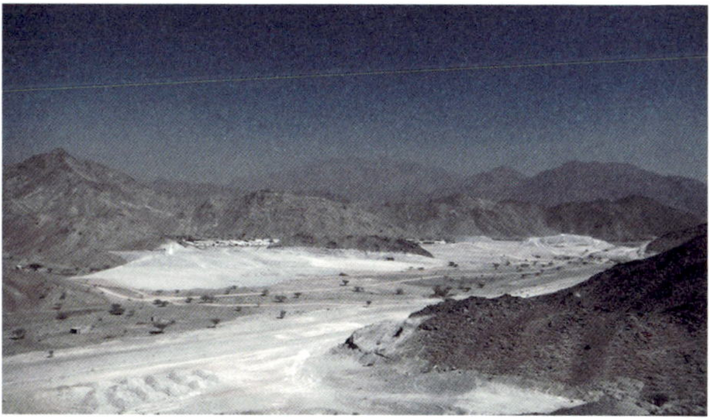

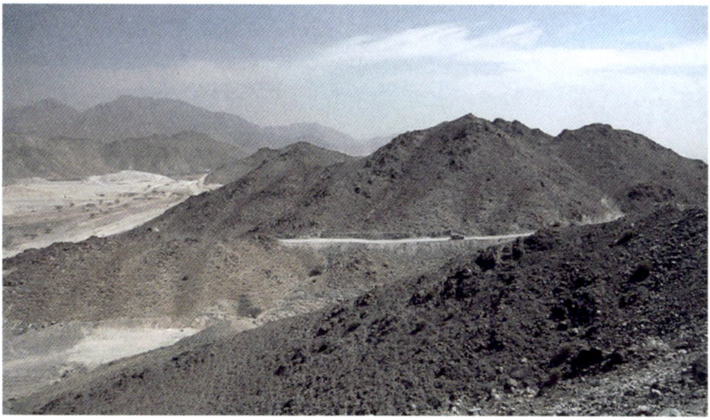

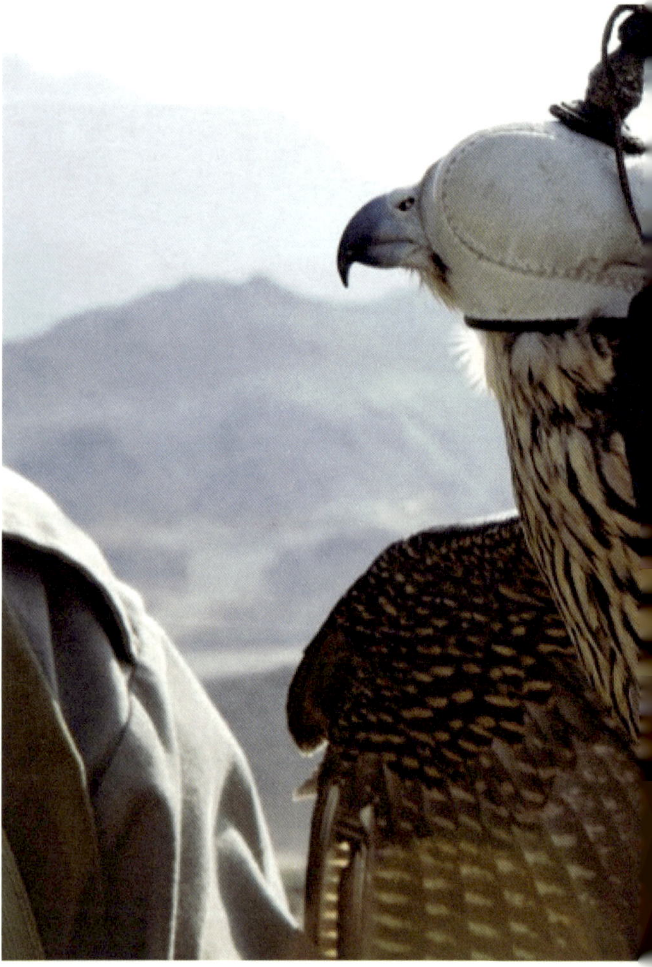

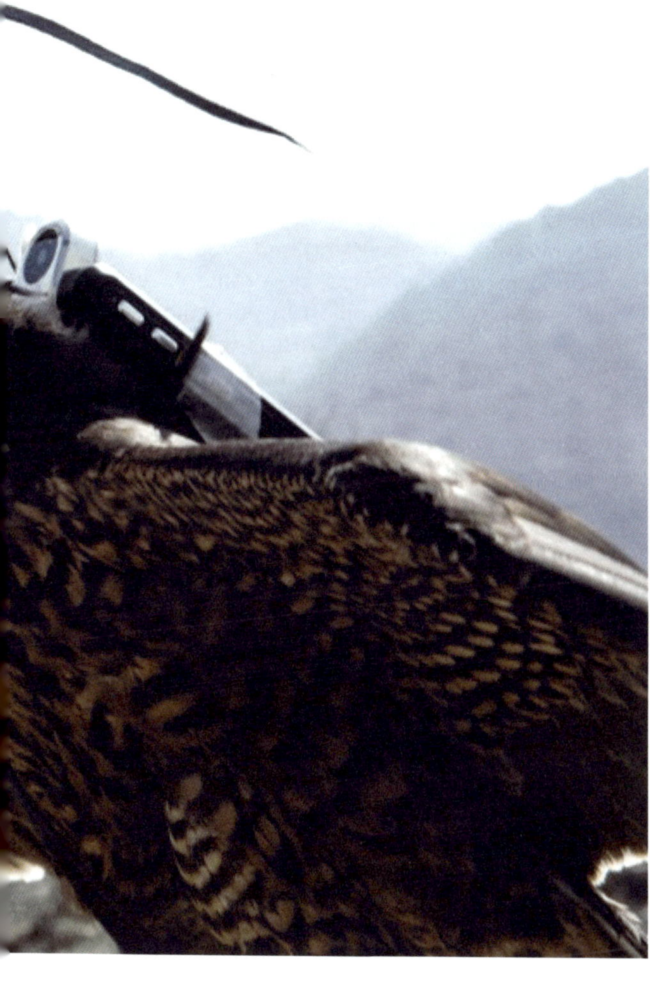

# DOUGLAS HUEBLER
# *VARIABLE PIECE NO. 4*, 1969

Page from *Secrets*: Variable Piece No.4, 1977

*Variable Piece No. 4 NYC, May 1969* was included in the exhibition *Software*, which opened at the Jewish Museum in New York in winter 1970. The works exhibited in *Software* explored the common ideological ground between Conceptual art's preoccupation with logical systems and propositional formulae, and the emergence of data processing and cybernetics as a motivating force in business, government, and science. The *Software* exhibition in particular sought explicitly to link Conceptual artists with the recent innovation of software, linking the idea of software with works where machines or audience members carried out instructions based on a script or protocol developed by the artist.

Huebler's work for the exhibition, whose scripted character is self-evident, took a whimsical approach to information exchange and interactivity. In *Variable Piece No. 4,* visitors were invited to write down a secret and leave it in a box; after twenty-four hours—to ensure anonymity—the secrets would be taken by the gallery and redistributed. Over 1,800 secrets collected during the exhibition were collated in a book, published two years later. Over time, the focus of this artwork, gathering secrets and their disclosure, takes on a more ominous tone, as if predicting society's obsession with disclosure—amply demonstrated in social media—as well as the ubiquity of forms of self-surveillance and data mining.

VARIBLE PIECE 4
NEW YORK CITY.

Visitors to the SOFTWARE exhibition are invited to participate in the transposition of information from one location to another by following the procedure described below:

1. Write or print on this paper an authentic personal secret that you have never revealed before: of course, do not sign it.
2. Slip the paper into the slot of the box provided at this location. Complete the exchange of your secret for that of another person by requesting a photo-copy of one previously submitted.

(To insure your anonymity incoming secrets will remain within the box for 24 hours before being removed to be photo-copied and joining the "library" of secrets for future exchange.)

May 1969 Douglas Huebler

Forms on which the above directions were printed were made available to all visitors at the exhibition SOFTWARE (Jewish Museum, NYC, September 16-November 8, 1970).

Nearly 1,800 "secrets" were submitted for exchange and have been transcribed exactly as written except that surnames have been edited: all are printed in this book and join with this statement as final form of this piece.

March, 1973 Douglas Huebler

## ON KAWARA
## *I AM STILL ALIVE*, 17.3.1995

Telegram to Hinrich Weidemann; 20.2 × 26.2 × 3.5 cm

On Kawara was among the first generation of Conceptual artists to reject traditional principles of pictorial or sculptural organization in favor of abstract principles of information, measurement, and quantification. He devoted most of his artistic life to measuring the passage of time in relation to his own life and movements, and to exploring the process through which humans, inevitably, both produce and consume information. Among his better known works are the paintings of numerical dates made on the one datum they depict; and the series of telegrams and postcards stating *I Got Up* (1968–79), as well as *I Went* (1968–79) documenting meticulously his own trajectories and sent to friends and acquaintances on a daily basis. The series *I Am Still Alive* began in 1970, and consists of almost nine hundred telegrams sent on an irregular basis.

In 2009, Pall Thayer, an Icelandic-American digital media artist, set up a Twitter account under the name of On Kawara, programming a Twitterbot to issue Kawara's phrase, "I Am Still Alive," every morning at ten o'clock. At first, Thayer neither asked Kawara's permission nor publicly announced the project. Nor did the fictive Kawara Twitter feed "follow" anyone else. Yet, people began following it, and when the feed had reached one hundred followers, Thayer admitted authorship. Yet he did not stop the project, allowing the Twitterbot to continue posting, even after Kawara's death in 2014, and to this day, it continues to post the iconic message concerning Kawara's continuing existence. "Life," here, has become spectral—a spectrality that exceeds the singular life of the artist, and perhaps is characteristic of its status in today's communication matrix.

ZCZC AYY074 WCF396 7445408 WUF-EX-9507502963117

DPXX CO UDNX 013

TDEL NEW YORK NY 013/011 16 1738

HINRICH WEIDEMANN

STUBENRAUCHSTR 41

12161BERLIN

I AM STILL ALIVE

ON KAWARA

NNNN

## KORPYS/LÖFFLER
## *PERSONEN INSTITUTIONEN OBJEKTE SACHEN*, 2014

3-channel HD video installation, color, sound; 21′46″

Since the early 1990s, the work of artist duo Andree Korpys and Markus Löffler has questioned where power and control are situated—particularly the architectural sites of historical and political events. In their recent work, *Personen Institutionen Objekte Sachen* (People Institutions Objects Things), they have constructed a three-channel video documenting their long-term surveillance of the soon-to-be-completed Berlin headquarters of the Federal Intelligence Service (*Bundesnachrichtendienst* or BND) at Chausseestraße in Berlin-Mitte. The new BND headquarters will amalgamate the work of the current two sites—one in Berlin and another in Pullach, near Munich—and employ 4,000 people on one site. The installation's title refers to the data management system PIOS (persons, institutions, objects, things), developed in the 1970s for computer investigation and criminal-data processing, thus both literally and conceptually Korpys/Löffler have turned the tables on the security service—the monitors have become the monitored.

As Germany's only overseas intelligence service, the BND gathers both military and civil intelligence, acting as an early-warning system to alert the German government to threats from abroad. Heavily dependent on wiretapping and surveying international electronic communications, it collects and evaluates information on a diverse range of topics from international non-state terrorism and information warfare to drug trafficking, money laundering, and illegal migration. Bundestag investigations resulting from Edward Snowden's NSA revelations revealed that the

BND reportedly stores 220 million sets of metadata every day from "foreign dialed traffic." This daily harvest of metadata is archived for ten years, in the interest of "long-term analysis" (quoted from Wikipedia).

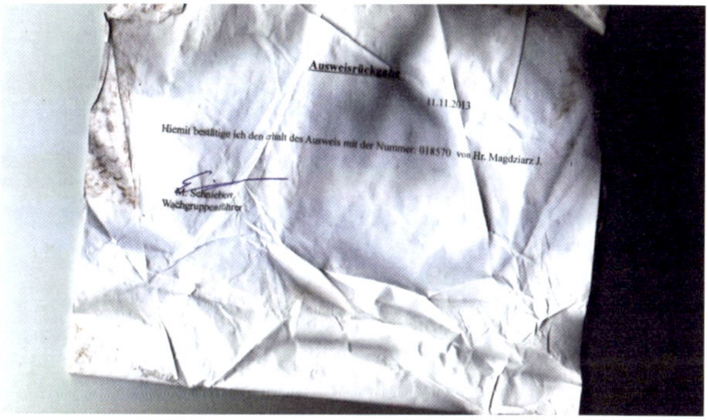


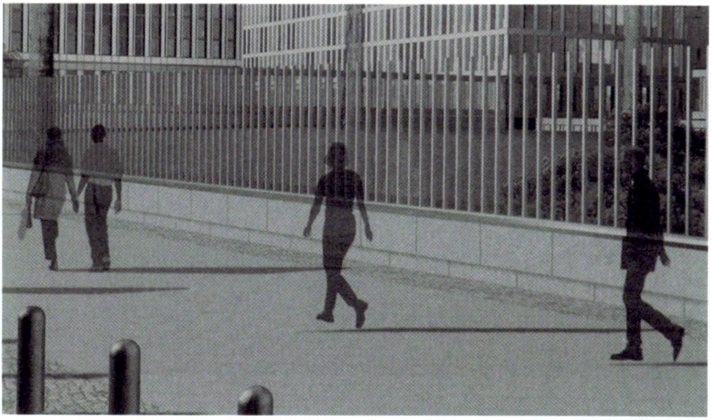

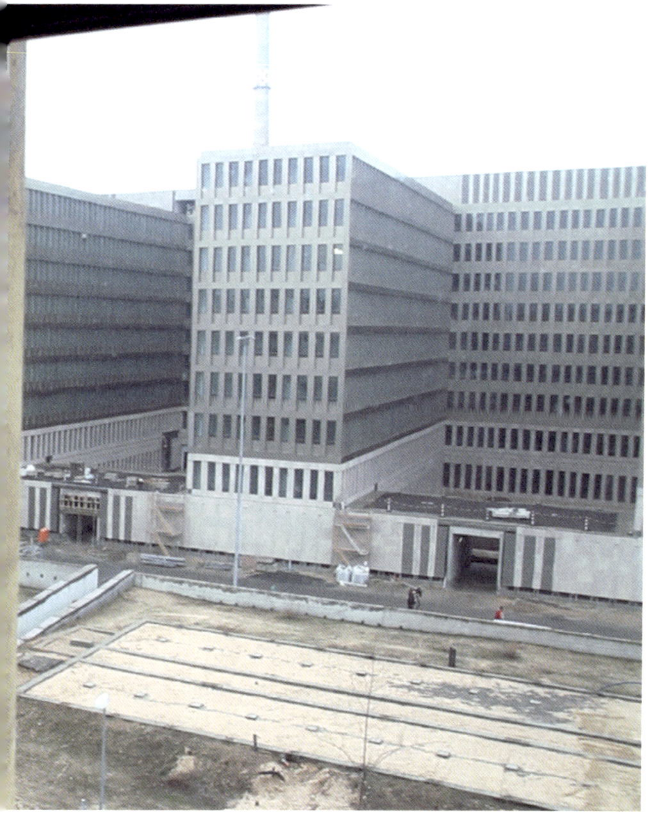

## !MEDIENGRUPPE BITNIK
## *DELIVERY FOR MR. ASSANGE—ASSANGE'S ROOM*, 2014

Mixed-media installation

*Assange's Room* is a detailed reconstruction of WikiLeaks founder Julian Assange's study at the Ecuadorian embassy in London, where he has lived since being granted political asylum in 2012. The room is not re-created from photographs or plans, but purely from the memory of !Mediengruppe Bitnik who visited Julian Assange on various occasions. The work is part of the series *Delivery for Mr. Assange*. It follows the live online performance piece, where, on January 16, 2013, the artists sent a parcel to Julian Assange, containing a hidden camera. Images of the parcel's progress through the postal system were uploaded automatically to Bitnik's website and their Twitter account as it traveled through various postal bags, vans, and delivery centers. Upon delivery, Julian Assange executed a triumphal, live on-camera performance for the benefit of several thousand Twitter followers.

In August 2012, the Ecuadorian embassy was surrounded by British police to impede Julian Assange's plan to leave the country. With *Delivery for Mr. Assange*, Bitnik intervened in a diplomatic crisis costing the UK government over ten million pounds. The stalemate around the embassy is one of the rare physical manifestations of the ongoing crisis between the powers-that-be and the internet-freedom *aficionados*. Due to the police cordon, Julian Assange is confined to the highly regulated interior of the embassy. The few visitors who are admitted cannot enter the building without undergoing security processes and do not know exactly what the interior looks like—yet this is the space from which

WikiLeaks still operates and reaches millions of people worldwide.

The life-size replication presents the "world" of Assange and his daily physical experience. A human body entrapped in a building. An existence more restricted than imprisonment. By moving Assange's work and influence out of the virtual, into a real-world bodily domain, Bitnik creates a tangible sketch of a daily life from which the visitor can walk freely in and out. By materializing an otherwise abstract question of confinement, control, and counter-power, we experience more acutely the paradox of one nation-state nervously observing the other state from within.

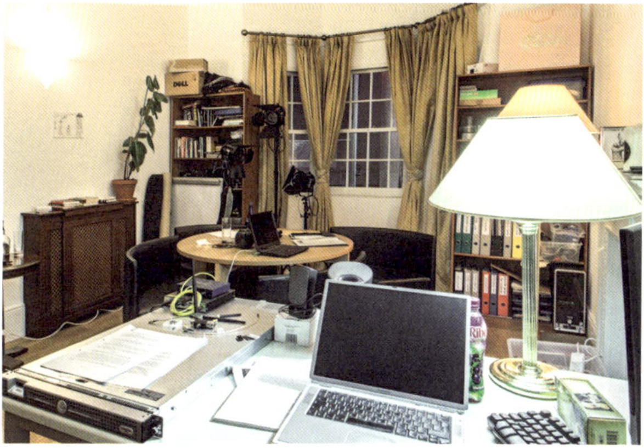

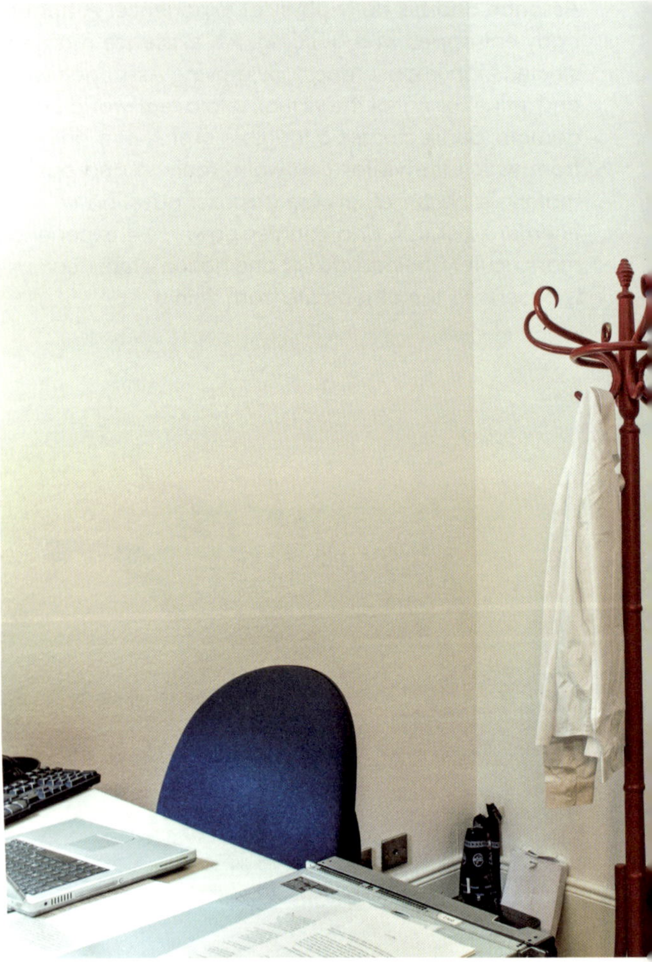

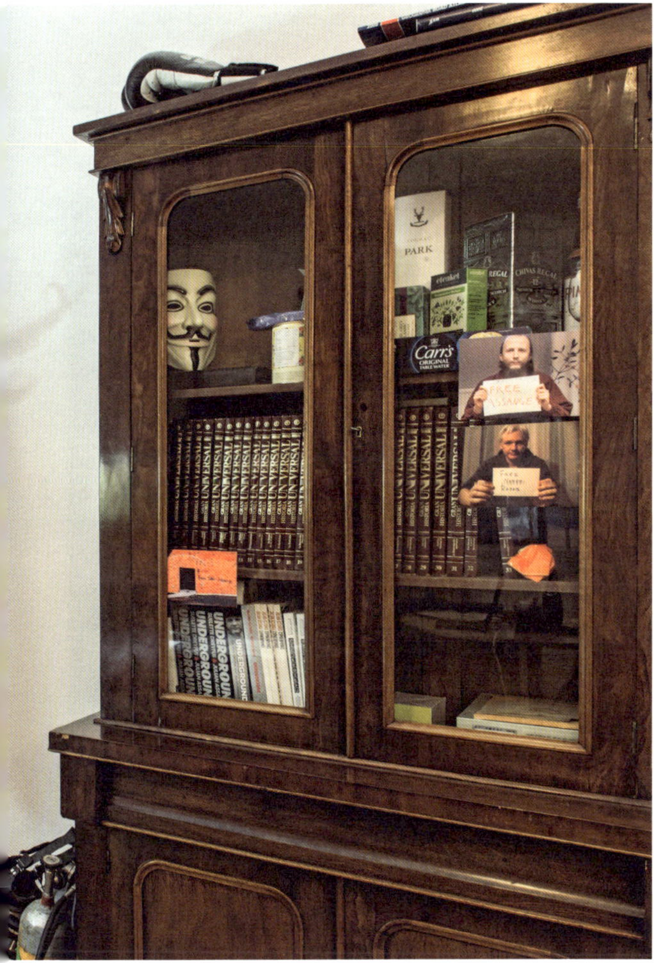
PARK
Carr's
ORIGINAL
TABLE WATER
CHIVAS REGAL
UNIVERSAL
UNDERGROUND
FREE
ASSANGE

# HENRIK OLESEN
# *HOW DO I MAKE MYSELF A BODY (7)*, 2008

Details; 3 computer collages, behind glass, felt-tip pen, ballpoint pen (from a series of 19 collages); 29.7 × 21 cm

British scientist Alan Turing is known today as a mathematical genius whose work paved the way for modern computing and what came to be known as "artificial intelligence." In the 1930s, Turing developed a theoretical model for a protean computing machine, the basis for today's computers, and during World War Two worked in the famous code-breaking unit of the UK Government Code and Cypher School, where his work on breaking the cyphers used by Germany's Enigma coding machine has been credited with shortening the war by several years.

In *How Do I Make Myself a Body* Henrik Olesen, however, engages with Turing's personal life, marked by the tragic consequences of the criminalization of non-normative sexuality. In 1954, nine years after the war's conclusion and with over a decade spent in government service, Turing was dead, having committed suicide two years after a criminal conviction for homosexual acts saw him stripped of his security clearance and forced to undergo chemical castration. Within Alan Turing's story, Olesen finds not only an account of the criminalization of the homosexual's body, but a more complex narrative about the interplay of different notional bodies. Turing's physical body and his artificially constrained libido are there, but so are other types of bodies Turing's genius envisioned, cyborgian man-machines created by the juncture of human and non-human intelligence.

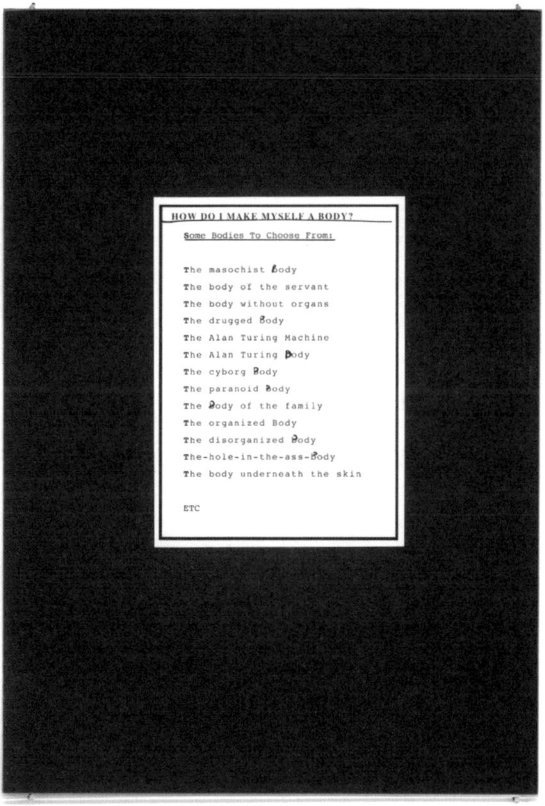
HOW DO I MAKE MYSELF A BODY?
Some Bodies To Choose From:
The masochist Body
The body of the servant
The body without organs
The drugged Body
The Alan Turing Machine
The Alan Turing Body
The cyborg Body
The paranoid Body
The Body of the family
The organized Body
The disorganized Body
The-hole-in-the-ass-Body
The body underneath the skin
ETC

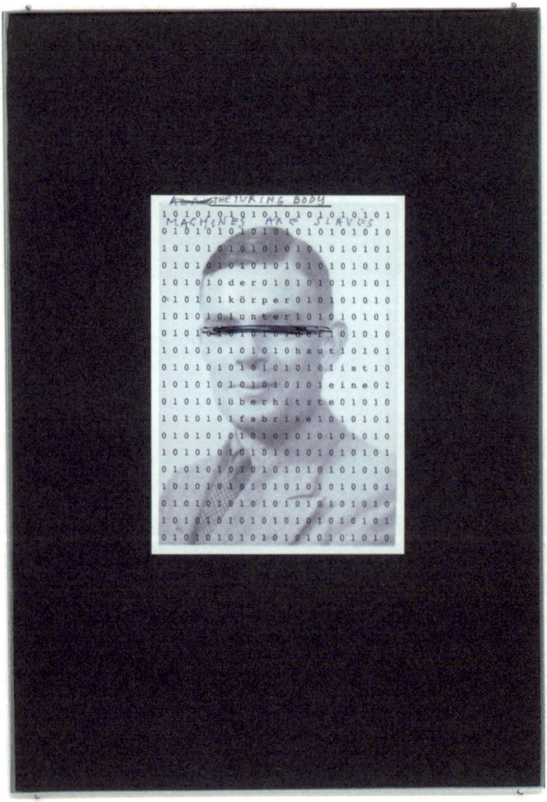
THE TURING BODY
MACHINES ARE SLAVES
der
körper
unter
haut
ist
eine
überhitzte
fabrike

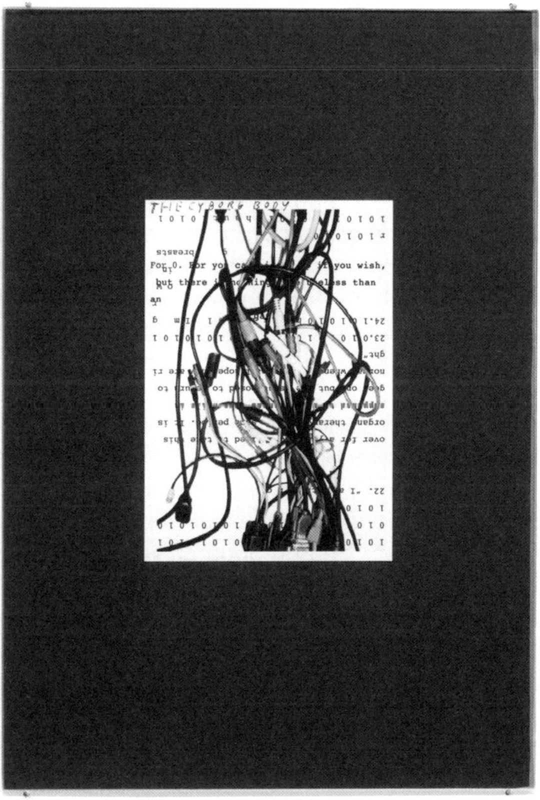
THE CYBORG BODY

# JULIEN PRÉVIEUX
# *PATTERNS OF LIFE*, 2015

HD Video/2K, color, sound; 16′
Dancers: Camille de Belfon, Grégory Dominiak, Allister Madin, Ninon Raux, Yann Saiz

*Patterns of Life* deals with the history of the technological capture of human movement within the genre of a dance film. For this video, loosely based on a text by Grégoire Chamayou entitled "Patterns of Life: A Short History of Schematic Bodies," Julien Prévieux has enlisted five dancers from the Paris Opera to develop dance choreographies based on six different experiments, studies, or technologies—presented in chronological order and accompanied by a narration—concerned in different ways with the task of extracting objectifiable patterns from bodies in motion, and the way this data is applied to reorganize, control, and encapsulate individual and group movement and behavior.

The film begins with dance schemes derived from earlier use of chronophotography in motion studies, some conducted by Lillian and Frank B. Gilbreth, colleagues of the pioneer of industrial efficiency, Frederick Taylor. They developed an apparatus, the "chronocyclegraph," which, using long-exposure photography traced sequential movements. Here the gesture—for instance, of a factory worker—is captured in order to reconstruct and remodel it in a search for greater efficiency within the factory regime. Later on, the film engages with studies involving the ways in which thought is unconsciously telegraphed through eye movement, to the development of tracking technologies, such as the electronic-monitoring device used for house arrest, and then to routines based on technologies that actually circumscribe movements—such as auditory devices that create virtual enclosures. The video concludes by addressing the contemporary preoccupation with data mining, and the consequent shift from looking for things to looking for "patterns of activity"—the very form of analysis that underwrites "targeting" today, both in the military context of the "war on terror" as well as in consumer culture and advertising.

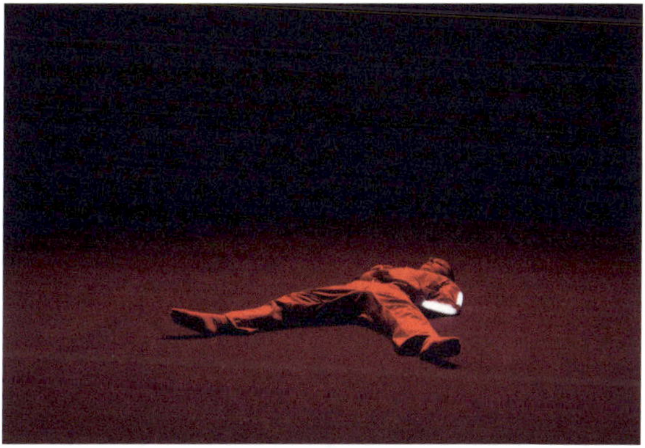

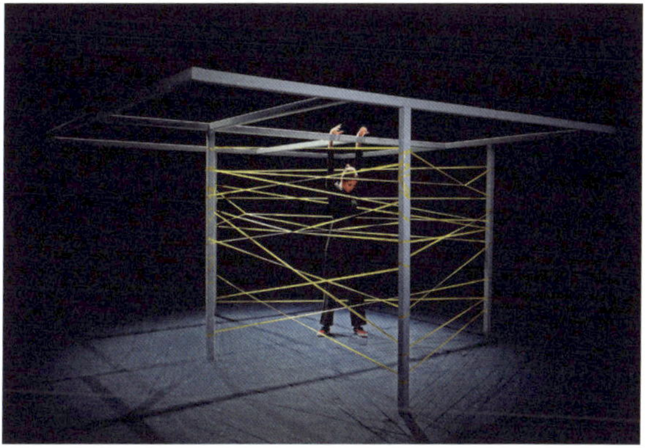

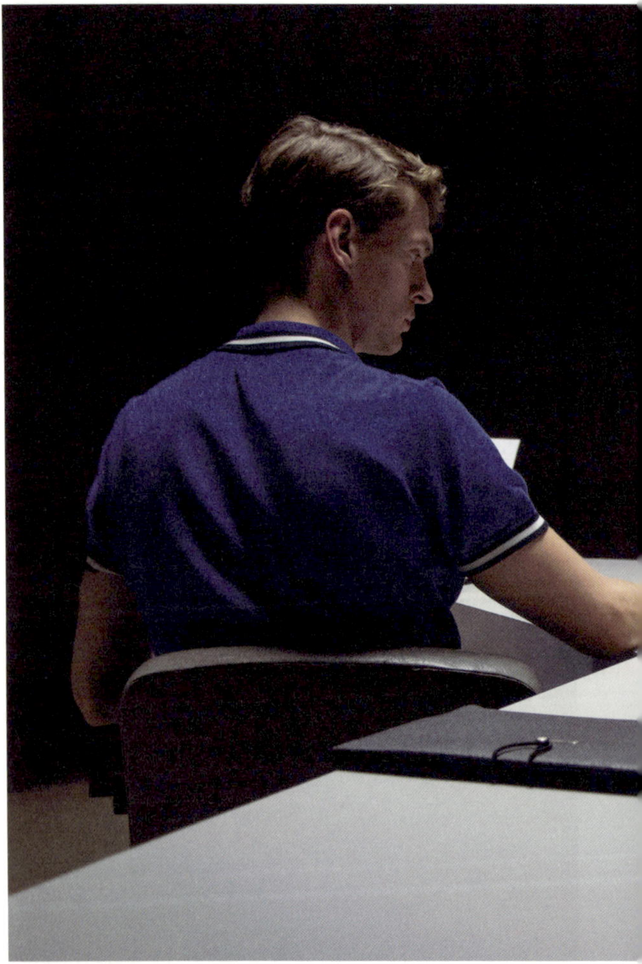

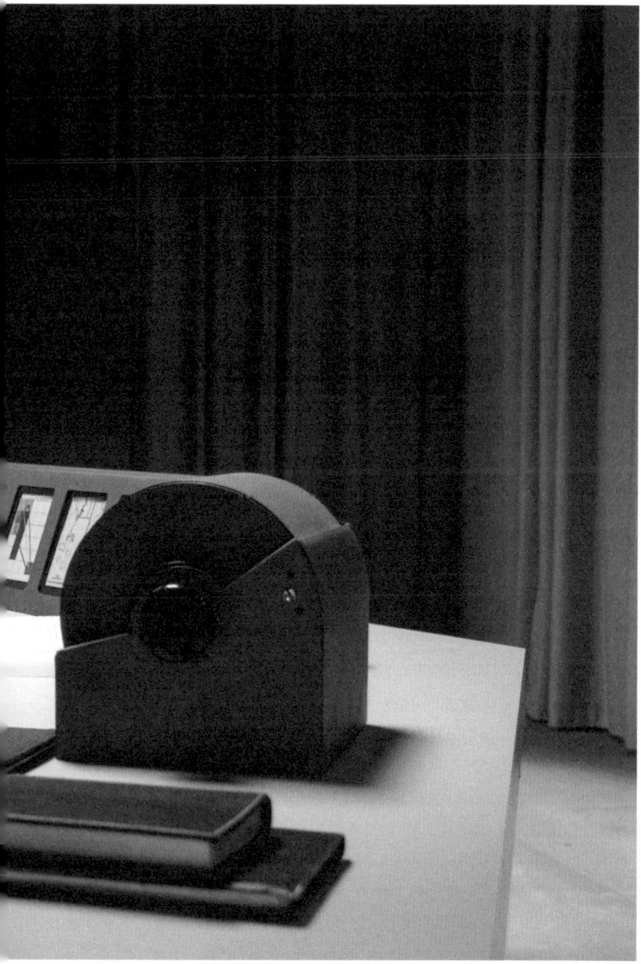

# JON RAFMAN
## *BITSA PARK, MOSCOW, RUSSIA,* 2010
## *3081 VALMONT ROAD, BOULDER, COLORADO,* 2012
## *26 WATER STREET, ST. CATHERINE, ONTARIO*

Photographs each 101.6 × 162.5 cm and 180.58 × 101.6 cm

Artist, filmmaker, and essayist Jon Rafman presents himself as an archivist, cataloguing artifacts culled from the virtual realms that surround us. His ongoing project, the straightforwardly named series, *The Nine Eyes of Google Street View*—of which three images are presented here—takes its title from the nine-camera system used by Google in its Street View mapping service. For Rafman, such images constitute a unique sort of digital typology. Roland Barthes' term, *punctum*, which he used to describe that unexpected photographic detail that captivates our attention and makes us look twice, aptly describes what attracts Rafman to an individual image and determines his choice in retrieval from among the millions of other Google Street View images that exist. The three images presented from his series all capture a moment of surprise made the more remarkable by being entirely a product of happenstance.

Google Street View images offer up the photographic act as contingency in its purest, most aesthetically unmotivated form. Yet these photographs are also part of a global project of intelligence-gathering motivated by explicitly commercial ends. They are thus highly determined. It is this tension between contingency and determination which Rafman's selections capture, an aesthetic by-product of the largely autonomic procedures upon which the internet relies to make its space intelligible and navigable.

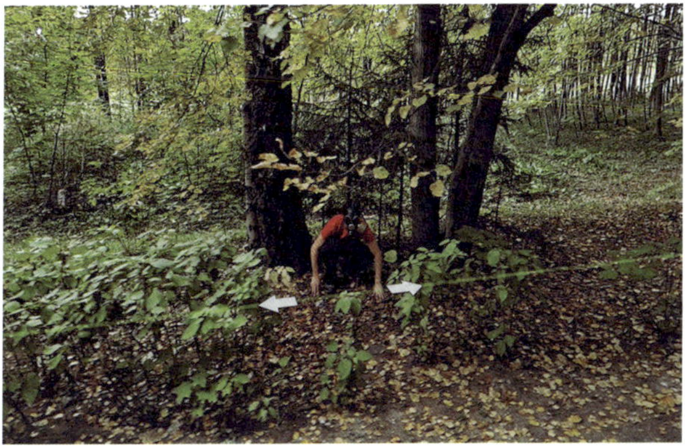

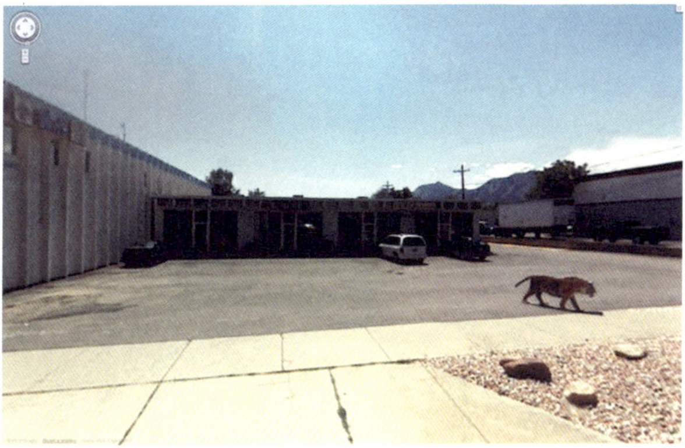

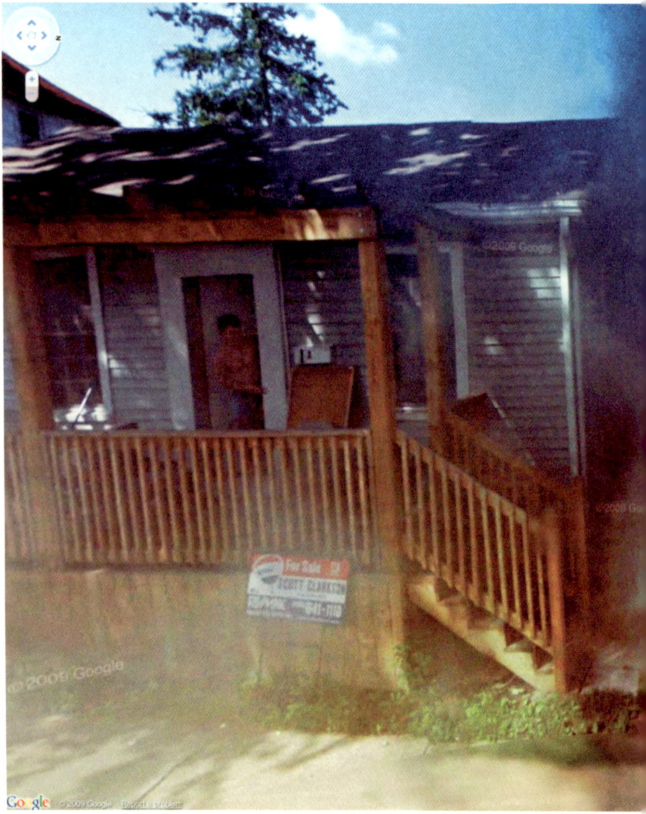
© 2009 Google
For Sale
SCOTT CLARKSON

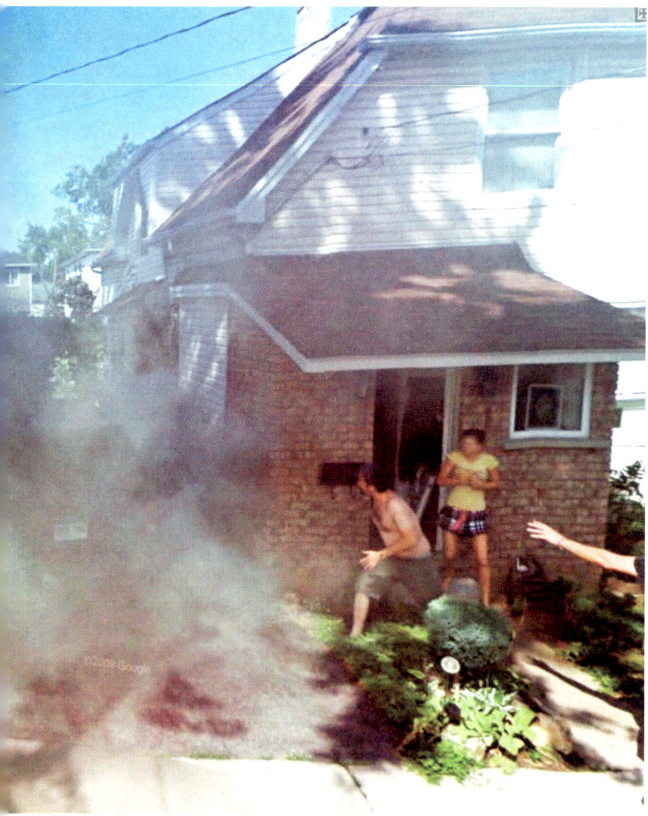

## MILJOHN RUPERTO
## *JANUS*, 2014

Animated by Aimée de Jongh; Digital video with sound, 3′30″; loop

Miljohn Ruperto's work imbues the famous, bivalent figure of the rabbit-duck with tragic significance. First published in the German humor magazine *Fliegende Blätter* in 1892, the rabbit-duck is a prime example of a class of optical illusions, the *Kippfigur* (multistable figure), which has long fascinated cognitive scientists. We see either duck or rabbit, but not both simultaneously. Yet this image cannot be reduced to the combination of duck and rabbit, for the eye oscillates between the two choices. In Ludwig Wittgenstein's *Philosophical Investigations* of 1953, this act of apprehension led to speculations about what changed in the external world in the instant that an internal act of cognition takes place, conditioning us to apply a certain interpretative scheme, a "seeing-as."

Ruperto's animated rabbit-duck is not merely a problem of logic, but is cast in a more tragic vein. By linking his version to Janus, the Roman god whose faces look to the past and the future, Ruperto extends the question of ambiguity beyond the problem of cognition. In the context of *Nervous Systems*, this *Kippfigur* held in suspense may also allude to the paradoxical status of identity-formation in contemporary capitalism, which is seeking to "mine" the tacit schemes of knowledge and interpretation embedded in subjectivity, but which also leads to the attunement of these very subjectivities to the patterns and schemes thus normatively circumscribed.

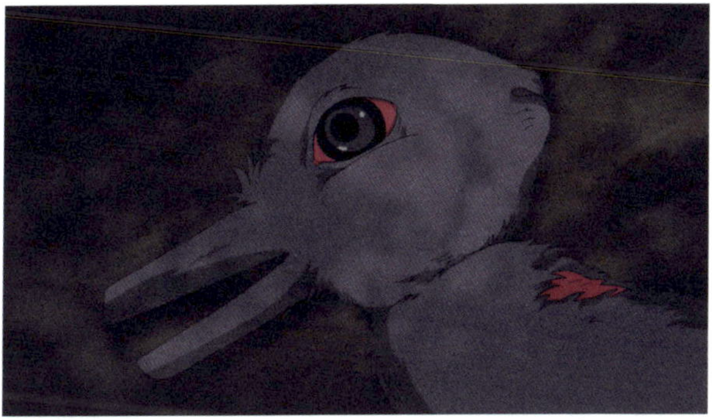

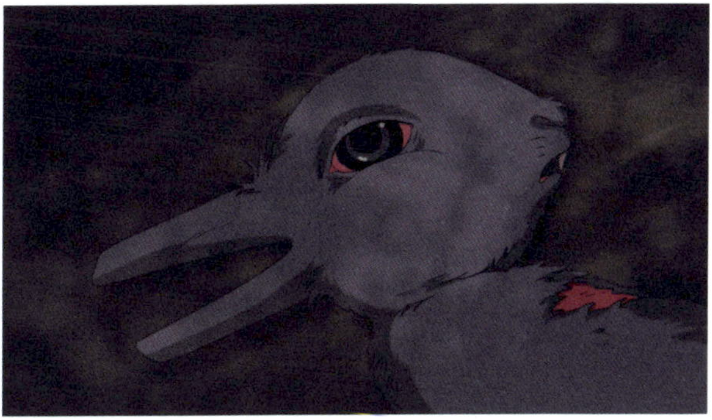

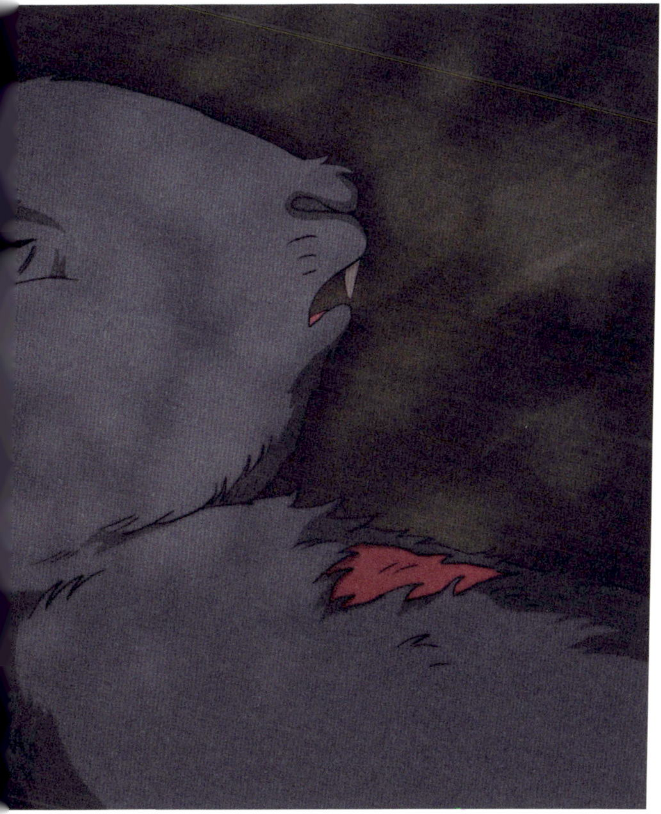

## RYBN.ORG
## *ALGORITHMIC TRADING FREAK SHOW,* 2013–14

Mixed-media installation: 4 vitrines with electronics and objects; dimensions variable

RYBN, a French collective formed in 1999, since its inception has sought to pursue extradisciplinary investigations. The ambition of this field, as cultural theorist Brian Holmes defined it, is to undertake rigorous investigations outside the ordinary subject matter of aesthetic production—finance, biotechnology, geography, urbanism, psychiatry, and so on. The piece shown, consists of material extrapolated from research undertaken for a work of 2011—*ADM VIII*, a bot which trades securities on the world market. Launched at ZKM Karlsruhe, the bot *ADM VIII* was an assemblage of modular programs employing open-source software. With an initial capitalization of 10,000 US dollars, it had been programmed not to make a profit, but merely to remain in operation until the account upon which it drew reached a zero balance.

In preparation for the launch of *ADM VIII*, RYBN's members immersed themselves in the history of trading software and the algorithms such programs use, in order to understand more about how they work and what their use implies for the future of the financial markets. As carefully guarded secrets, only algorithms that prove unprofitable become public. RYBN compiled hundreds of scientific articles and press reports about automated-trading software, searching for faulty algorithms, uncovering those that have proved successful.

The organization of *Algorithmic Trading Freak Show* is much like a cabinet of curiosities or a specimen collection. Laid out on long tables are a collection of diagrammatically rendered algorithms with evocative names—Sniper, Sumo, Guerilla, etc.—creating a repository of the failures of computer-based trading.

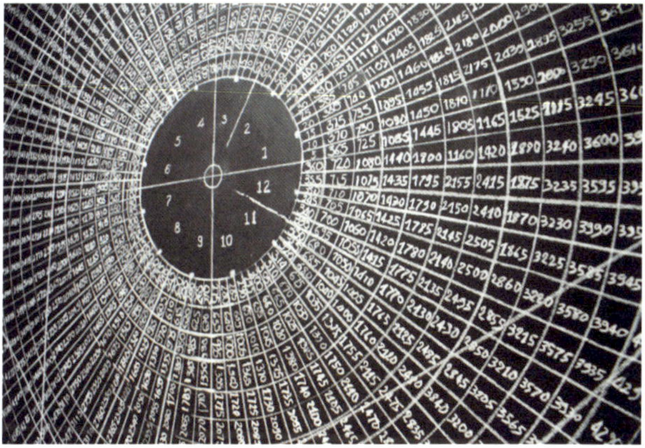

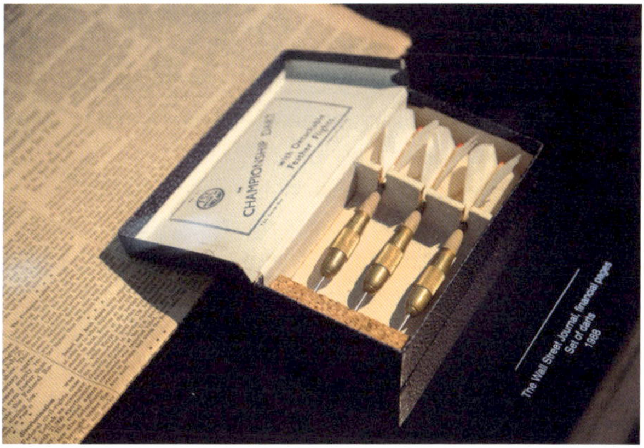

# DIERK SCHMIDT
## *"ICH WEISS WAS … WAS DU NICHT WEISST…"— WHEN OPINION BECOMES AN OCCASION FOR CALCULATION*, 2001/2006; *IBM STICKS ON HOLLERITH*, 2007

Oil on PVC foil and oil on mirror foil (diptych); 281 × 201.5 cm; diptych ca. 96.3 × 152.5 cm; 96 × 131 cm; Oil on PVC foil; 98.3 × 392 cm

A central question Dierk Schmidt addresses in his work is what form History painting might take in today's media-saturated age. In his painting cycle Schmidt depicted a fictitious episode of the well-known German TV talk show *Sabine Christiansen*, and painted variously mirrored scenes from the episode on large-scale PVC films, thus echoing the editing room as a site of image-construction. Broadcast on March 21, 2001, the episode, allegedly entitled "When Opinion Becomes an Occasion for Calculation," had Christiansen's guests gathered to discuss the contentious topic of compensation for forced labor during the National Socialist era—an admittedly late initiative to come to terms with this as-yet neglected aspect of Nazi history and German businesses, which was stirring a major public debate at the time. Yet it appeared that the association of major German firms deliberately delayed the processes of reaching an agreement over compensation, thus winning time while many of the victims were passing away from old age.

The time also saw the publication of the book *IBM and the Holocaust* by American journalist Edwin Black. An exhaustively researched account of the close relationship between the pioneering American company and the Nazi regime, Black documents the Nazi's use of the Hollerith punch card (produced by its IBM-owned subsidiary, DEHOMAG) in classifying individuals by nationality, race, creed, physical disability, and so on. As the slow rate of disbursement in Germany's compensation program had become a national scandal, significantly, in one painting of the cycle Schmidt depicts the moment when an audience member launched a "slimy" (a viscous green children's toy) at Wolfgang Gibowski, spokesman for the Foundation Remembrance, Responsibility and Future (Stiftung EVZ).

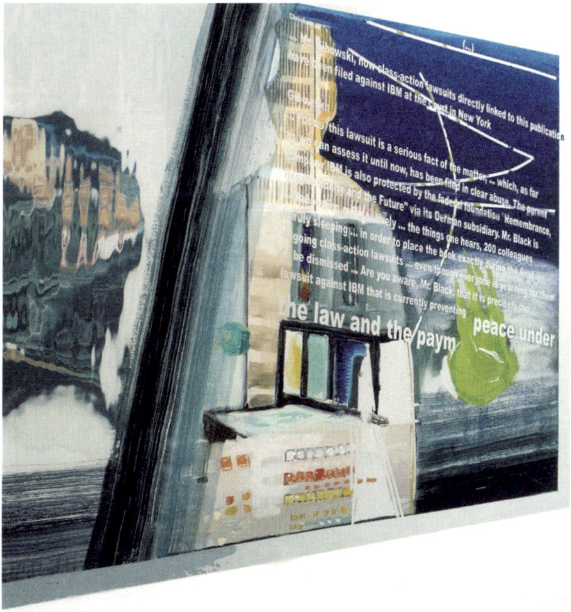

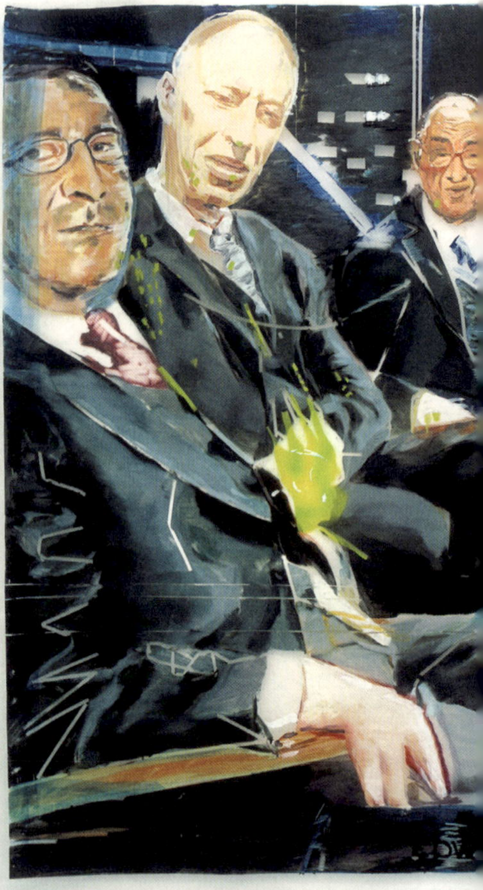

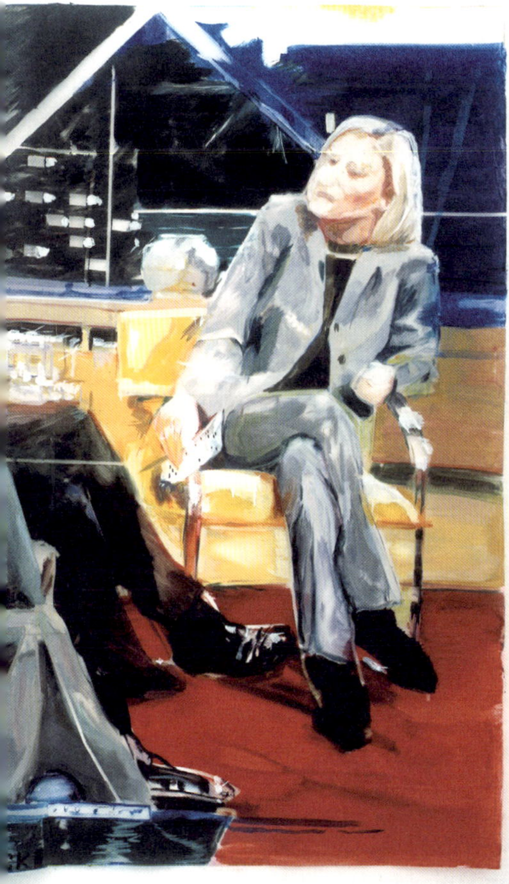

## EYAL SIVAN AND AUDREY MAURION
## *AUS LIEBE ZUM VOLK*, 2003

Film, color, sound; 88′

When the Democratic Republic of Germany collapsed in 1989, it is estimated that the Ministry of State Security (or *Stasi*) had 91,000 full-time employees and 300,000 informants (or "unofficial employees"). One outcome of this myriad network of informers was an enormous archive housing files on over six million individuals, and endless hours of video surveillance and taped interviews—an analogue precursor of the data-mining technologies employed today by government and big business.

A common post-GDR assessment of the Stasi is of a bureaucracy staffed by near-automatons, blindly following the dictates of their paranoid superiors. In *Aus Liebe zum Volk*, filmmakers Eyal Sivan and Audrey Maurion portray a far more complex reality, based on the book *Ausgedient. Ein Stasi-Major erzählt* by East German author Reinhardt O. Hahn. It is a first-person account by one Major S., a career Stasi officer who four months after the Ministry's disintegration took stock of his career, offering up a highly personal defense of his complicity in creating the GDR security state.

Using archival footage culled from the Stasi Records Agency (BStU), Stasi training films, recordings of interrogations and surveillance, and material from private and public archives, Sivan and Maurion seamlessly knit Major S.'s account, voiced by the actor Axel Prahl, into a montage composed from these varied sources. The conjunction creates a chilling discordance between the bathos of Major S.'s words and the nature of the Stasi's authoritarian project.

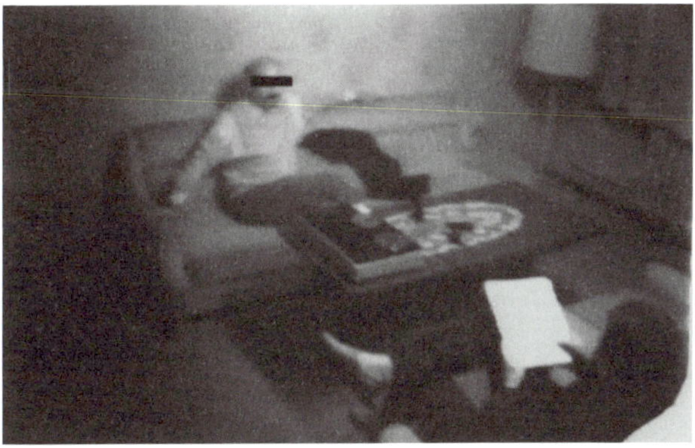

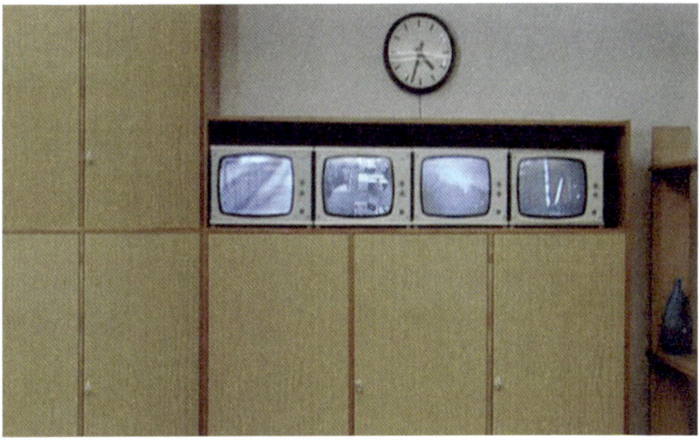

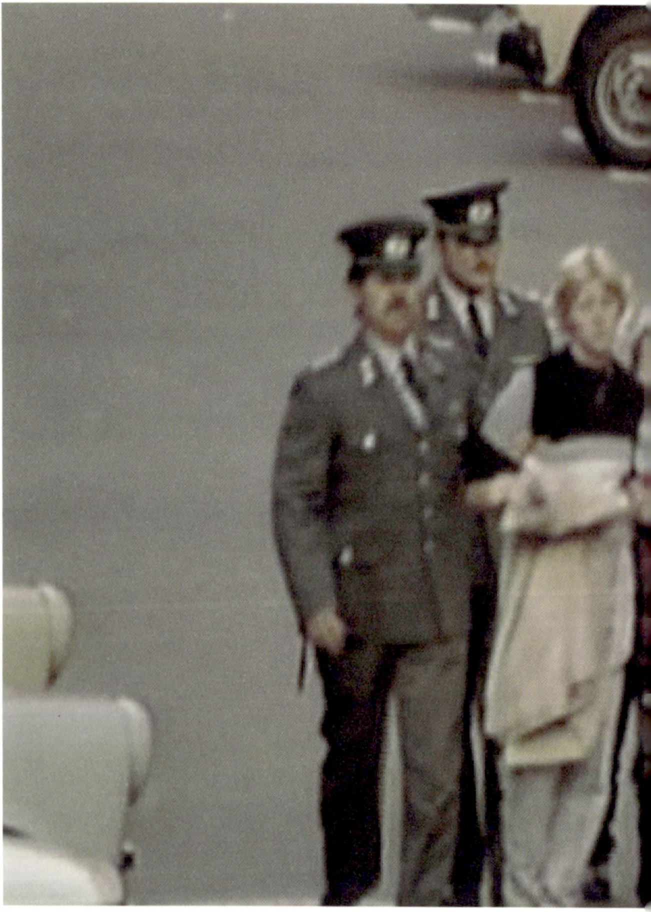

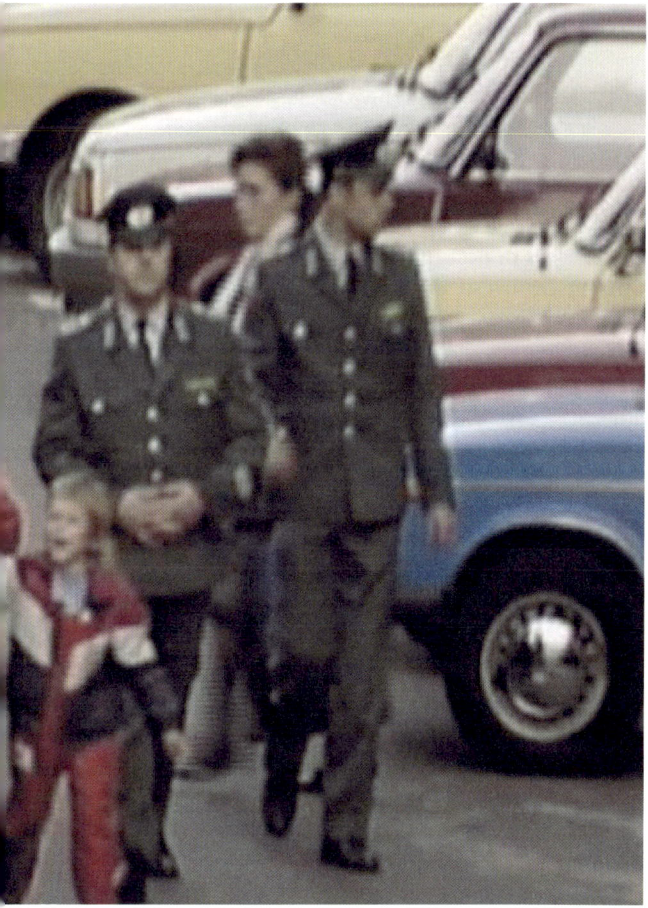

## JÜRG SPILLER
## *PAUL KLEE: FORM- UND GESTALTUNGS-LEHRE, BAND 2: UNENDLICHE NATURGESCHICHTE,* 1970

Book, Schwabe & Co. Verlag, Basel, page 285

In 1970, the second in a two-volume collection of Paul Klee's aesthetic writings was published, edited by the artist Jürg Spiller. Derived from essays, unpublished writings, and preparatory lecture notes, this volume, entitled *The Nature of Nature*, presented Klee's multifaceted analysis of natural forms, including his self-analysis of *Grid Dance*, a watercolor from 1935. Swedish geographer Torsten Hågerstrand and French philosopher Gilles Deleuze subsequently used Klee's *Grid Dance* analysis in their critique of the use and function of statistical aggregates in technologically advanced societies. Over the statistically derived "dividual," Hågerstrand advocated the indivisible human being, whose "lived corporeality could be represented through "chronogeography," "traceable and measurable paths in space-time." Deleuze employed this same terminology to describe the shift from the mass/individual pair to a more fluid form of power in which the individual was conceived in terms of statistical attributes, facilitating processes of control that did not require mechanisms of confinement for their effectiveness.

In the mutations undergone by power post-internet, we have subsequently seen big data merge with chronospatial mapping techniques, in which data-collection and individual tracking technologies merge. This combination is also suggested by Klee's morphosis of ground into figure, which seems to presage a conception of the individual less and less separable from the cumulative data that can be extrapolated from his or her existence. As French theorist Grégoire Chamayou notes, such a conception belongs to an entirely different form of power, whose formal attributes are shared by policing, military reconnaissance, and marketing. "It might well be," he writes, "that we are entering *targeted societies*."

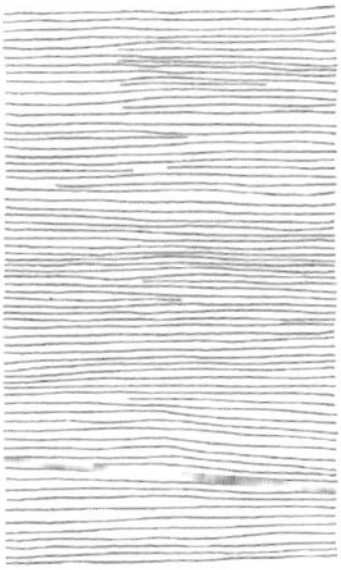

1

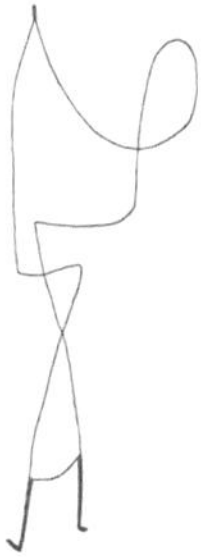

2

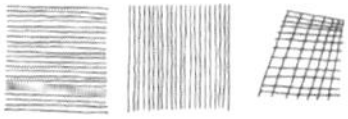

3

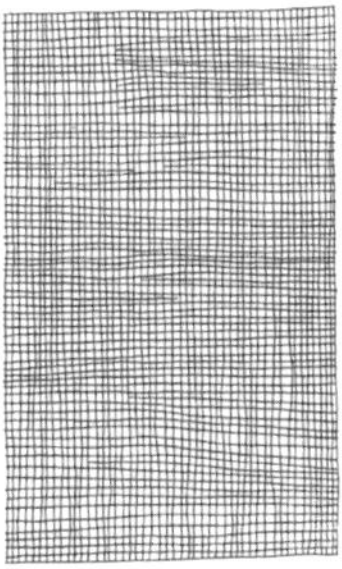

4

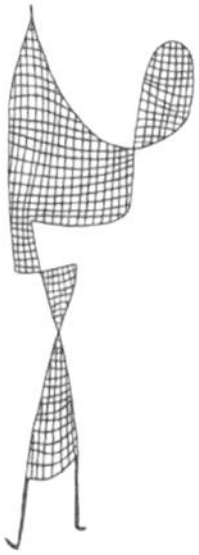

5

# DEBORAH STRATMAN
# *HACKED CIRCUIT*, 2014

HD video, color, sound; 15'05"

In the times of a ubiquitous war, where security concerns act as a template for far-reaching interventions into democratic societies, the distinction of what constitutes actual experience, itself the result of growing paranoia, ultimately becomes blurred and a matter of ideological concern. This blurring and its impacts on the perception of reality are at the heart of Deborah Stratman's film.

The work superimposes two scenes of paranoiac enactment: a scene in which a character takes apart his entire apartment in search of a hidden microphone, and scenes where we see Foley artists enact the paranoia by re-creating the scene's soundtrack. The reference here is to Francis Ford Coppola's film *The Conversation* from 1974, which revolves around a surveillance expert played by Gene Hackman, and whose reception ultimately was framed by the unfolding events of the Watergate scandal.

In Stratman's film, a single lengthy tracking shot oscillates between the interior and exterior of a Foley stage in Burbank, California, where a group of Foley artists are reproducing the ambient soundtrack of this iconic scene of film history. Convincing filmic reality, as is well known and easily experienced, depends to a large degree on the soundtrack acting in support of, and as an interpretative aid to the dominant sense of sight. The focus on the Foley artists, who reproduce sound effects for cinema in real time by providing precisely synchronized high-fidelity recordings, reveals a similar paranoiac crack in the texture of (filmic) representation, pertaining to the fact that our suspension of disbelief is largely a construction, created by the painstaking work of sonic reconstruction.

Stratman, who has previously taken up the subject of government surveillance in her work, here approaches the topic obliquely. Caul takes his apartment apart, and the Foley artists re-create the dismantled sound of the original film, carefully mimicking Hackman's actions: Like Russian nesting dolls, processes of construction and fabrication are imbricated within one another.

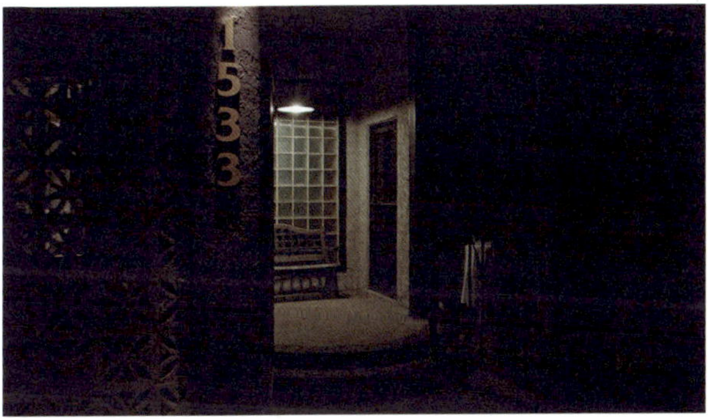


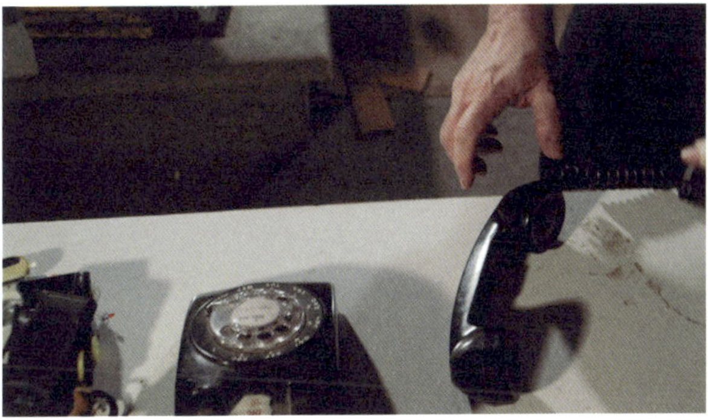

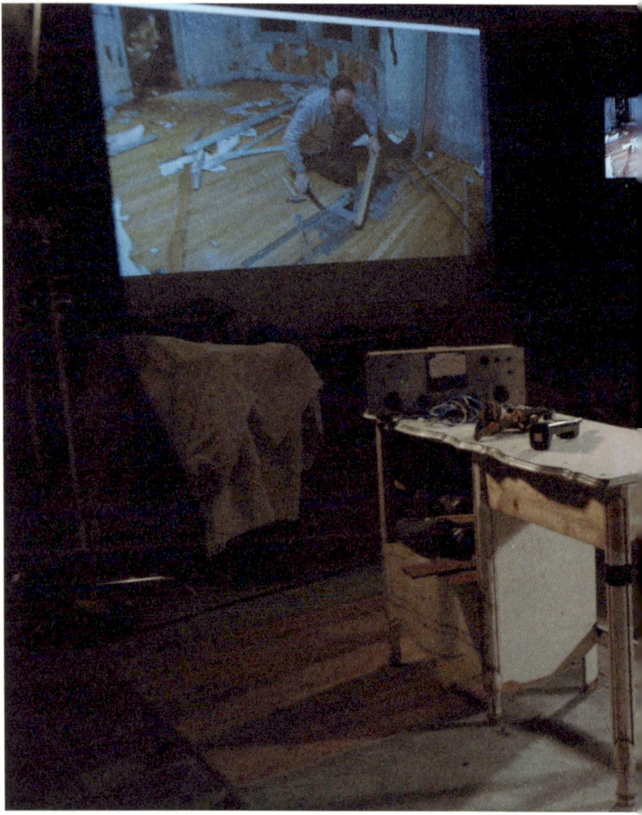

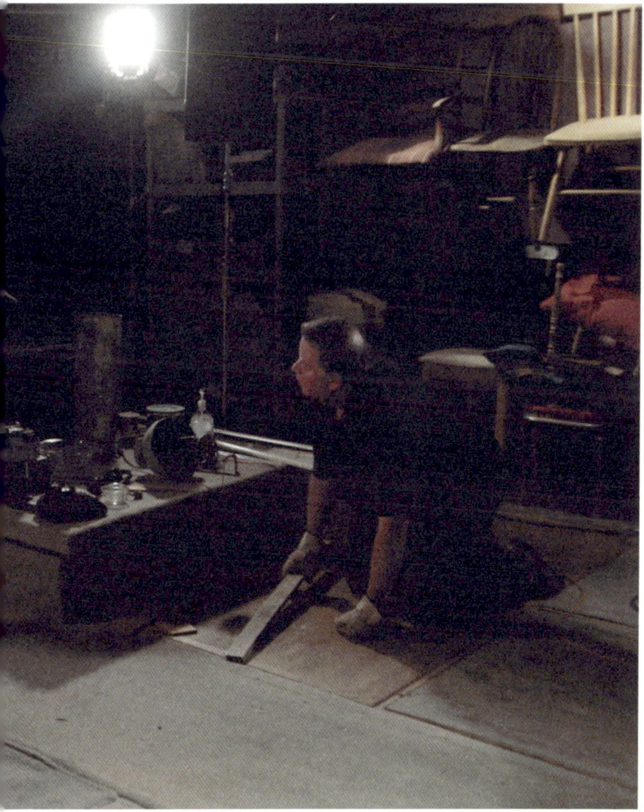

# ALEX VERHAEST
# *DINNER SCENE,* 2014

Interactive video installation; 9′

The recent work of Alex Verhaest subtly interweaves today's networked communication environment with the humanistic tradition of the Northern Renaissance. Her multifaceted work, *Temps Mort / Idle Times*, is fundamentally a reflection about our ever-failing relationship with time and the temporal paucity one experiences while using social media. It uses a loose, skeletal structure to gather a heterogeneous series of works around a common narrative: the effect of the suicide of an absent *pater familias* on his family, who find themselves simultaneously incapable of mourning or adequately dealing with the loss, and are accorded a specific subjective position in relation to this event, conveyed through a series of portraits.

In *Dinner Scene*, the family have been assembled in a tableau consciously aping Lucas Cranach the Elder's *The Last Supper*, interspersed with shots referencing the luxuriant still lives of Pieter Claesz and Willem Claesz Heda. The dead father's offspring are gathered around "Angelo," the narrator, and are depicted both before and after hearing of their father's passing. They are thus suspended in a psychological limbo, their ambivalence precipitating a profound psychic blockage, manifested in a series of lugubrious monologues. This video, which at first glance is easily mistaken for a static work, is activated via mobile phone, when visitors telephone "Peter," whose number is distributed on a business card.

Verhaest's critique of social media is nuanced. What *Dinner Scene* attempts to illustrate is the gulf between the limited emotional options expressible on social media and the psychic complexities that so often overwhelm us in real life.

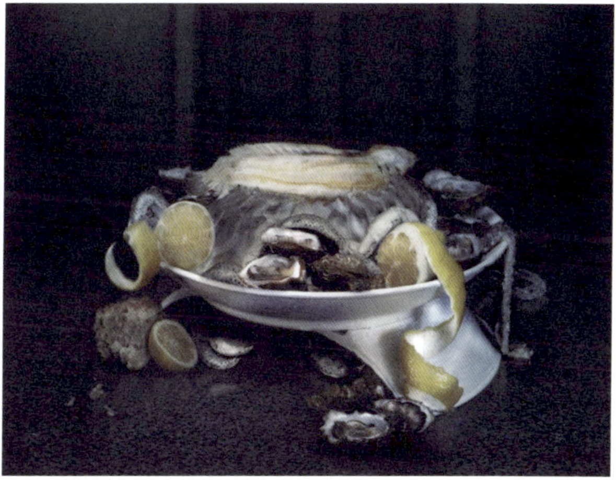

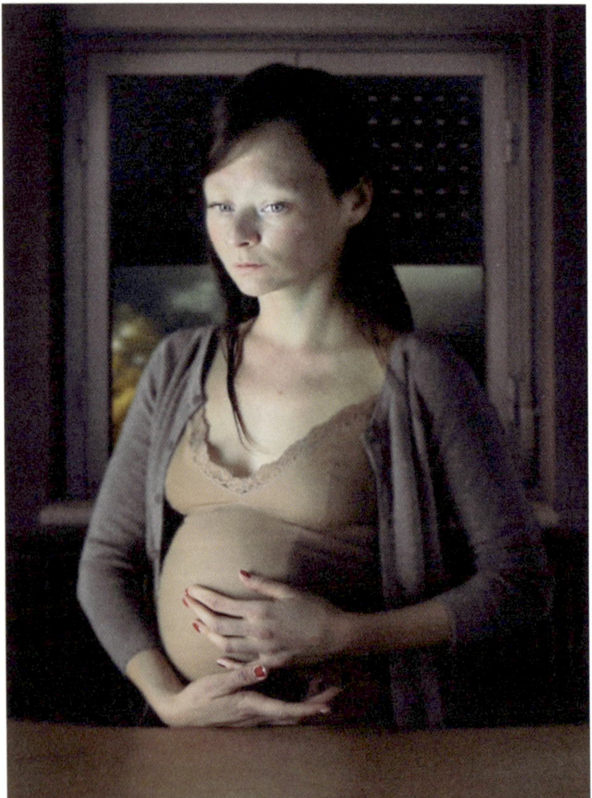

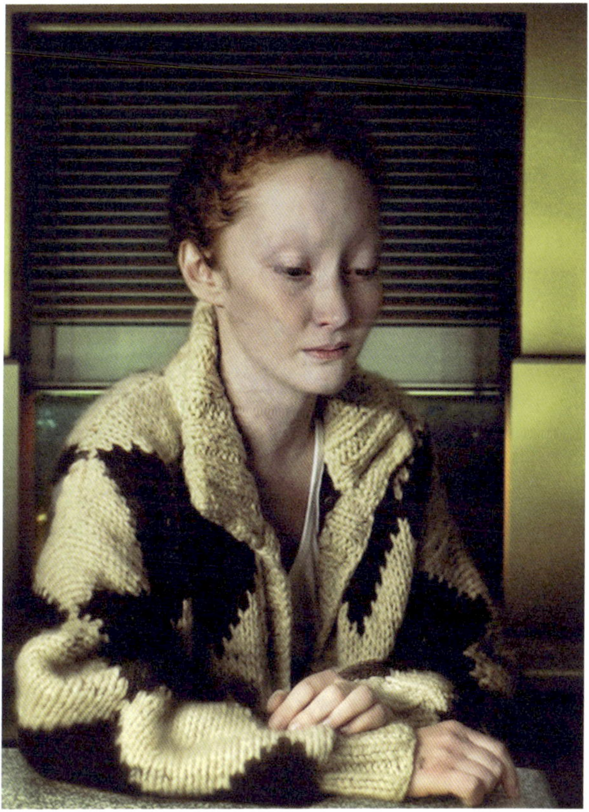

## STEPHEN WILLATS
## *I DON'T WANT TO BE LIKE ANYONE ELSE,* 1977

Details; Panel 2, 3 and 4; photographic prints, ink, Letraset text, gouache on card; six-panel work; each panel 109 x 76 cm

Stephen Willats, an early proponent of Conceptual art, often renders diagrammatic representations of social relations, reminiscent of cybernetic connection schemes, as abstractions that derive from his long-term engagements with specific communities, where he investigates the relationship between architecture, social systems, and the individual self. Willats, one of the few artists of his generation who engaged with the rise of information and systems theory, created his own idiosyncratic vision of cybernetics in the service of the social. In Willats' work from 1977, *I Don't Want To Be Like Anyone Else*, graphic lines map out the position of a woman in her social and physical surrounding. The panel texts represent questions that in the 1970s were at the core of the struggle of women battling with their normative position in society; who, according to Willats, were forced into a passivity which foreclosed participation in their own cultural identity, but which also reflect concerns of identity and freedom in the age of liberal consumerism.

The series *I Don't Want To Be Like Anyone Else* is set in Avondale Estate in Hayes, West London, and environs, chosen for being typical of the context in which most members of post-war British society were compelled to live. Within this tension of uniformity and individuality, translated into a formal play with specificity and abstraction, Willats created a dynamic structure that forced viewers to confront the hegemonic codes that mold individuals into specific ideological roles, as well as the ways in which these codes become naturalized by context and particularity. In the context of *Nervous Systems*, the work embodies a form of reflexive social quantification. It represents a historical momentum, where the social sciences and cybernetics had inherited the promises of progress and modernization, just before the rise of the ubiquitous data-sphere.

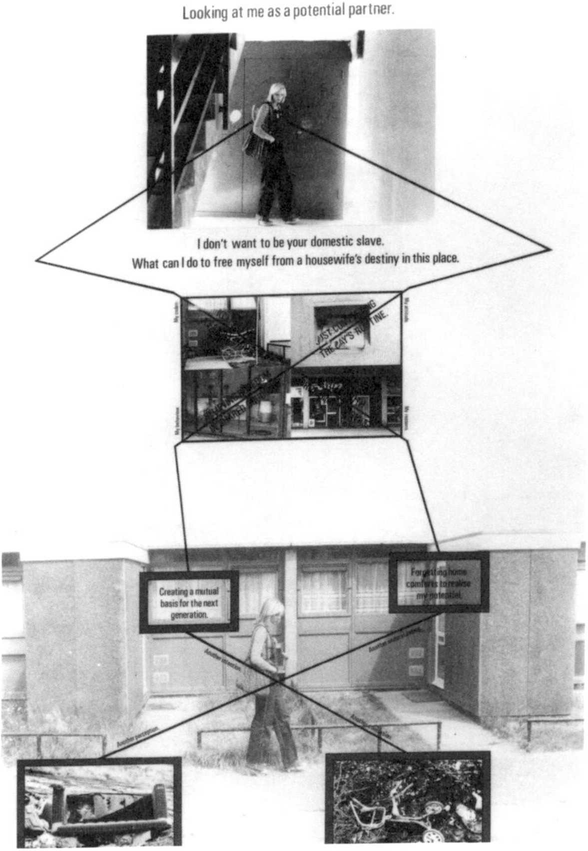

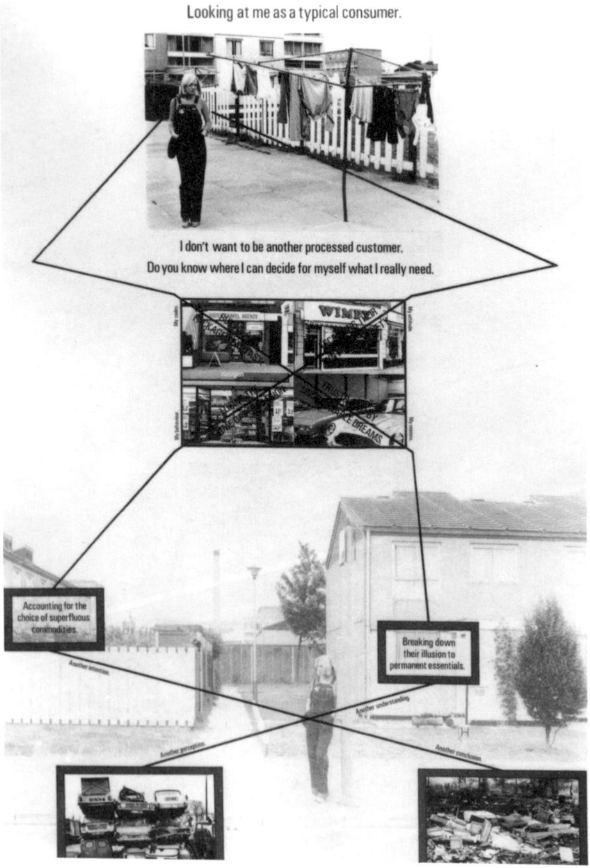

Looking at me as a typical consumer.
I don't want to be another processed customer.
Do you know where I can decide for myself what I really need.
Accounting for the choice of superfluous commodities.
Breaking down their illusion to permanent essentials.
Another intention.
Another understanding.
Another perception.
Another conclusion.

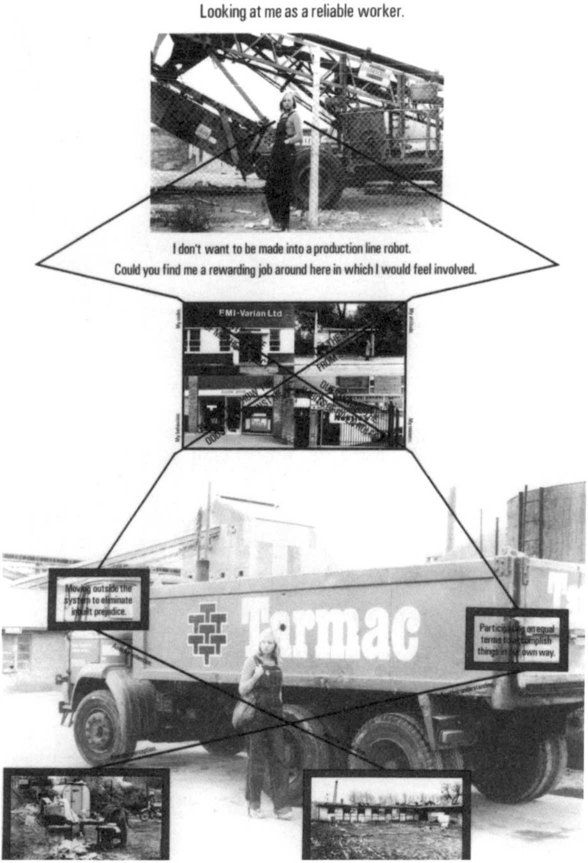
Looking at me as a reliable worker.
I don't want to be made into a production line robot.
Could you find me a rewarding job around here in which I would feel involved.
EMI-Varian Ltd

# INSTALLATION SHOTS

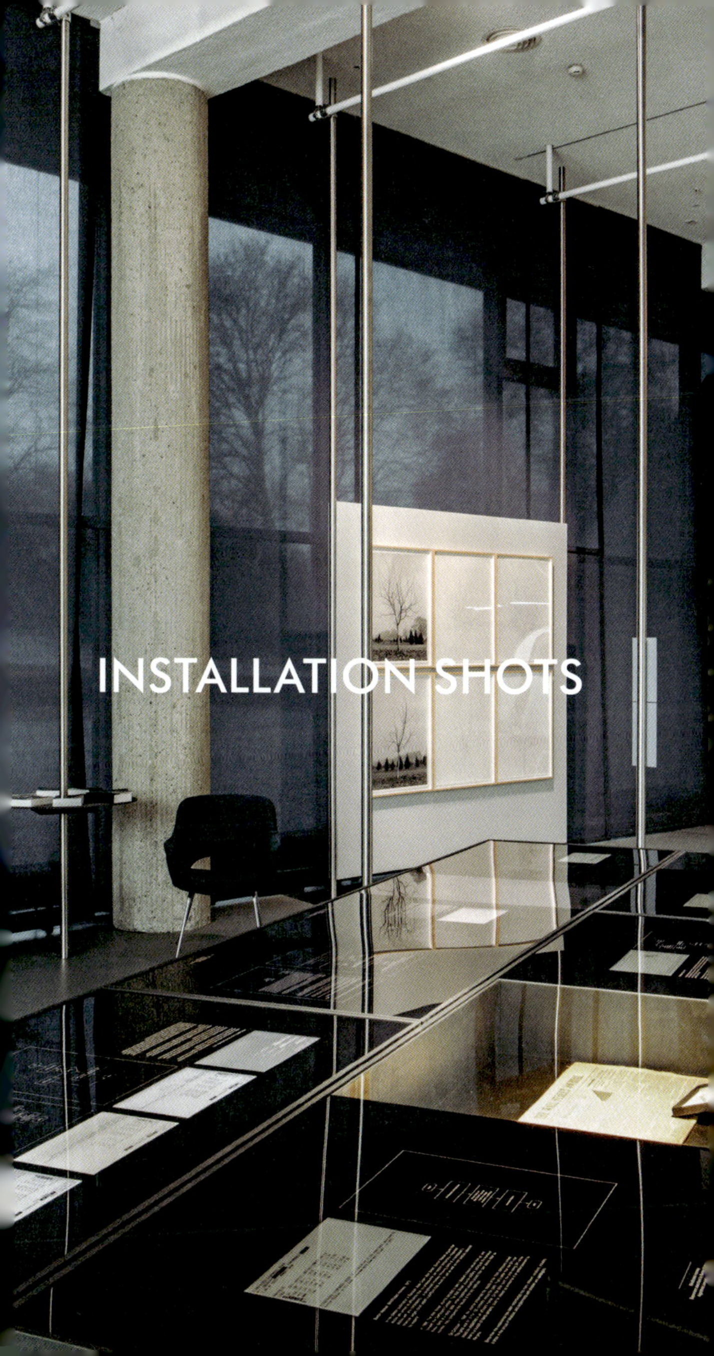

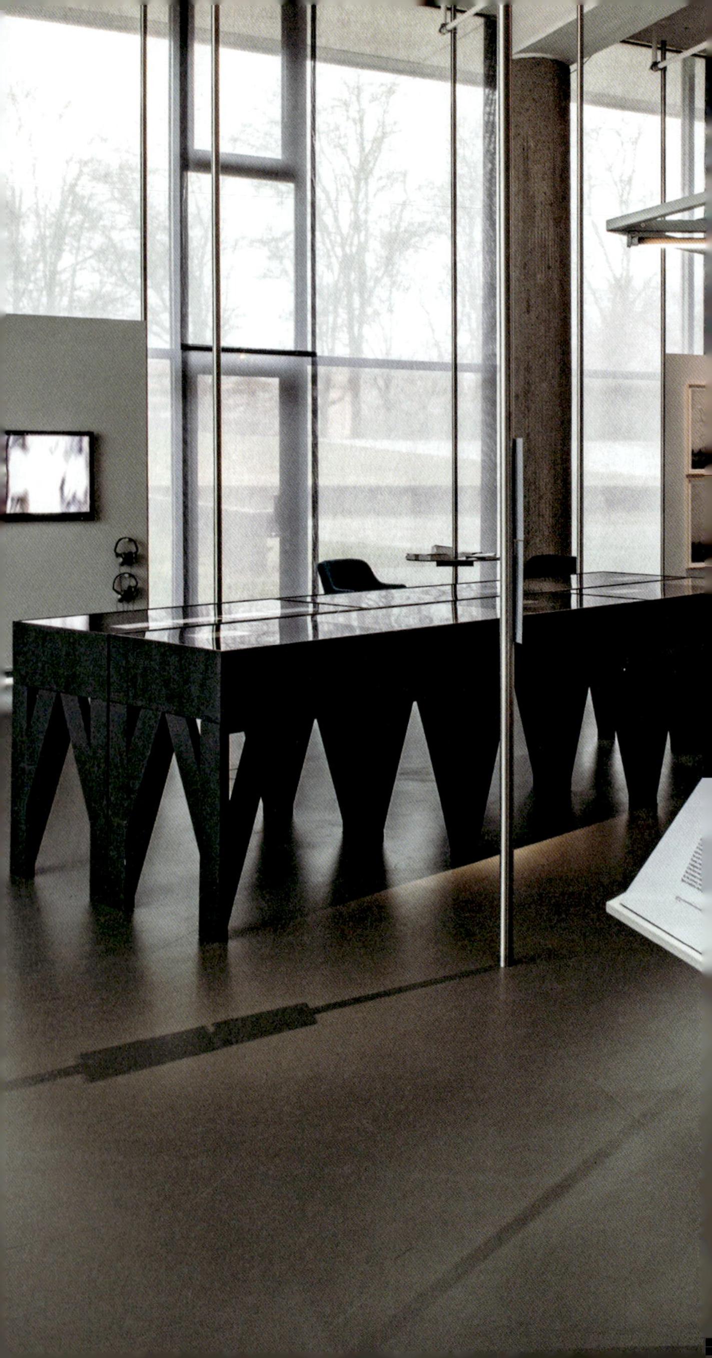

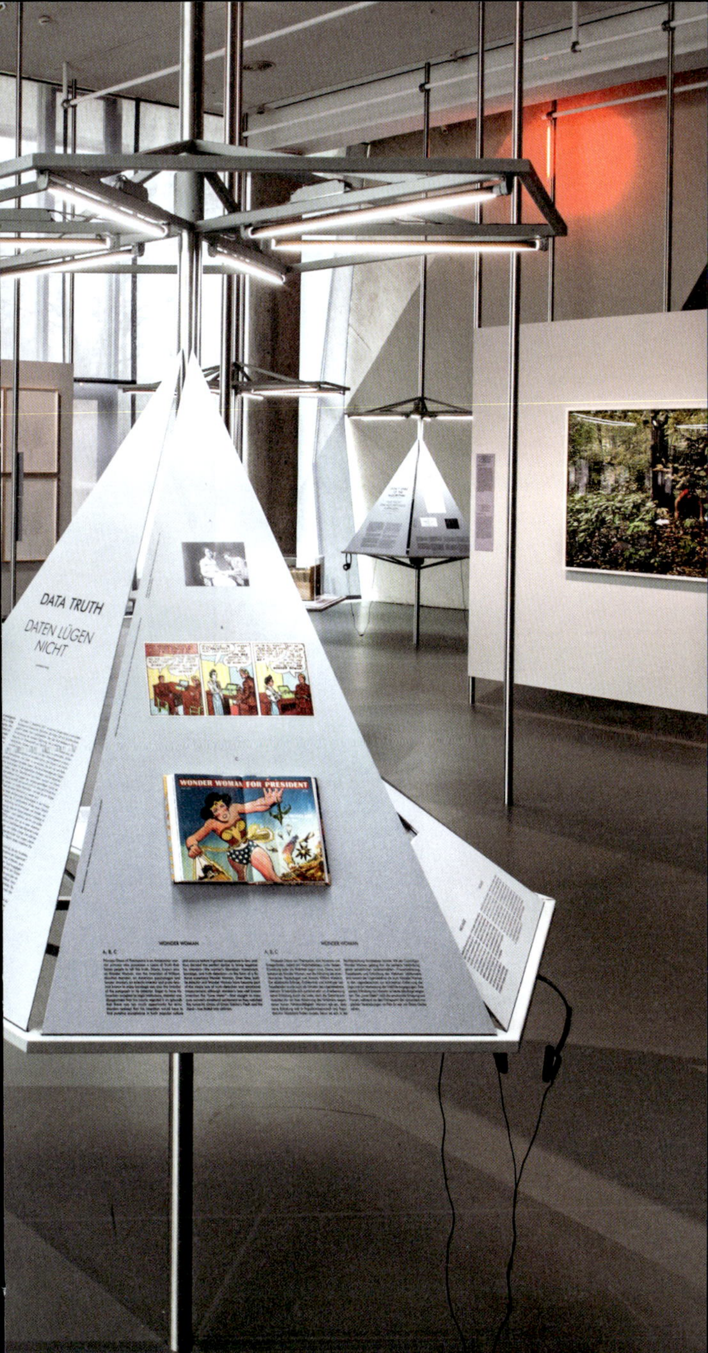

DATA TRUTH
DATEN LÜGEN NICHT
WONDER WOMAN FOR PRESIDENT
WONDER WOMAN
WONDER WOMAN

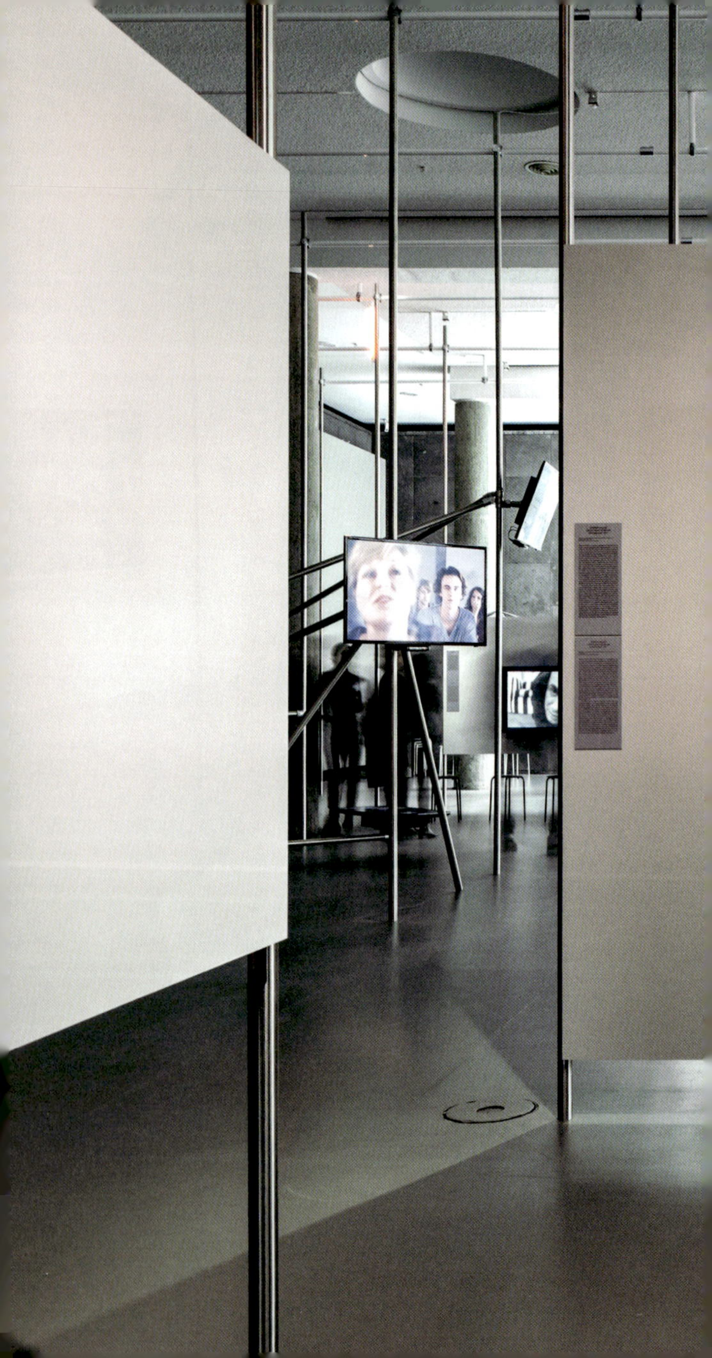

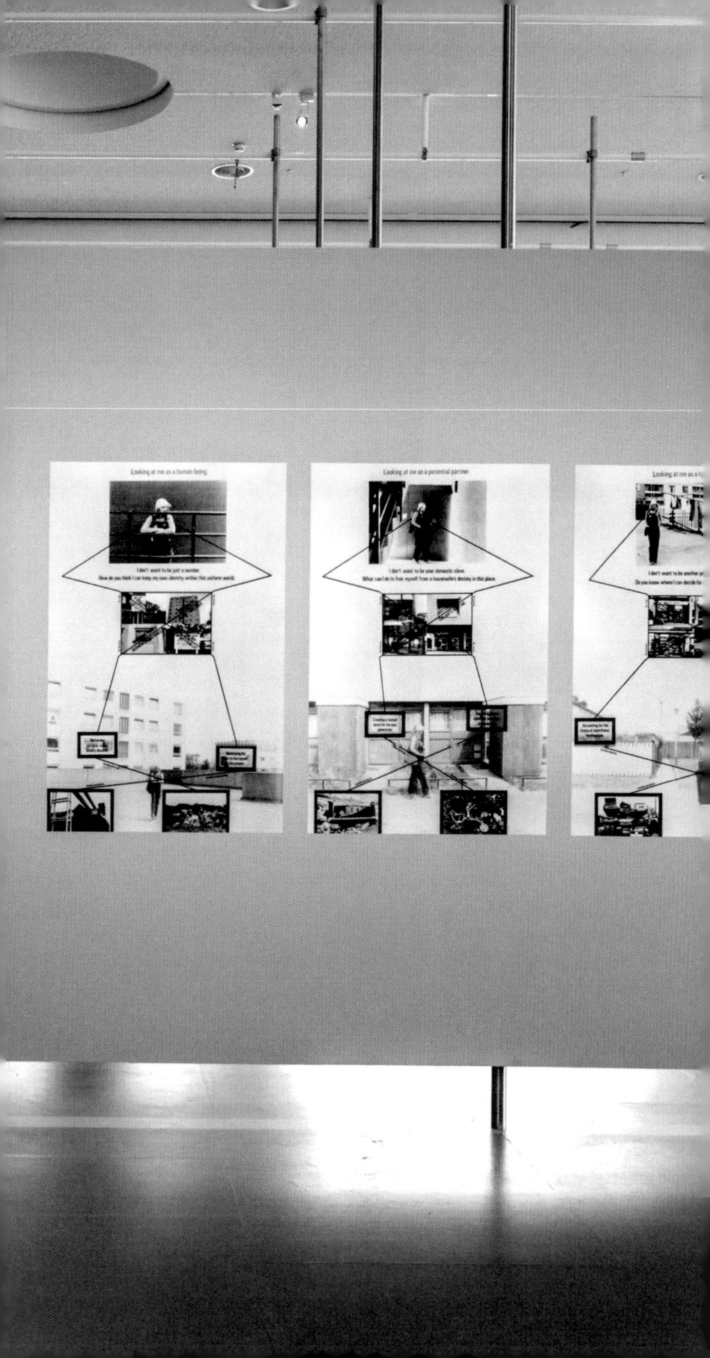

Looking at me as a human being.
I don't want to be just a number.
How do you think I can keep my own identity within this uniform world.
Looking at me as a potential partner.
I don't want to be your domestic slave.
What can I do to free myself from a housewife's destiny in this place.

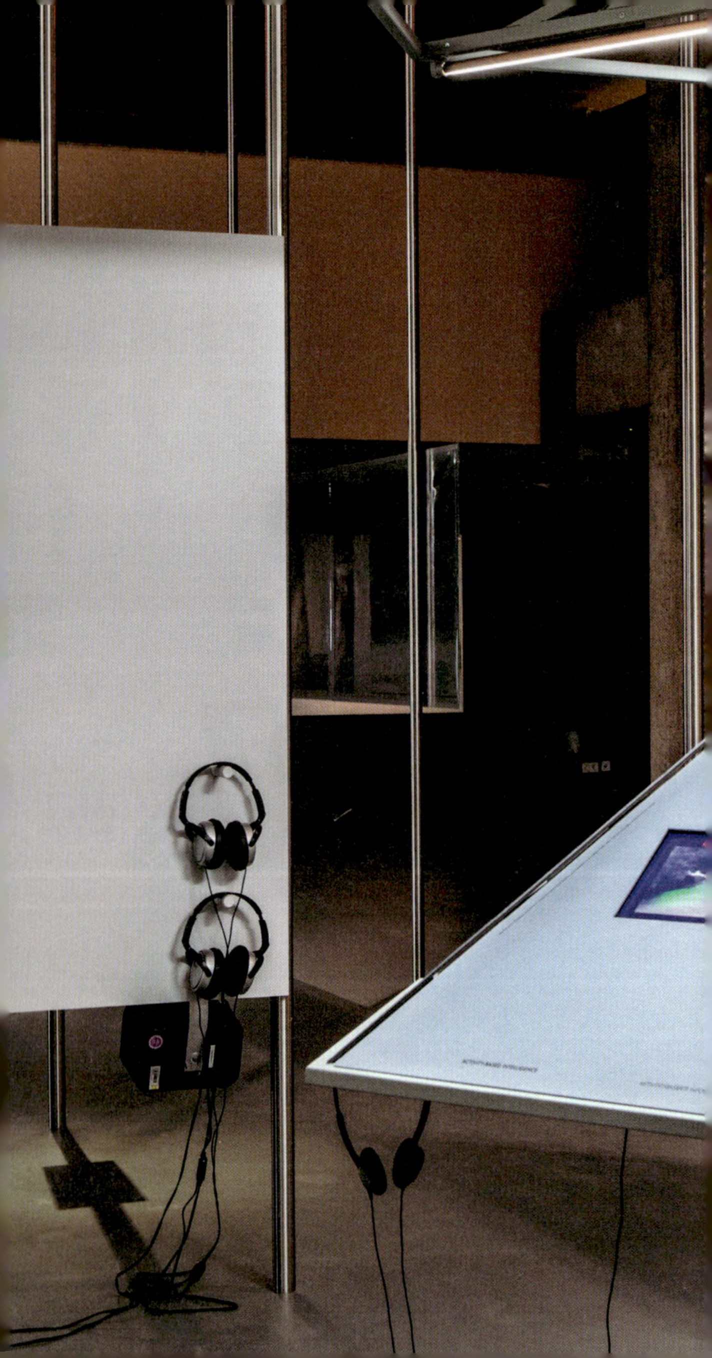

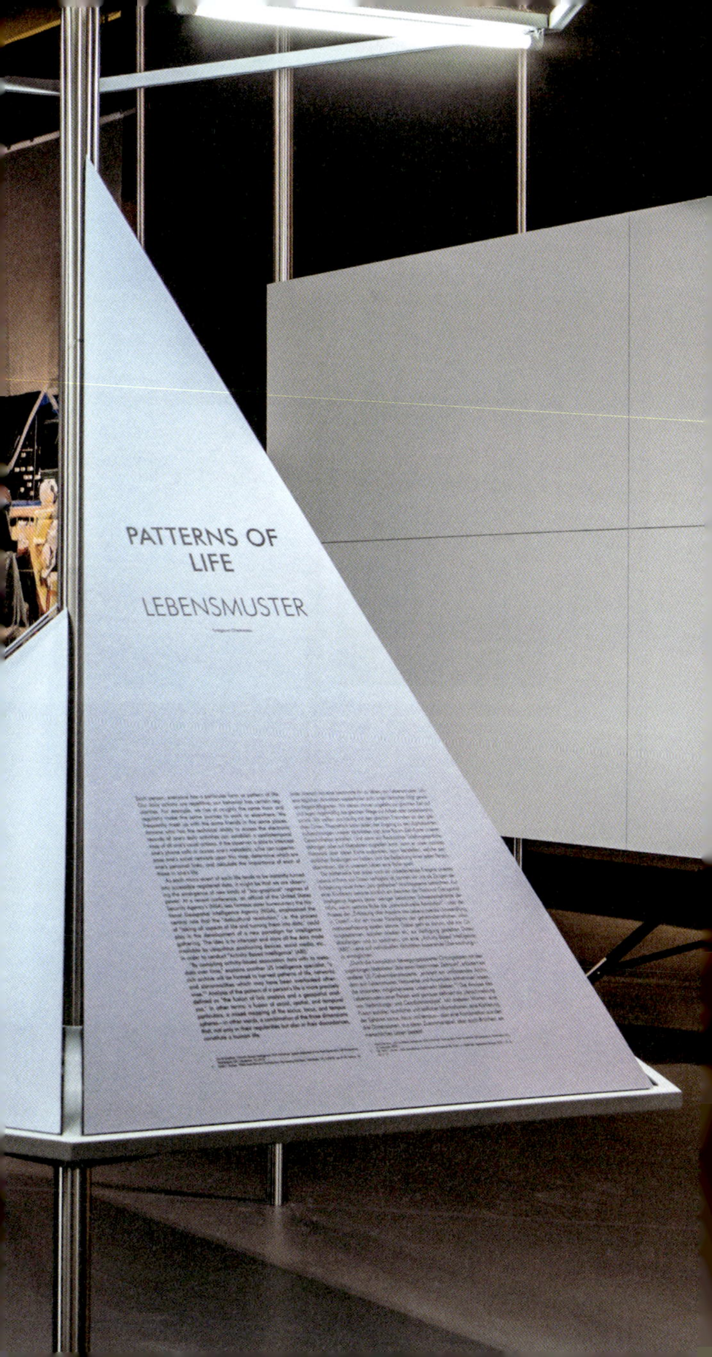
PATTERNS OF
LIFE
LEBENSMUSTER

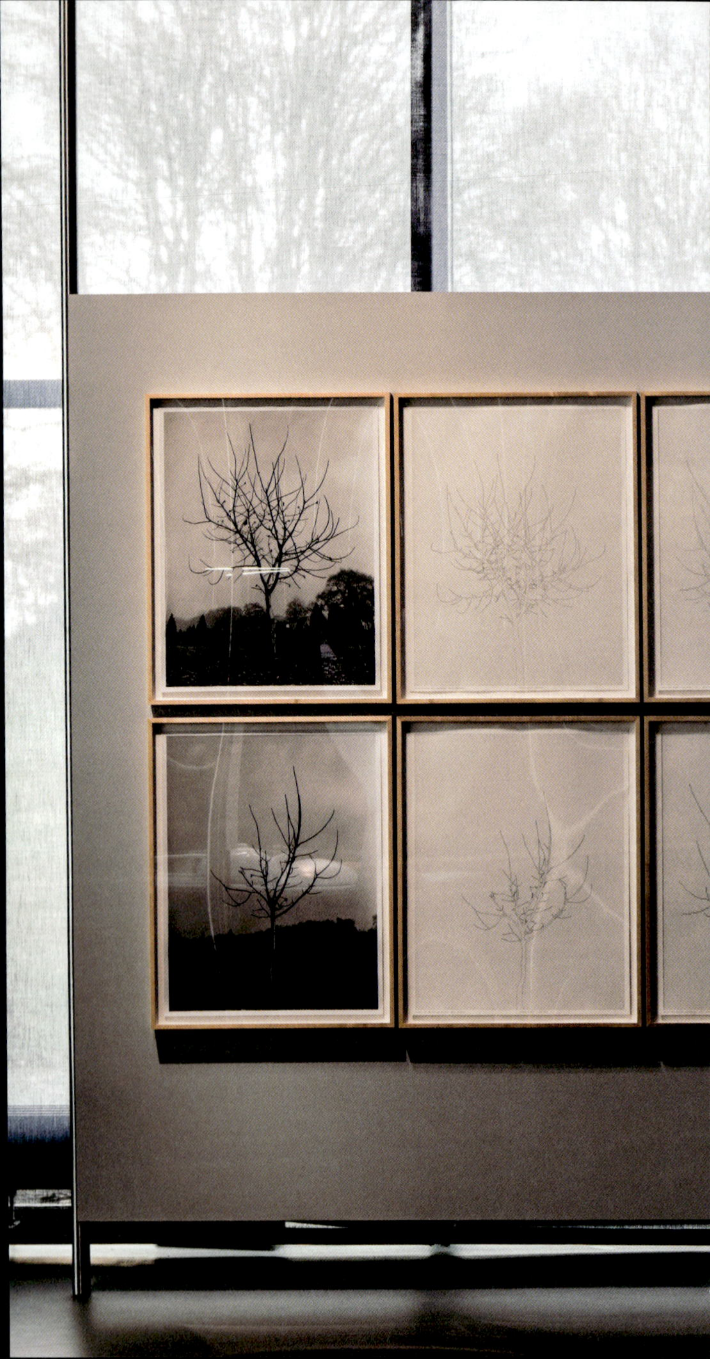

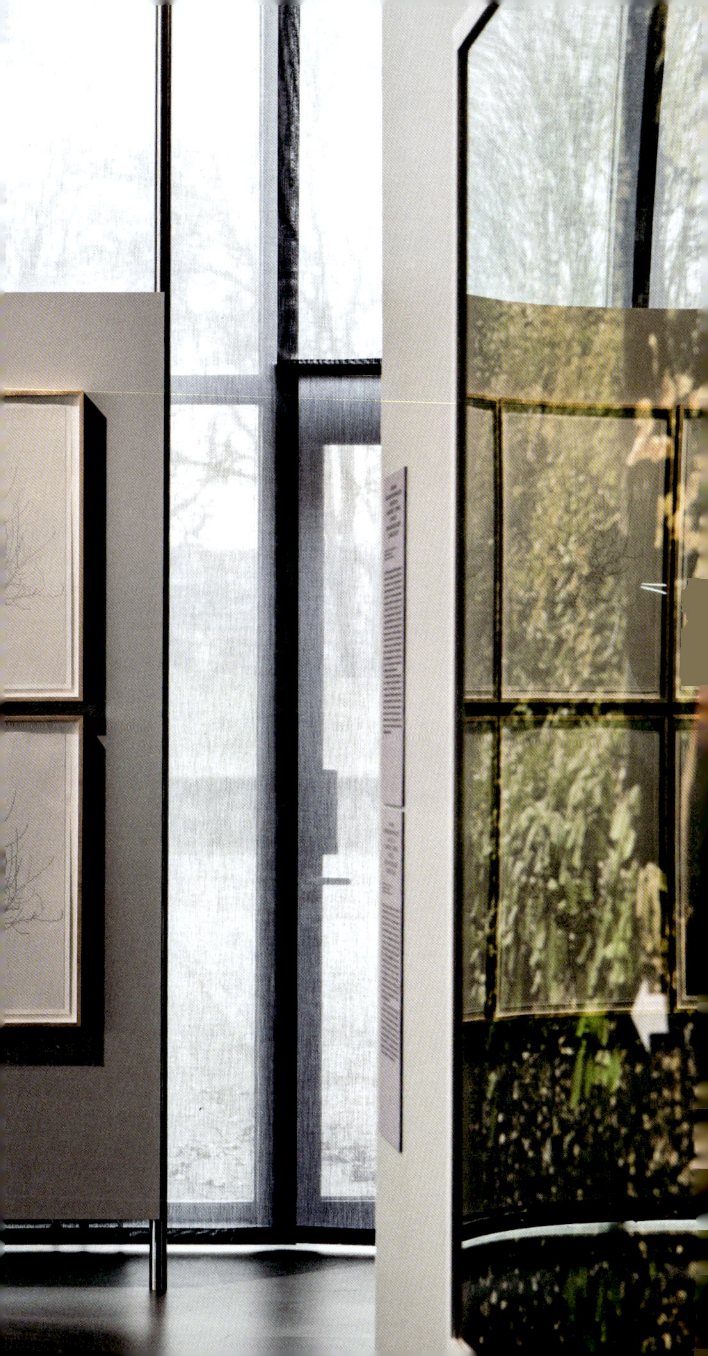

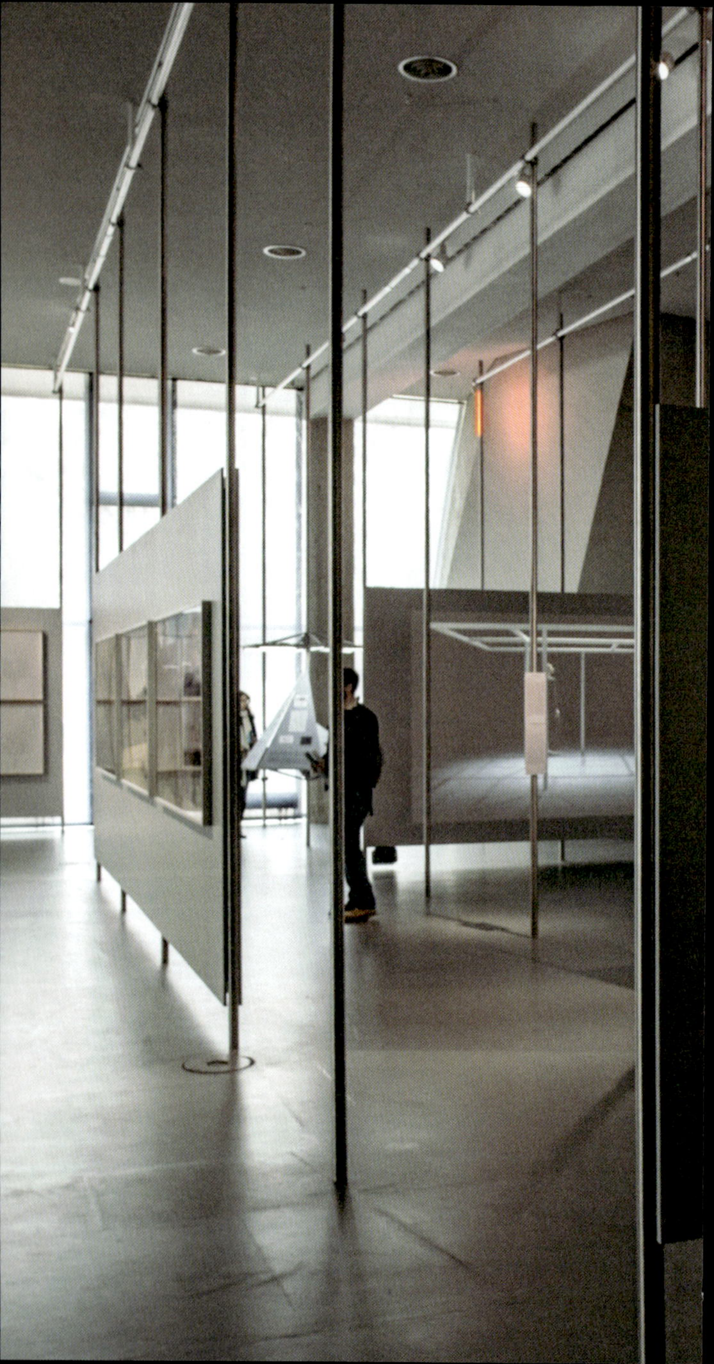

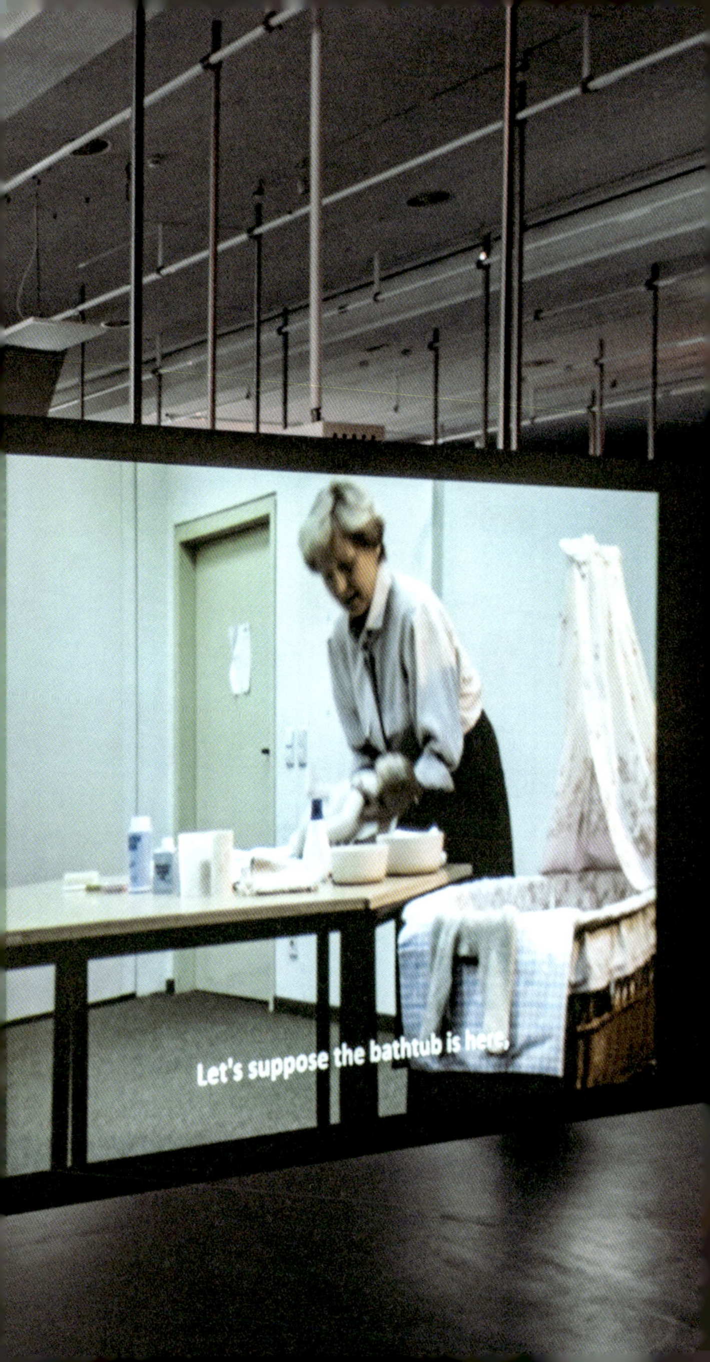
Let's suppose the bathtub is here.

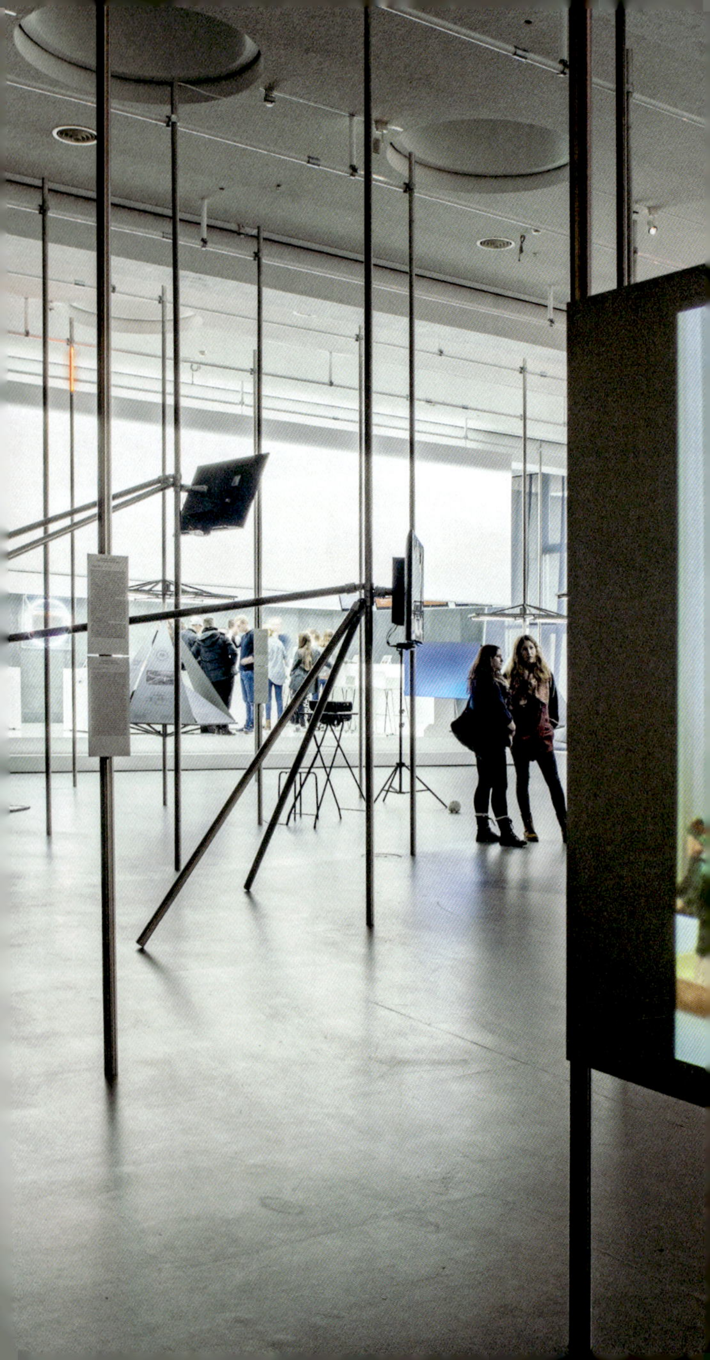

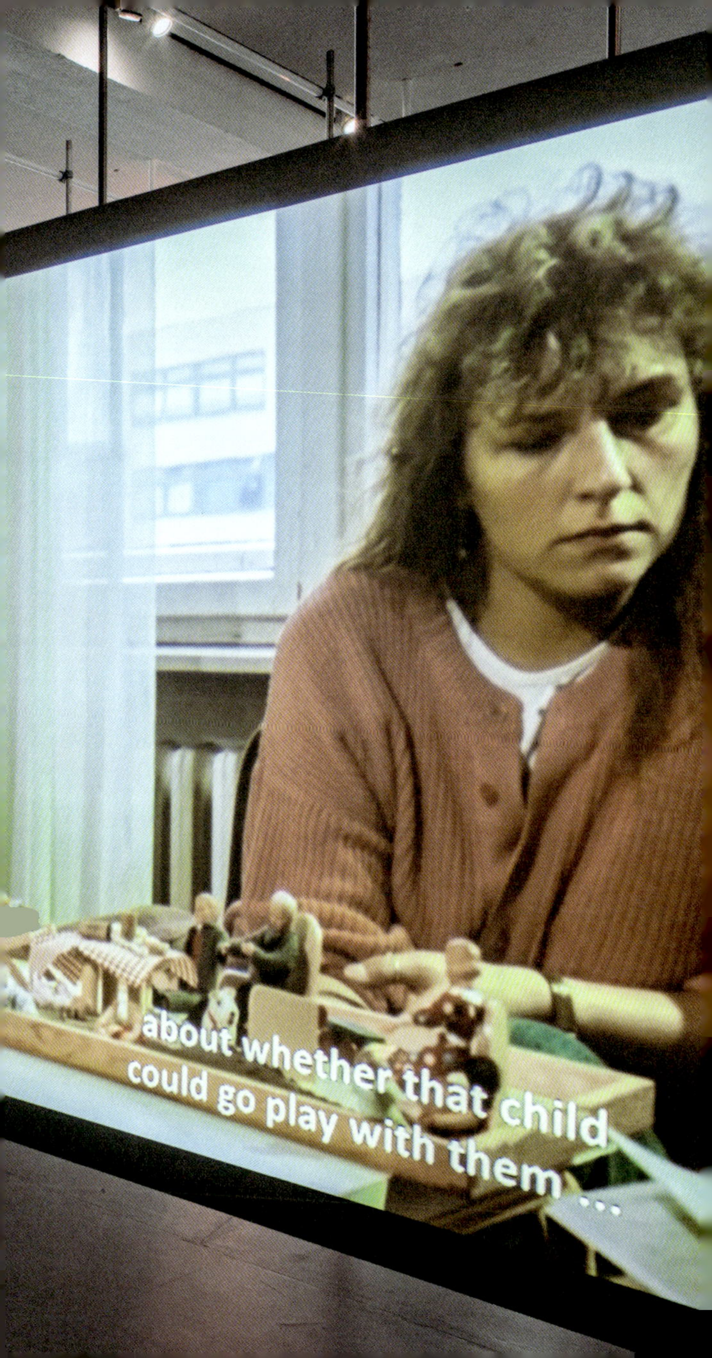
about whether that child
could go play with them ...

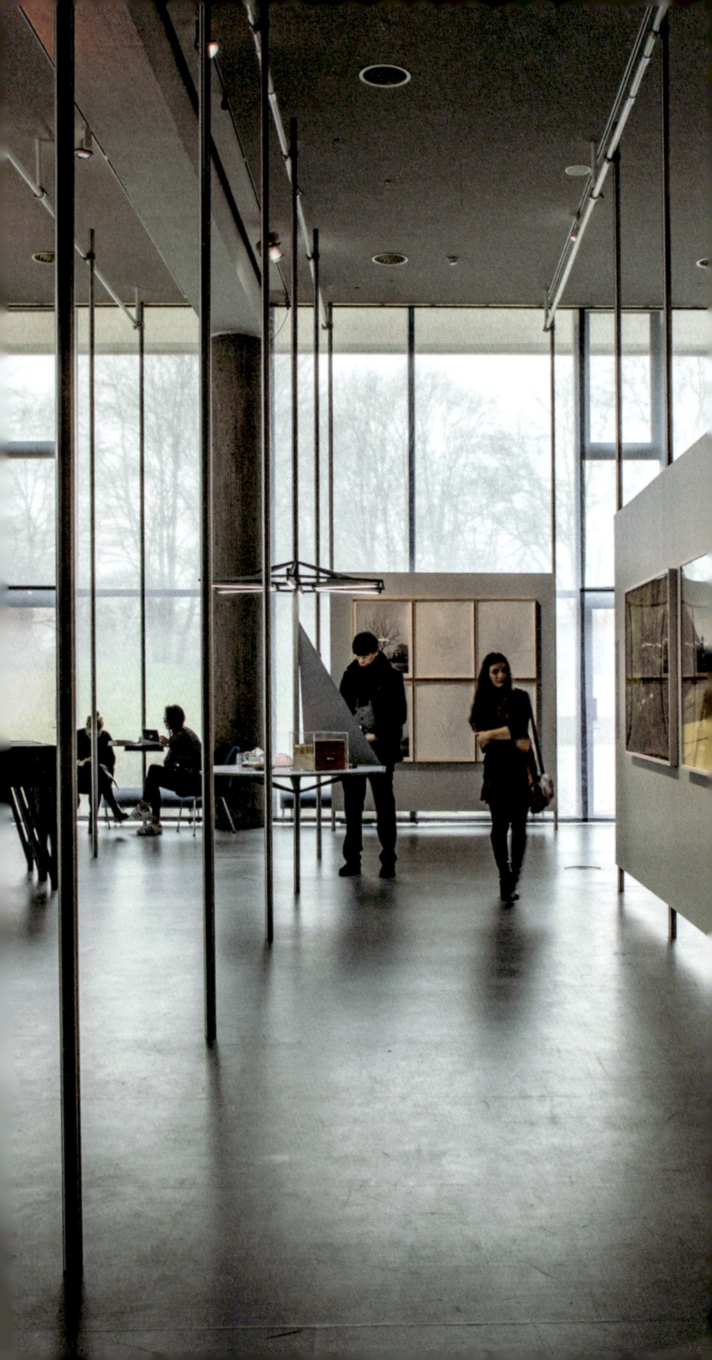

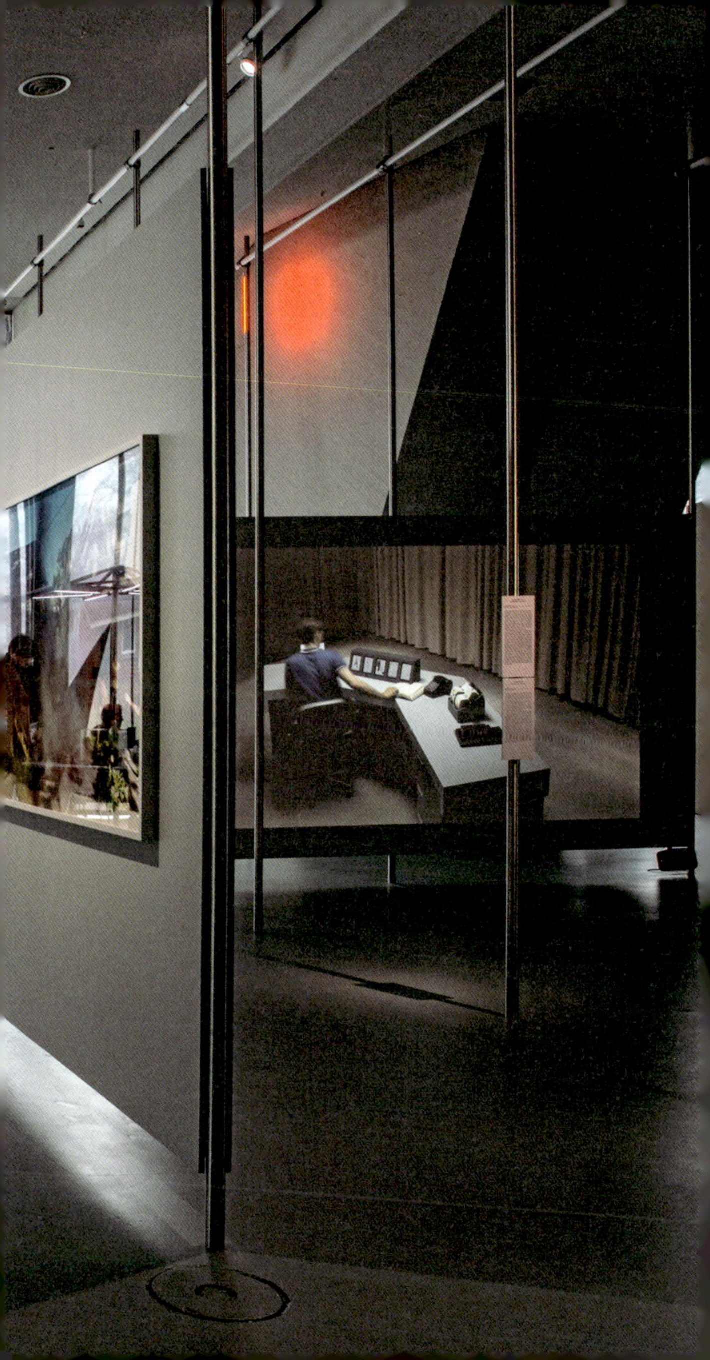

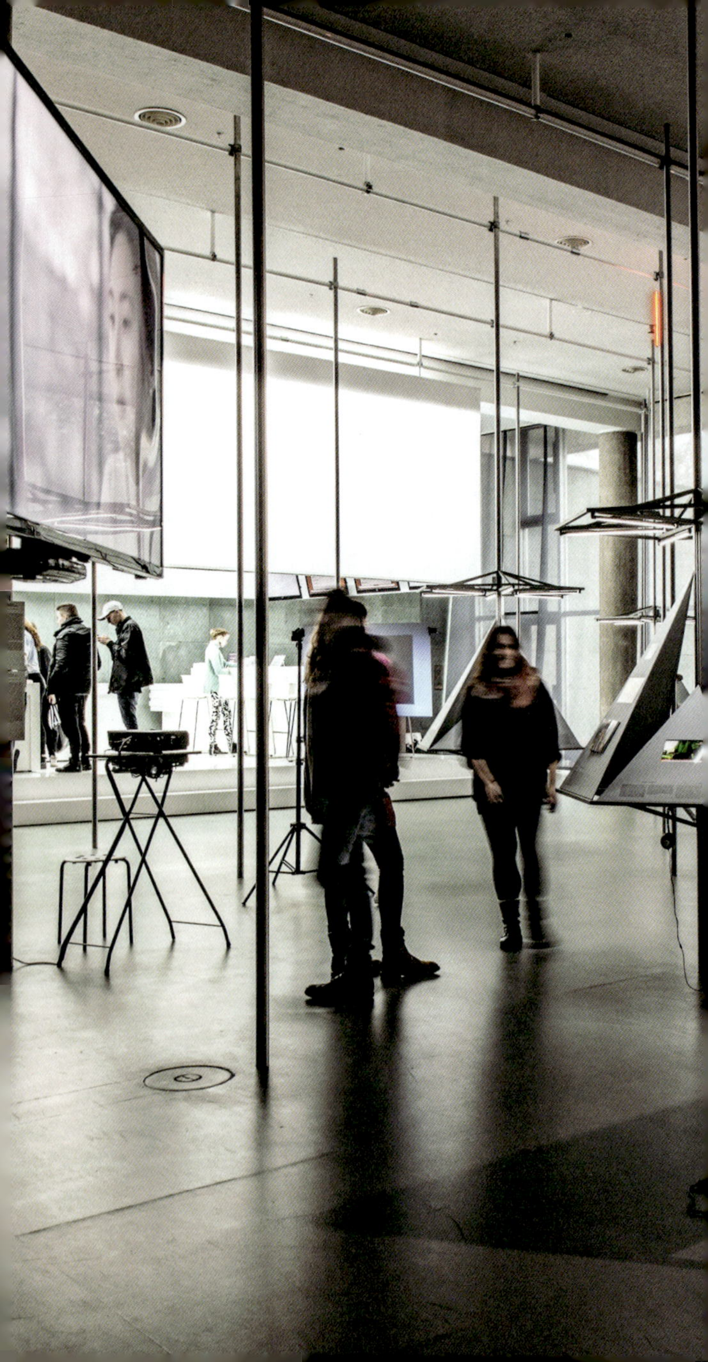

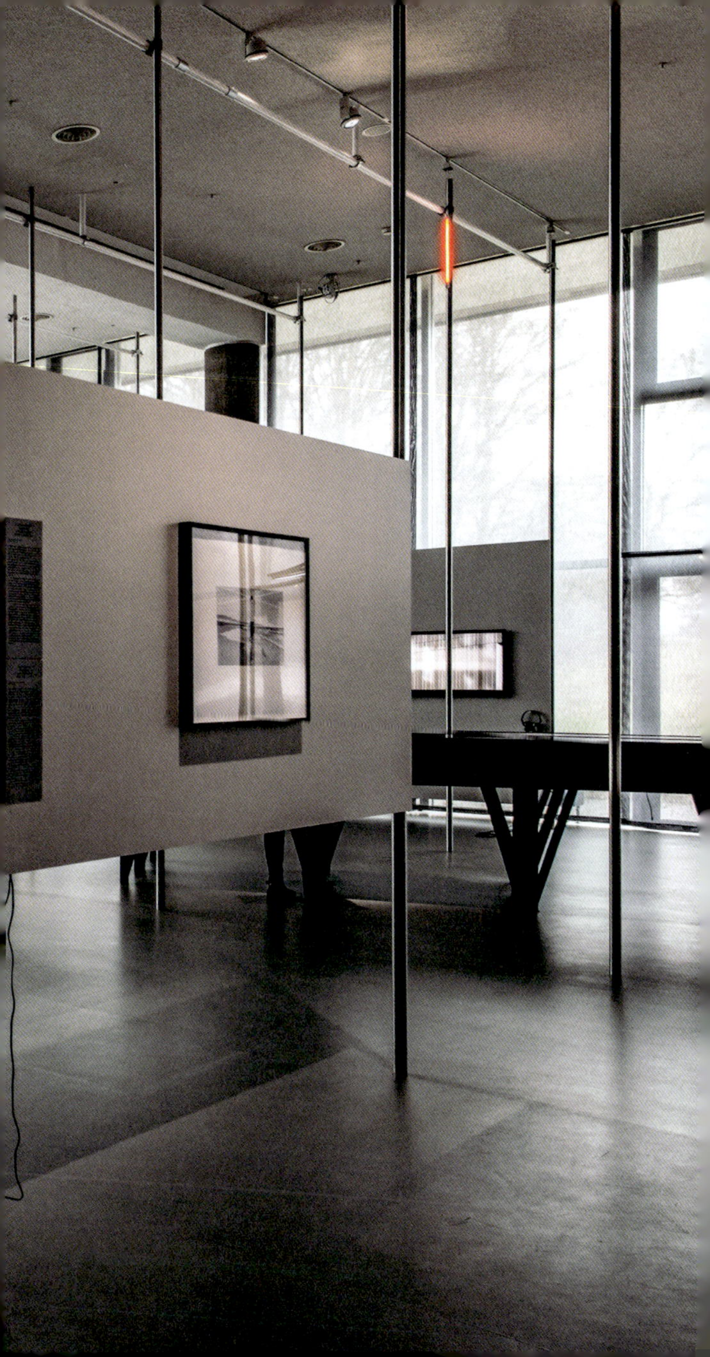

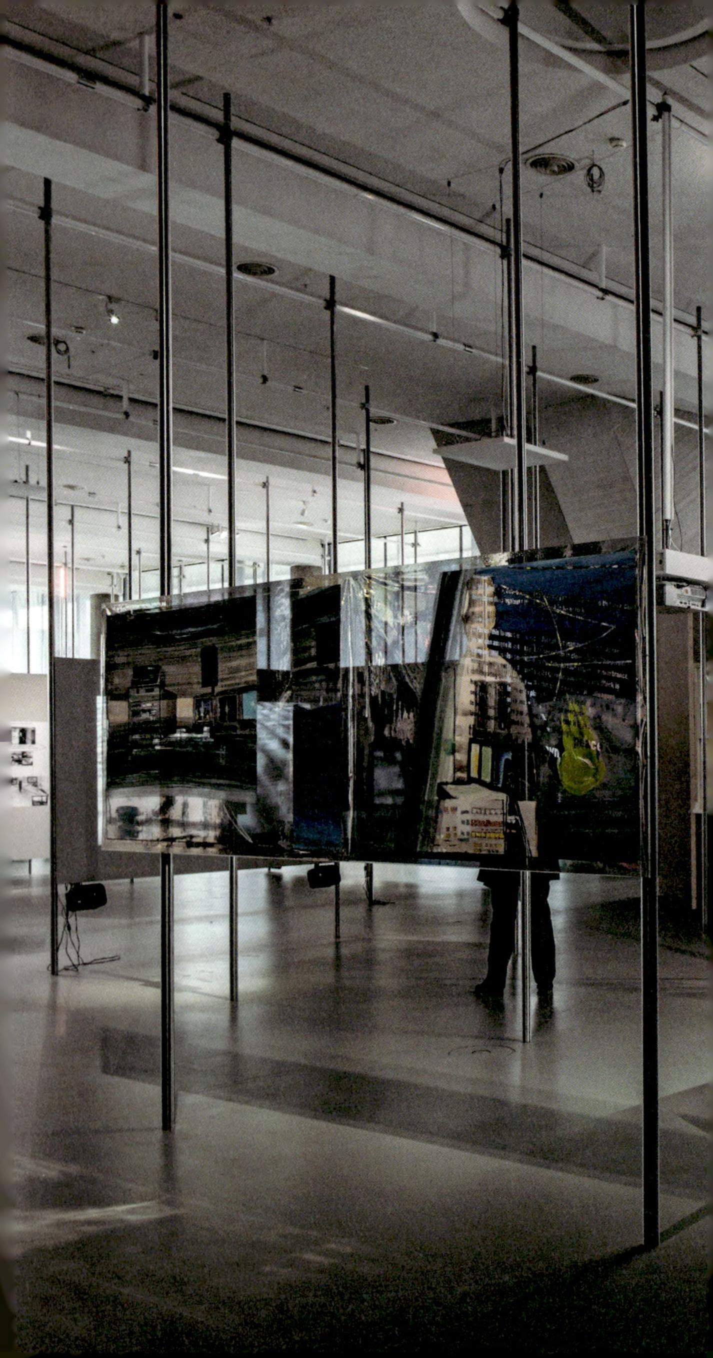

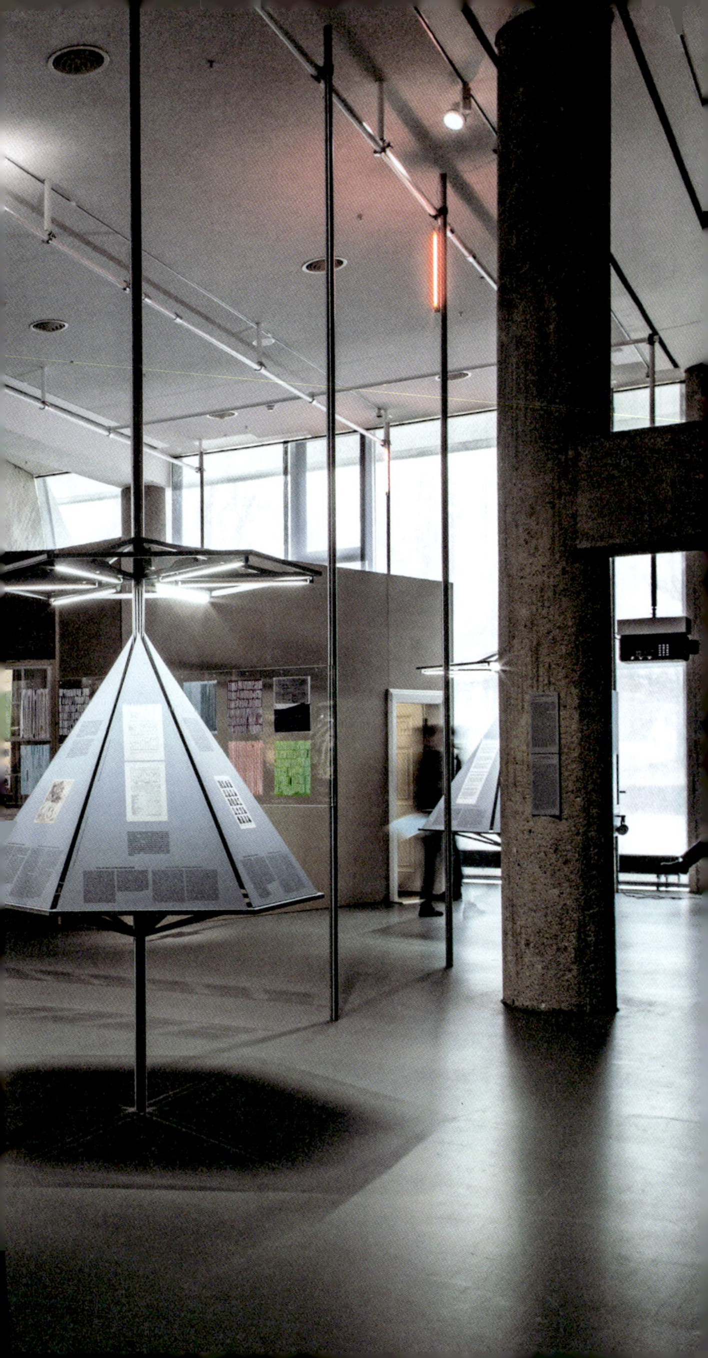

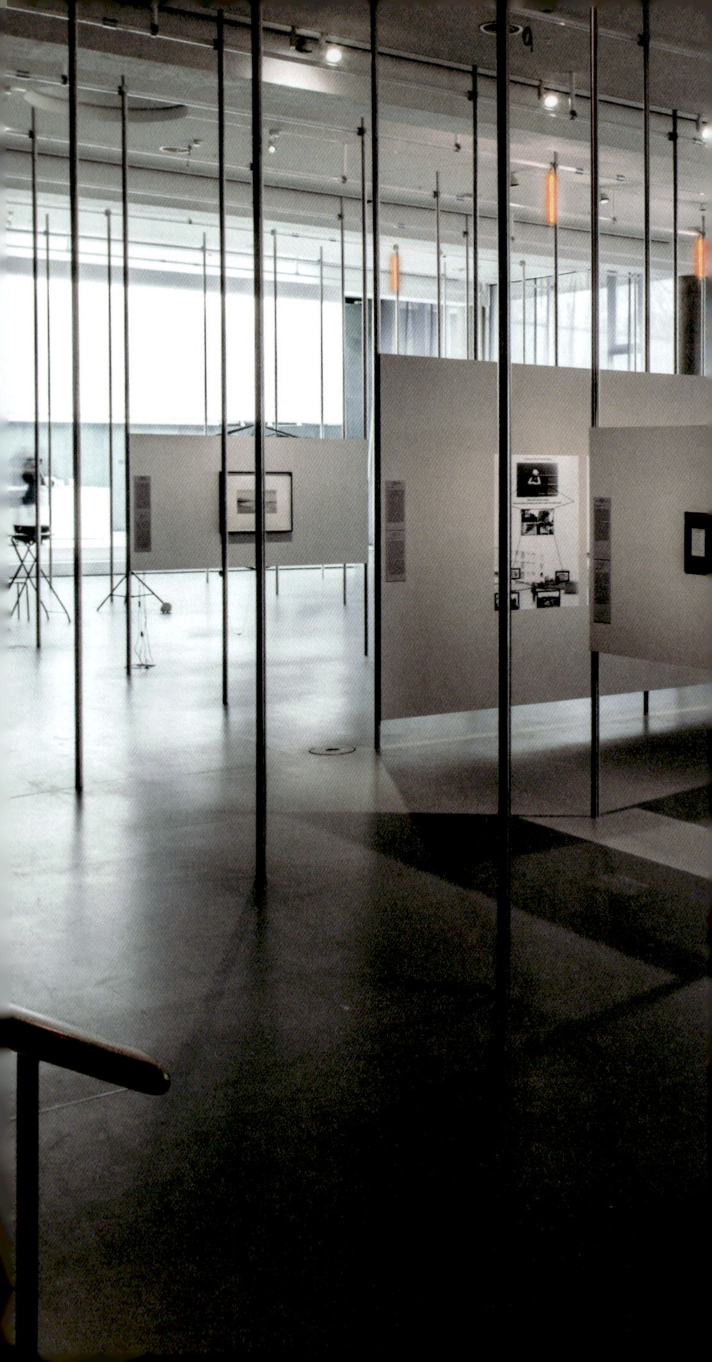

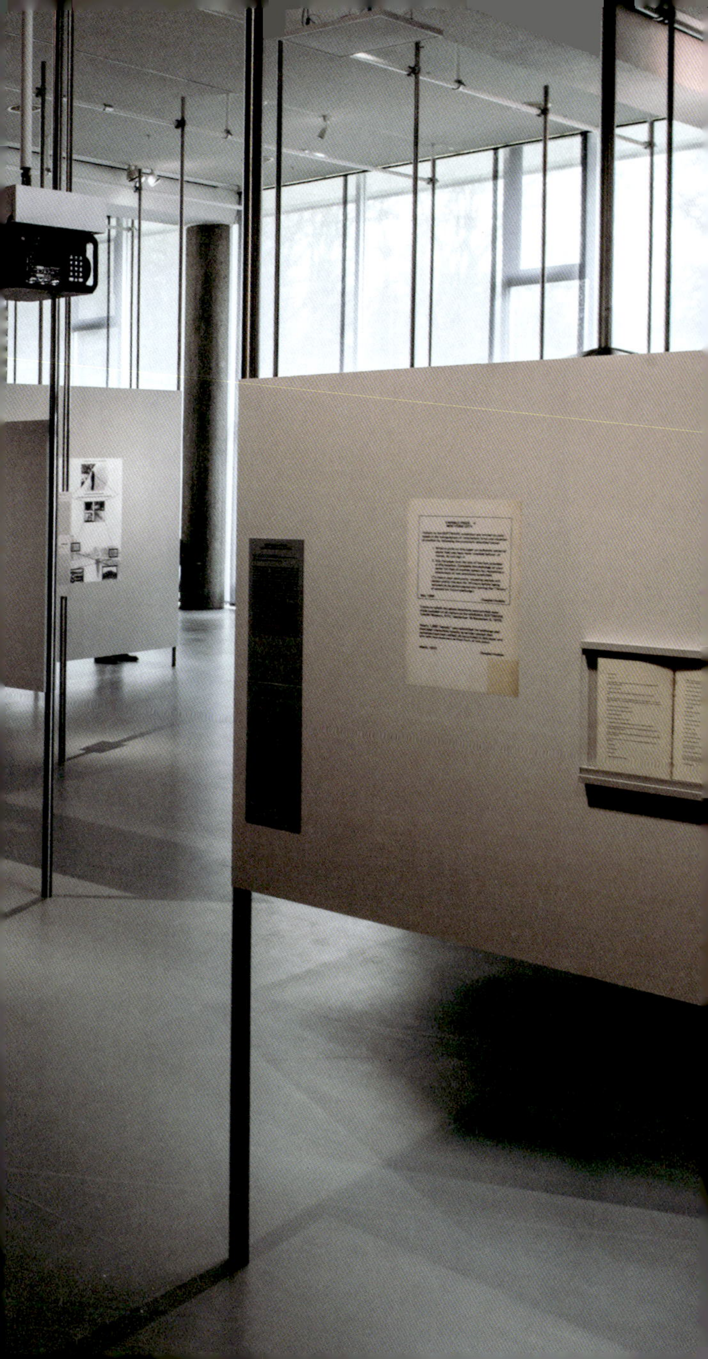

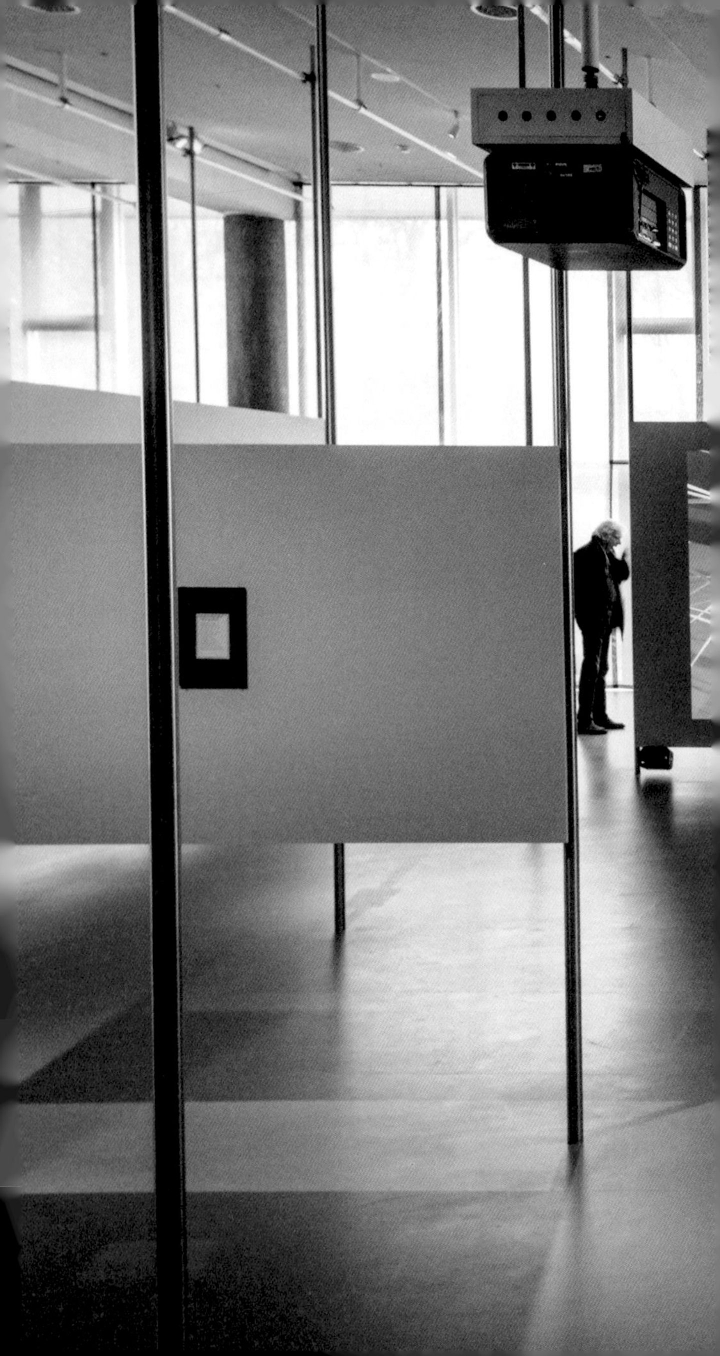

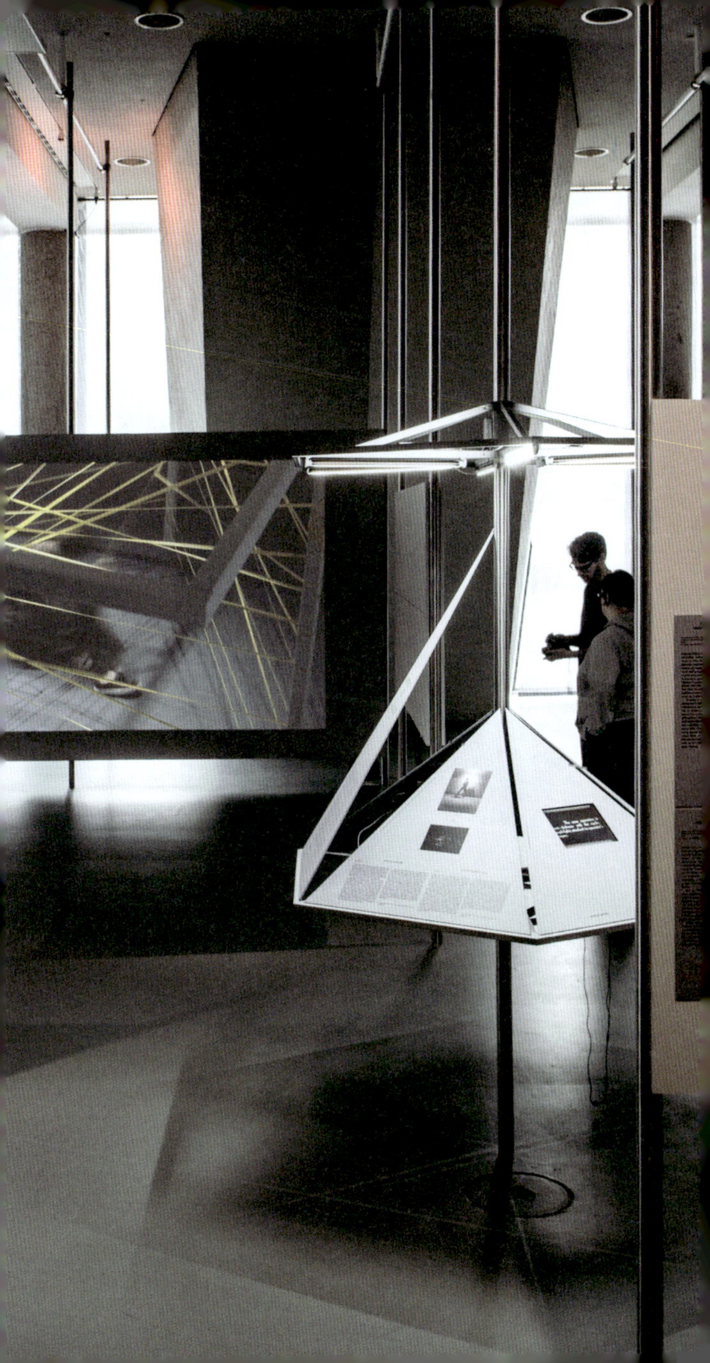

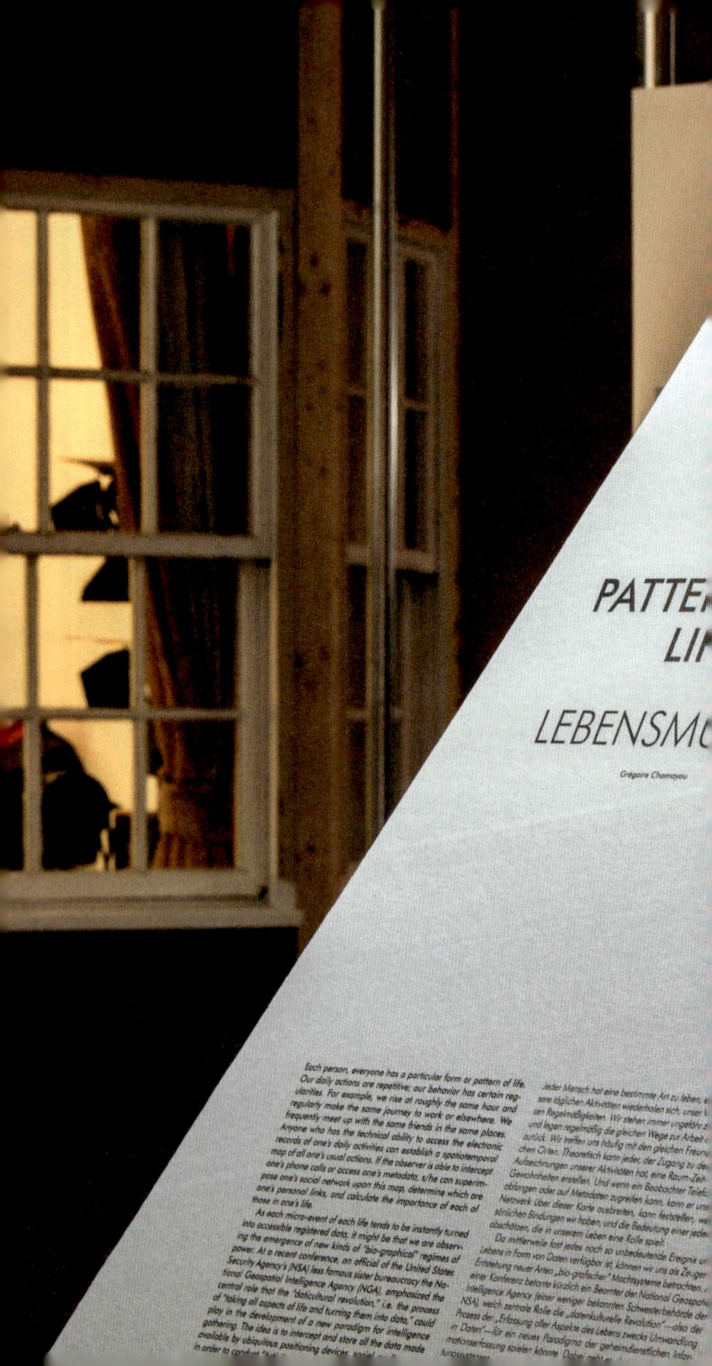
PATTER
LIF
LEBENSMU
Grégoire Chamayou
Each person, everyone has a particular form or pattern of life. Our daily actions are repetitive; our behavior has certain regularities. For example, we rise at roughly the same hour and regularly make the same journey to work or elsewhere. We frequently meet up with the same friends in the same places. Anyone who has the technical ability to access the electronic records of one's daily activities can establish a spatiotemporal map of all one's usual actions. If the observer is able to intercept one's phone calls or access one's metadata, s/he can superimpose one's social network upon this map, determine which are one's personal links, and calculate the importance of each of those in one's life.
As each micro-event of each life tends to be instantly turned into accessible registered data, it might be that we are observing the emergence of new kinds of "bio-graphical" regimes of power. At a recent conference, an official of the United States Security Agency's (NSA) less famous sister bureaucracy the National Geospatial Intelligence Agency (NGA), emphasized the central role that the "daticultural revolution," i.e. the process of "taking all aspects of life and turning them into data," could play in the development of a new paradigm for intelligence gathering. The idea is to intercept and store all the data made available by ubiquitous positioning devices,
Jeder Mensch hat eine bestimmte Art zu leben,
sere täglichen Aktivitäten wiederholen sich, unser
sen Regelmäßigkeiten. Wir stehen immer ungefähr
und legen regelmäßig die gleichen Wege zur Arbeit
zurück. Wir treffen uns häufig mit den gleichen Freun
chen Orten. Theoretisch kann jeder, der Zugang zu de
Aufzeichnungen unserer Aktivitäten hat, eine Raum-Zeit-
Gewohnheiten erstellen. Und wenn ein Beobachter Telef
abfangen oder auf Metadaten zugreifen kann, kann er un
Netzwerk über dieser Karte ausbreiten, kann feststellen, w
sönlichen Bindungen wir haben, und die Bedeutung einer jede
abschätzen, die in unserem Leben eine Rolle spielt.
Da mittlerweile fast jedes noch so unbedeutende Ereignis u
Lebens in Form von Daten verfügbar ist, können wir uns als Zeuge
Entstehung neuer Arten „bio-grafischer" Machtsysteme betrachten.
einer Konferenz betonte kürzlich ein Beamter der National Geospati
Intelligence Agency (einer weniger bekannten Schwesterbehörde de
NSA), welch zentrale Rolle die „datenkulturelle Revolution"—also der
Prozess der „Erfassung aller Aspekte des Lebens zwecks Umwandlung
in Daten"—für ein neues Paradigma der geheimdienstlichen Infor-
mationserfassung spielen könnte.

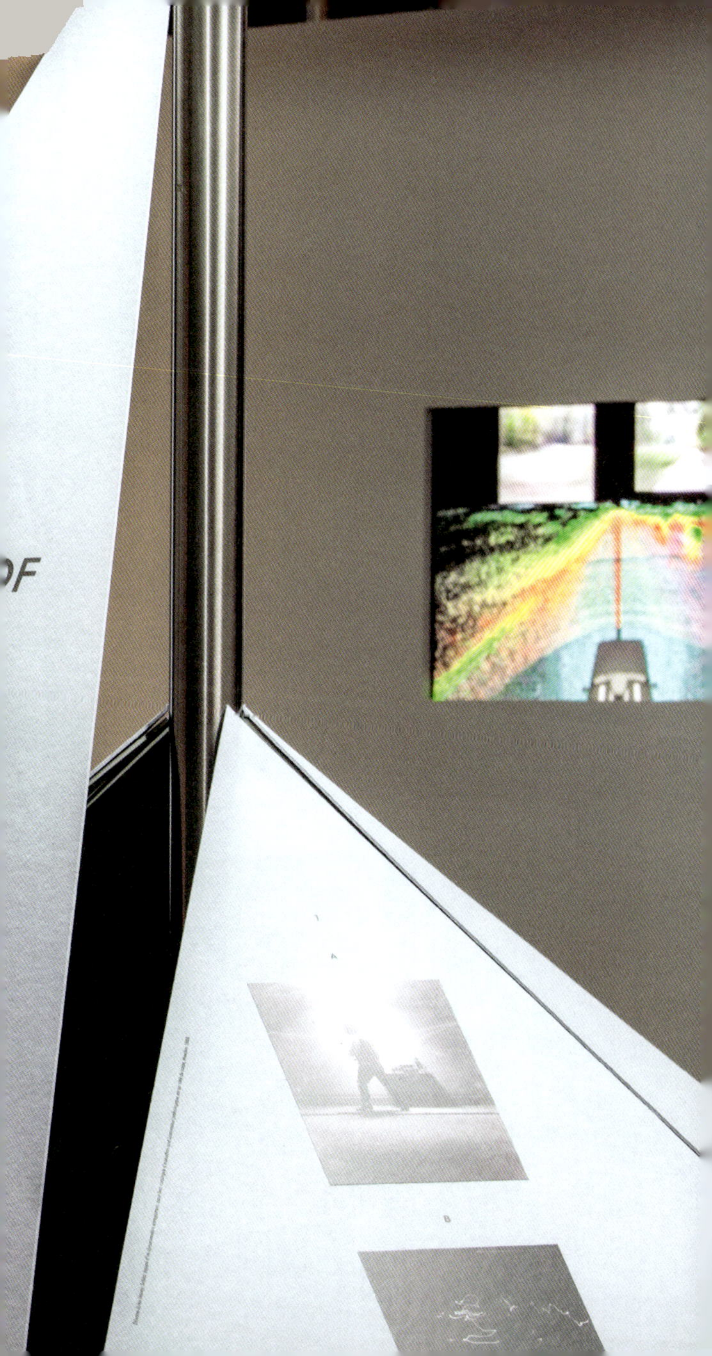
OF
A
B

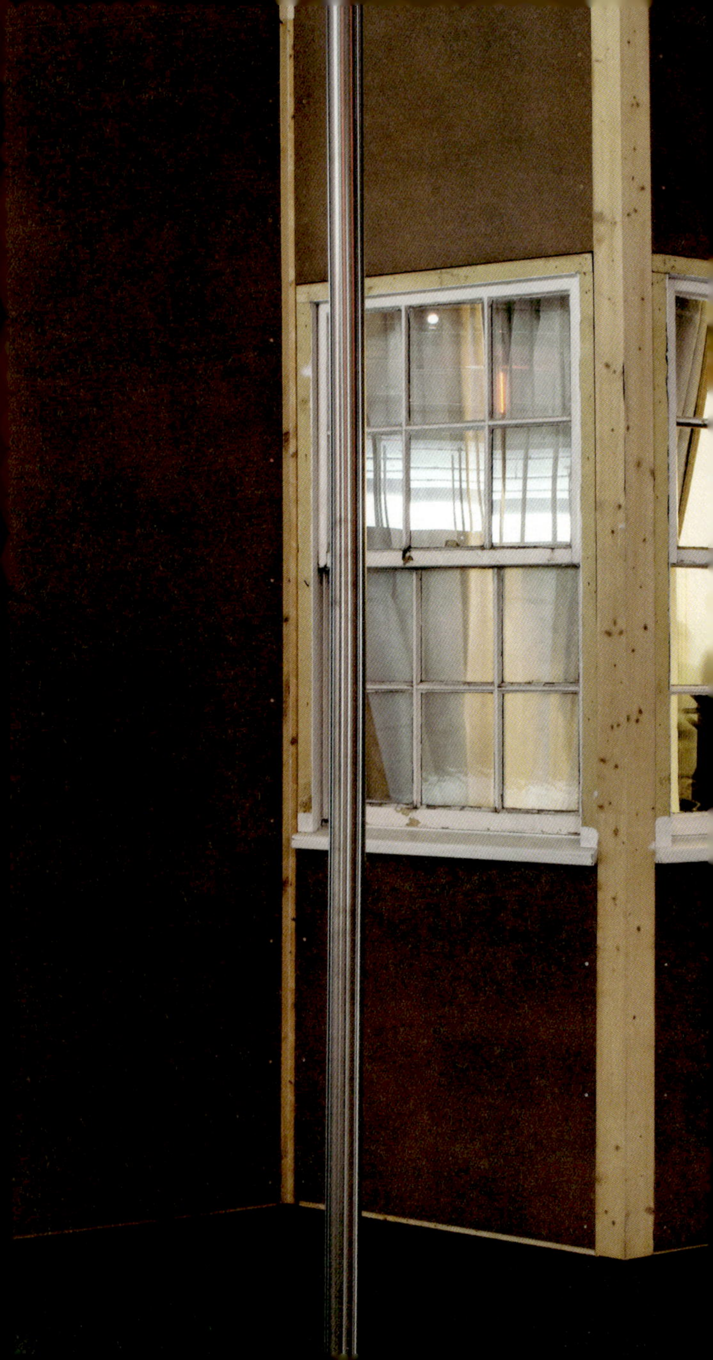

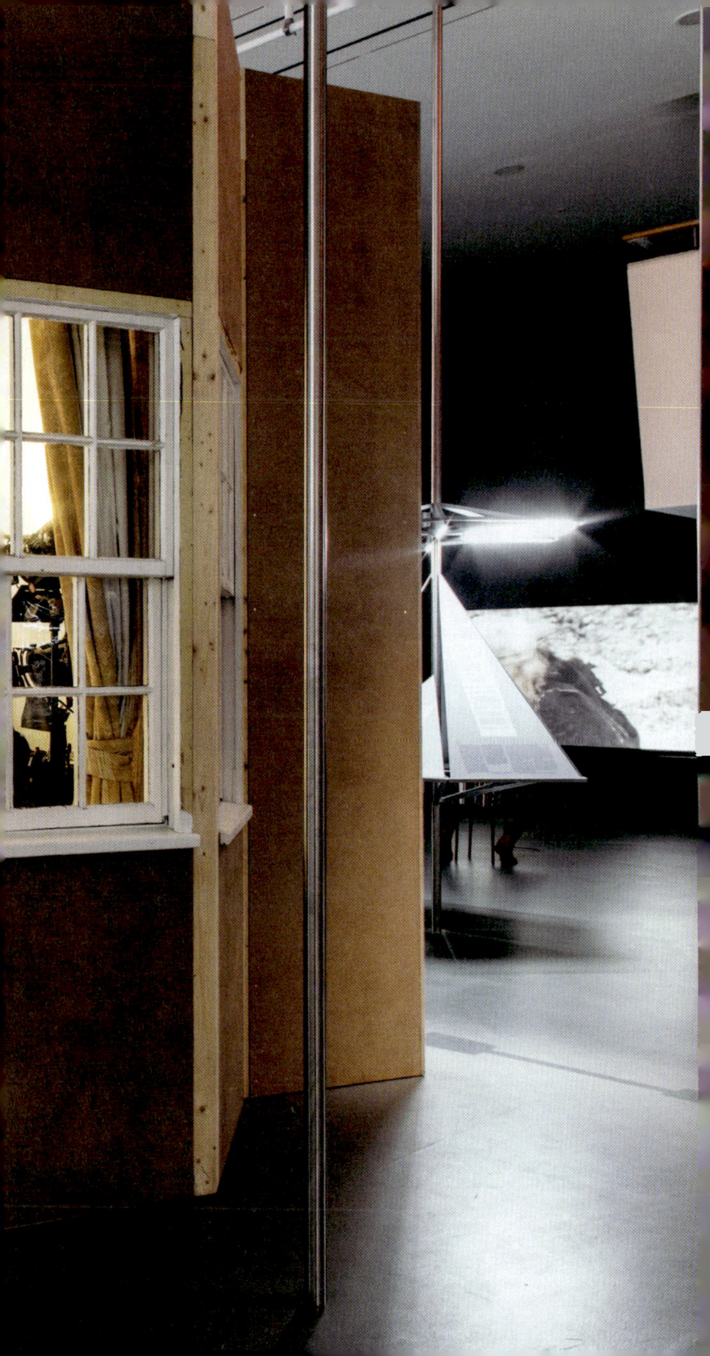

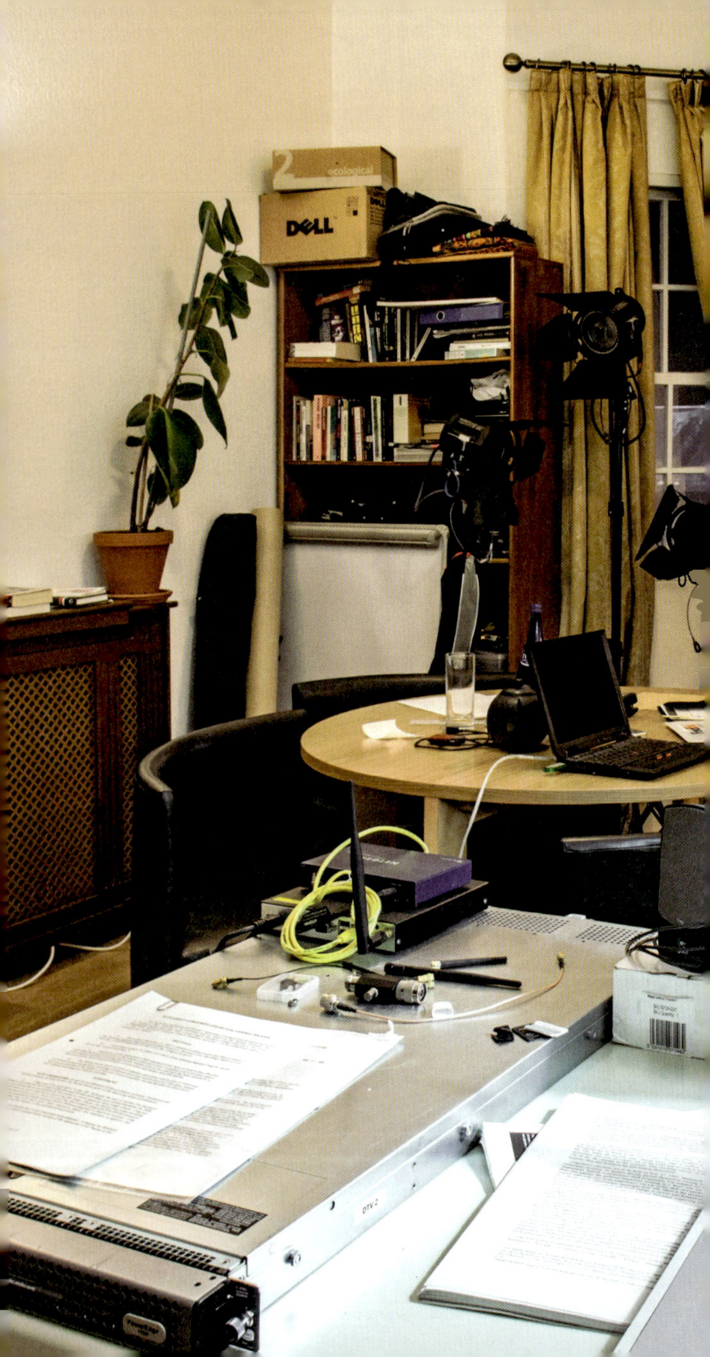
ecological
DELL
DTV 2

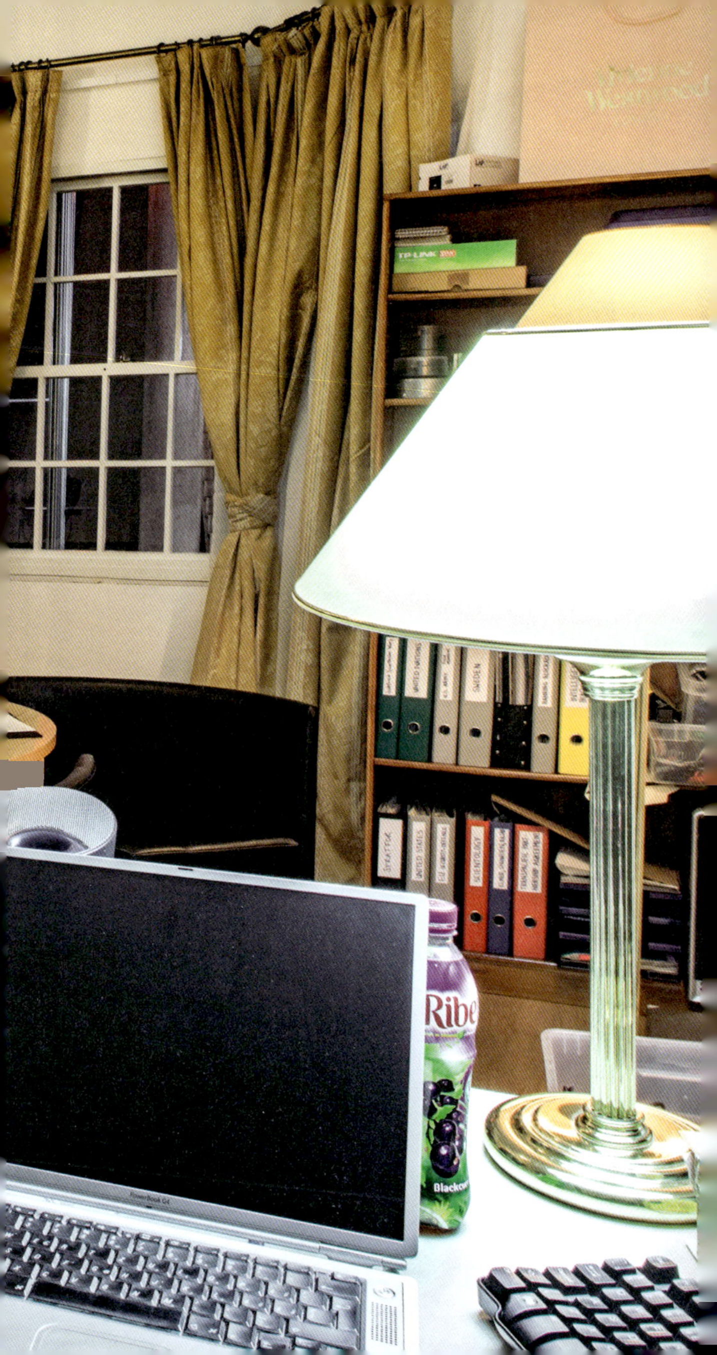
TP-LINK
UNITED NATIONS
SWEDEN
UNITED STATES
SCIENTOLOGY

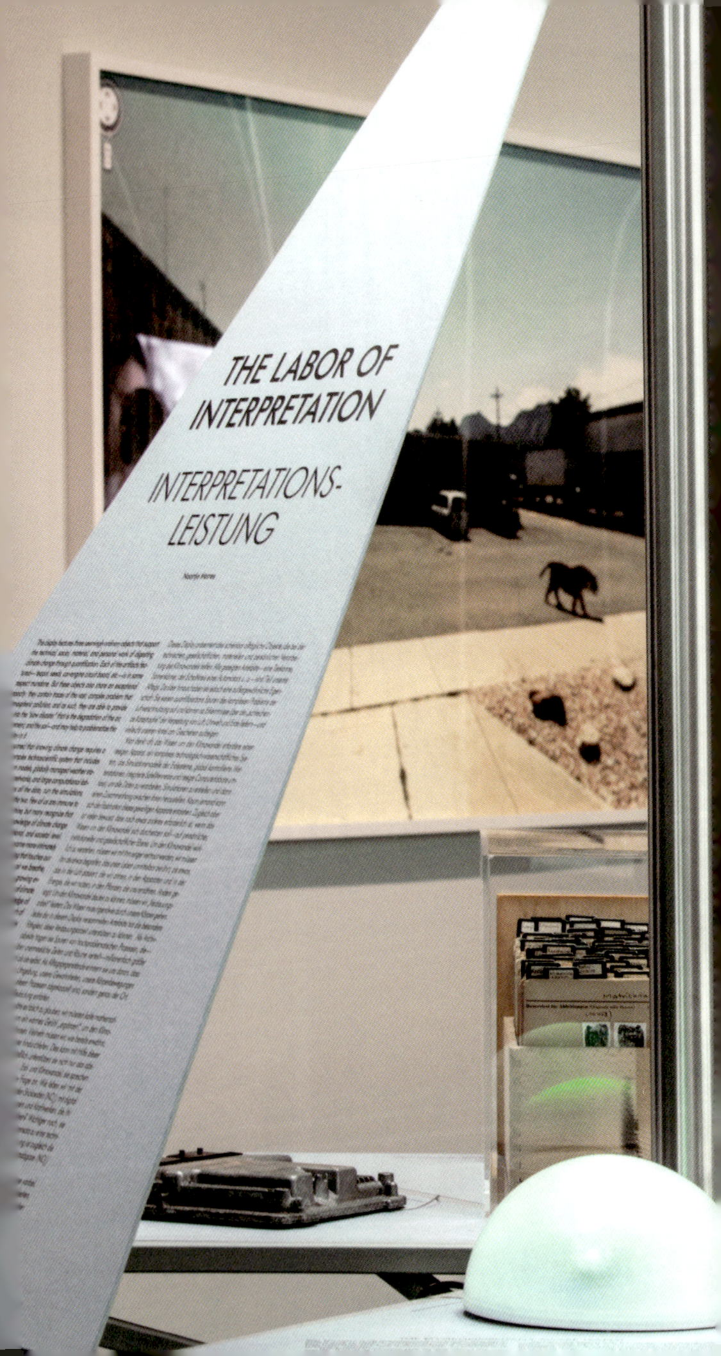
THE LABOR OF INTERPRETATION
INTERPRETATIONS-LEISTUNG

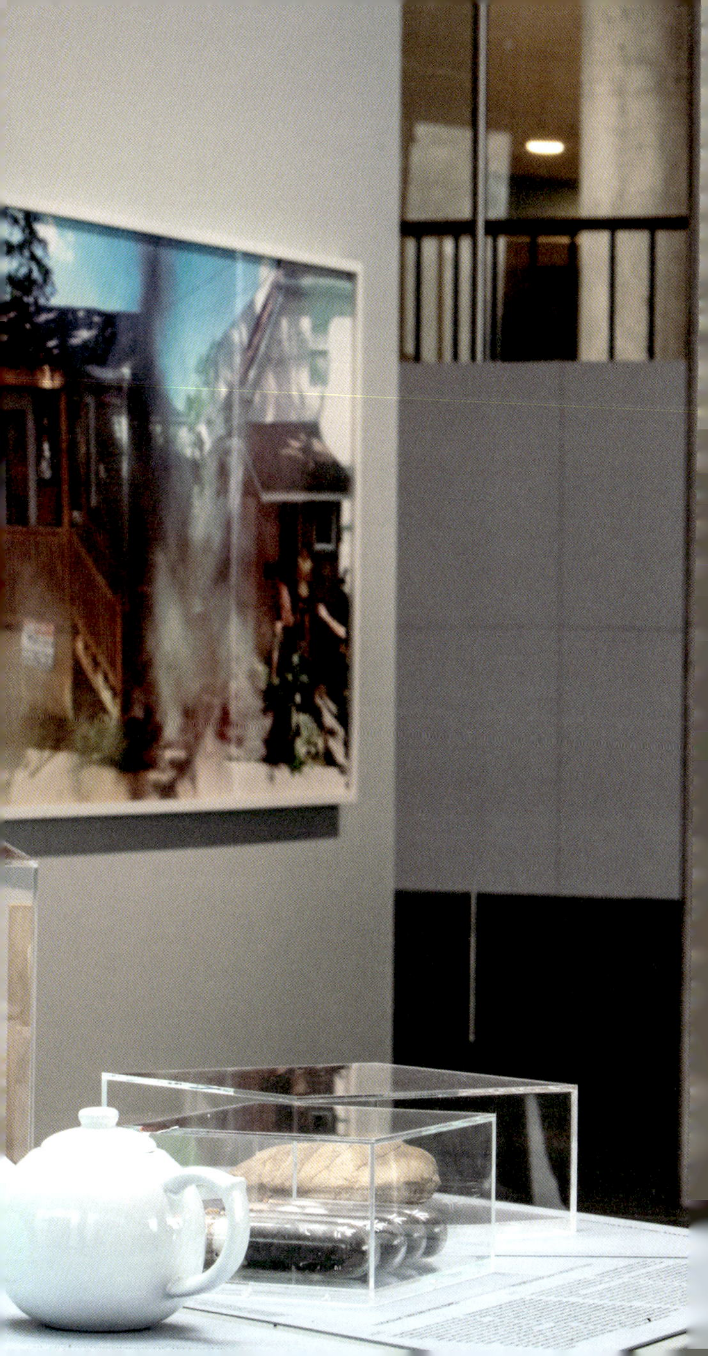

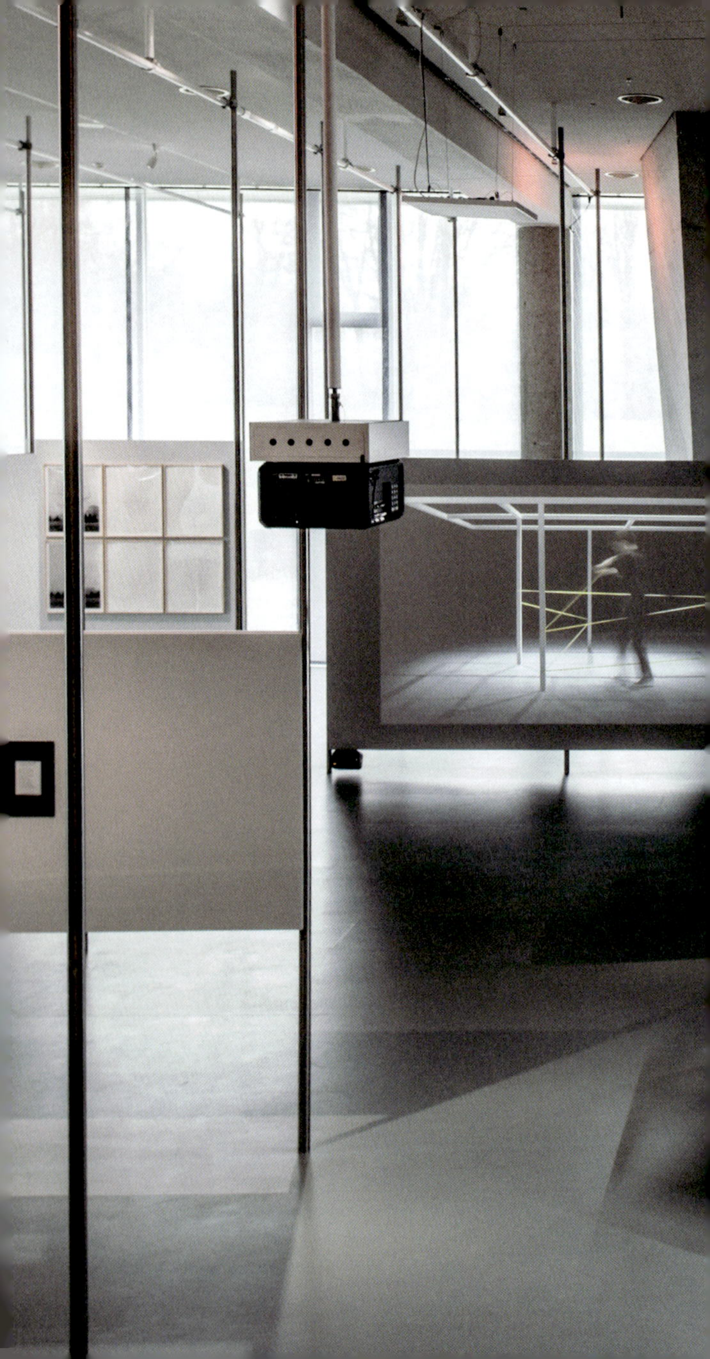

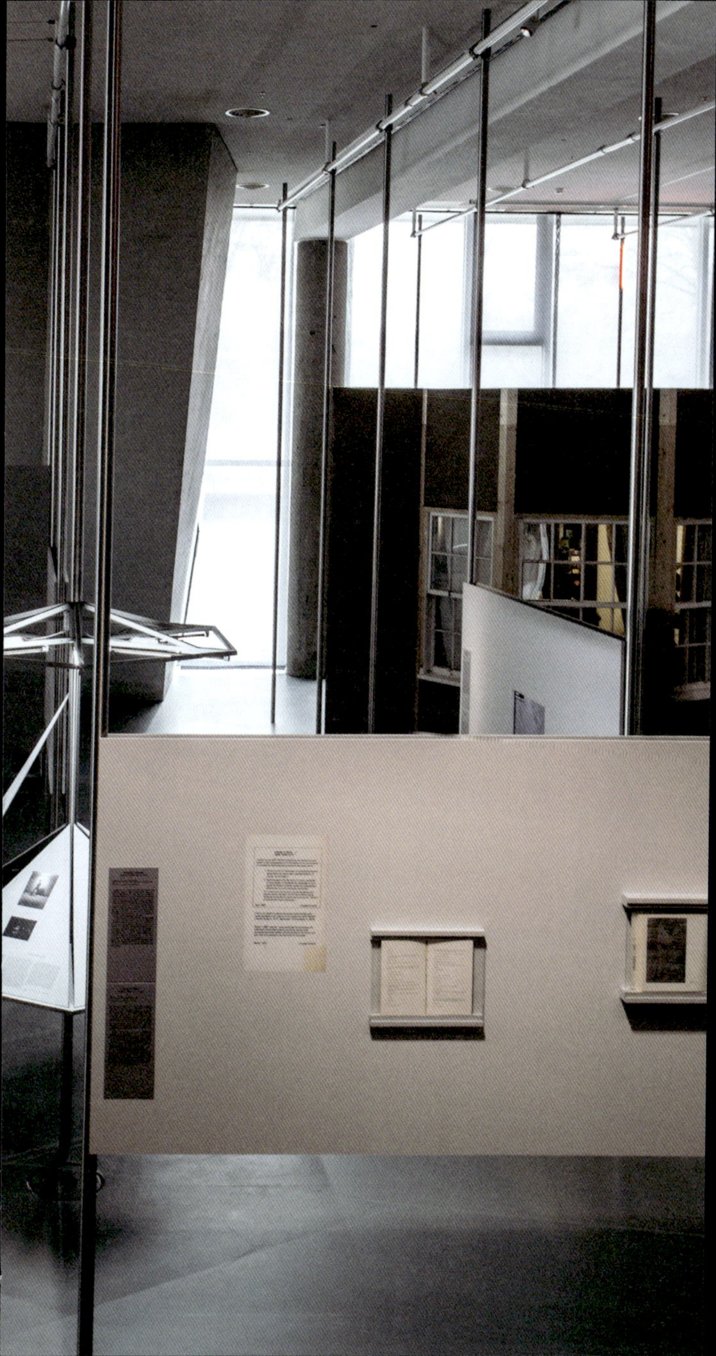

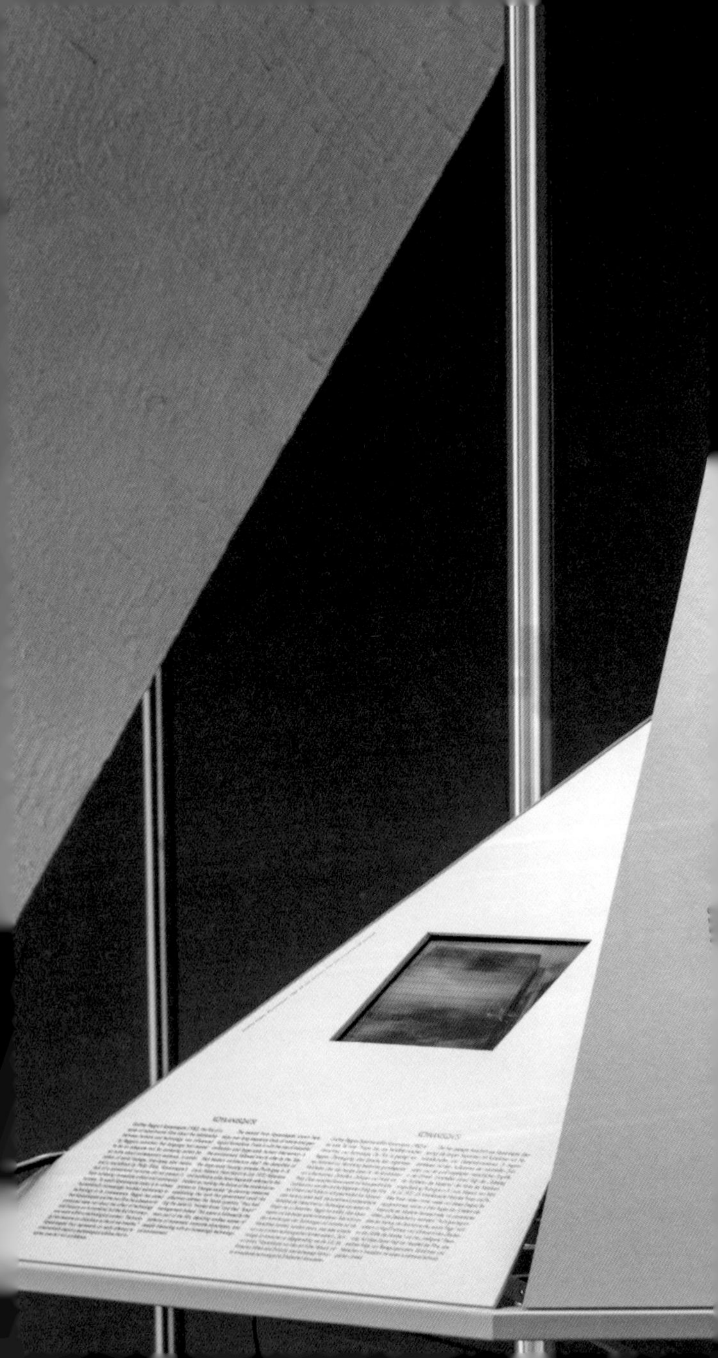

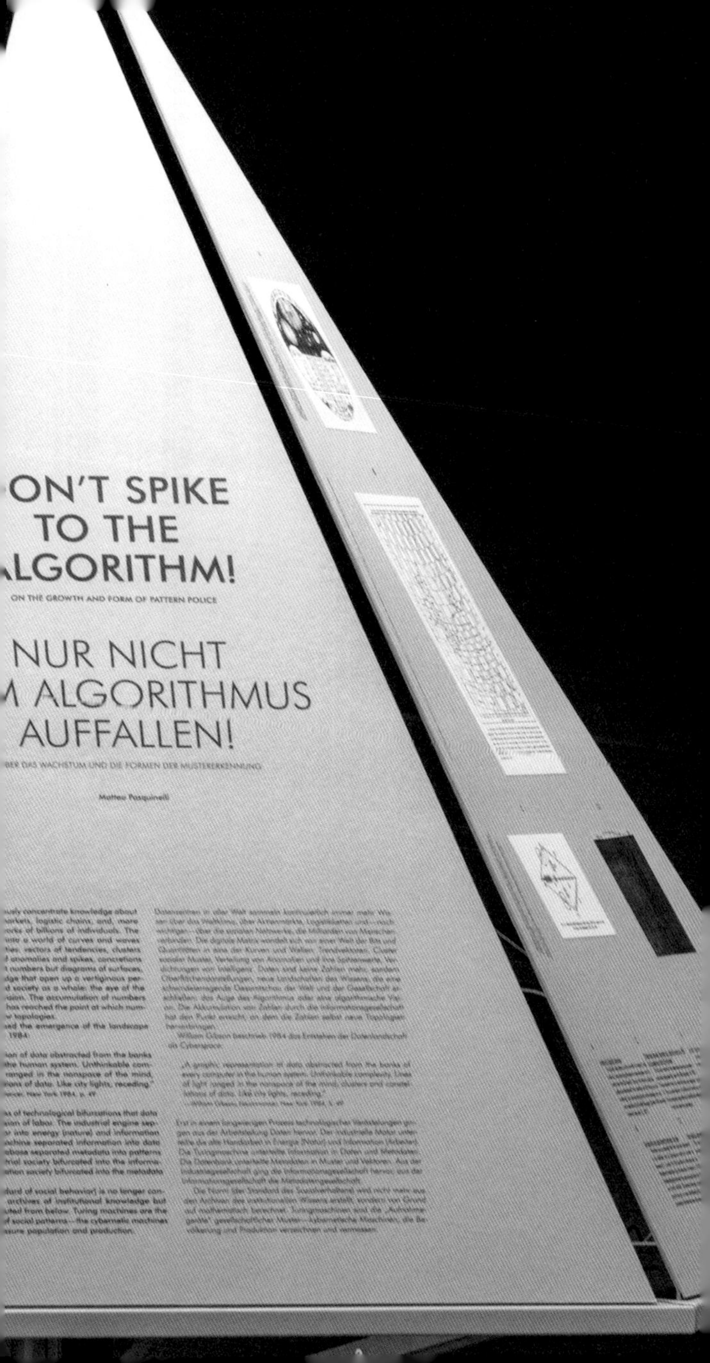
ON'T SPIKE
TO THE
LGORITHM!
ON THE GROWTH AND FORM OF PATTERN POLICE
NUR NICHT
ALGORITHMUS
AUFFALLEN!
Matteo Pasquinelli

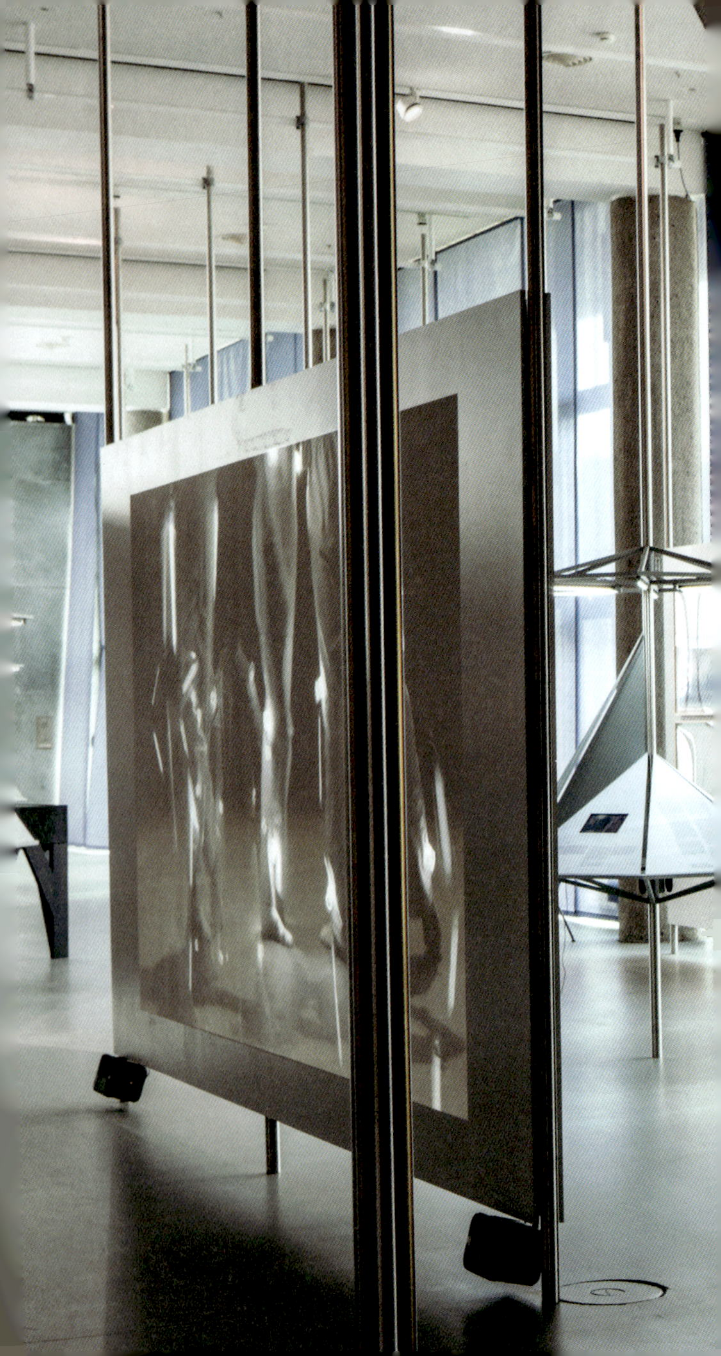

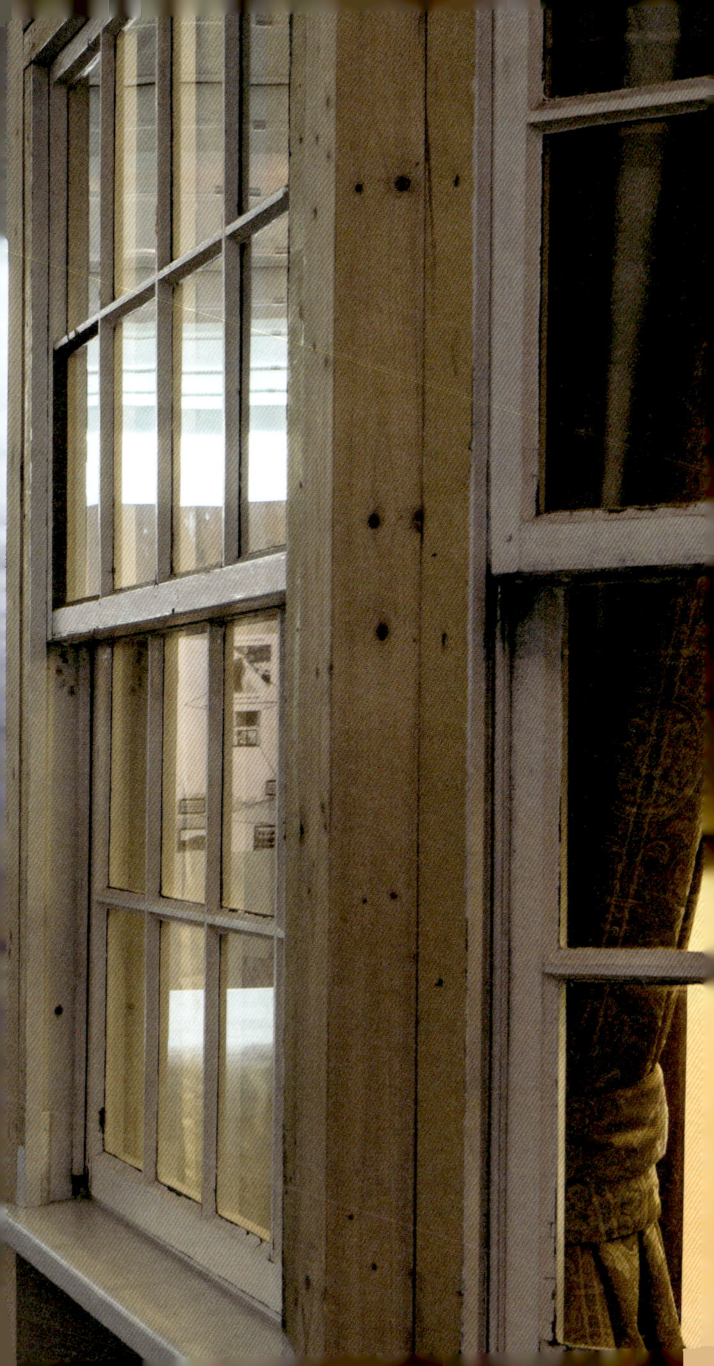

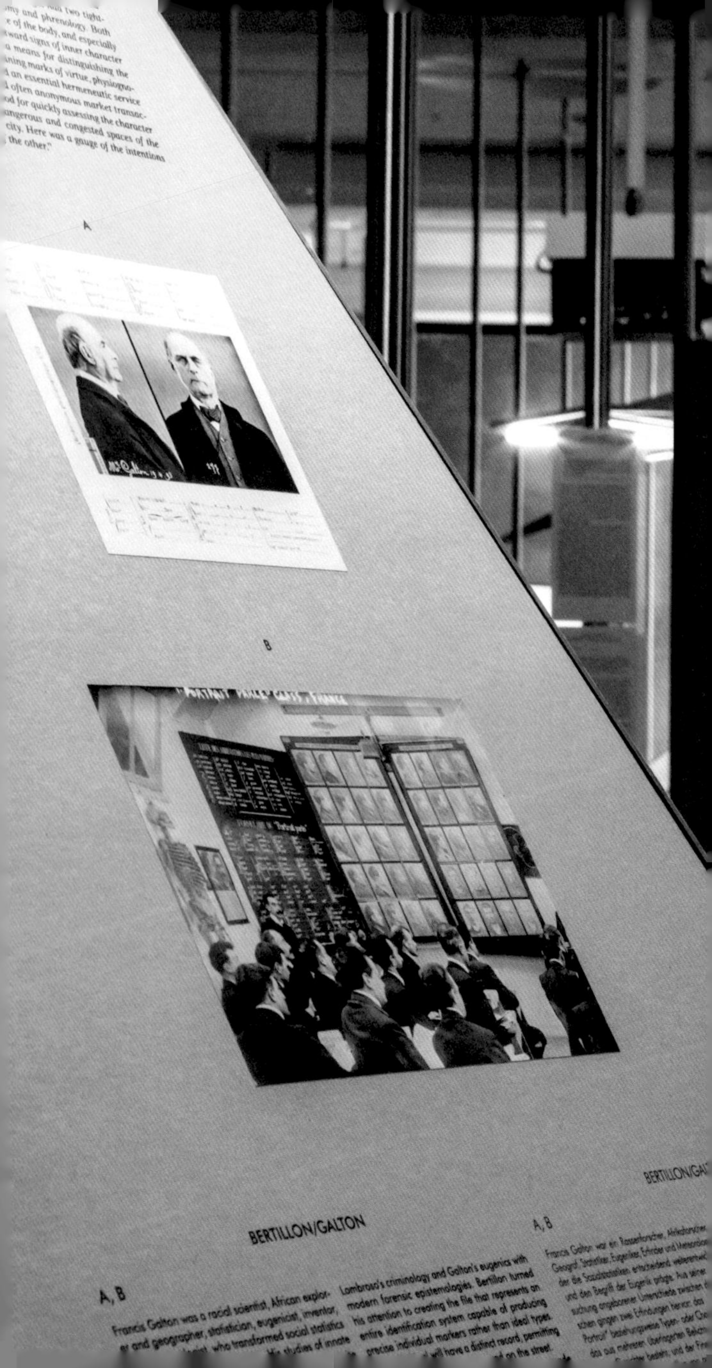

and two tight-
my and phrenology. Both
of the body, and especially
ward signs of inner character
a means for distinguishing the
ning marks of virtue, physiogno-
an essential hermeneutic service
often anonymous market transac-
od for quickly assessing the character
angerous and congested spaces of the
city. Here was a gauge of the intentions
the other."
A
B
BERTILLON/GALTON
A, B
Francis Galton was a racial scientist, African explor-
er and geographer, statistician, eugenicist, inventor,
who transformed social statistics
His studies of innate
Lombroso's criminology and Galton's eugenics with
modern forensic epistemologies. Bertillon turned
his attention to creating the file that represents an
entire identification system capable of producing
precise individual markers rather than ideal types.
will have a distinct record, permitting
on the street.
BERTILLON/GAL
A, B
Francis Galton war ein Rassenforscher, Afrikaforscher,
Geograf, Statistiker, Eugeniker, Erfinder und Meteorolog
der die Sozialstatistiken entscheidend weiterentwic
und den Begriff der Eugenik prägte. Aus seiner
suchung angeborener Unterschiede zwischen
schen gingen zwei Erfindungen hervor: das
Porträt" beziehungsweise Typen- oder
das aus mehreren überlagerten Belich

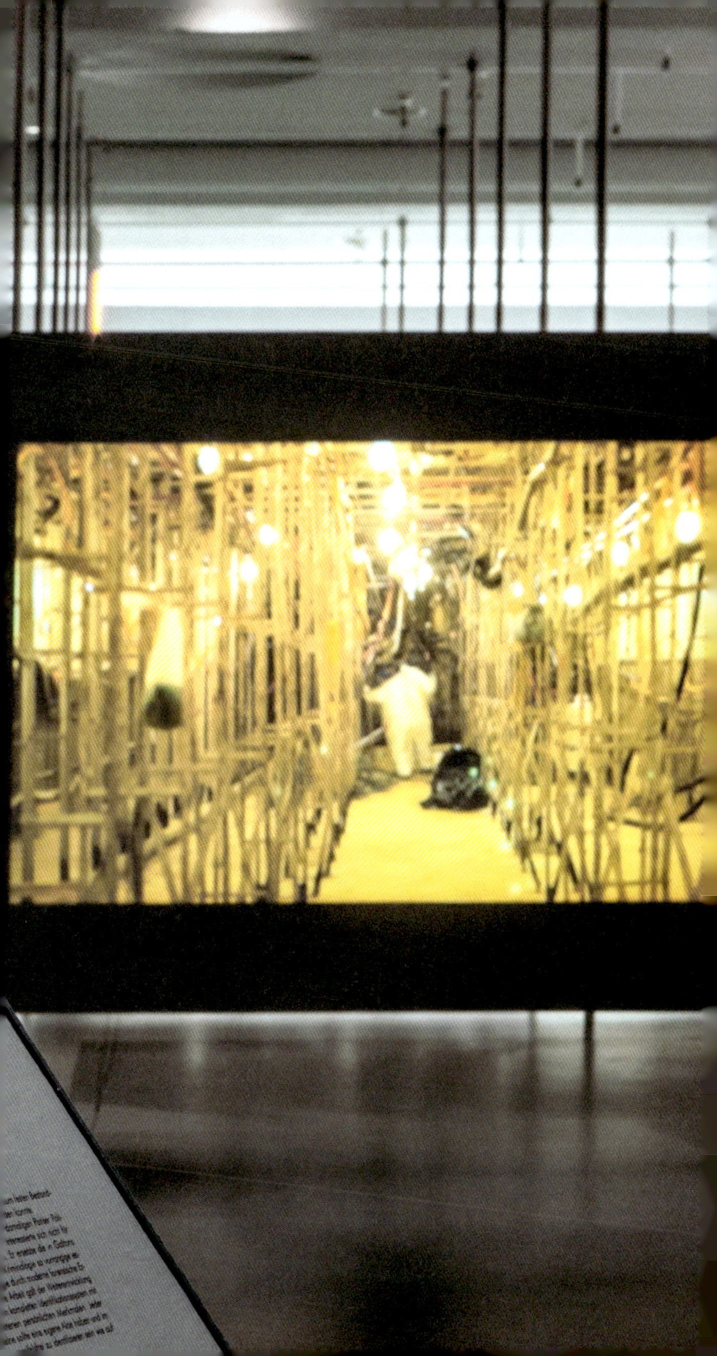

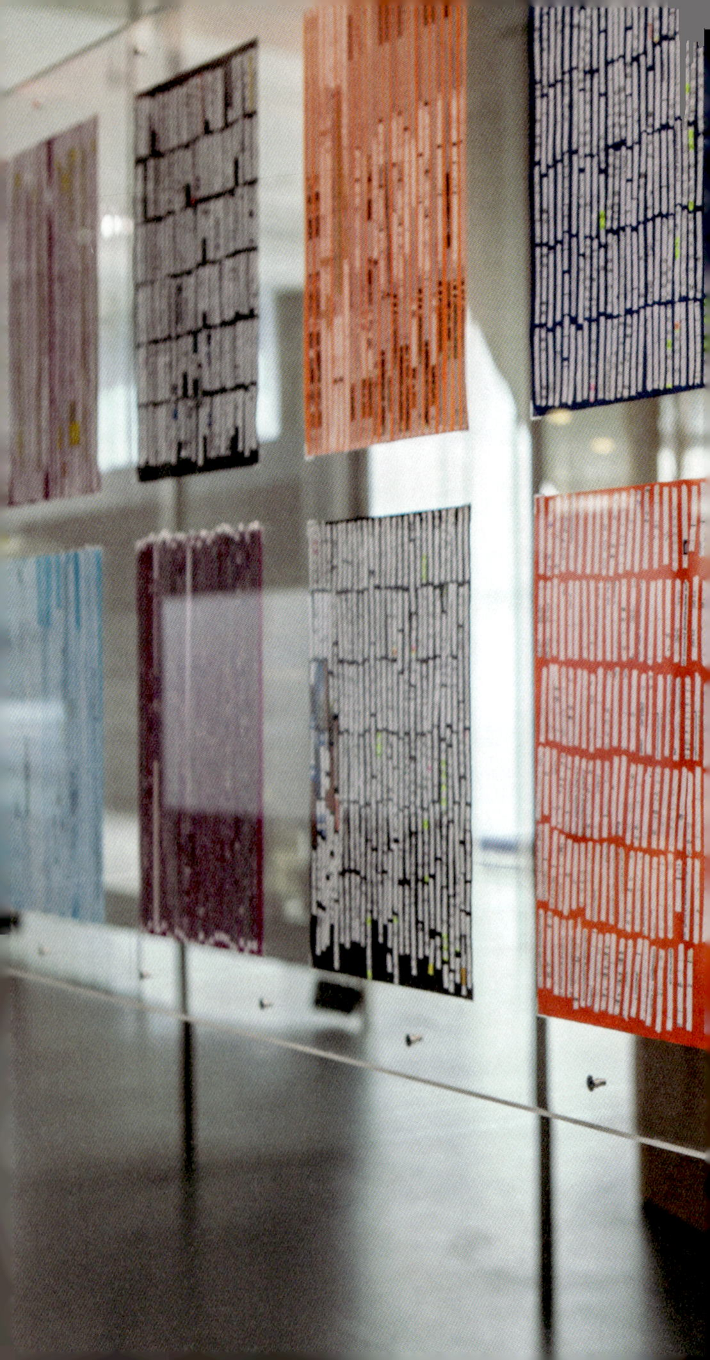

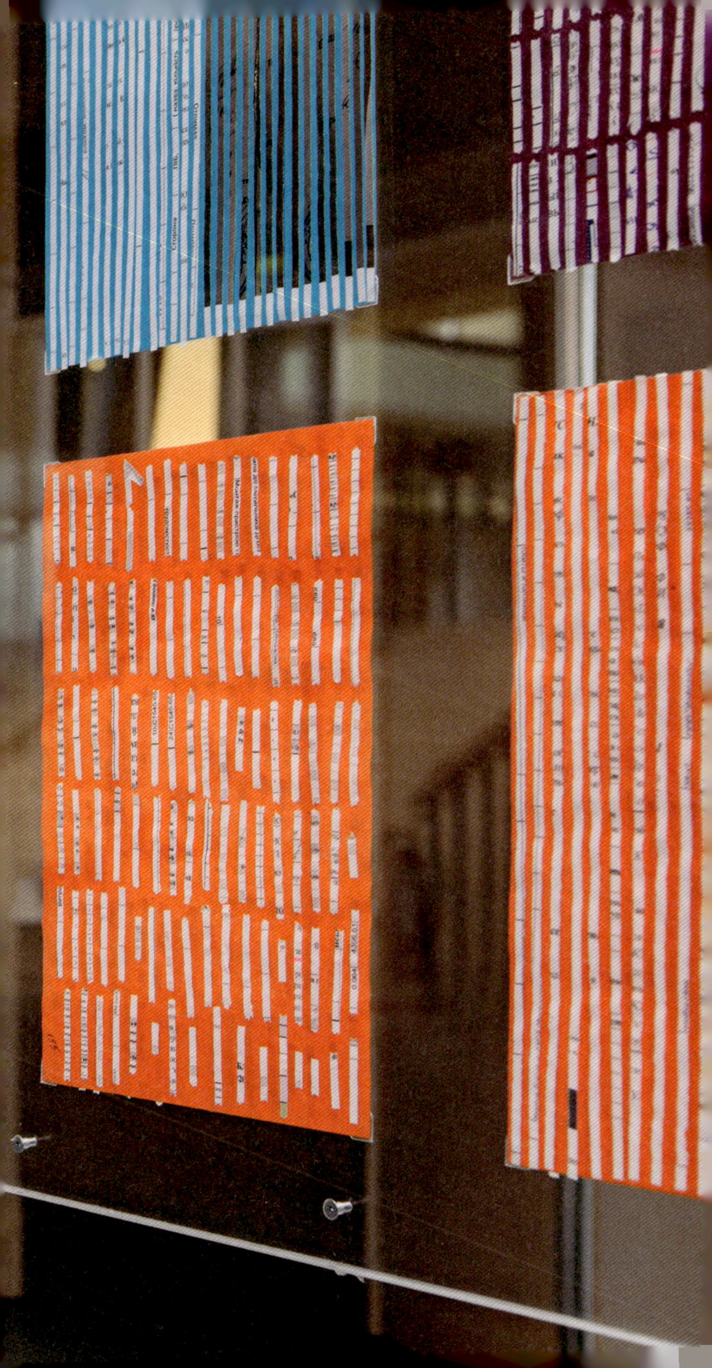

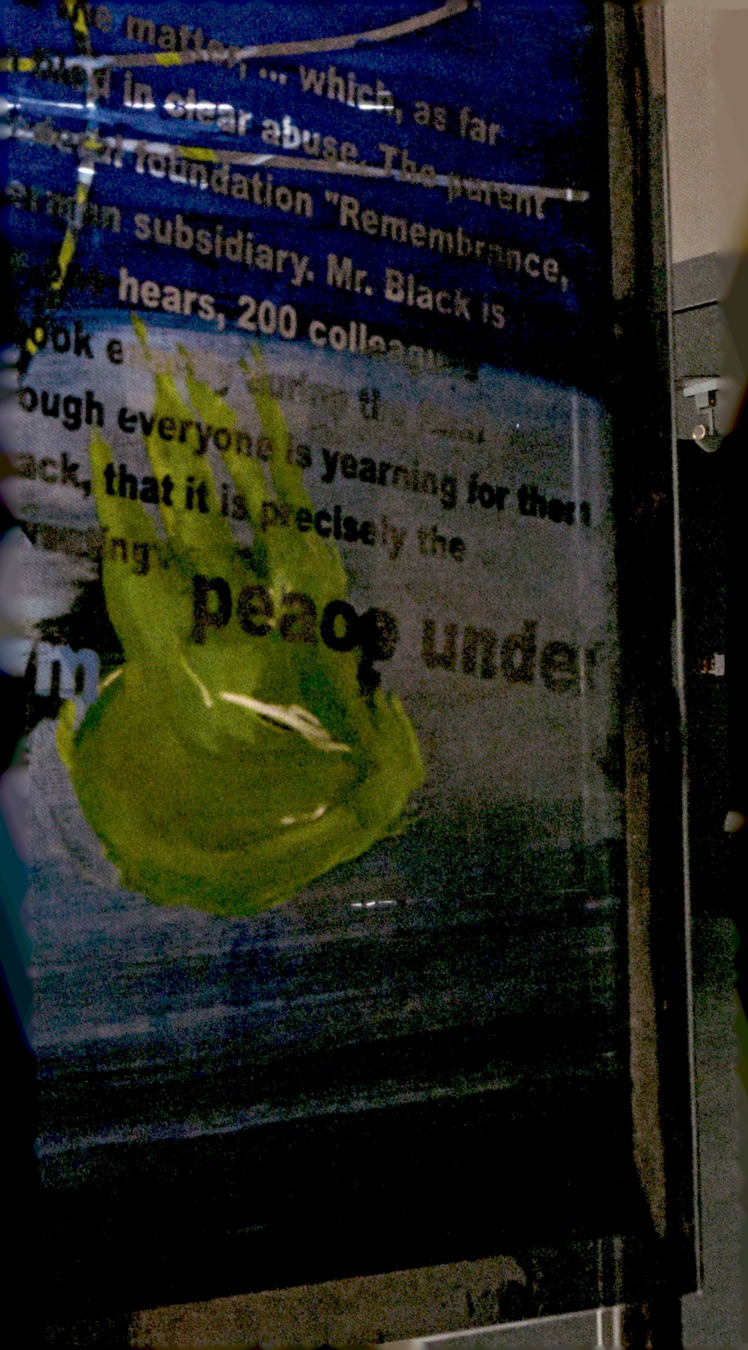
matter, ... which, as far
in clear abuse. The parent
foundation "Remembrance,
subsidiary. Mr. Black is
hears, 200
everyone is yearning for them
that it is precisely the
peace under

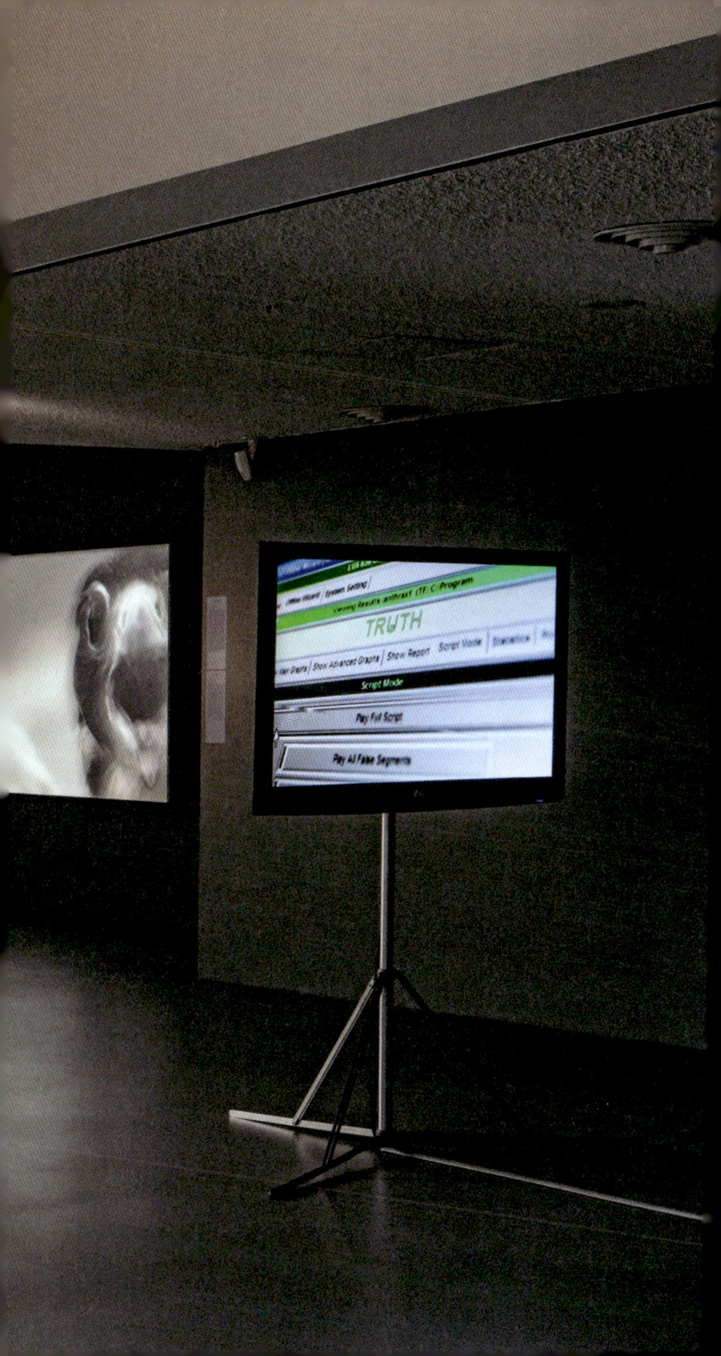
System Setting
TRUTH
Show Advanced Graphs
Show Report
Script Mode

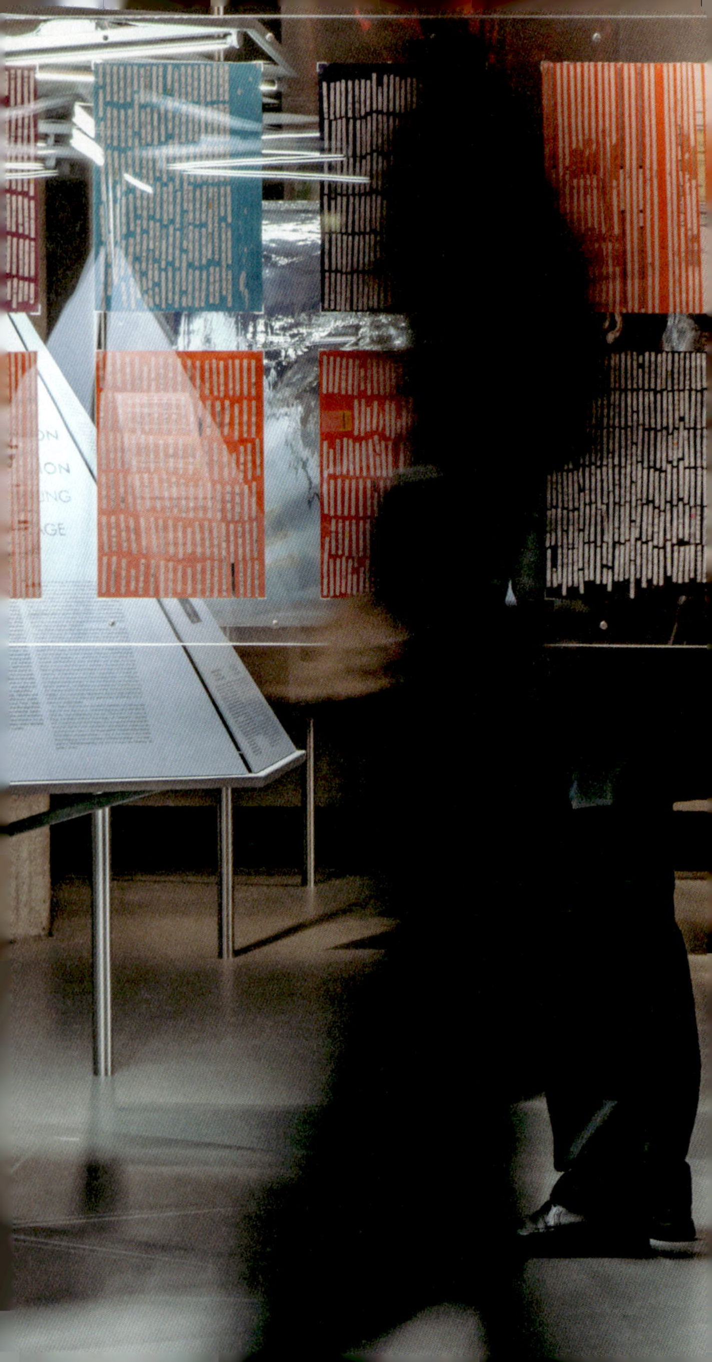

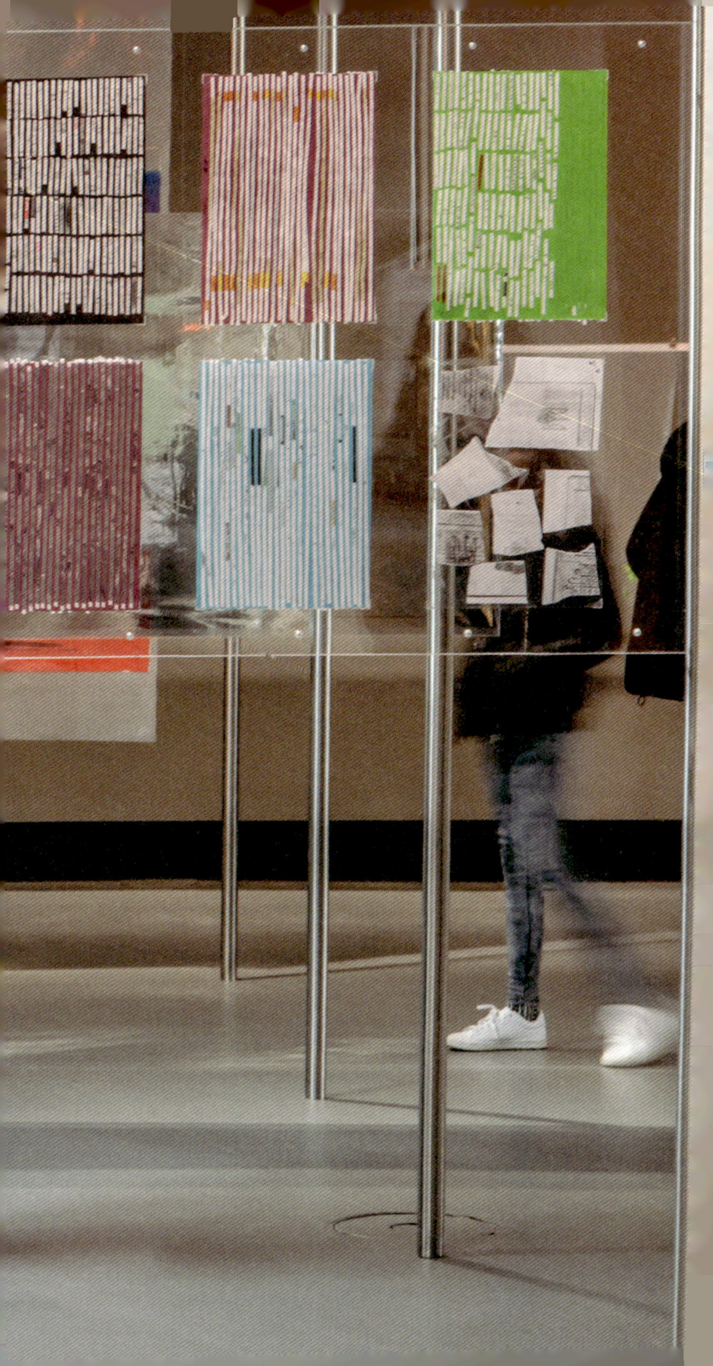

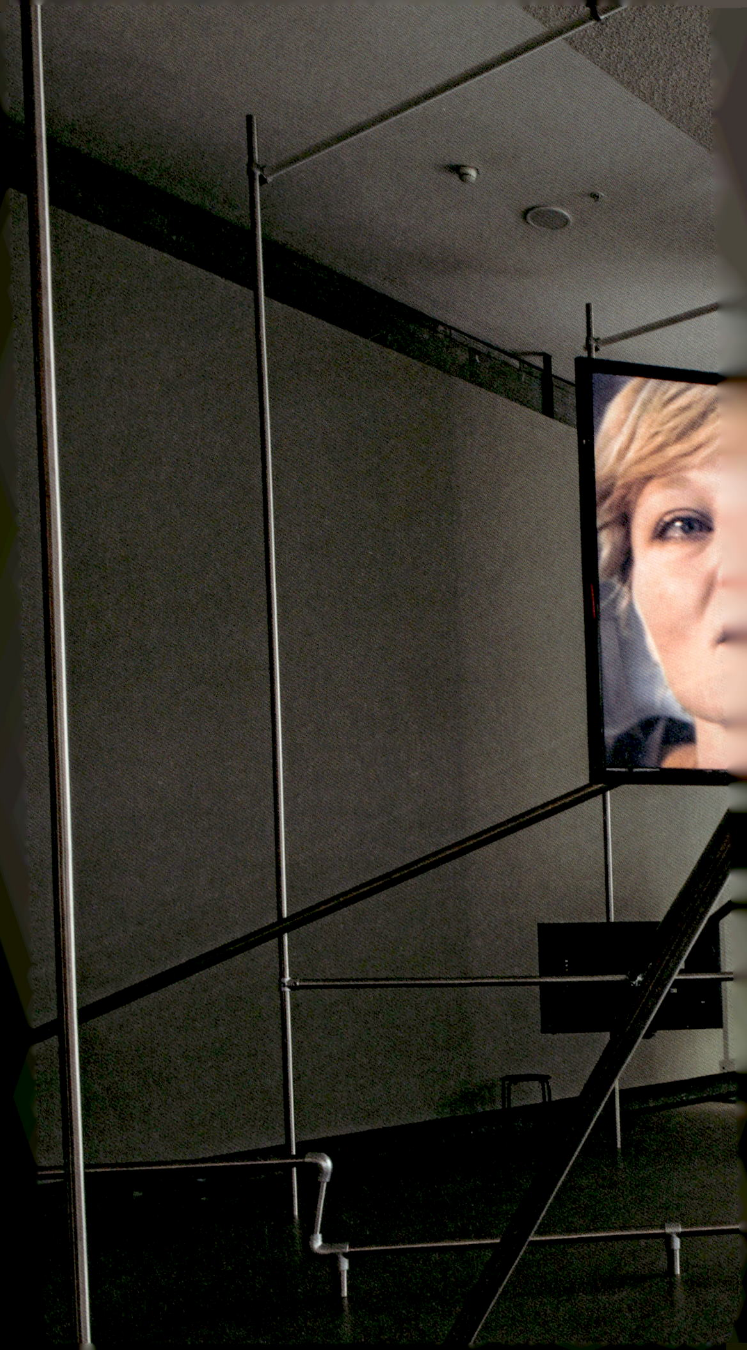

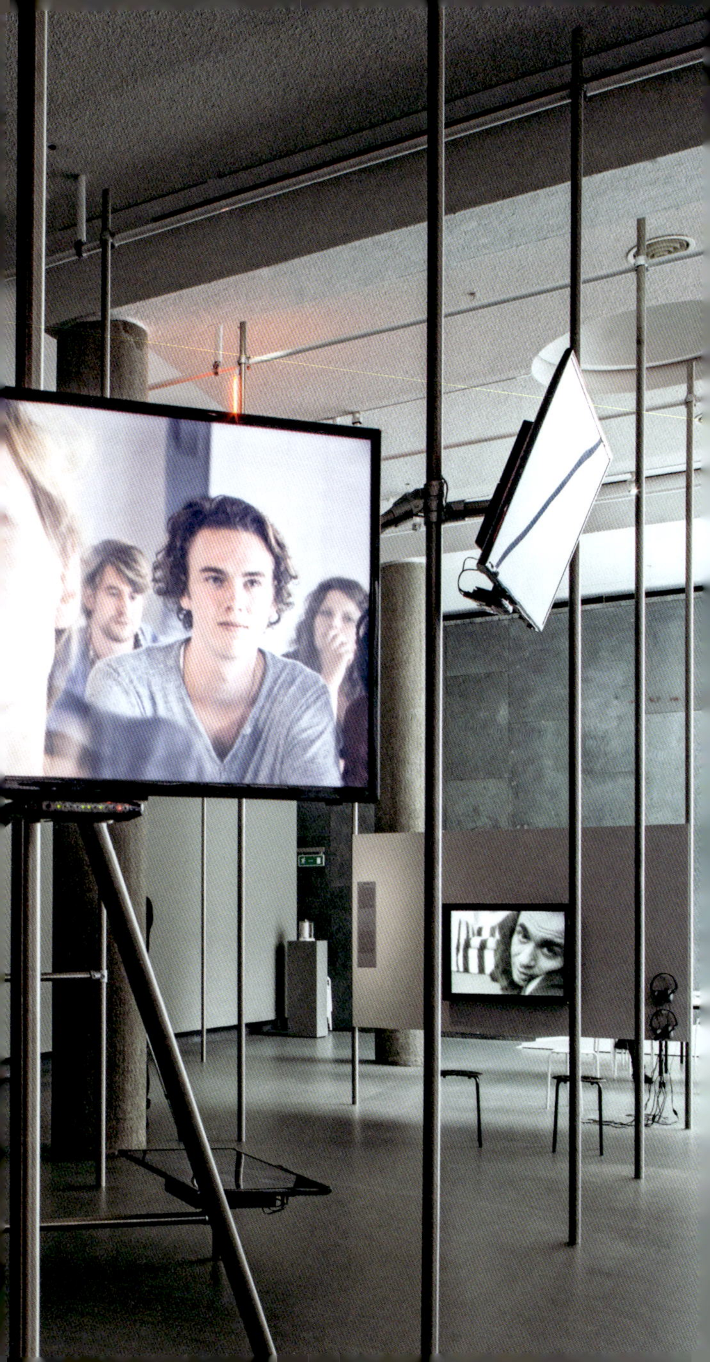

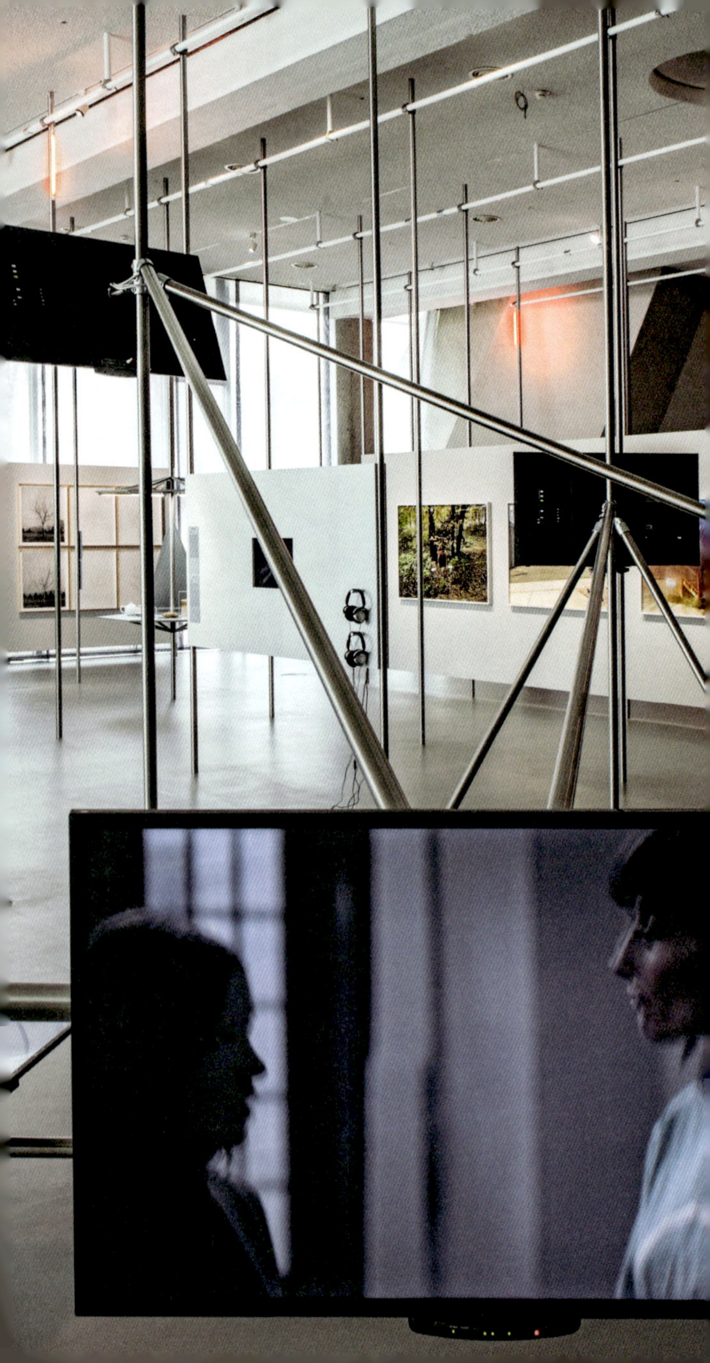

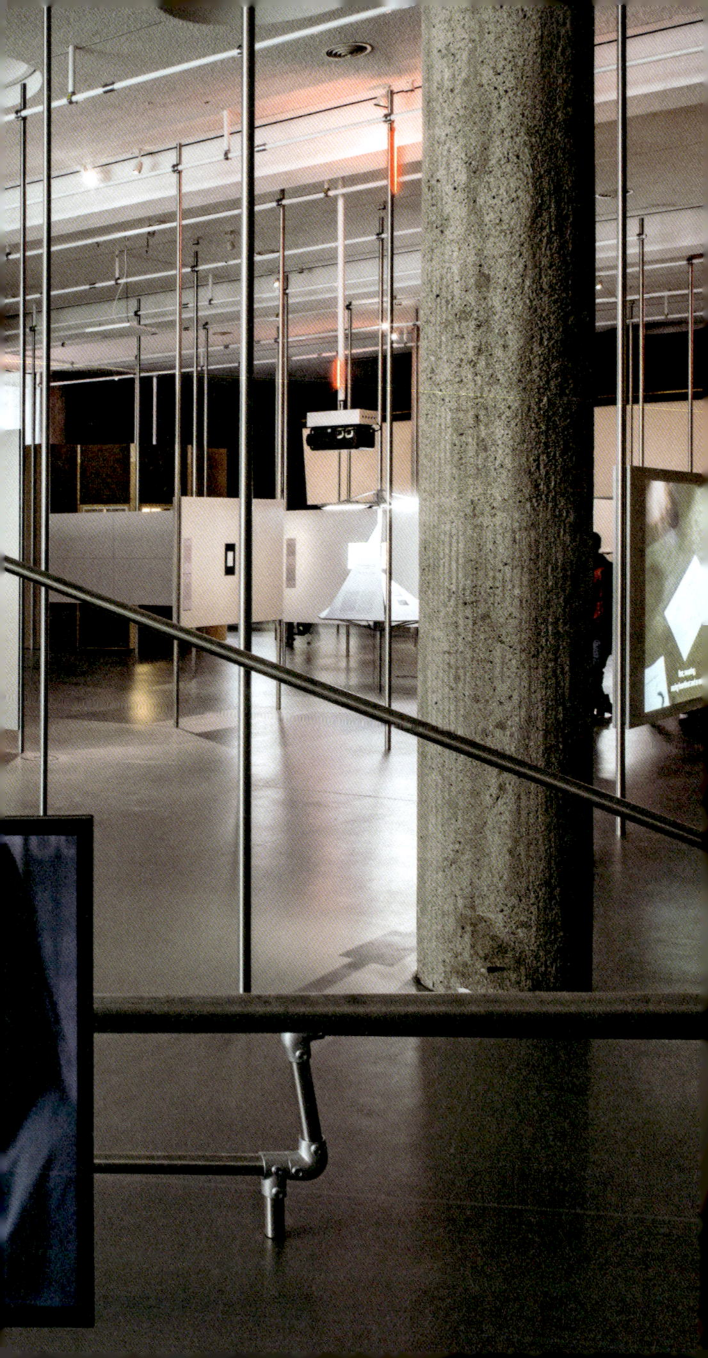

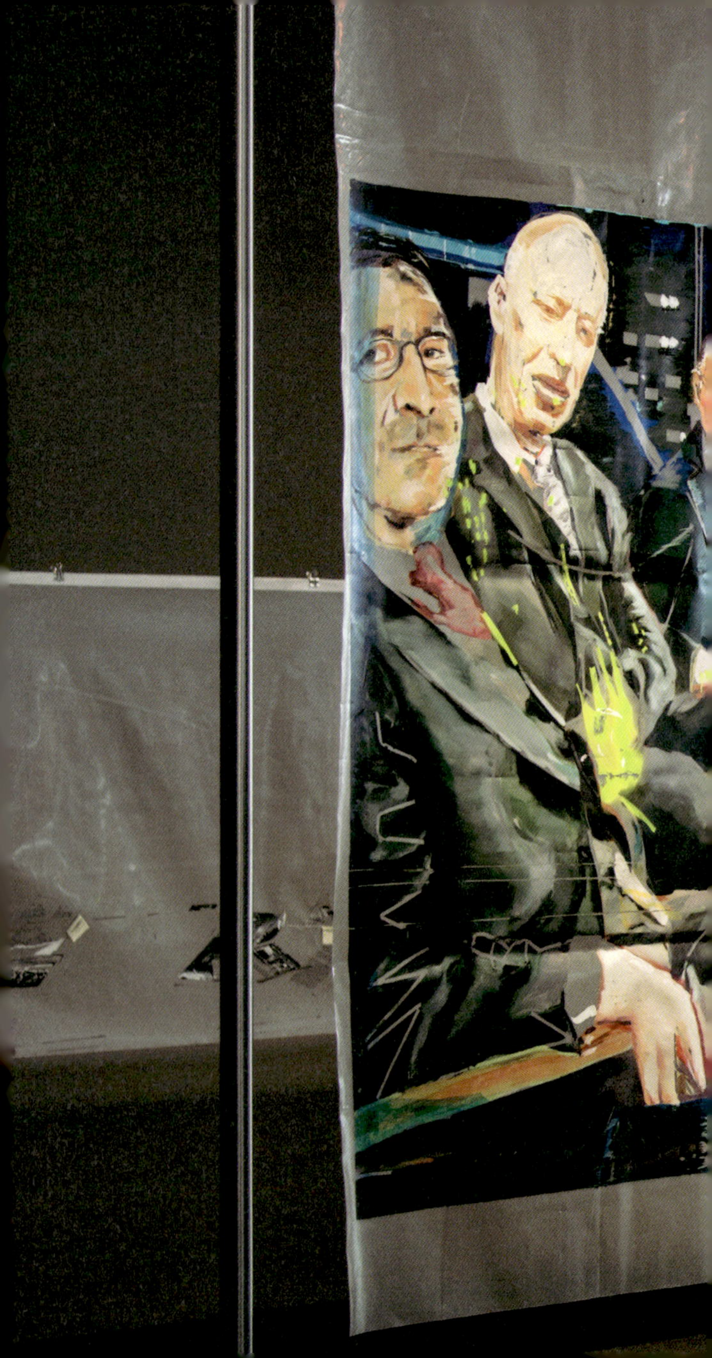

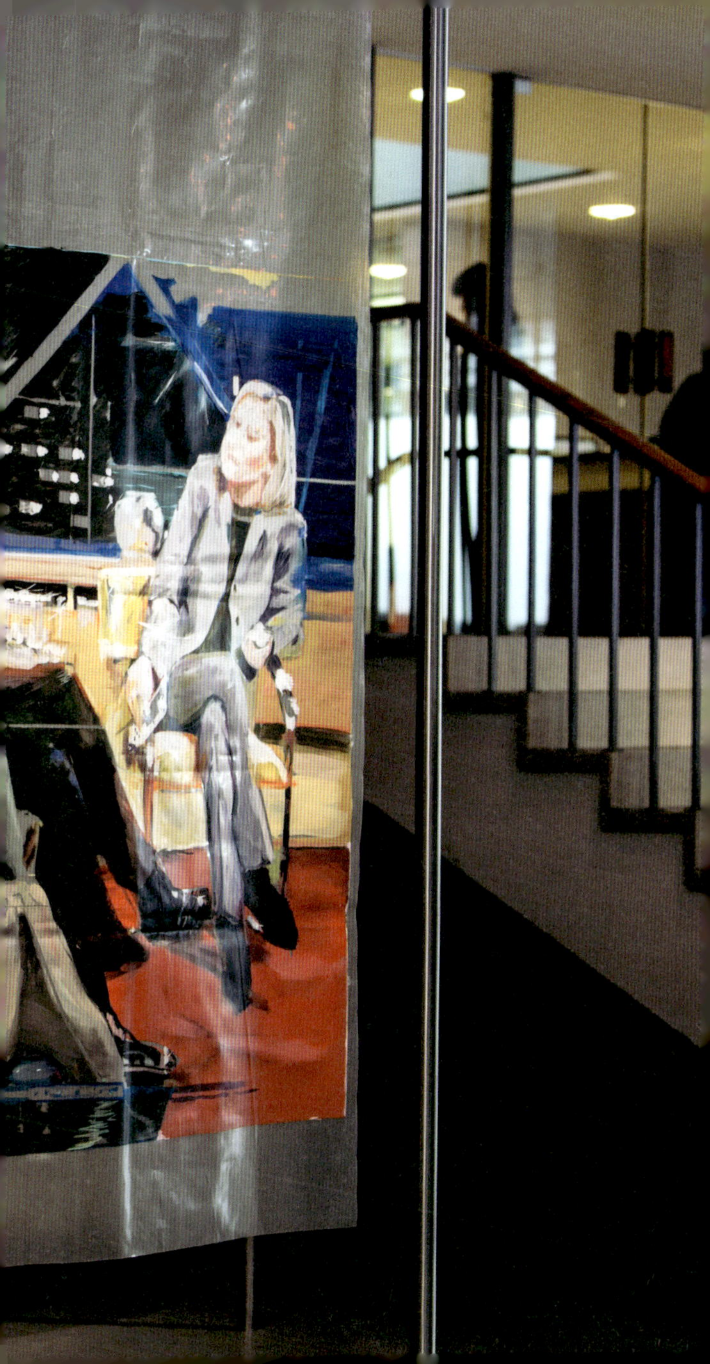

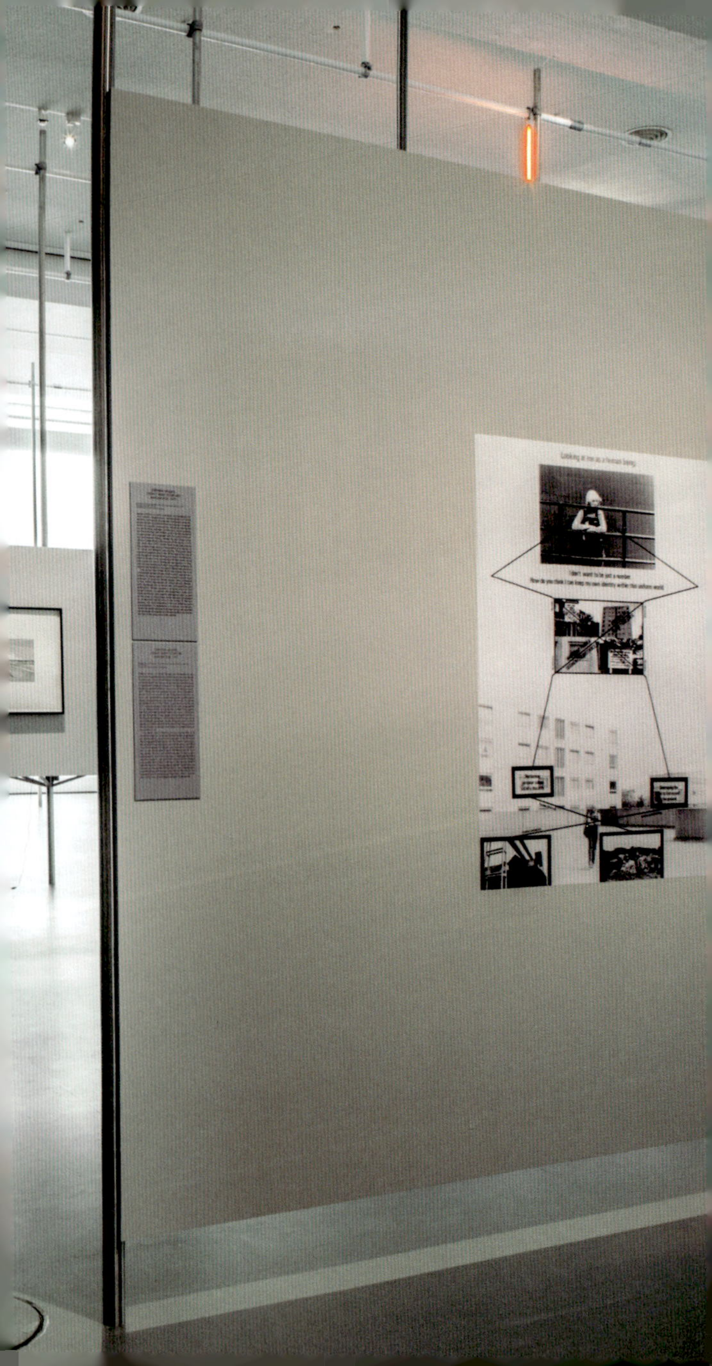
Looking at me as a human being
I don't want to be just a number

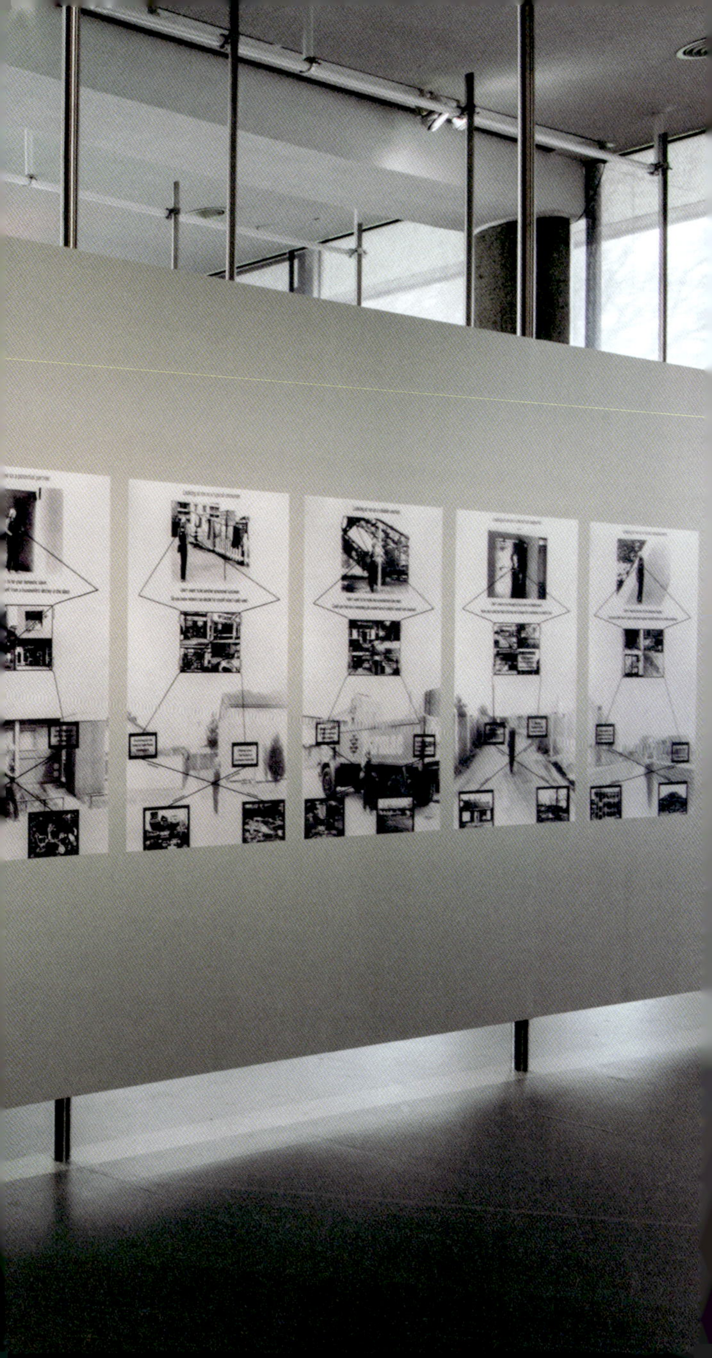

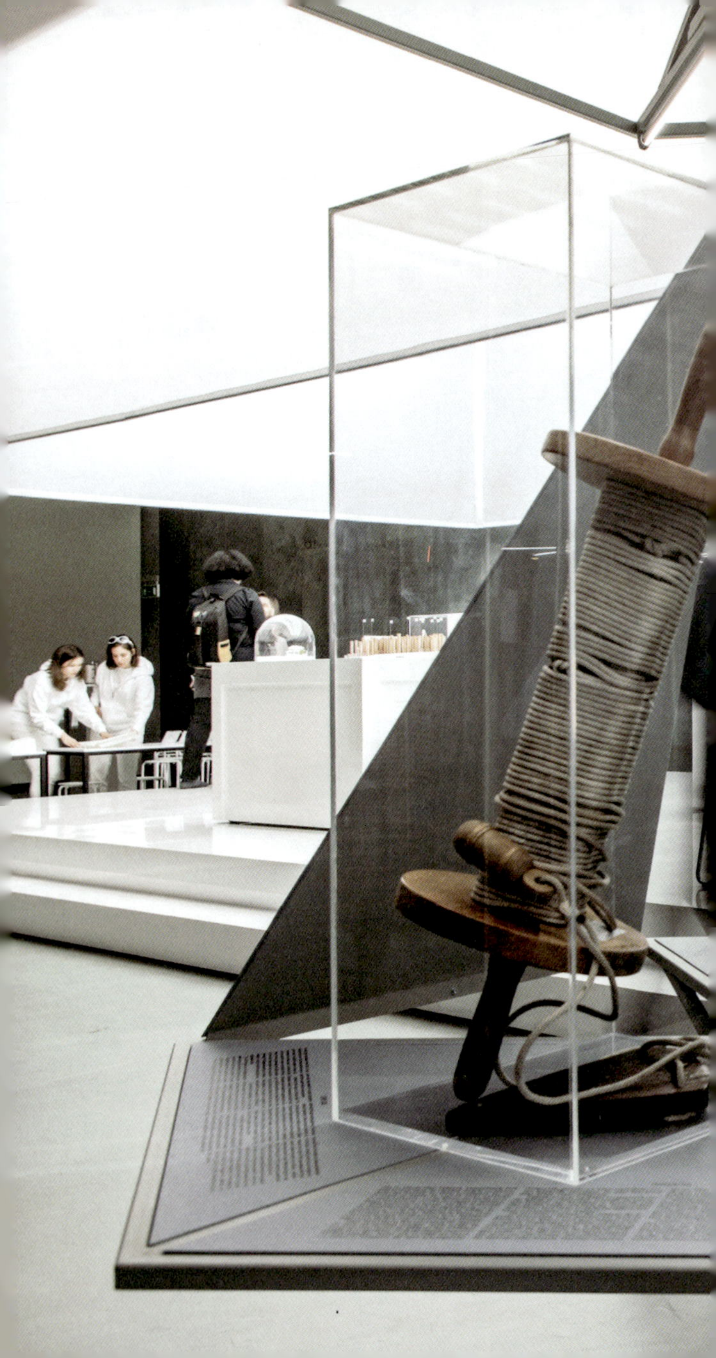

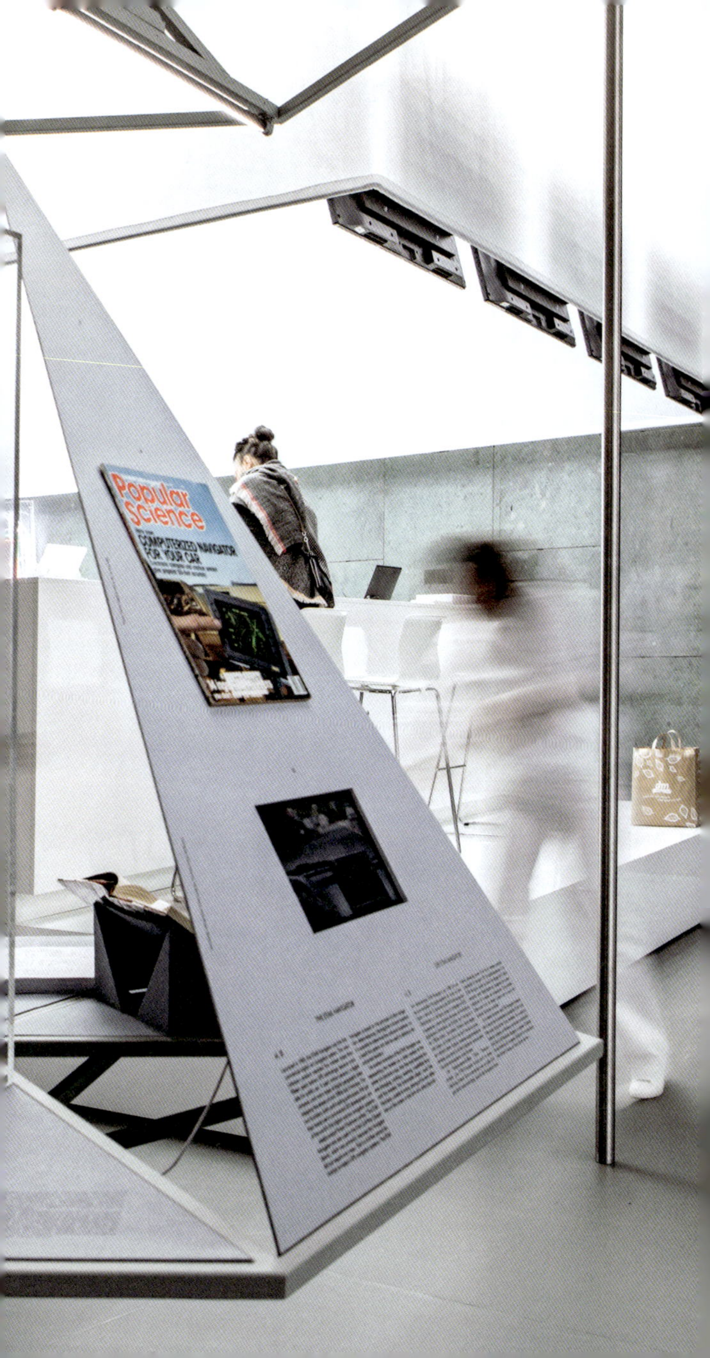
Popular Science
COMPUTERIZED NAVIGATOR FOR YOUR CAR

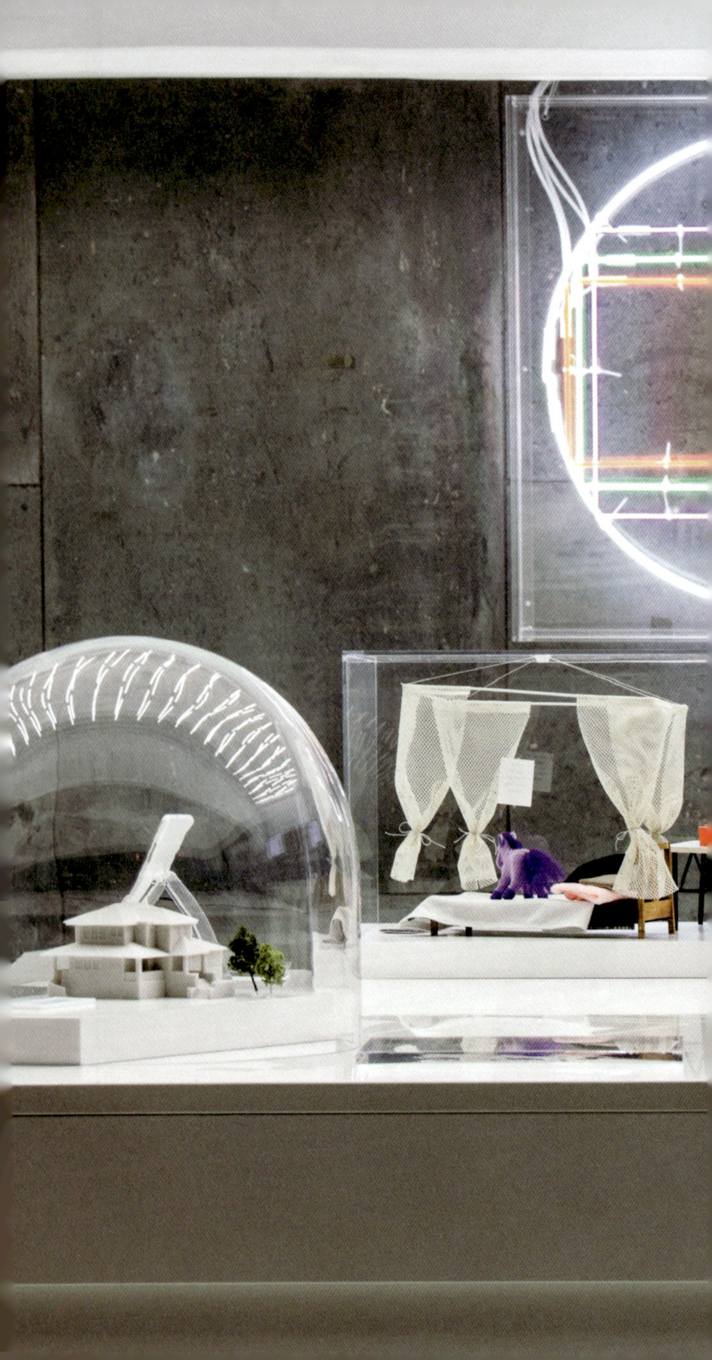

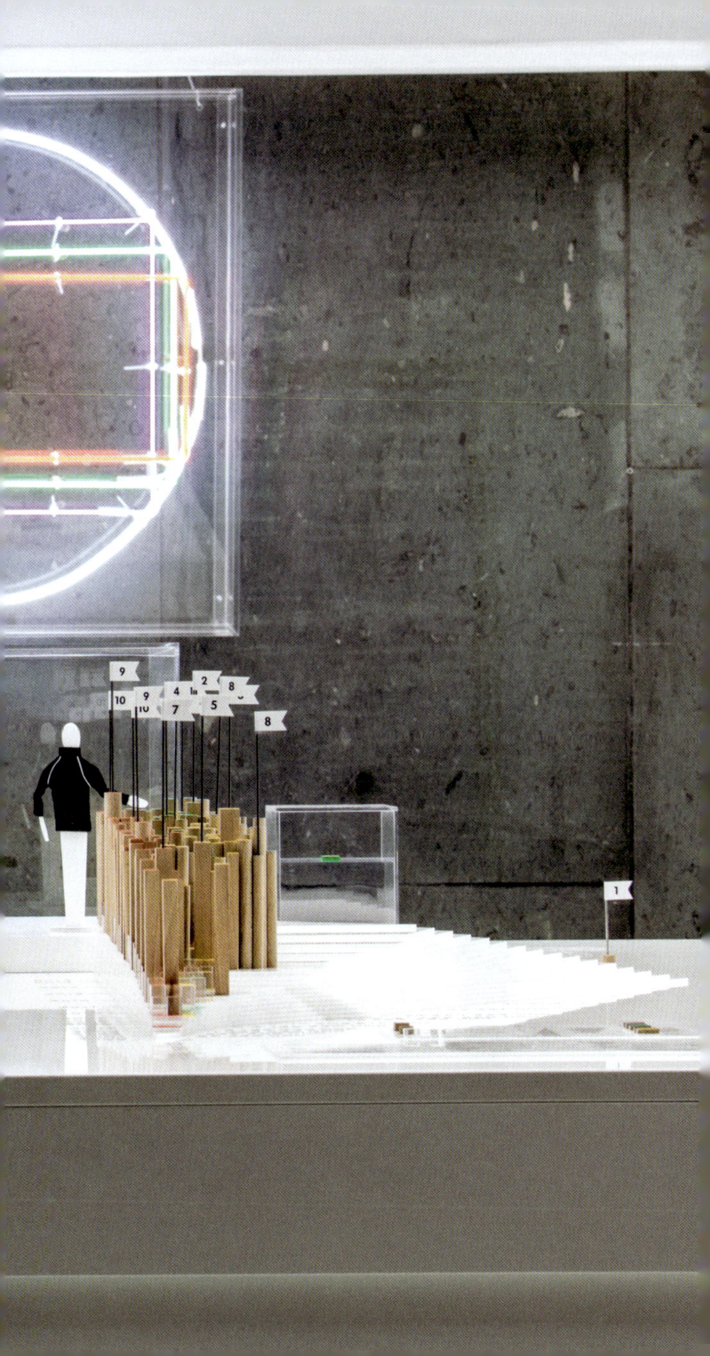
9
10
9
10
4
2
8
7
5
8
1

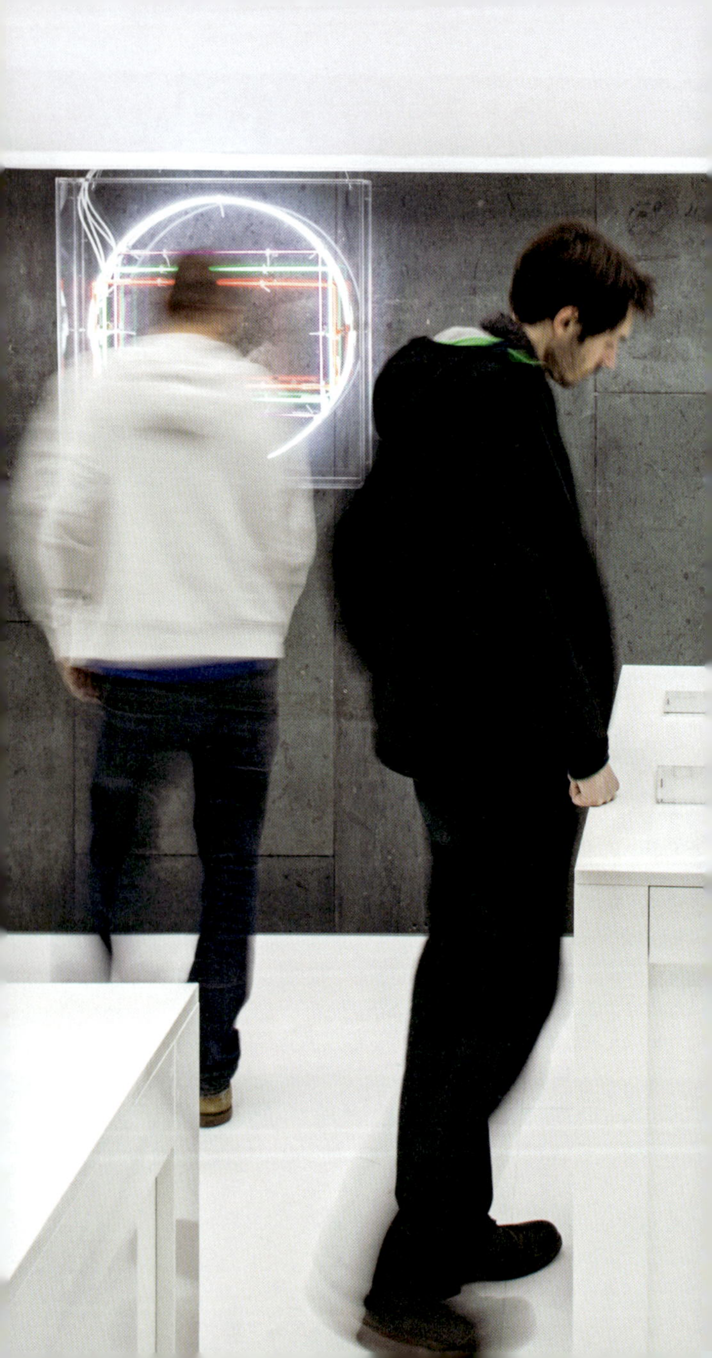

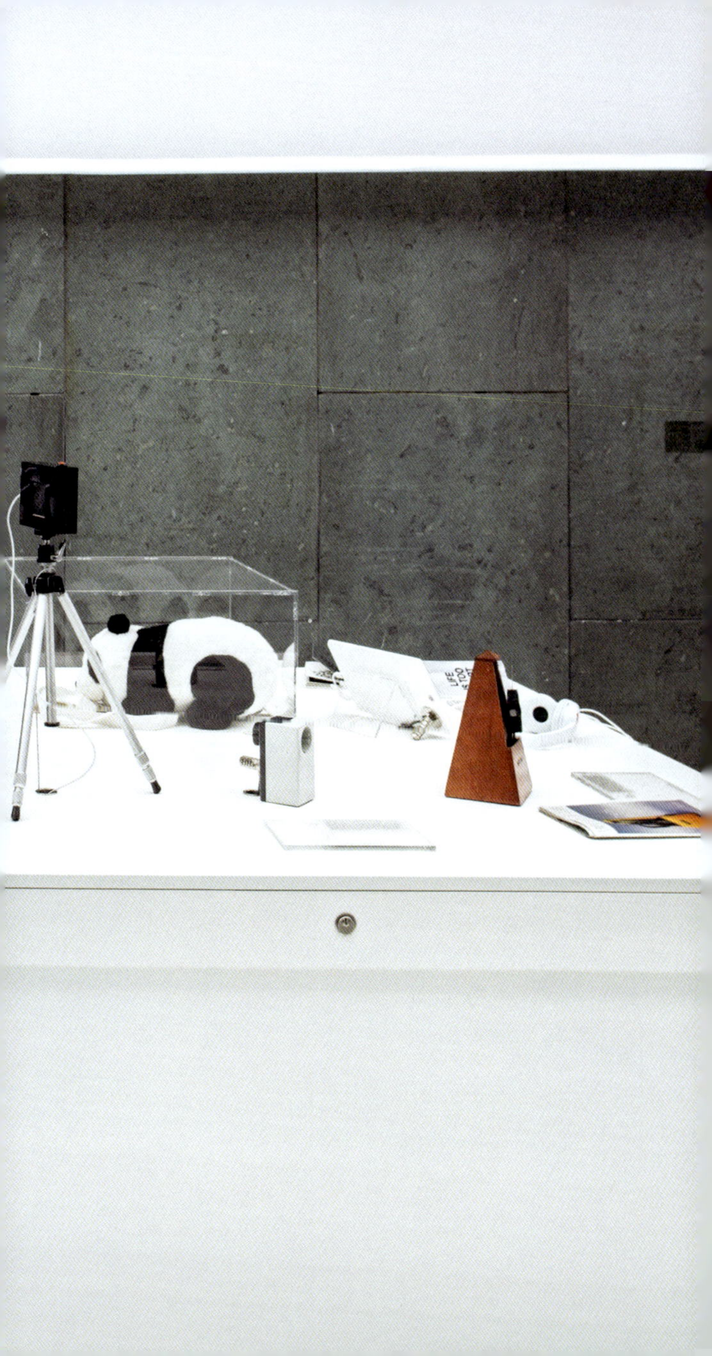
LIFE

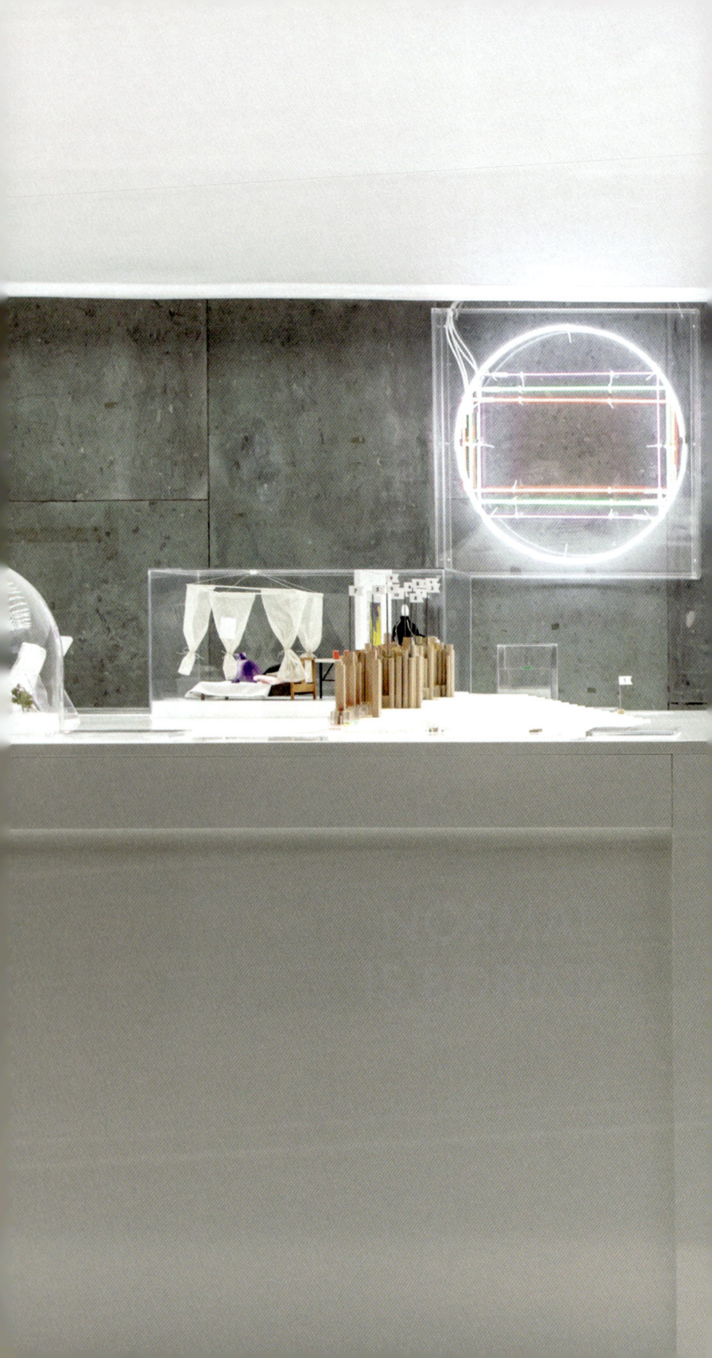

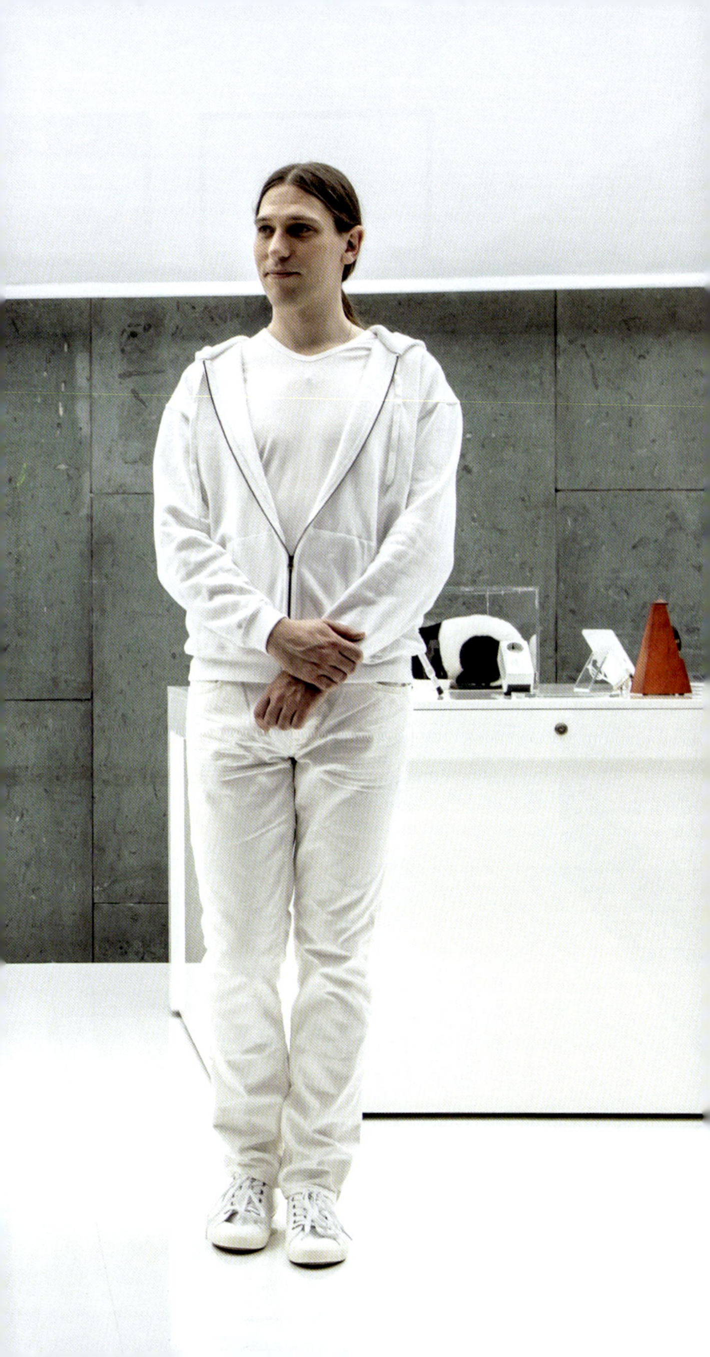

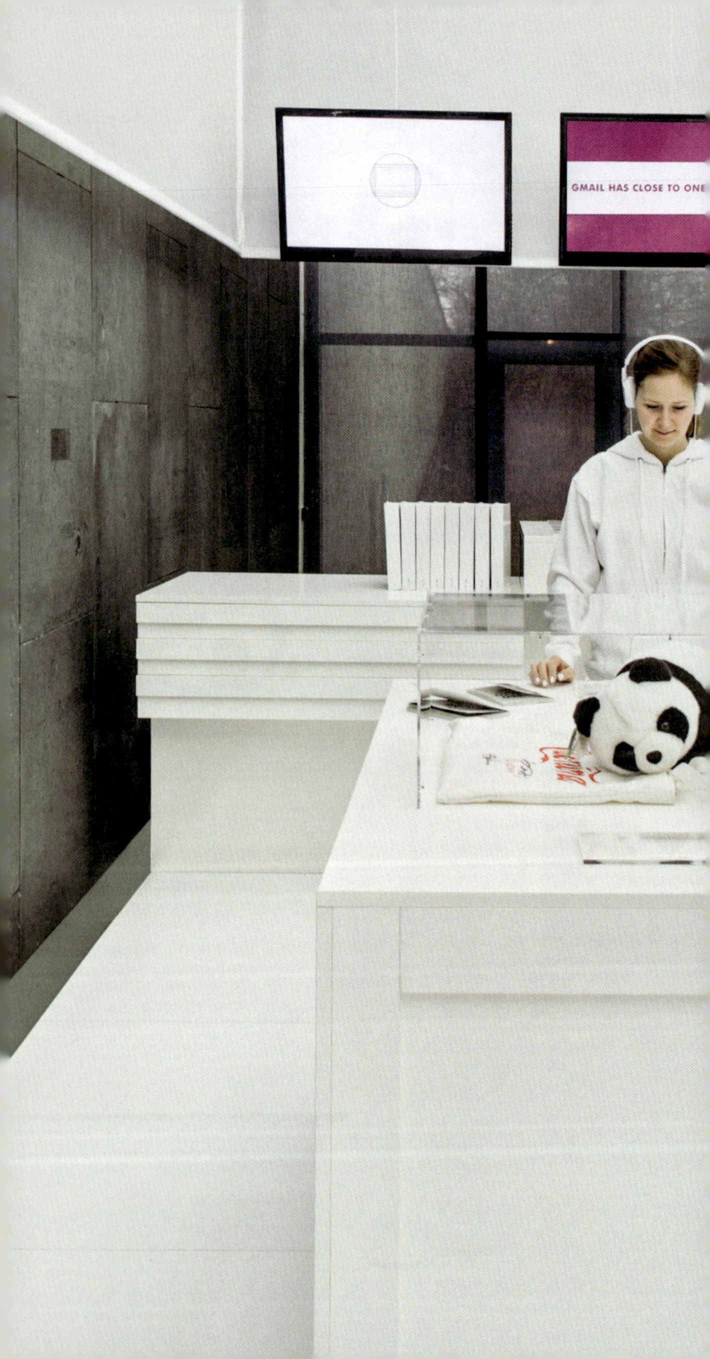
GMAIL HAS CLOSE TO ONE

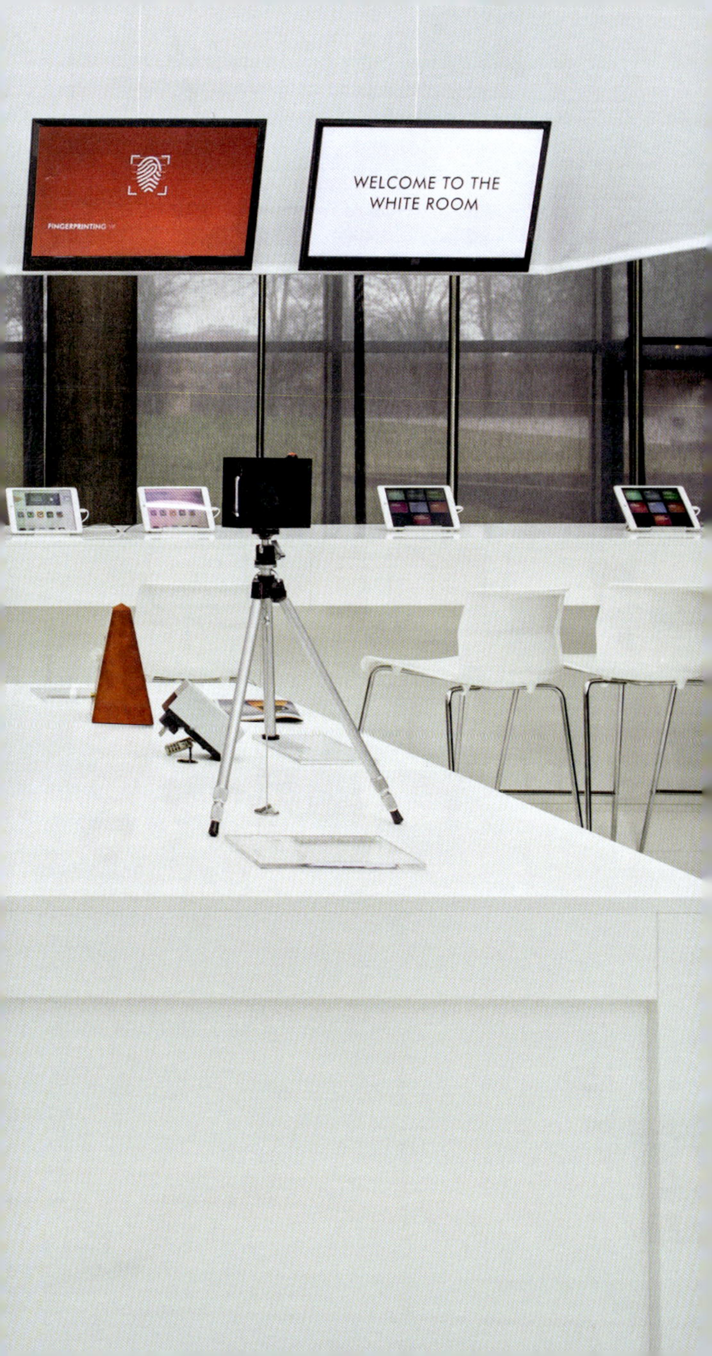

FINGERPRINTING
WELCOME TO THE
WHITE ROOM

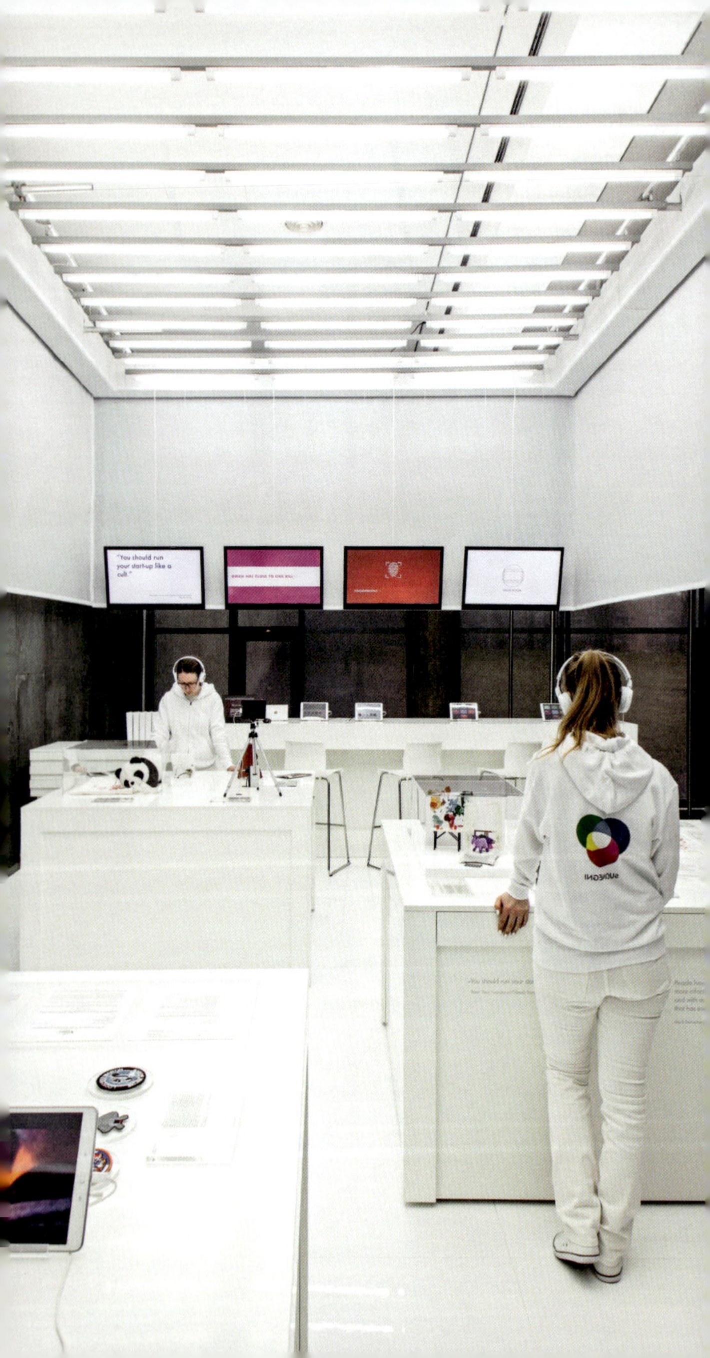
"You should run your start-up like a cult."

# TRIANGULATIONS

GRÉGOIRE CHAMAYOU

*PATTERNS OF LIFE*

Once upon the time, human beings were able to live their lives without leaving much trace. Their wanderings impressed footprints in the sand or in the mud, but, soon, the next storm would come in and wash away the fleeting local vestiges of their earthly journey. Later on, the minuscule events of their ordinary existences began to project a growing shadow of a new kind, made of paper trails and scriptural records. It was yet to fall on modern generations to witness the far-reaching expansion of this long process of capture.

Today, designers in San Francisco offer strange jewelry for purchase: small geometric medallions that look like spiderwebs or crystalline structures. Their patterns are actually those of the routes you have taken. Meshu—this is the name of this small high-tech silversmith business—uses the geolocation data collected by your smartphone in order to extract the schematic map of your peregrinations. The visualization of your chronospatial data generates a graph that then may serve as a model to carve out your personalized pendant in either metal or wood. The spatialized history of your travels, therefore, becomes a cryptic sign worn as ornamental jewelry. It is also a personalized emblem, the expression of a new art of portraiture.

Each person, everyone has a particular form or pattern of life. Our daily actions are repetitive; our behavior has certain regularities. For example, we rise at roughly the same hour and regularly make the same journey to work or elsewhere. We frequently meet up with the same friends in the same places. Anyone who has the technical ability to access the electronic records of one's daily activities can establish a spatiotemporal map of all one's usual actions. If the observer is able to intercept one's phone calls or access one's metadata, s/he can superimpose one's social network upon this map, determine which are one's personal links, and calculate the importance of each of those in one's life.

As each micro-event of each life tends instantly to be turned into accessible registered data, it might be that we are observing the emergence of new kinds of "bio-graphical" regimes of power. At a recent conference, an official of the United States Security Agency's (NSA) less famous sister bureaucracy the National Geospatial Intelligence Agency (NGA), emphasized the central role that the "daticultural revolution," i.e. the process of "taking all aspects of life and turning them into data," could play in the development of a new paradigm for intelligence gathering. The idea is to intercept and store all the data made available by ubiquitous positioning devices, social media, etc. in order to conduct "Activity-Based Intelligence" (ABI).[1]

"By compiling activity-based association data with its metadata over time," explains another US Intelligence specialist, "a rich archive will be formed to harvest patterns of life, networks and abnormalities which may have been overlooked otherwise."[2] Analysis of the pattern of a person's life is more precisely defined as "the fusion of link analysis and a geospatial analysis." In other terms: a fusion of social, spatial, and temporal particulars, a mixed mapping of the *socius*, *locus*, and *tempus* spheres—in other words, a combination of the three dimensions that, not only in their regularities but also in their discordances, constitute a human life.

1 David Gauthier, "Activity-Based Intelligence: NGA Initiatives" (paper presented at the Next Generation ISR Symposium, Washington, DC, December 10, 2013).

2 Keith L. Barber, "NSG Expeditionary Architecture: Harnessing Big Data," *Pathfinder*, 10, 5 (2012): 8–10, here 10.

## MOTION CAPTURE

At the end of the nineteenth century Georges Demenÿ, an assistant to the physiologist Étienne-Jules Marey devised a new method for visualizing the patterns of a pathological gait: attaching light bulbs to the body with a harness and taking long-exposure photographs in the dark, he could then graphically follow the luminous trajectories of the limbs.

In the first decade of the nineteenth century, two disciples of Frederic Taylor, Lillian and Frank B. Gilbreth developed a similar method for other purposes. They invented an apparatus they called the "chronocyclegraph." After having affixed small electrical bulbs on a worker's hand, they would take long-exposure photographs of the operator while the task was being executed. Thus they obtained the image of a "continuous path of a cycle of motions" appearing in white lines on the photographic emulsion. "I believe," explained an enthusiastic young engineer, "a good method of illustrating how a motion model helps one to visualize is to compare it with the wake left by an ocean liner."[3]

These orbits should be not only visualized but also modeled in order to gain greater transformation. If one analyzes the trajectories of the gestures, it is in order to simplify them, to rid them of their useless detours: it is the principle of "waste elimination." Modelization is a prelude to standardization: "through a comparison of graphs or models showing the paths of different operators doing the same kind of work, it is possible to deduce the most efficient method and to make this a standard."[4] The Gilbreths also sculpted the movement models into three dimensions with wire and used them "to teach the path

3 Frank B. Gilbreth and Lillian M. Gilbreth, *Applied Motion Study*, New York 1917, 207.
4 Ibid., 91.

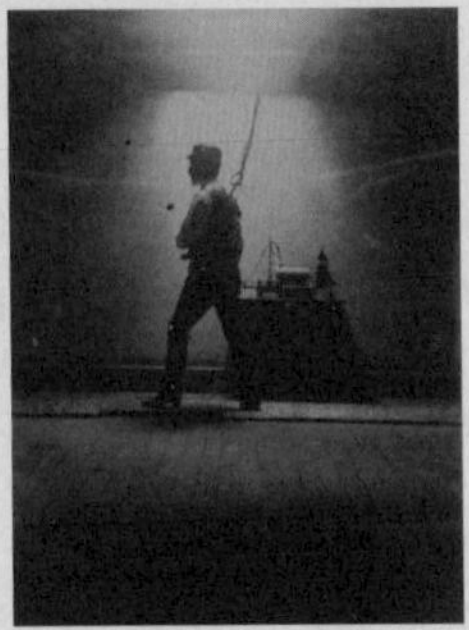

▲

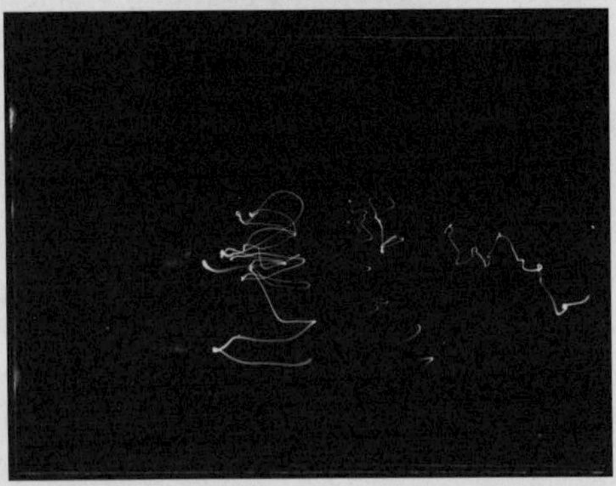

▲

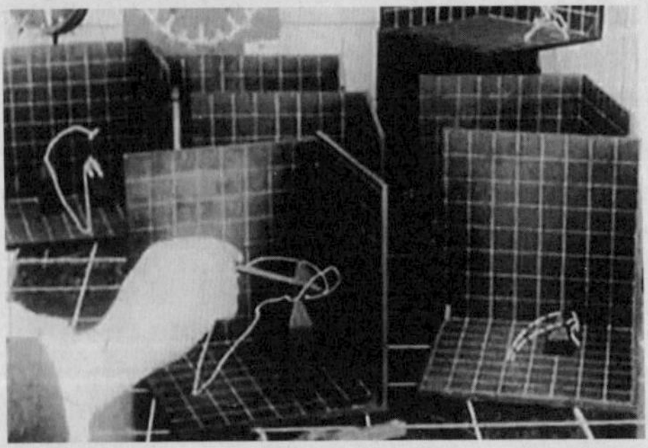

▲▲

▲ Étienne-Jules Marey, *Soldat équipé d'un dynamomètre enregistreur, pour leur catalogue d'exposition* and *Locomotion pathologique sur un côté du corps*, Meudon 1888.
▲▲ Frank B. Gilbreth, *The Original Films of Frank B. Gilbreth*, 1910–24, 32 min.

of the motion" to operators. The worker's gesture, reconstructed in a laboratory, re-enters the workshop in modified form, this time as a thread by which to conduct productive bodies to conform to their dance.

## TIME-GEOGRAPHY

In his 1956 *Theory of the Dérive*, Guy Debord described a map of Paris drawn by an urban sociologist, depicting "all the movements made in the space of one year by a student living in the 16th Arrondissement." "Her itinerary," he remarked, "forms a small triangle with no significant deviations, the three apexes of which are the School of Political Sciences, her residence and that of her piano teacher."[5]

The cartographic *objectivation* of a life form was taken as a starting point for a poetical and political critique of daily life. This critique of life's narrowness, its routines, and the reduction of the lifeworld they articulate, Debord concluded: "Such data—examples of a modern poetry capable of provoking sharp emotional reactions (in this particular case, outrage at the fact that anyone's life can be so pathetically limited) ... will undoubtedly prove useful in developing *dérives* (drifts)."[6]

Also during the 1960s, an innovative movement in human geography undertook to revolutionize the discipline: this was the project of chronogeography or time-geography. The fundamental idea was that one could give an account of human lives by treating them as paths within time-space. This implied, among other things, the invention of new kinds of maps, which would articulate time to space. Torsten Hågerstrand, one of the founding fathers of this methodology,

5 Guy Debord, "Theory of the dérive," in: Ken Knabb (ed. and tr.), *The Situationist International Anthology*, Berkeley, CA 1981, 50. Debord is refering to a map reproduced in Paul Henry Chombart de Lauwe, *Paris et l'agglomération parisienne*, Vol. 1, Paris 1952, 106.

6 Debord, "Theory of the dérive," 50.

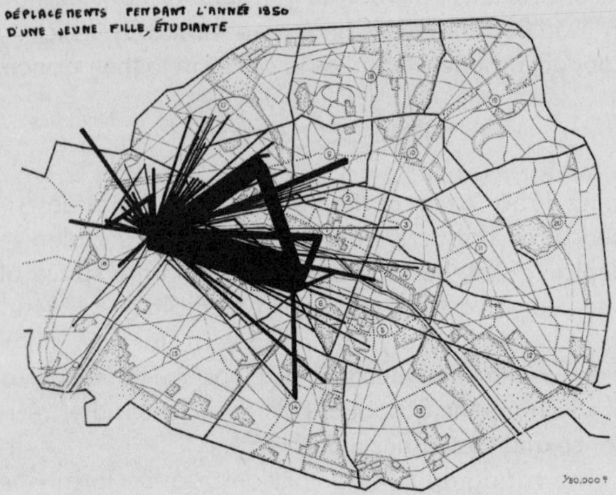


▲

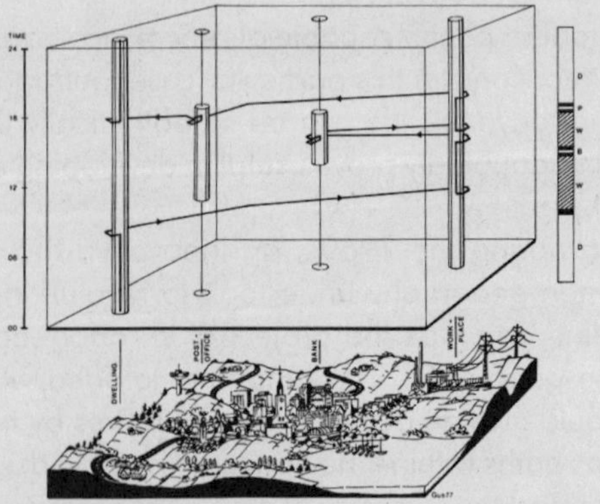


▲▲

▲ Martine Alibert / M. Le Bas (eds.), *Quartier Et Milieu Bourgeois Aux Alentours De La Place Victor Hugo*, Paris 1951.

▲▲ Bo Lenntorp, "A time-geographic simulation model of individual activity programs," in: Tommy Carlstein et al. (eds), *Timing Space and Spacing Time II: Human Activity and Time Geography*, London 1978.

summed up its postulate as follows: "In time space the individual describes a *path* ... the concept of life path (or path of it such as the day path, the week path, etc.) can easily be shown graphically if we agree to collapse a three-dimensional space into a two-dimensional plain..., and use a perpendicular direction to represent time."[7] Nowadays, this kind of cartographic representation has been integrated into powerful Geographical Information Systems (GIS) used for geovisual analytics research.

But, along the way, the fundamental postulate of time-geography, according to which individual biographies can be tracked as "life paths in time-space," is in the process of becoming the epistemological basis of other sorts of practices of power.

## ACTIVITY-BASED INTELLIGENCE

In 2010, the highest authorities in the United States Intelligence community laid down the principles of a new paradigm: "Activity-Based Intelligence." The geographer Derek Gregory describes it as "a sort of militarized rhythm analysis, even a weaponized time-geography" based on the use of programs "that fuse and visualize geospatial, temporal and intelligence data from multiple sources ('combining the where, the when and the who') as a three-dimensional array that replicates the standard time-geography diagrams."[8]

This methodology is based on the use of data mining applied to trajectories of movements in order to discover, within a gigantic assortment of paths, periodic patterns or signatures corresponding to characteristic segments of habits. Within such a model, by "accumulating tracks over time," one can, for example,

7 Torsten Hågerstrand, "What about people in regional science?," *Papers of the Regional Science Association*, 24, 1 (1970): 6–21, here 10.

8 Derek Gregory, "Lines of descent," *Open Democracy* (November 2011), online http://www.opendemocracy.net/derek-gregory/lines-of-descent (accessed 01/22/2016).

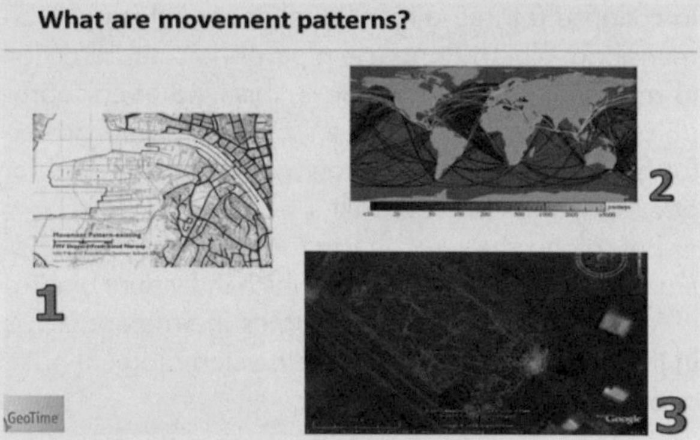


▲

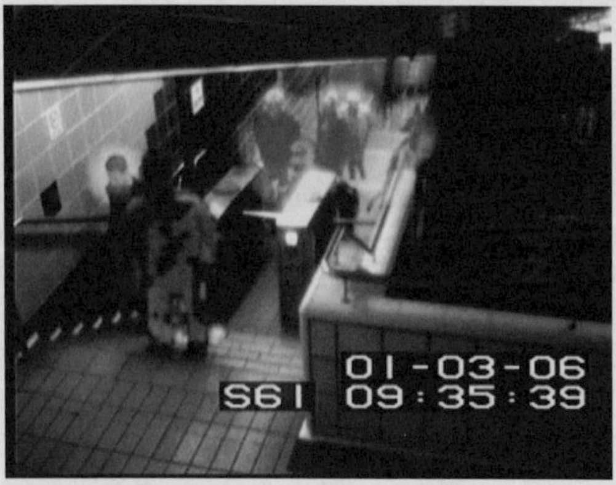


▲▲

▲ Uncharted, *GeoTime Webinar: Human Movement Pattern*, 2012, 24 min.

▲▲ Mehrsan Javan Roshtkhari and Martin D. Levine, *Anomalous Event Detection and Localization in Surveillance Video*, 2011, 3.59 min.

"model the movement patterns of pedestrians and detect anomalies from learned behavioral trends."[9]

The rationality that orders such a work of detection relies on a normative divide, a certain conception of what is normality. But their notion of the normal is, in fact, strictly empirical: it is *learned* by the machine on the basis of an analysis of frequencies and repetitions in given sets of activities. It is, then, a discrepancy with such patterns of regularities—an *anomaly*, rather than an *abnormality*—that will trigger the red-orange alert on the analyst's screen.

One of the classical issues with such a conception of normality is that, as the French medical philosopher Georges Canguilhem explained, "we would necessarily have to treat as abnormal (that is to say, we believe, pathological) every *anomal* individual, every carrier of anomalies—every individual aberrant in relation to a specific, statistically defined type."[10] While a singular discrepancy can be interpreted in various ways, for instance "as a failure or as an attempt, as a fault or as an adventure,"[11] a paranoid apparatus immediately tends to flag it up as a potential threat: "ALERT."

Somewhat ironically, it seems that within societies where the dominant ideology held sacred the individual freedom to follow one's own way of life, the singularity of such a route soon ends up being automatically signaled as suspicious. Another way to put this is that, in such regimes of knowledge and power, a potential target appears fundamentally as a drift.

9 Kevin Streib et al., "Interactive Visualization and Behavior Analysis for Video Surveillance," SIAM Data Mining (SDM 10), International Conference on Data Mining (ICDM), Columbus, OH, 2010.
10 Georges Canguilhem, *Knowledge of Life*, New York 2008, 127.
11 Ibid., 125.

AVERY F. GORDON WITH
ANSELM FRANKE

# *QUANTIFICATION AND THE SOCIAL QUESTION*

Methods of quantification, identification, mapping, and standardization are at the core of both industrial capitalism and modern statecraft. Dating from the period of the colonial plantations and the financial transactions of early capitalism that enabled them, the emerging system of measuring, counting, surveying, and accounting expanded into a vast web of quantitative technologies, designed to organize and police humans, increase their productivity, and extract wealth. This vast web of bureaucratic procedures and mathematical operations, having grown exponentially since the beginning of industrialization, has culminated in the information technologies in use today. The diverse practices and divergent protocols that make up these procedures, ranging from economics to the natural sciences to state administration and the rules that govern the treatment of prisoners, nevertheless, form a single frontier, a single self-sustaining fabric, of which Big Data is arguably but the latest iteration. While social scientists sought to apply the classificatory and objectivist methods of the natural sciences to social facts and processes, like all methods of classification, the procedures of these practices did not simply describe an existing reality, but sought to reduce, subjugate, and transform it, often with unintended consequences. These maps of the social are as the political scientist and anthropologist James C. Scott noted, "abridged maps": simplifications that render the complexity of social life administrable and inscribe it into a matrix while simultaneously changing social life. Since this method of inducing general laws and patterns from particulars formed an essential part of the legitimization of structural inequality and violence, the quantitative social sciences met with conflict from the outset. Situated at a crossroads of social struggles, social science offered a means to demystify the causes of social ills, and thus fight ignorance on the one hand, while on the other offering a positivist and reductionist "naturalization" of given relations and systemic inequalities.

It is at this tipping point, where supposedly objective and neutral data speaks for ideology, that the conflict over "positivism," and what constitutes social knowledge and "facts," takes place to this day. Today, the focus is no longer on classification and segregation, but on attribution and prediction, and the hedging of risks. As the legal theorist, Antoinette Rouvroy suggests in her essay, "The end(s) of critique: data-behaviourism vs. due-process," the data maps of both individual and collective behavior are generated from "infra-" and "supra-individual data." Thus, although they present us consistently with "personalized" echoes of our quantifiable selves, actually, they bypass any encounter with reflexive human subjects, in favor of the "computational, preemptive, context- and behavior-sensitive management of risks and opportunities," yet they also engulf us in echo chambers. Merely in trying to figure out what effects a personal credit score, for instance, today, results in a possible reduction of one's personal credit score. There is growing evidence that the algorithmic underwriting of digital culture and media, not unlike the "positivist" data that would re-inscribe and essentialize social symptoms in the past, reinforce bias and structural discrimination on an increasingly greater scale. A data-augmented reality becomes an echo chamber of the law of the great number.

> *On the other hand, however, average opinion does not represent an approximate value of truth, but instead the socially average illusion. In the latter, there participate what unreflective social research imagines to be its* ens realissimum*: those questioned, the human subjects. Their own nature, their being as subjects, depends upon the objectivity, upon the*

*mechanisms which they obey, and which constitute their concept. This can only be determined, however, if one perceives in the facts themselves the tendency which reaches out beyond them. That is the function of philosophy in empirical social research. If it is not realized or suppressed, if merely the facts are reproduced then such a reproduction is at the same time a corruption of facts into ideology.*
—Theodor W. Adorno[1]

## HERMAN HOLLERITH AND THE INVENTION OF THE DATA PUNCH-CARD SYSTEM FOR THE 1890 UNITED STATES CENSUS BUREAU

The census or head count is as old as the history of cities and statehood, purportedly originating with the Babylonians in 3800 BC. The age of modern data processing begins with the introduction of Hollerith's tabulator into the Eleventh United States Census in 1890—the same census that declared the "frontier" closed, and thus nominally put an end to the expansionist phase of colonization in North America. The 1890 census marks an era of technological intensification that witnesses a wave of rapid electrification, among other industrial, political, and social developments.

The American statistician Herman Hollerith developed the Hollerith machine in response to a competition by the US Census Bureau. The electric machine read holes, punched into paper cards, to tabulate the population data. The breakthrough created near-automatization of the sorting mechanism, as the machine read, counted, and sorted the punched cards whose holes represented the population data gathered by census-takers. The punch-card technology spread globally, enabling modern states to administer more

1 Theodor W. Adorno, "Sociology and Empirical Research," in: Theodor W. Adorno et al., *The Positivist Dispute in German Sociology*, tr. Glyn Adey and David Frisby, London 1976, 86.

intensely their populations and workforces. In 1924, Hollerith's Tabulating Machine Company developed into the International Business Machines Corporation, later known as IBM.

By 1935, the Social Security Act signed by Franklin D. Roosevelt won IBM a government contract for the biggest data-gathering enterprise to date, managing employment records of twenty-six million working Americans and three million employers. At the same time, IBM leased to the National Socialist government in Germany, via a subsidiary, custom-designed Hollerith solutions able to process millions of punch cards for the organization of the railroads, the forced labor system, and the concentration camps. As Edwin Black has shown in his study *IBM and the Holocaust* from 2001, Hollerith's tabulator enabled the targeting of European Jews—leading to confiscation of their property, ghettoization, deportation, enslaved labor, and, ultimately, annihilation.

> *Population comes to appear above all else as the ultimate end of government.... Government has as its purpose not the act of government itself, but the welfare of the population, the improvement of its condition, the increase of its wealth, longevity, health, etc; and the means that the government uses to attain these ends are themselves all in some sense immanent to the population; it is the population itself on which government will act either directly through large-scale campaigns, or indirectly through techniques that will make possible, without the full awareness of the people, the stimulation of birth rates, the directing of the flow of population into certain regions or activities, etc.*
> —Michael Foucault[2]

2 Michael Foucault, "Governmentality," in: Graham Burchell et al. (eds), *The Foucault Effect: Studies on Governmentality*, Chicago, IL 1991, 100.

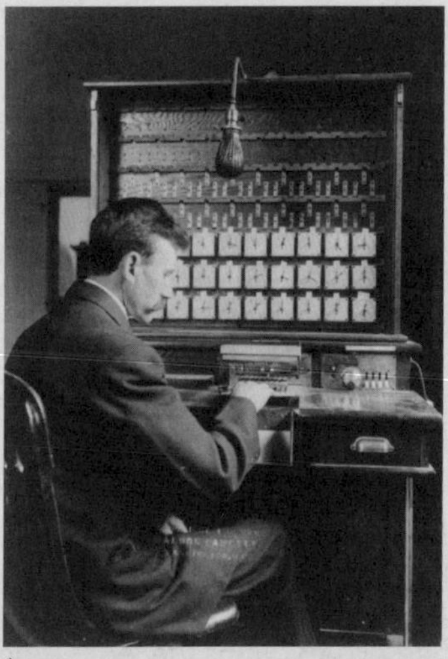

▲

## MAP OF LONDON'S POOR BY CHARLES BOOTH

Between 1886 and 1903, Charles Booth, an English social researcher and reformer from a wealthy Liverpool shipping family, undertook a comprehensive survey of poverty, industry, and religion entitled *Inquiry into the Life and Labour of the People of London*, the third and final version published in seventeen volumes in 1902/03. When Booth began the study, England was at the height of its imperial power. The "social question" was already in its second iteration following the wave of worker militancy throughout Europe in the 1830s and 1840s, the defeat of the 1848 revolutions, and the brutal suppression of the Paris Commune in 1871, which again raised the specter of communism, communal luxury, and an end to the acceptance of misery as a way of life.

▲ Hollerith Electric Tabulator, *US Census Bureau*, Washington, DC 1908.

The Booth study, comprising a team of twenty researchers, was unprecedented in its scope and influence. Its statistical data on living and working conditions, the organization of trades and industries, migration patterns, and leisure and religious activities set within the larger urban environment, was widely used by reformers, parliamentarians, and social science researchers. Perhaps best known for the maps, which charted levels of poverty and wealth street by street, *Life and Labour* is considered to have put the study of poverty on a firm scientific basis. Booth was well aware of the stakes of the project, which presumably accounts for the fact that he only included quantitative information in the published volumes. Yet much of that quantifiable information was calculated from interviews and observations the team made while accompanying the police and School Board Visitors, the latter keeping detailed records of every house and its occupants, which they generously shared, bibles in hand, with the Booth team. The published volumes obscured the crucial role the police and the regulatory agents of the state played in enabling the social researcher to cross into zones of the city in which normally they would not be welcomed, and the role of the state in ordering knowledge about poverty.

Already in 1844, Friedrich Engels had undertaken his own study of life and labor entitled *The Condition of the Working Class in England*, which focused on the industrial city of Manchester in the north of England. It began: "The real conditions of the life of the proletariat are so little known among us that even the well-meaning 'societies for the uplift of the working classes,' in which our bourgeoisie is now mistreating the social question, constantly start out from the most ridiculous and preposterous judgments concerning the condition of the workers. We Germans more than anybody else stand in need of a knowledge of the facts concerning this question." It is not so much facts that Marx and Engels will provide, but a completely different analytic framework to that dominating the so-called social question. Marx and Engels are clear: capitalism as a system is the problem. The social question as given is misdirected: the organization of the whole of society needs questioning.

> *When we consider bourgeois society in the long view and as a whole, then the final result of the process of social production always appears as the society itself, i.e. the human being itself in its social relations. Everything that has a fixed form, such as the product etc., appears as merely a moment, a vanishing moment, in this movement.... The conditions and objectifications of the process are themselves equally moments of it, and its only subjects are the individuals, but individuals in mutual relationships, which they equally reproduce and produce anew.*
> —Karl Marx[3]

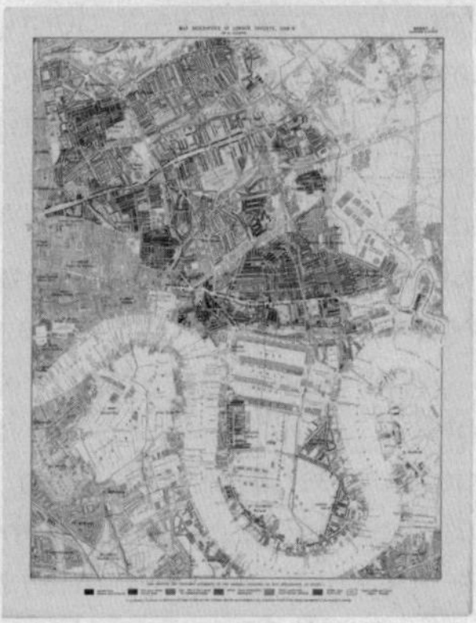

▲

▲ Charles Booth, "Eastern District," in: *Life and Labour of the People of London*, London 1898–99.

3 Karl Marx, *Grundrisse: Foundations of the Critique of Political Economy*, tr. Martin Nicolaus, Notebook VII, London 1993, 643–4.

## W.E.B. DU BOIS, THE PHILADELPHIA NEGRO

W.E.B. Du Bois' *The Philadelphia Negro: A Social Study*, published in 1899, was the first major social scientific study of the social and economic life of African Americans to make use of quantitative data. The extensive study of Philadelphia's Seventh Ward appeared as debates about the status of African Americans, twenty-five years after emancipation, were provoked by the publication of the 1890 census and by a growing hysteria over black crime and "disorder." Similar to Booth's study, Du Bois and his one assistant Isabel Eaton surveyed every household in the Ward, creating maps as well as elaborate tables and charts that were new to the presentation of social science results. As Booth's study had found, crime, policing, and prison appeared to be central to the lives of working class and poor people in England's cities as well as in America's. Unlike the Booth study, however, the police were not collaborators: Du Bois and his wife lived in the poorer area of the Ward for over a year during the study. More importantly, the explanation for crime and imprisonment rates—where African Americans represented 12 percent of the population but comprised 30 percent of the prison population—was located in the history of slavery and the emancipation experience, consisting as it did in convict-leasing, discrimination in the Southern courts, mob violence, and the "drawing of the color line." Despite its extraordinary range: meticulous data collection, its singular treatment of the residents of the Seventh Ward as people whose future mattered, and sponsorship by the wealthy Susan P. Wharton, *The Philadelphia Negro* received no accolades, ignored by both the academic profession and research-funding bodies until after the centennial of its publication.

250 *The Negro Criminal.* [Chap. XIII.

| | |
|---|---|
| Theft . . . . . . . . . . . . . . . . . . . . . . . | 243 |
| Serious assaults on persons . . . . . . . . . . . . | 139 |
| Robbery and burglary . . . . . . . . . . . . . . . | 85 |
| Rape . . . . . . . . . . . . . . . . . . . . . . . | 24 |
| Other sexual crimes . . . . . . . . . . . . . . . | 23 |
| Homicide . . . . . . . . . . . . . . . . . . . . . | 16 |
| All other crimes . . . . . . . . . . . . . . . . . | 11 |
| Total . . . . . . . . . | 541 |

Following these crimes from year to year we have:

| Crime. | 1885. | 1886. | 1887. | 1888. | 1889. | 1890. | 1892. | 1893. | 1894. | 1895. | Total. |
|---|---|---|---|---|---|---|---|---|---|---|---|
| Theft, etc. . . . . . . . . | 20 | 21 | 23 | 13 | 24 | 39 | 20 | 32 | 23 | 28 | 243 |
| Robbery and burglary . . . | 2 | 8 | 8 | 5 | 5 | 9 | 7 | 14 | 19 | 8 | 85 |
| Serious assaults . . . . . . | 10 | 9 | 11 | 15 | 9 | 12 | 9 | 19 | 18 | 27 | 139 |
| Homicide . . . . . . . . . . | . | . | 3 | 2 | 5 | . | 2 | 1 | 1 | 2 | 16 |
| Sexual crimes . . . . . . . | 6 | 7 | 7 | 4 | 4 | 4 | 4 | 5 | 3 | 3 | 47 |
| All others . . . . . . . . . | 2 | . | 1 | 1 | . | . | . | 2 | 3 | 2 | 11 |
| Total . . . . . . . . . | 40 | 45 | 53 | 40 | 47 | 64 | 42 | 73 | 67 | 70 | 541 |

The course of the total serious crime for this period may be illustrated by this diagram:

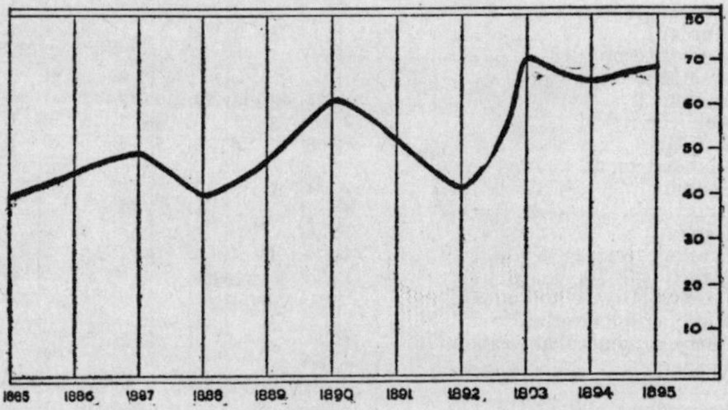


Drawing a similar diagram for the different sorts of crime we have:

▲ W.E.B. Du Bois, *The Philadelphia Negro: A Social Study*, Philadelphia, PA 1899, 250–51.

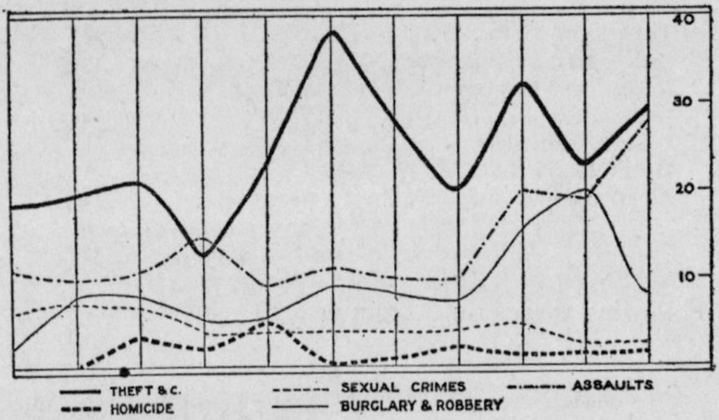


In ten years convictions to the penitentiary for theft have somewhat increased, robbery, burglary and assault have considerably increased, homicide has remained about the same, and sexual crimes have decreased. Detailed statistics are given in the following table:

CRIMES OF 541 CONVICTS IN EASTERN PENITENTIARY, 1885–1895.

| Crimes. | 1885. | 1886. | 1887. | 1888. | 1889. | 1890. | 1892. | 1893. | 1894. | 1895. |
|---|---|---|---|---|---|---|---|---|---|---|
| Assault and battery . . . . . . . | 3 | . | 1 | 2 | . | 1 | . | . | . | . |
| Aggravated assault and battery . . | 3 | 3 | 3 | 7 | 3 | 6 | 3 | 6 | 6 | 9 |
| Assault to kill . . . . . . . . . | 4 | 6 | 7 | 6 | 6 | 5 | 4 | 13 | 11 | 17 |
| Manslaughter . . . . . . . . . | . | . | . | 1 | 3 | . | 1 | 1 | . | 1 |
| Murder . . . . . . . . . . . | . | . | 3 | 1 | 2 | . | 1 | . | 1 | 1 |
| Assault to murder . . . . . . . | . | . | 1 | . | . | . | . | . | . | . |
| Assault to steal . . . . . . . . | . | . | . | . | . | . | 2 | . | 1 | 1 |
| Larceny . . . . . . . . . . . | 20 | 21 | 23 | 13 | 24 | 39 | 17 | 27 | 22 | 28 |
| Robbery . . . . . . . . . . . | 2 | 3 | 3 | 1 | . | 4 | 3 | 5 | 9 | 6 |
| Burglary . . . . . . . . . . . | . | 5 | 5 | 4 | 5 | 5 | 4 | 9 | 10 | 2 |
| Embezzlement . . . . . . . . . | . | . | . | . | . | . | . | 1 | . | . |
| Sodomy . . . . . . . . . . . | 2 | 1 | 1 | 3 | 2 | 3 | 2 | . | . | 1 |
| Abortion . . . . . . . . . . . | 1 | . | . | . | . | . | 1 | . | . | . |
| Rape . . . . . . . . . . . . | 1 | . | . | . | . | . | . | 2 | 1 | . |
| Attempt to rape . . . . . . . . | 1 | 6 | 1 | 1 | 1 | 1 | 1 | 3 | 2 | 1 |
| Incest . . . . . . . . . . . | 1 | . | . | . | . | . | . | . | . | . |
| Keeping bawdy house . . . . . . | . | . | 4 | . | . | . | . | . | . | 1 |
| Enticing female child . . . . . . | . | . | 1 | . | 1 | . | . | . | . | . |
| Carrying concealed weapons . . . | 1 | . | . | . | . | . | . | 1 | . | . |
| Forgery . . . . . . . . . . . | 1 | . | . | . | . | . | . | . | 1 | 1 |
| False pretence . . . . . . . . . | . | . | . | 1 | . | . | 1 | | 1 | . |
| Receiving stolen goods . . . . . | . | . | . | . | . | . | 2 | 4 | 1 | . |
| Mayhem . . . . . . . . . . . | . | . | . | . | . | . | . | 1 | . | . |
| Indecent exposure . . . . . . . | . | . | . | . | . | . | . | . | . | 1 |
| Conspiracy . . . . . . . . . . | . | . | . | . | . | . | . | . | 1 | . |
| Total . . . . . . . . | 40 | 45 | 53 | 40 | 47 | 64 | 42 | 73 | 67 | 70 |

▲ W.E.B. Du Bois, *The Philadelphia Negro: A Social Study*, Philadelphia, PA 1899, 250–51.

> *The main result of my schooling had been to emphasize science and the scientific attitude.... I determined to put science into sociology.... I was going to study the facts, any and all facts, concerning the American Negro and his plight, and by measurement and comparison and research, work up to a valid generalization....*
>
> *Two considerations thereafter broke in upon my work and eventually disrupted it: first, one could not be a calm, cool, and detached scientist while Negroes were lynched, murdered, and starved; and secondly, there was no such definite demand for scientific work of the sort that I was doing. I regarded it as axiomatic that the world wanted to learn the truth.... This was, of course, but a young man's idealism.*
>
> —W.E.B. Du Bois[4]

## CRIMINAL ANTHROPOLOGY: VISUAL STIGMATA

The Italian criminologist and physician Cesare Lombroso's theory of the "criminal man" was probably the most influential doctrine to emerge from the anthropometric tradition, and significantly directed the development of criminology. Lombroso's basic claim, based on thousands of measurements of both living and dead convicts, was that criminality was innate, an arrested evolutionary development, which tied criminality to savagery. Lombroso believed that members of the "criminal race" were identifiable by certain visual signs or stigmata, and when Galton began photographing the facial features of known criminals, Lombroso followed, adapting photographic composites into his work. Members of the "criminal race" had thicker skulls and simpler cranial

4 W.E.B. Du Bois, *Dusk of Dawn: An Essay Toward an Autobiography of a Race Concept*, San Diego, CA 1940, Chapter 4: "Science and Empire," 67–8.

structures, longer arms, receding foreheads, asymmetrical faces, scant beards, woolly hair, swollen lips, twisted noses, precocious wrinkles, darker skin, inverted sexual organs, and so on. Lombroso was particularly obsessed with prostitutes and anarchists and in his study of American and European anarchists, he found the degenerative characteristics common to natural-born criminals in an overwhelming number of cases, including those of the Parisian anarchists, whom he studied alongside the French criminologist Alphonse Bertillon.

While the whole notion of the visual stigmata of the criminal may seem antiquated, it is still in use. This particular branch of criminology, which barely differs from its late nineteenth- and early twentieth-century versions in its racial profiling, is influential today in the policing of gangs, with its vast photographic and informational archives. It also underwrites all current and planned security and surveillance systems, from routine DNA identification to iris-recognition scans, which promise predictive preemption of the individual's danger to society. Seemingly easy identification of a person's race—the experience of knowing it unconsciously or knowing it without doubt—is central to racism and to the means by which groups of people can be classified, surveyed, and disciplined. The criminal needs his or her stigmata too, and Lombroso was one of the first to provide it.

> *The protean oral 'texts' of the criminal and pauper yield to a 'mute testimony' that 'takes down' (that diminishes in credibility, that transcribes) and unmasks the disguises, the alibis, the excuses and multiple biographies of those who find or place themselves on the wrong side of the law. This battle between the presumed denotative univocality of the legal image and the multiplicity and presumed duplicity of the criminal voice is played out during the remainder of*

*the nineteenth century. In the course of this battle a new object is defined—the criminal body—and, as a result, a more extensive "social body" is invented. We are confronting, then, a double system: a system of representation capable of functioning both honorifically and repressively. To the extent that bourgeois order depends upon the systematic defense of social relations based on private property, to the extent that the legal basis of the self lies in the model of property rights, in what has been termed "possessive individualism," every proper portrait has its lurking, objectifying inverse in the files of the police. In other words, a covert Hobbesian logic links the terrain of the "National Gallery" with that of the "Police Act."*
—Allan Sekula[5]

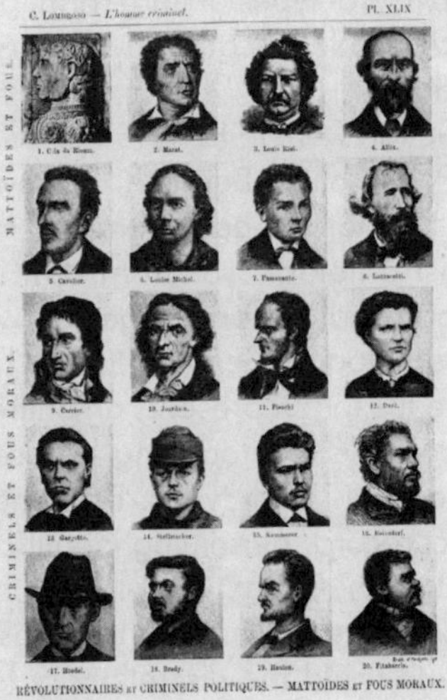


▲

▲ Cesare Lombroso, *L'homme criminal: atlas*, Paris 1895.

5 Allan Sekula, "The Body and the Archive," *October*, 39 (Winter 1986): 3–64, here 6–7.

## BERTILLON/GALTON

Francis Galton was a racial scientist, African explorer and geographer, statistician, eugenicist, inventor, and meteorologist, who transformed social statistics and coined the term eugenics. His studies of innate human differences led to two inventions: composite portraiture and fingerprinting, both of which were of great interest to Alphonse Bertillon. A member of the police force and a biometrics researcher, Bertillon pioneered the anthropometric system of criminal identification, the basis for twentieth-century surveillance, criminal identification, and profiling. Photographic recording of criminals began in the 1840s, but Bertillon's standardization of the procedure in the late 1880s was enabled by Galton's superimposition of multiple photographs to create an ideal type or "natural kind." Galton's discovery of types of fingerprint patterns was crucial to making identification by fingerprinting the norm in policing.

In 1893, Galton went to Paris to visit Bertillon, then chief of the Paris Police. Bertillon, however, was not interested in the natural-born criminal. He replaces the essentialist ontology, so prominent in Lombroso's criminology and Galton's eugenics, with modern forensic epistemologies. Bertillon turned his attention to creating the file that represents an entire identification system capable of producing precise individual markers rather than ideal types. Each individual will have a distinct record, permitting identification in the file room and on the street.

In order for police power to function as a mode of governance—to wield the discretionary force necessary to dispose of present threats to social order and to avert future dangers to it—the police will need to learn to systematize law, knowledge, procedure, and anticipation, and learn how to acquire the indifference necessary for policing on an industrial global scale. Bertillon's system is very important in this process.

> *We can speak then of a generalized, inclusive archive, a shadow archive that.... contains both the traces of the visible bodies of heroes, leaders, moral exemplars, celebrities, and those of the poor, the diseased, the insane, the criminal, the nonwhite, the female, and all other embodiments of the unworthy. The clearest indication of the essential unity of this archive of images of the body lies in the fact that by the mid-nineteenth century a single hermeneutic paradigm had gained widespread prestige. This paradigm had two tightly entwined branches, physiognomy and phrenology. Both shared the belief that the surface of the body, and especially the face and head, bore the outward signs of inner character.... In claiming to provide a means for distinguishing the stigmata of vice from the shining marks of virtue, physiognomy and phrenology offered an essential hermeneutic service to a world of fleeting and often anonymous market transactions. Here was a method for quickly assessing the character of strangers in the dangerous and congested spaces of the nineteenth-century city. Here was a gauge of the intentions and capabilities of the other.*
> —Allan Sekula[6]

6 Allan Sekula, "The Body and the Archive," 10–12.

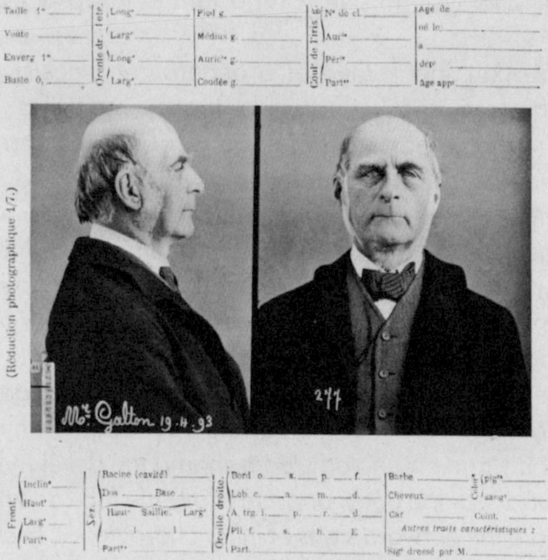


▲

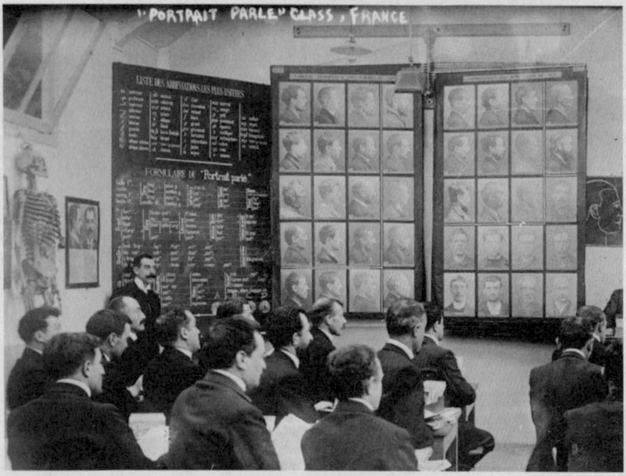


▲▲

▲ Alphonse Bertillon, "Alphonse Bertillon's photograph and record of Francis Galton," in: *Karl Pearson: The Life, Letters, and Labors of Francis Galton, Vol. 2*, Cambridge 1893.
▲▲ Bain News Service, *"Portrait Parle class, France,"* New York 1910–15.

ORIT HALPERN

# *THE "SMART" MANDATE*

*The city is primarily a communications center, serving the same purpose as a nerve center in the body.... All this applies to the nature of cities in times of peace as much as in times of war ... the traffic jams in streets and subways, the jams on the telephone circuits—jams which fray our nerves and squander our time—are evidence that our cities as they now exist are not nearly in their best possible form.*

—Karl Deutsch[1]

## NERVOUS SYSTEM

After World War Two, environments became increasingly understood as networked landscapes facilitating communication and information flow as the keys to security and survival. These spaces were not envisioned as stable utopian forms, but as "nervous" networks undergoing constant change.This transformation in ideas of territory and security then refracted and advanced broader shifts in the concept of reason, rationality, and intelligence, as well as psychology, and consciousness[2] emerging from the cybernetic and communication sciences, which would go on to inform everything from finance and options-trading equations, to environmental psychology, urban planning, and design. The post-war social sciences were repositories for techniques that transformed what had once been questions of political economy, value production, and the organization of human desire and social relations to problems of circulation and communication by way of a new approach to modeling intelligence and agency.[3] This epistemology of the "nervous" network created an ongoing opportunity

1 Accessed from the MIT Archives, Wiener Papers, box 29A, folder 638.

2 Paul Erickson et al., *How Reason Almost Lost Its Mind: The Strange Career of Cold War Rationality*, Chicago, IL 2013.

to entangle calculation and life by literally correlating the nervous system with financial, territorial, and political systems. Cyberneticians and architects imagined a world of neural processing, what we might label now a "smart" or "cognating" planet where our very nerves could be directly linked to networks.

Today, the "smart mandate" has become perhaps one of the governing notions of global polity, creating novel infrastructures, and methods, in fact instruments, which now underpin our design practices across many fields and have come to organize environment, economy, energy-supply chains, food and medicine distribution, and of course, security. What is most remarkable about the emerging discourse of "smart" networked environments is the argument that corporations claim to "infuse intelligence into decision-making"[4] in order to facilitate a new level of complexity and global integration. One must ask about what forms of instrumentation will produce this "decision-making"; what methods, techniques, and processes are those global corporate entities suggesting?

3 See: Orit Halpern, *Beautiful Data: A History of Vision and Reason*, Durham, NC 2014, Chapter 3. See also: Herbert Simon, "A Behavioral Model of Rational Choice," *The Quarterly Journal of Economics*, 69, 1 (1955): 99–118, here 101; Hunter Crowther-Heyck, *Herbert A. Simon: The Bounds of Reason in Modern America*, Baltimore, MD 2005, and *Economics, Bounded Rationality and the Cognitive Revolution*, Northhampton, MA 1992.

4 See: Council on Foreign relations, a discussion on "A Smarter Planet: The Next Leadership Agenda," online http://www.cfr.org/technology-and-foreign-policy/smarter-planet-next-leadership-agenda/p17696 (accessed 01/31/2016).

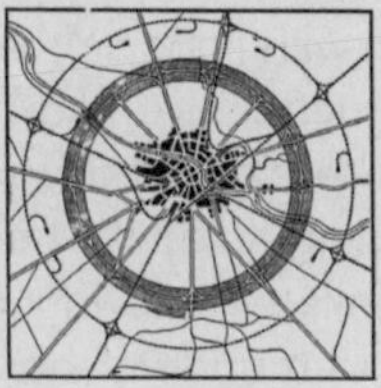

▲

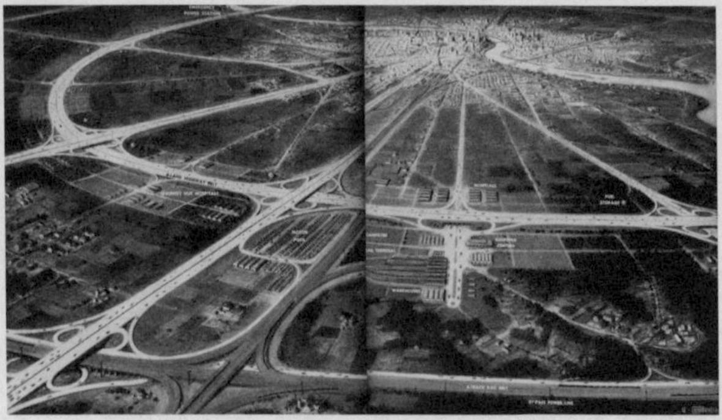

▲

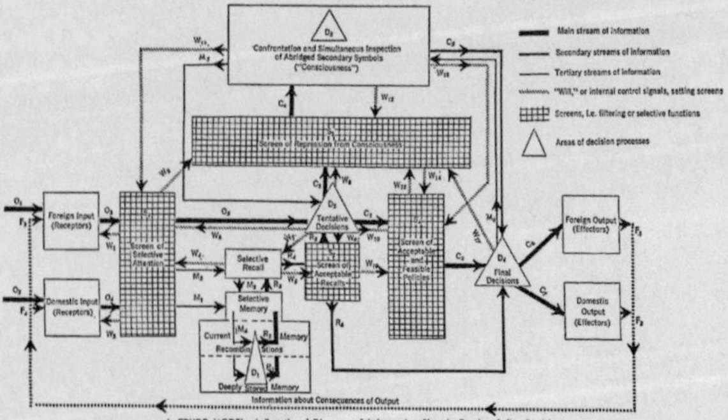


A CRUDE MODEL: A Functional Diagram of Information Flow in Foreign Policy Decisions.

▲▲

▲ Karl Deutsch, Georgio de Santillana, Norbert Wiener, "How US Cities can Prepare for Atomic War–Cities vs. A-Bombs," *Life*, December 18, 1950.

▲▲ Karl Deutsch, "Crude model: Functional Diagram of Information Flow in Foreign Policy Decisions," in: *The Nerves of Government. Models of Political Communication and Control*, New York 1963.

## NETWORKS

*What we thought we were doing (and I think we succeeded fairly well) was treating the brain as a Turing machine; that is, as a device which could perform the kind of functions which a brain must perform if it is only to go wrong and* ***have a psychosis****.*
—Warren S. McCulloch[5]

In 1943, inspired by cybernetician Norbert Wiener's work on anti-aircraft defense and the idea that machines and minds might be thought together through the language of logic and mathematics, the psychiatrist Warren McCulloch and the logician Walter Pitts at the University of Illinois at Urbana-Champaign, decided to take quite literally the machine-like nature of human beings. Their article "A Logical Calculus of Ideas Immanent in Nervous Activity," appearing in the *Bulletin of Mathematical Biophysics*, has now come to be one of the most commonly referenced pieces in cognitive science, philosophy, and computer science. There are a series of moves by which neurons could be made equivalent to logic gates, and therefore "thought" made materially realizable from the physiological actions of the brain.

The model of the neural net put forward in "A Logical Calculus" has two characteristics of note that are critical in producing our contemporary ideas of rationality, and transforming ideas of methodology.[6]

5 Quoted in: John von Neumann, "The General and Logical Theory of Automata," in: William Aspray and Arthur Burks (eds), *Papers of John von Neumann on Computing and Computer Theory*, Pasadena, CA 1948/1986, 422 (my emphasis). For more on automata theory, see also: William Aspray, *John von Neumann and the Origins of Modern Computing*, Cambridge, MA 1990.

6 The model has been reviewed elsewhere; here, I briefly outline the work focusing on epistemology. See: Lily E. Kay, "From Logical Neurons to Poetic Embodiments of Mind: Warren S. McCulloch's Project in Neuroscience," *Science in Context*, 14, 4 (2001): 591–614; Tara Abraham, "(Physio)Logical Circuits: The Intellectual Origins of the McCulloch–Pitts Neural Networks," *Journal of the History of the Behavioral Sciences*, 38 (Winter 2002): 3–25.

130 LOGICAL CALCULUS FOR NERVOUS ACTIVITY

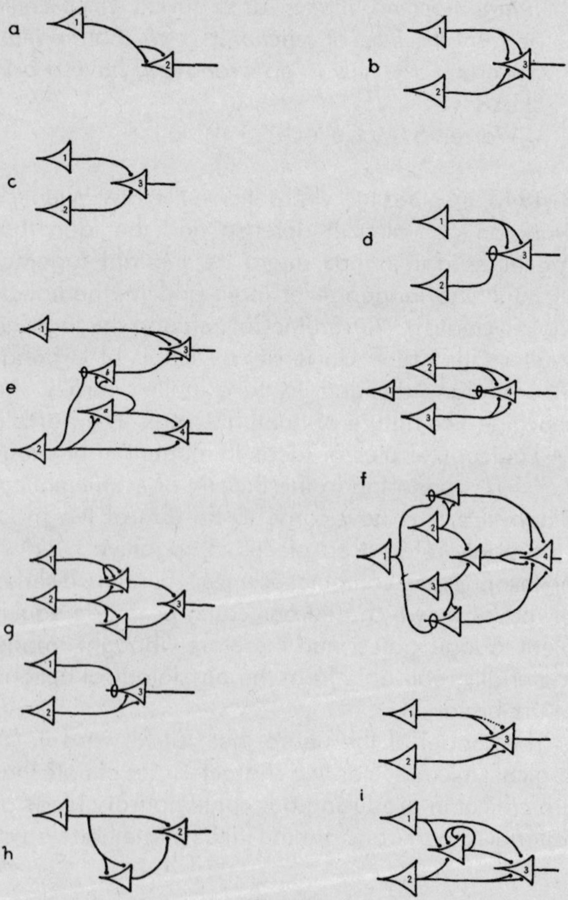


FIGURE 1

▲ Warren S. McCulloch and Walter Pitts, "A Logical Calculus of the Ideas Immanent in Nervous Activity," in: *Bulletin of Mathematical Biophysics, Vol. 9*, s.l. 1943, 115–33.

The first claim is that every firing of a neuron has a "semiotic character"; that is, it may be rendered mathematically as a proposition.[7] To support this claim, Pitts and McCulloch imagined each neuron as operating on an "all-or-nothing" principle when firing electrical impulses over synaptic separations; that is, the pair interpreted the fact that neurons possess action potentials and delays, as equivalent to the ability to effect a discrete decision. This effect affirms or denies a fact (or activation). From this follows the claim that neurons can be thought of as signs (true/false), and nets as semiotic situations, or communication structures (just like the structured scenarios of communication theory).[8] This discrete decision (true or false, activate or not) also made neurons equivalent to logical propositions and Turing machines.

## PANDEMONIUM

In 1958, inspired by neural-net models of machine learning, Oliver Selfridge an engineer at MIT and later consultant for the United States National Security Agency (NSA) on pattern recognition, envisioned an architecture for pattern recognition labeled "Pandemonium."[9]

The Pandemonium architecture is a "bottom-up," instead of "top-down" approach to software architecture. The system is comprised of "demons" programs running quasi-autonomously in a decentralized manner as background processes. Each demon has a tightly constrained task on which to work, and there are parallel demons at different layers, all working simultaneously.

7 The logic used in the article was taken from Rudolf Carnap, with whom Pitts had worked.
8 Warren S. McCulloch and Walter Pitts, "The Logical Calculus of Ideas Immanent in Nervous Activity" (1943), in: Warren S. McCulloch, *Embodiments of Mind*, Cambridge, MA 1965, 21–4.
9 Branden Hookway, *Pandemonium: The Rise of Predatory Locales in the Post-War World*, Cambridge, MA 1999.

For instance, one demon deals with horizontal strokes. Such a demon comprised of a neural-net cluster, or a series of logic gates, emits a "shriek" (which is equivalent to a neural "fire" or "do not fire" in a "yes"/"no" or "true"/"false" statement) whose intensity is proportionate to how closely the data fits its search and decision-making criteria (i.e. louder for letters A or T that contain straight lines, less loud for 0 or S). At the next hierarchical level, a cognitive demon would be attentive to the shrieks of the demon population below it, and would assign a value based on the relative "weights" or intensities of the shrieks (how many nets had fired). Other demons would be simultaneously performing disparate tasks at this level, subjecting the letter to grids of various kinds, and the data they gathered would be continually funneled up the demon hierarchy, until finally, a judgment is rendered by the decision-making demon according to which part of the network "yelled" loudest. Cumulatively more signals coming from a certain region of the network linked to particular shapes indicate closer similarity to the letter in question.[10]

The Pandemonium model for character recognition marks a historical shift in the forms of reason and logic being applied to constructing intelligence. The principal is to facilitate machine learning without having to fully represent a problem; allowing machines to deal with what today we might label "fuzzy" or "wicked" problems. This is both a pragmatic engineering approach, and a new epistemology for defining intelligence and learning in machines and other organisms. Selfridge, in writing the paper, argued without apology or question that this decentralized model is clearly closer to the "natural" way that human cognition works, because it works! This double displacement of both nature and

10 Oliver G. Selfridge, "Pandemonium: A Paradigm for Learning" (paper presented at the Mechanisation of Thought Processes: Proceedings of a Symposium held at the National Physical Laboratory, London, November 24–27, 1958.)

ontology renders digital computers and animals into information-processing machines. As Branden Hookway has noted, this idea of machine learning is also "predatory"; the world becomes a standing reserve of data, continuously assimilated into the networked architecture of pattern-recognizing agents.[11]

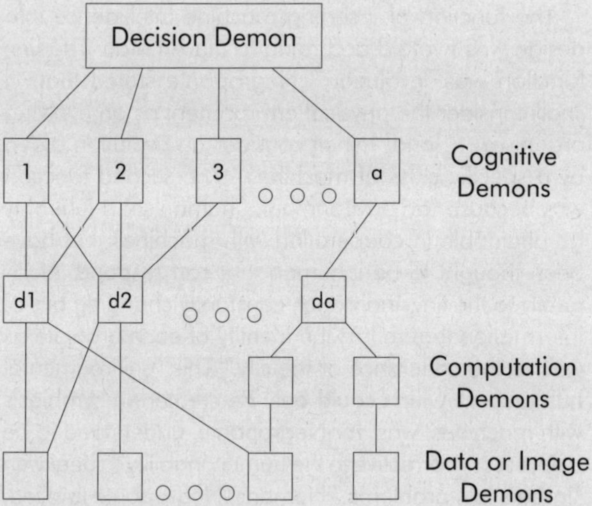


▲ Adapted from: Oliver Selfridge, "Pandemonium model," in: *Pandemonium: a Paradigm for Learning*, London 1959.

11 Hookway, *Pandemonium*.

## RESPONSIVE ENVIRONMENTS

In the 1970s, architecture-digital media became a central idea in design. Nicholas Negroponte, leader of the Architecture Machine Group (ArcMac), the predecessor of what is now the Media Lab at MIT, introduced his vision of computer-aided design in a famous book titled *The Architecture Machine*. Negroponte had the idea of unifying television, film, print publishing, and architecture. With this imaginary of integrating all media into unified platforms, came a new conception of machine learning and intelligence.

The function of inserting machine intelligence into design was twofold according to the ArcMac. The first function was "evolution." Negroponte stated that, "I shall consider the physical environment as an evolving organism … [and] I shall consider an evolution aided by a specific class of machines." The second function was because "an environmental humanism might only be attainable in cooperation with machines that have been thought to be inhuman that can respond intelligently to the tiny, individual, constantly changing bits of information that reflect the identity of each urbanite as well as the coherence of the city." This "environmental humanism," which could only be created in symbiosis with machines, was, for Negroponte, understood to be a necessary corrective to the human inability to deal with "large-scale problems." Humans, Negroponte implied, simply were not good pattern seekers, they could not see systemic problems resulting from changes over time or changing contexts. Human beings were either specific or abstract, but they could not negotiate the space between the highly local and the global. Machines arguably could assist in this function.[12] Computing can thus be understood to serve two related functions for the ArcMac—the

12 Nicholas Negroponte, *The Architecture Machine*, Cambridge, MA 1970, 3.

automation of change and the production of new practices that could scale between the individual and the urban environment or, even, the planet.

These concepts of computer-aided design demanded a redefinition of intelligence, one no longer beholden to the human. "Computer-aided design cannot occur without machine intelligence, in fact it would be dangerous without it … [and that intelligence] must have a sophisticated set of sensors, effectors, and processors to view the real world directly and indirectly. Intelligence is a behavior."[13] The form of intelligence being put forward is behavioral, sensory, and decentralized, literally adopted from neural nets and the "pandemonium" architecture; an intelligence, perhaps "smartness," now out in the world. In computer-aided design, as in machine learning, the necessity of predicting or representing future states was replaced by an incremental demand-to version in order to, in the words of the laboratory, "demo or die."

## COMPUTERIZED ENVIRONMENTS

"Computing isn't about computing anymore. It's about living," Negroponte was once cited as saying.[14] This life world, he argued in a later interview was to be a "machine … [conceived as both] a 'cybernetic world model' and a 'behaviourist laboratory for observation and experimentation.'"[15] Now envisioned as "omnipresent," "behaviorist," and "cybernetic," computing was imagined as consuming abstract life itself. Increasingly, this "life" would occur in a new architecture full of sensors and include the extension of computerized intelligence into the environment.

13 Ibid., 1.

14 See online http://www.brainyquote.com/quotes/authors/n/nicholas_negroponte.html#iP4yl7eJt0kBQzrS.99 (accessed 01/31/2016).

15 Theodora Varduli, "Nicholas Negroponte: An Interview," *openArchitecture(s)*, October 27, 2011, online https://openarchitectures.wordpress.com/2011/10/27/an-interview-with-nicholas-negroponte/ (accessed 01/31/2016).

In an installation made for the path-breaking and infamous *Software* exhibition of 1970 held in the Jewish Museum in New York, the group demoed a microworld, titled *SEEK*. This demo world was one where its inhabitants (albeit not human) were surrounded by an environment entirely managed by machines. The exhibit consisted of a small group of Mongolian desert gerbils, chosen, according to Negroponte, for their "curiosity" and "inquisitive" nature. Placed into an environment of Plexiglass-mirrored blocks that was constantly rearranged by a robotic arm, the basic concept was that the mechanism would observe the interaction of the gerbils within their habitat (the blocks), and would gradually "learn" their "living preferences" by observing their behavior, and how they moved the blocks. The gerbils were there to introduce chance, and non-mechanical behavior into the environment, an unpredictable element. The theory was that the machine would homeostatically try to maintain the "city," and the gerbils would mess up this model; subsequently, the machine would have to learn about how the gerbils changed the environment and attempt to return the system to equilibrium.

This experiment in rethinking the nature of intelligence, or perhaps even life, unfortunately went quite badly, or perhaps creatively, depending on your point of view. Over the duration of the exhibition the computers constantly ceased working (the problem ended up being both the software and the hardware), the museum almost went bankrupt, and the gerbils, in their computer environment, confused the computer, wrought havoc on the blocks, and ended up aggressively attacking each other and became unwell. When Negroponte's computerized environment broke down at the Jewish Museum, the art critic Thomas Hess wittily stated his position in an *Art News* editorial. He described the gerbils as covered in excrement and shadowed by the broken arms of the robot, "Artists who become seriously engaged in technological processes might remember," he concluded, "what happened to four charming gerbils."[16] No one thought to ask, or could ask, whether gerbils wished to live in a block-built micro-world. No one could ask, because conversations in this case were now interactions and behaviors, without translation. This demo, which was now a world, was subtly mutating from a "conversation" between machines and animals, to a network between agents that found its first perhaps comprehensive actualization in the installation at the Jewish Museum. The world rendered as a demonstration or a prototype, one where death is not a failure but the very rationale for increasing the penetration of computing into life.

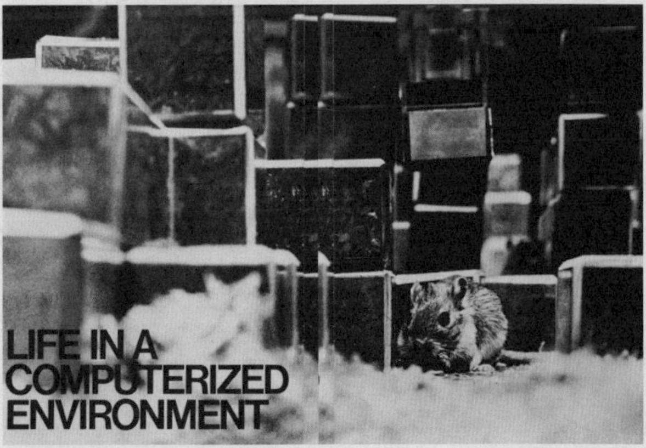


▲ Harry Shunk and John Kender, *Software—Information Technology: Its New Meaning For Art*, New York 1970.

16 Thomas Hess, "Gerbils Ex Machina," *Art News*, December 1970, 23.

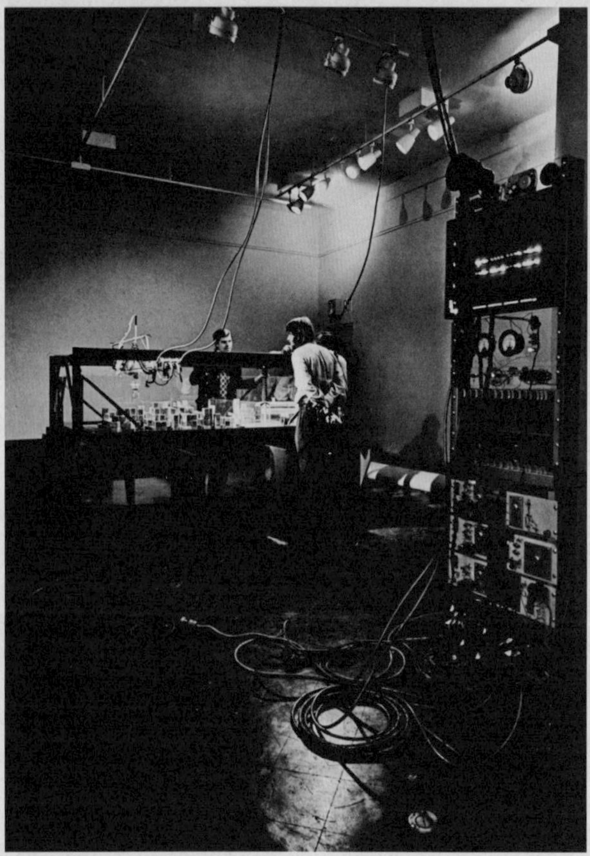

▲ Harry Shunk and John Kender, *Software—Information Technology: Its New Meaning For Art*, New York 1970.

## IMMERSION

Having failed with "conversations" between machines and animals, the ArcMac turned to immersion. One of the culminating demos for the ArcMac, the first three-dimensional digitally mediated responsive environments ever built, was the 1978 Aspen moviemap,[17] commissioned by the US Military Defense Advanced Research Projects Agency (DARPA), inspired by use of simulated environments by the Israelis in Operation Entebbe in Uganda in 1976. There are no computers to be seen, this was not envisioned as a model. It is Aspen. As Michael Naimark, an artist who worked on the project has written, "Aspen [is a] verb … Aspen is known for two processes, or 'verbs' relating to heritage and virtuality. One is to 'moviemap' … the other is to 'Aspenize,' the process by which a fragile cultural system is disrupted by tourism and growth."[18] One can extrapolate from this quote that the moviemap is not a representation, but an operation, a way to live, a way to be in the world. One can also summate that whether disruptive or emergent, the architects, designers, and engineers of this project imagined it not as a room, or simply an interface, but as a "cultural system" and an entire ecology.

Aspen was the first fully, in Negroponte's words, "responsive" environment, an individualized but networked way to negotiate space, a new form of life, to answer, perhaps to the seeming ruins of modern urbanity. This model now is considered the predecessor of many first-shooter games, military simulation in both battlefield and post-traumatic stress disorder (PTSD) treatment, and Google Earth.

17 https://www.youtube.com/watch?v=Hf6LkqgXPMU.

18 Michael Naimark, "Aspen the Verb: Musings on Heritage and Virtuality," *Presence Journal*, 15, 3 (2006), online http://www.naimark.net/writing/aspen.html (accessed 08/01/2014). Personal Interview with Michael Naimark on August 12, 2013.

In the original film demo, the questions of race, urbanization, war, and society fade into the calm embrace of interaction. We are forced to confront what it means to live in this eternally extendable computer-enhanced world. What had started therefore as game theories around military concerns, and then the simulations of artificial intelligence, had now become about total life.

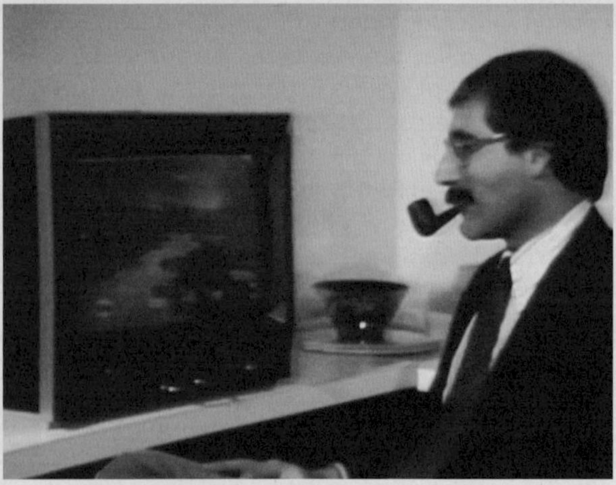

▲ MIT Architecture Machine Group, *Interactive Movie Map—A Surrogate Travel System*, Aspen, 1981.

BEN HAYES

# *ANATOMICAL PARANOIA*

In physiology, the nervous system comprises the network of nerve cells and fibers that transmit impulses between parts of the body. The hyperconnectivity engendered by globalization and information technology can be viewed in much the same way, with events in one place producing impulses that reverberate across the globe. This reverberation has become synonymous with emerging markets, capital flight, and economic shock. International responses to crime and terrorism mean that fear and its consequences now manifest in other globalized systems.

In a process that took shape in the 1990s, and expanded rapidly under the "war on terror," governments across the world have placed statutory obligations on both public and private bodies to police users of their services and networks. In practice, this means that organizations must identify threats and take action to mitigate the risks they pose. The outsourcing of risk management and aversion—which is underpinned by strict sanctions for non-compliance, or failures in "due diligence"—has come to affect everything from telecommunications to air travel, banking to charities, education to public health. How do these new arteries of suspicion function, and what impact do they have?

Edward Snowden has laid bare the degree of control governments exert over our communications infrastructure, but less thought has gone into the parallel processes in other key areas of social and material life. It is not simply a case of the few watching over the masses; surveillance and risk management, which have been dispersed throughout the body politic, are imposed upon entities ill-equipped to perform such functions. Their fear of being held culpable for inaction has produced chronic overreaction both at the collective and individual level—an anatomical paranoia that manifests itself in local alarm and arbitrariness.

Bank tellers, schoolteachers, as well as others, transformed into the arbiters of risk, show how the occasion of risk is also the opportunity for profit making,[1] with private interests among the primary beneficiaries of society's newest fears and convulsions. The items featured also demonstrate the personal impact upon those deemed risky or suspicious through the impulses of those whose duty now is to act as modern-day informants. This suggests that for all the promises of efficiency and security, these extraordinary measures may be incapable of delivering. Unable to satisfy the system's ever-diminishing appetite for risk, the only certainty is the constant tightening and revision of the rules.

By juxtaposing the complexity of the system with the simplicity of its outcomes, the overall intention is to demonstrate the actual consequences of the bureaucratic management of risk upon both the watcher and the watched. Who are the innocent and guilty parties? Why?

1 Michael Dillon, "Global Security in the 21st Century: Circulation, Complexity and Contingency," ISP/NSC Briefing Paper 05/02, London 2005.

## FINANCIAL RISKS

In 1990, a little-noticed Financial Action Task Force (FATF) comprising organized crime specialists from the Group of Seven (G7) countries, produced forty detailed recommendations to combat money laundering. The rationale was that drug cartels and other criminal organizations were moving money around the world with ease, and that checks were required within the global financial system to prevent complicity and corruption.

The FATF's recommendations—subsequently adopted and implemented by the European Union, United Nations, the World Bank, and International Monetary Fund—have been regularly updated since inception of the regulations. These require banks and other financial service providers to undertake extensive surveillance of customers; including "due diligence" to ensure that account-holders and financial transactions have no links to organized crime, terrorism, corruption, or any other criminal activity. In addition, institutions are obliged to keep all account and transaction records for a minimum period of ten years and report "suspicious financial transactions" to national Financial Intelligence Units (FIU). Failure to perform these duties has significant consequences: fines of billions of dollars for lapses in "due diligence" by banks, and bank staff under threat of prosecution and jail for failure to file suspicious transaction reports where there are grounds to do so. Globally, tens of thousands of so-called "sustrans" are filed every day.

However, as vetting customers for involvement in criminal activities is not something that banks are particularly well equipped to do, they have (re-)outsourced some of their "due diligence" obligations to specialist companies. This, in turn, has created a vast global compliance industry whose primary purpose is not simply to stop the flow of "bad money" to "bad

2014

IMPORTANT NOTICE: CLOSURE OF ACCOUNTS

Further to our meeting today, I am writing to conform that has recently conducted a general review of its portfolio of customers and has concluded that provision of banking services to now falls outside of our risk appetite. In accordance with clause 7 of our Buisness Banking Terms and Conditions, we are therefore giving you two months' notice of our decision to close your accounts. Unless you tell us in writing that you want us to close your accounts earlier, we will close them on 22 September 2014. If there are funds in your accounts when they are closed, we will send a cheque for the cleared funds (provided no payments are outstanding). Of any of your accounts are overdrawn when they are closed, you will need to repay the outstanding balance immediately. Please see below for the list of accounts which this letter refers to:

**What you should do now**

You will need to make alternative banking arrangements as we are not prepared to open another account for you. When you accounts are closed, please destroy all unused cheques and cards we have issued to you. (As a security measure, you should out these into at least six pieces)

I appreciate that this may cause you some inconvenience and we will do our best to assist you with this change. I am sorry we are unable to continue to provide you wish banking services, but do thank you for your custom to date.

Yours sincerely,

Area Commerical Director

**HIGHLY RESTRICTED**

people," but also to deliver profits to their shareholders by devising ever-more ingenious and profitable means to distinguish the risky and suspicious from the *bona fide* and the normal.

One such company is World-Check, a compliance service acquired by Thompson-Reuters for 530 million dollars in 2011,[2] which has been accused of aggressively profiling and blacklisting millions of people.[3] Illustrated above is a typical "de-risking" letter where a bank notifies customers of the closure of their account without any explanation as to why. According to *The Economist*, "in most cases banks are not ending relationships because they have evidence of malfeasance. They are doing so simply because the costs and hassle of checking on their correspondents outweigh the measly profits they generate."[4]

## RADICAL INTERVENTIONS

Since July 1, 2015, the United Kingdom Counter-Terrorism and Security Act 2015 has imposed a legal duty upon local UK authorities, prisons, National Health Service trusts, and the education sector, from pre-school to university, to prevent and detect "radicalism" and "extremism." The idea is that potential terrorist sympathizers and recruits are identifiable before they become a threat to national security. The "Prevent" strategy requires staff of designated bodies to report suspicions to the police, who then determine the appropriate course of action. This leaves potentially innocent people vulnerable to a visit from counter-terrorism police, surveillance, or compulsory attendance on a "deradicalization" program.

2 https://risk.thomsonreuters.com/?ref=world-check.com.

3 Namir Shabibi and Ben Bryant, "Vice News Reveals the Terrorism Blacklist Secretly Wielding Power Over the Lives of Millions," *Vice News*, February 4, 2016, online https://news.vice.com/article/vice-news-reveals-the-terrorism-blacklist-secretly-wielding-power-over-the-lives-of-millions (accessed 02/13/2016).

4 "Poor correspondents," *The Economist*, June 14, 2015, 10.

In the short time the Act has been in force, it has had a chilling and at times scarcely believable impact on the UK education sector. For example, a kindergarten teacher reporting children as young as three over concerns about "radicalization," nine- and ten-year-olds invited to fill out a questionnaire to assess whether their religious and political views raise cause for concern. And a teenager visited at home by counter-terrorism police after taking to school a "Boycott, Divestment, and Sanctions" (BDS)-movement leaflet (in support of Palestinian human rights).

Featured are excerpts from the draft Statutory Guidance on "Keeping children safe in education" (2015), issued by the Department for Education. It explains that "extremism" is "vocal or active opposition to fundamental British values, including democracy, the rule of law, individual liberty and mutual respect and tolerance of different faiths and beliefs," and explains the measures that educational establishments must take if they suspect "radicalization," defined as "the process by which a person comes to support terrorism and forms of extremism."

Shown alongside the guidance is a letter of apology from a British university to a student, who was questioned about his attitudes to homosexuality, ISIS, and al-Qaeda after an official at Staffordshire University spotted him reading a textbook entitled *Terrorism Studies*—in fact, the topic of his Masters program.[5] Despite the apology, the student has since quit his studies.

5 Randeep Ramesh and Josh Halliday, "Student accused of being a terrorist for reading book on terrorism," *the Guardian*, September 24, 2015.

DRAFT

**Further information on preventing radicalisation**

51. Protecting children from the risk of radicalisation should be seen as part of schools' wider safeguarding duties, and is similar in nature to protecting children from other forms of harm and abuse. During the process of radicalisation it is possible to intervene to prevent vulnerable people being radicalised.

52. Radicalisation refers to the process by which a person comes to support terrorism and forms of extremism [13]. There is no single way of identifying an individual who is likely to be susceptible to an extremist ideology. It can happen in many different ways and settings. Specific background factors may contribute to vulnerability which are often combined with specific influences such as family, friends or online, and with specific needs for which an extremist or terrorist group may appear to provide an answer. The internet and the use of social media in particular has become a major factor in the radicalisation of young people.

53. As with other safeguarding risks, staff should be alert to changes in children's behaviour which could indicate that they may be in need of help or protection. Staff should use their judgement in identifying children who might be at risk of radicalisation and act proportionately which may include making a referral to the Channel programme.

**Prevent**

54. From 1 July 2015 specified authorities, including all schools (and since 18 September 2015 all colleges) as defined in the summary of this guidance, are subject to a duty under section 26 of the Counter-Terrorism and Security Act 2015 ("the CTSA 2015"), in the exercise of their functions, to have "due regard [14] to the need to prevent people from being drawn into terrorism" [15] This duty is known as the Prevent duty. It applies to a wide range of public-facing bodies. Bodies to which the duty applies must have regard to statutory guidance issued under section 29 of the CTSA 2015 ("the Prevent guidance"). Paragraphs 57-76 of the Prevent guidance are concerned specifically with schools (but also cover childcare).

55. The statutory Prevent guidance summarises the requirements on schools in terms of four general themes:

* Schools and colleges are expected to assess the risk of children being drawn into terrorism, including support for extremist ideas that are part of terrorist ideology. This means being able to demonstrate both a general understanding of the risks affecting children and young people in the area and a specific understanding of how to identify

[13] Extremism is vocal or active opposition to fundamental British values, including democracy, the rule of law, individual liberty and mutual respect and tolerance of different faiths and beliefs. We also include in our definition of extremism calls for the death of members of our armed forces, whether in this country or overseas.
[14] According to the Prevent duty guidance 'having due regard' means that the authorities should place an appropriate amount of weight on the need to prevent people being drawn into terrorism when they consider all the other factors relevant to how they carry out their usual functions.
[15] "Terrorism" for these purposes has the same meaning as for the Terrorism Act 2000 (section 1(1) to (4) of that Act).

16

▲ Excerpt: Department of Education, "Further information on preventing radicalization," in: *DRAFT: Keeping children safe in education. Statutory guidance for schools and colleges*, London.

individual children who may be at risk of radicalisation and what to do to support them. Schools and colleges should have clear procedures in place for protecting children at risk of radicalisation. These procedures may be set out in existing safeguarding policies. It is not necessary for schools and colleges to have distinct policies on implementing the Prevent duty.

* The Prevent duty builds on existing local partnership arrangements. For example, governing bodies and proprietors of all schools should ensure that their safeguarding arrangements take into account the policies and procedures of Local Safeguarding Children Boards. The Prevent guidance refers to the importance of Prevent awareness training to equip staff to identify children at risk of being drawn into terrorism and to challenge extremist ideas. Individual schools are best placed to assess the training needs of staff in the light of their assessment of the risk to pupils at the school of being drawn into terrorism. As a minimum, however, schools should ensure that the designated safeguarding lead undertakes Prevent awareness training and is able to provide advice and support to staff on protecting children from the risk of radicalisation.

* Schools and colleges must ensure that children are safe from terrorist and extremist material when accessing the internet in schools.

56. The Department for Education has also published advice for schools on the Prevent duty. The advice is intended to complement the Prevent guidance and signposts other sources of advice and support.
Channel

57. School and college staff should[16] understand when it is appropriate to make a referral to the Channel programme. The Channel is a programme which focuses on providing support at an early stage to people who are identified as being vulnerable to being drawn into terrorism. It provides a mechanism for schools to make referrals if they are concerned that an individual might be vulnerable to radicalisation. An individual's engagement with the programme is entirely voluntary at all stages.

58. Section 36 of the CTSA 2015 places a duty on local authorities to ensure Channel panels are in place. The panel must be chaired by the local authority and include the police for the relevant local authority area. Following a referral the panel will assess the extent to which identified individuals are vulnerable to being drawn into terrorism, and, where considered appropriate and necessary consent is obtained, arrange for support to be provided to those individuals. Section 38 of the CTSA 2015 requires partners of Channel panels to co-operate with the panel in the carrying out of its functions and with the police in providing information about a referred individual. Schools and[17] colleges which are required to have regard to Keeping Children Safe in Education are listed in the CTSA 2015 as partners required to cooperate with local Channel panels 17.

---

[16] Guidance issued under section 36(7) and section 38(6) of the CTSA 2015 in respect of Channel is available at: https://www.gov.uk/government/publications/channel-guidance

[17] Such partners are required to have regard to guidance issued under section 38(6) of the CTSA 2015 when cooperating with the panel and police under section 38 of the CTSA 2015

University

United Kingdom

2015

Dear Mohammed

I wish to express my sincere apology for the upset that you have suffered as a result of the conversation that took place in the University 2015 and the events that followed it.

I do not possess any particular knowledge or experience of terrorism and radicalisation, and I have only attended a short training session on how to identify students who might be at risk of being radicalised. As a result, I did not know if I should have been concerned about elements of the conversation that took place and I wanted to talk it through with my senior manager. In order to do so, I required your student number in case it was deemed necessary to follow up any concerns with you, hence my request to security.

The combination of the content of our discussion and my lack of experience in this arena, caused me to consider whether this was something that may fall within the 'prevent' agenda. I discussed the conversation with my senior manager and he reassured me that there was nothing to be concerned about.

I would therefore like to reiterate that I genuinely regret the distress that has been caused to you and that I hope you are able to accept my heartfelt apology.

Yours sincerely

▲ Letter to a student, British university, 2015.

Mohammed

University

United Kingdom

2015

Dear Mohammed

Thank you for attending the mediation meeting on 2015, At the end of that meeting we agreed that I would discuss your request that provides you with an apology for the incident in the University 2015. I believe that a letter of apology has now been sent to you

In addition, we also agreed that I would provide a written response to the remedies which you set out in your C1 form, dated I shall deal with each of these in turn below.

First, on behalf of the University, I very much regret the distress that has been caused to you. I recognise that the train of events which commenced on 2015 are deeply troubling to you and, in my comments below, I set these in some context and also describe the work that the University will be putting in place to manage our respective statutory duties to secure freedom of speech and to prevent people being drawn into terrorism.

I also confirm that the University remains committed to proving a space in which students can study and fully exercise freedom of speech within the law.

As you know, the Counter-Terrorism & Security Act 2015 imposes a duty on the University to have due regard to the need to prevent people from being drawn into terrorism. This is a very broad duty, devoid of detail, but is underpinned by statutory guidance which must be taken into account in interpreting how the University should discharge its duty. While the guidance is more extensive than the statutory duty, it contains insufficient detail to provide clear practical direction in an environment such as the University's. In particular, the guidance requires university staff to understand the risk of radicalisation in their area and to build the capabilities to deal with it. It therefore requires understanding of the difference between the intellectual pursuit of radical ideas and radicalisation itself and where the latter or its potential is evident, to take steps to prevent it developing further. In practice, such distinctions can be a significant challenge and can be vulnerable to error particularly in the absence of extensive experience in dealing with such sensitive matters. Though the statutory duty is not yet in force, some University staff have been introduced to this agenda through Prevent training. We recognise that further training for appropriate staff is now required, particularly in the context of the Counter-Terrorism & Security Act 2015, and this will be put in place over the following months. In addition, we will also establish policy and procedures to support staff in terms of their responsibilities to both secure freedom of speech and to prevent people being drawn into terrorism, including protocols for staff to raise concerns within the University.

did complete a Prevent training course in That course did not provide staff with a procedure to raise concerns within the University and, as noted above, actions are now being taken to codify our approach to this issue.

Finally, I am sorry that this incident occurred and for the distress it has caused you. It has exposed weaknesses in our approach to staff training in this area and we will now seek to remedy that both with further training for appropriate staff but also with the creation of written guidance and procedures for staff.

Please let me know if you would wish to meet with me again to discuss this further.

Yours sincerely

## STANDARDIZING SUSPICION

The free movement of ideas, people, and capital—the very attributes for which globalization is celebrated—relies upon the common protocols and international standards used in telecommunications, travel, and finance. Standardization is the process of developing and implementing technical standards. Developed during the Industrial Revolution to regulate the production of components used in manufacturing, the unglamorous process of standards setting has come to play a crucial if overlooked role in globalization.

Over the past two decades, obscure intergovernmental organizations have begun standardizing security protocols to combat terrorism and other organized crime. We have already seen how the FATF has set global standards for financial surveillance, "due diligence," and risk profiling in the financial sector. Similar processes of mandatory social sorting are also at work in the area of border control, travel surveillance, document security, identity management, and counter-radicalization.

Since 9/11, this process has become turbo-charged, with increasing international security obligations imposed by forums that are beyond any meaningful democratic control. The result is a growing body of international regulations that places the demand for security and surveillance ahead of any other societal value.

The Timeline illustrates how current practices in these areas were introduced, computerized, globalized, and "securitized," placing significant obligation on national policy and practice as well as the private sector. Shown after the Timeline is an agreement between the European Union and the United States of America, providing the latter with access to European airline passenger-reservation databases.[6]

6 The identity project, "Another Paris–Mexico flight barred from US airspace," *Papers, Please!* Blog, posted June 7, 2010.

**1858** British administrators in India begin using fingerprints on "native" contracts

**1880** British surgeon in Japan publishes article in *Nature* on fingerprint identification

**1888** Argentinian police officer makes the first fingerprint identification in a criminal case

**1896** International Association of Chiefs of Police (IACP) establishes Bureau of Criminal Identification (BCI)

**1901** Fingerprint classification system piloted by British police in India

**1915** International Association for Identification (IAI) established in the USA

**1920** League of Nations agrees to standardize passports

**1924** FBI establishes ID Division

**1952** American Airlines introduces first electronic reservations system

**1959** First standards for machine-readable banking records agreed

**1964** American Airlines introduces first automated airline reservations system

**1969** International Civil Aviation Organization (ICAO) begins to explore different approaches for machine-readable travel documents

**1973** Society for Worldwide Interbank Financial Telecommunication (SWIFT) founded in Brussels

**1975** Terrorisme, radicalisme, extrémisme et violence internationale (TREVI) framework established by European Council of Ministers

**1980** ICAO issues Document 9303: "A Passport with Machine Readable Capability"

**1980** FBI establishes world's first computerized fingerprint database

**1989** International Financial Action Task Force (FATF) established

**1995** ICAO begins exploring inclusion of fingerprints and other "biometrics" in passports

**2000** EU sets up database containing fingerprints of all asylum seekers and refugees

**2001** 9/11 attacks in New York City, USA

**2003** ICAO agrees use of Radio-frequency Identification (RFID), photographs, fingerprints, and iris scans in passports. Smiling banned

**2004** EU agrees to include fingerprints in all passports (states outside the Schengen area opt out)

**2004** EU agrees to give US Department of Homeland Security (DHS) access to European airline-reservation systems

**2004** USA starts fingerprinting all third-country nationals entering the USA

**2006** UN establishes Working Group on "Radicalization and Extremism that Lead to Terrorism"

**2008** EU agrees mandatory fingerprinting of all visa applicants

**2008** EU adopts Regulation mandating inclusion of fingerprints in all residence permits

**2010** EU and USA agreement on Terrorist Finance Tracking Program (TFTP)

**2010** ICAO issues guidelines on Advance Passenger Information (API) for security purposes

**2013** EC proposes mandatory fingerprinting of all third-country nationals entering EU

**2014** EC pilots "Smart Borders" that will record all entry, exit, and movement across the EU

**2015** EU security and intelligence agencies given access to European airline passenger-reservation systems

▲ International Security Regulation Timeline 1858–2015.

Also shown are documents belonging to Paul-Emile Dupret, an advisor in the European Parliament, who was on an Air France flight from Paris to Mexico City when the aircraft was refused permission to enter US airspace, and diverted mid-flight, because he was on board. He had been detained and interrogated previously while transiting through the USA after visiting Venezuela and Nicaragua, as part of an official European Parliamentary delegation.

EN Official Journal of the European Union

**AGREEMENT**

**between the United States of America and the European Union on the use and transfer of passenger name records to the United States Department of Homeland Security**

THE UNITED STATES OF AMERICA,

hereinafter referred to also as 'the United States', and

THE EUROPEAN UNION,

hereinafter referred to also as 'the EU',

together hereinafter referred to as 'the Parties',

DESIRING to prevent and combat terrorism and serious transnational crime effectively as a means of protecting their respective democratic societies and common values;

SEEKING to enhance and encourage cooperation between the Parties in the spirit of transatlantic partnership;

▲

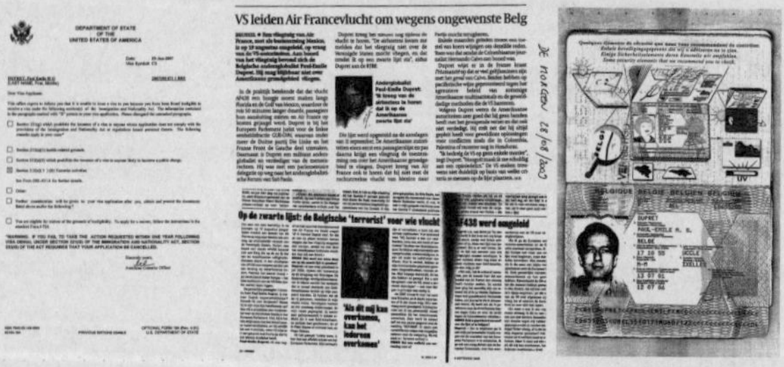

▲▲

▲ Excerpt: "Agreement between the United States of America and the European Union on the use and transfer of passenger name records to the United States Department of Homeland Security," in: *Official Journal of the European Union*, Brussels 2012.

▲▲ Excerpt: Documentation on the case of Member of European Parliament Paul-Emile Dupret.

TUNG-HUI HU

## *SOVEREIGNTY OF DATA*

The internet is typically understood as a borderless, bloodless, and democratizing technology. But it might be that data networks cause a largely unnoticed return to sovereign borders and to a sovereign's antiquated power to prosecute or even kill his or her subjects. This move occurs when user participation comes into uncomfortable contact with today's security regimes.

In recent years, many citizens have embraced a do-it-yourself approach to knowledge that relies on users to gather, sort, and visualize raw data, often to find hidden patterns or correlations. At the same time, these often-pleasurable opportunities for participation "enfold the [user]," in the words of theorists Eugene Thacker and Alexander Galloway, "into codified and routinized models of behavior." More and more, user behaviors are produced by a logic of security that divides a social body into inside and outside. The digital subject's relationship with the collective has been shaped by cultural anxieties and social panics over computer viruses, cyberporn, spam, and surveillance: each user, exhorts the United States Department of Homeland Security, has a "shared responsibility" for the nation's cybersecurity. As a result, users have increasingly taken it upon themselves to enforce the boundaries between an imagined "us" and those excluded from the network.

The sovereignty of data—the fusion of data technologies with sovereign power—is a submerged structure of violence that reverses our expectations about how data algorithms optimize and control life. This structure may become visible through live streaming and live interaction, but it is in fact what the philosopher Achille Mbembe calls a "necropolitics," a politics of death.

## MASS OBSERVATION

The British Mass Observation movement began in 1936, after the abdication of King Edward VIII, and recruited volunteers to report on themselves and their neighbors. The co-founders, anthropologist Tom Harrisson, surrealist poet Charles Madge, and filmmaker Humphrey Jennings, had meant to find out what people thought about Edward's abdication. This intention led to an "anthropology of ourselves," and in an early version of crowdsourcing, participants returned diaries and answered "directives," or questions, that were at once intimate and public. Reports compiled by Mass Observation included data on the subject of hair and personal hygiene, the effects of war on one's sex life, and the number of times the spit of a pub-goer landed in a spittoon. These seemingly unimportant phenomenon were particularly necessary subjects; as the narrator of Jennings' documentary film *Spare Time* (1939) puts it, "Spare time is a time when we have a chance to do what we like: a chance to be most ourselves."

Paramount. AH II 6 /B 31.3.39

Obs tried to work out some system of counts but it is very difficult. One interesting line is to get an idea of the numbers who hold their partners on different manners. Tried counts but they were impossible. But found that there were 9 positions for the man's right hand on his partners back :-

H45

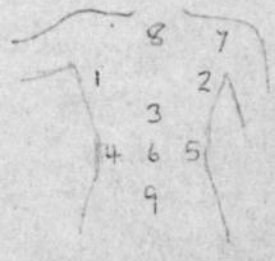


1. Under her left shoulder blade.
2. " " right " "
3. Centre of back (Correct hold)
4. Left side of her waist.
5. Right " " " "
6. Centre " " " "
7. On her right shoulder blade.
8. Just beneath her neck.
9. Below her waist.

Some have the palm of their hand on their partners body, others have the wrist only touching her body. In one or two cases neither hand nor wrist touched her body.

Not so easy to classify the holds women have of men.

There are first the holds of the hands (man's left, woman's right) and also the hold of the women's left hand and arm on the man's right ~~hand~~ arm and shoulder.

▲ Humphrey Jennings and Charles Madge (eds.), "Dancing Report", s.l. 1937.

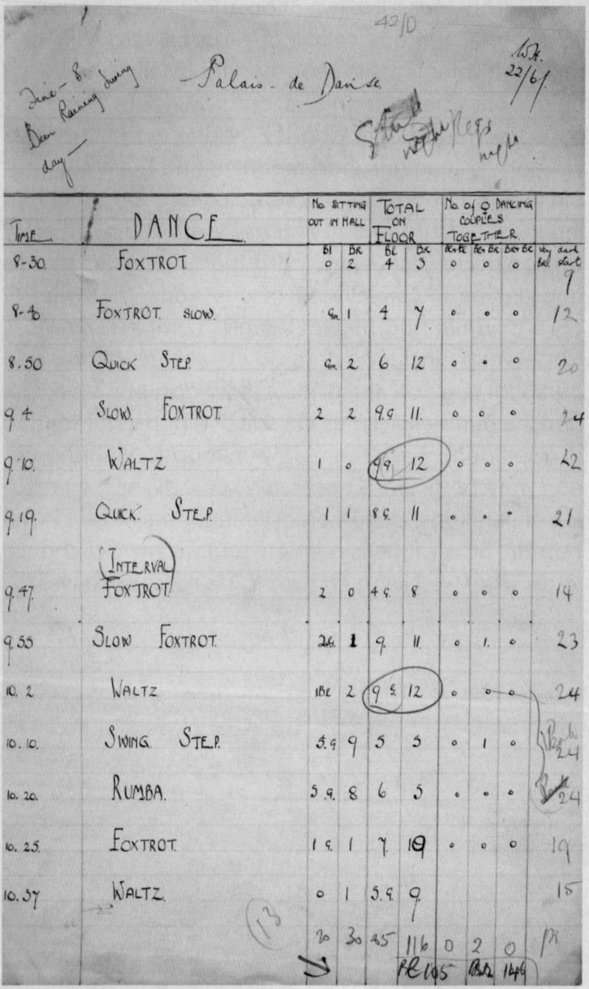

June 8. Been Raining during day — Palais-de-Danse — 22/6/

| Time | Dance | No. sitting out in hall Bl | Br | Total on floor Bl | Br | No. of ♀ dancing couples together Bl+Bl | Bl+Br | Br+Br | Very dark start |
|---|---|---|---|---|---|---|---|---|---|
| 8-30. | Foxtrot | 0 | 2 | 4 | 3 | 0 | 0 | 0 | 9 |
| 8-40 | Foxtrot slow | Gn. | 1 | 4 | 7 | 0 | 0 | 0 | 12 |
| 8.50 | Quick Step | Gn. | 2 | 6 | 12 | 0 | 0 | 0 | 20 |
| 9.4 | Slow Foxtrot | 2 | 2 | 9.9 | 11. | 0 | 0 | 0 | 24 |
| 9.10. | Waltz | 1 | 0 | 9 9 | 12 | 0 | 0 | 0 | 22 |
| 9.19. | Quick Step | 1 | 1 | 8 9. | 11 | 0 | 0 | - | 21 |
| 9.47. | (Interval) Foxtrot | 2 | 0 | 4 9. | 8 | 0 | 0 | 0 | 14 |
| 9.55 | Slow Foxtrot | 2 G. | 1 | 9. | 11. | 0 | 1. | 0 | 23 |
| 10. 2 | Waltz | 1 Bl | 2 | 9 9. | 12 | 0 | 0 | 0 | 24 |
| 10. 10. | Swing Step | 5.9 | 9 | 5 | 5 | 0 | 1 | 0 | Both 24 |
| 10. 20. | Rumba | 5 9. | 8 | 6 | 5 | 0 | 0 | 0 | [illegible] 24 |
| 10. 25. | Foxtrot | 1 9. | 1 | 7. | 19 | 0 | 0 | 0 | 19 |
| 10. 37 | Waltz | 0 | 1 | 5.9 | 9 | | | | 15 |
| | | 20 | 30 | 45 | 116 | 0 | 2 | 0 | [illegible] |
| | | | | Bl 105 | | Br 146 | | | |

▲

▲ Humphrey Jennings and Charles Madge (eds.), "Dancing Report", s.l. 1937.

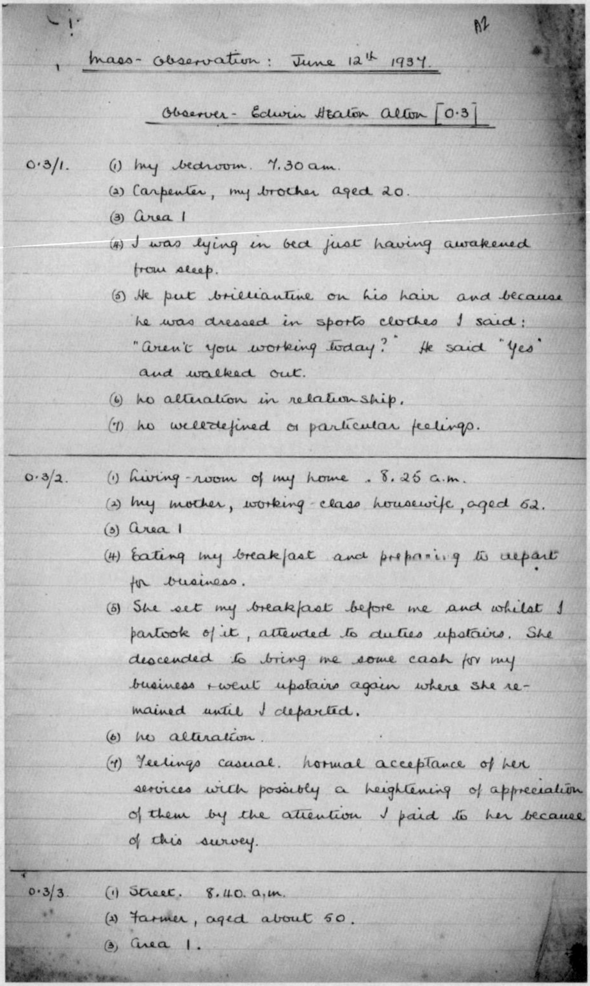

A2

Mass-Observation: June 12th 1937.

Observer- Edwin Heaton Alton [0·3]

0·3/1. (1) My bedroom. 7.30 am.
(2) Carpenter, my brother aged 20.
(3) Area 1
(4) I was lying in bed just having awakened from sleep.
(5) He put brilliantine on his hair and because he was dressed in sports clothes I said: "Aren't you working today?" He said "Yes" and walked out.
(6) No alteration in relationship.
(7) No welldefined or particular feelings.

0·3/2. (1) Living-room of my home. 8.25 a.m.
(2) My mother, working-class housewife, aged 62.
(3) Area 1
(4) Eating my breakfast and preparing to depart for business.
(5) She set my breakfast before me and whilst I partook of it, attended to duties upstairs. She descended to bring me some cash for my business + went upstairs again where she remained until I departed.
(6) No alteration.
(7) Feelings casual. Normal acceptance of her services with possibly a heightening of appreciation of them by the attention I paid to her because of this survey.

0·3/3. (1) Street. 8.40. a.m.
(2) Farmer, aged about 50.
(3) Area 1.

▲▲ Humphrey Jennings and Charles Madge (eds.), "Chemist's Diary," s.l. 1937.

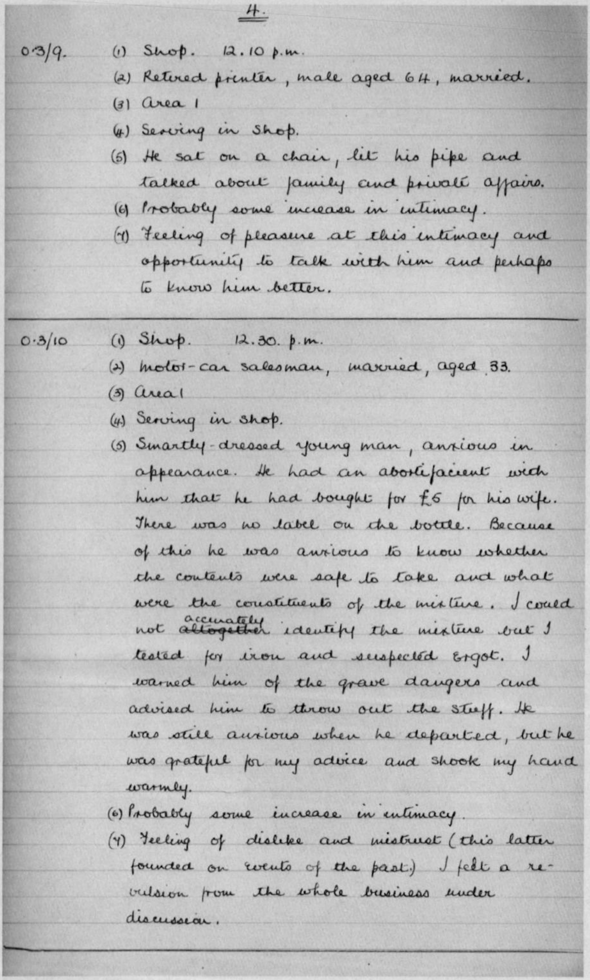

4.

0·3/9. (1) Shop. 12.10 p.m.
(2) Retired printer, male aged 64, married.
(3) Area 1
(4) Serving in shop.
(5) He sat on a chair, lit his pipe and talked about family and private affairs.
(6) Probably some increase in intimacy.
(7) Feeling of pleasure at this intimacy and opportunity to talk with him and perhaps to know him better.

---

0·3/10 (1) Shop. 12.30. p.m.
(2) motor-car salesman, married, aged 33.
(3) Area 1
(4) Serving in shop.
(5) Smartly-dressed young man, anxious in appearance. He had an abortifacient with him that he had bought for £5 for his wife. There was no label on the bottle. Because of this he was anxious to know whether the contents were safe to take and what were the constituents of the mixture. I could not ~~altogether~~ accurately identify the mixture but I tested for iron and suspected Ergot. I warned him of the grave dangers and advised him to throw out the stuff. He was still anxious when he departed, but he was grateful for my advice and shook my hand warmly.
(6) Probably some increase in intimacy.
(7) Feeling of dislike and mistrust (this latter founded on events of the past.) I felt a revulsion from the whole business under discussion.

▲

▲ Humphrey Jennings and Charles Madge (eds.), "Chemist's Diary," s.l. 1937.

## CYBERBUNKER

Despite their borderless appearance, digital net-works are increasingly fractured along territorial lines. To comply with country-specific laws on data sovereignty, Microsoft has started to locate German clients within German data centers; to bypass United States National Security Agency (NSA) surveillance, Brazil has discussed building an alternate, Brazil-only internet. Another sign of this resurgence in territorial thinking is the growth of data havens: data-hosting providers that claim to be physically untouchable by established states, typically by housing servers inside an impregnable bunker and occasionally by claiming to be located outside the boundaries of international law. CyberBunker was both: "located" in a nuclear bunker in Kloetinge, the Netherlands, CyberBunker spun a fanciful story of NATO forgetting to repatriate the structure to the Netherlands. Claiming it was no longer situated on Dutch soil, the bunker's new purchaser, Herman Xennt, a convicted drug trafficker, declared it a constitutional monarchy and himself the ruler. Using Photoshop, his associate, Sven Kamphuis (the so-called "Minister of Telecommunications") concocted pictures of a failed police attempt to storm the bunker as proof of the state's *de facto* recognition of its independence.

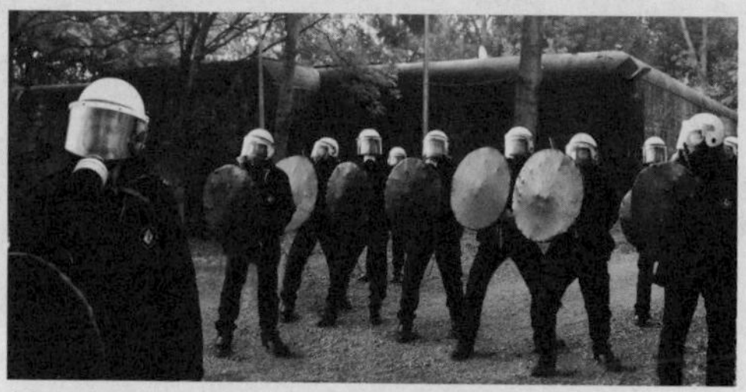

▲▲

▲▲ CyberBunker, *SWAT Team raids bunker*, Kloetinge, 2013.

## TECHNOPATRIOTS.COM

In 2007, Jon Healy, a conservative activist, installed a wireless network and five remote-controlled webcams on light poles and fences in Cochise County, Arizona, on the United States side of the border with Mexico. Healy's mother, who lived two miles from the border, signed on as a board member of Techno-Patriots and became its financial backer, explaining that: "The Mexican man is macho, and they consider beating their wives as part of the daily kind of thing. Impregnating is an important thing for them." With a ten-dollar donation, users on the Techno-Patriots website could sign up to watch the border from the comfort of their own home and help spot undocumented immigrants, which they could then report to Border Patrol officers for arrest.

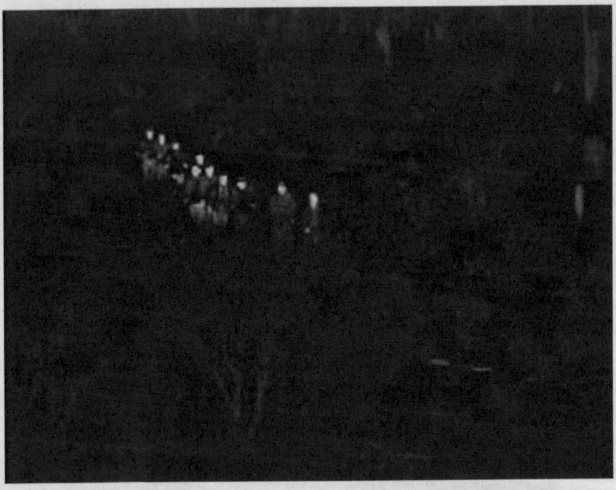

▲ Techno-Patriots, *Thermal Night Operation*, 2007, 00:55 min.

LAWRENCE LIANG

# *DATA TRUTH*

*Posters, placards, signs, symbols must be distributed, so that everyone may learn their significations. The publicity of punishment must not have the physical effect of terror; it must open up a book to be read.*
—Michel Foucault[1]

In the post-9/11 period, we have seen a sudden re-emergence of forensic technologies which had lain dormant for a while. From the polygraph and the truth serum to brain mapping—the latest addition to the forensic arsenal—there is a long history of how science and technology have sought to transform our understanding of the human body, of interiority, and make it machinically accessible. In doing so, the primary move is to transform the body into an archive of information and data that can then be rendered intelligible as "truth." The consequences of such technologies on civil liberties and human rights are immense: for instance, a court judgment from India held that lie-detection technologies do not violate the constitutional right against self-incrimination in which testimony and pure information are distinguishable, and that information obtained from the body is simply information *per se*.

These technologies have their roots in the statistical turn of the nineteenth century, which saw the rise of a new discipline known as criminalistics (combining criminology with statistics) and a belief that the body is both empirically knowable and in need of externally imposed principles of order and control. From the 1930s, there was a shift, where the human mind, emotions, and its links to ideas of the self—for a long time the domain of philosophers—became the subject of an emergent discipline: "new psychology," which attempted to remove subjectivity from psychology.

1 Michel Foucault, *Discipline and Punish: The Birth of the Prison*, tr. Alan Sheridan, New York 1979, Chapter 2, "The Gentle Way to Punishment," 111.

This was part of the larger development, characterized by art critic Jonathan Crary as the "appropriation of subjectivity."[2] By transforming emotional interiority into a visually present, quantifiable, controllable, and rationalized object of knowledge, the science of emotions depended on the mechanization of the body. In defining interiority, the manifestation of the brain, displayed via various verbal and instrumental examinations, revealed that character, personality, guilt, innocence, and accountability were no longer determined by actions, but by reactions, and not by intuition. Most of the technologies were employed to address racial-political anxieties.

In this world, the state as the nervous system literally accesses the data of the nervous system to produce an illusion of euphoric security. As in the past, in the contemporary era, the world of forensic fantasy does not exist merely within the domain of science and technology, but also frequently transposes itself into the world of popular culture, science fiction, and mass media. Forensic investigations of real crimes share space with criminal investigation fantasies, such as the contemporary TV series *CSI: Crime Scene Investigation*, even as forensic tapes are leaked and then broadcast on television, blurring the lines between the studio, the courtroom, and the laboratory, and establishing a new figure of authority—the expert who interprets data.

2 Jonathan Crary, *Techniques of the Observer: On Vision and Modernity in the Nineteenth Century*, London and New York, 1992, 148.

## WONDER WOMAN

Princess Diana of Themyscira is an Amazonian warrior princess who possesses a "Lasso of Truth" that forces people to tell the truth. Diana, known also as Wonder Woman, was the invention of William Moulton Marston, an American psychologist and lawyer. Marston, an eclectic inventor and proto-feminist known to enjoy bondage was also the inventor of the polygraph or lie detector. Eager to have his invention accepted by legal institutions, Marston was disappointed that the courts rejected it on grounds that there was too much opportunity for error. Marston realized that his invention would have to find putative acceptance in both popular culture and science before it gained acceptance in law, and thus devised the perfect device to bring together his interests—the women's liberation movement, bondage, and truth-detection—in the form of a fictional superhero Wonder Woman. Over time, both lie detector and Wonder Woman have become part of the staple lore of truth-detection and emotional measurement; although Marston's less well known invention the "Love Meter"—that sought to measure women's emotional excitement as they watched the romantic climax of Greta Garbo's *Flesh and the Devil*—has faded into oblivion.

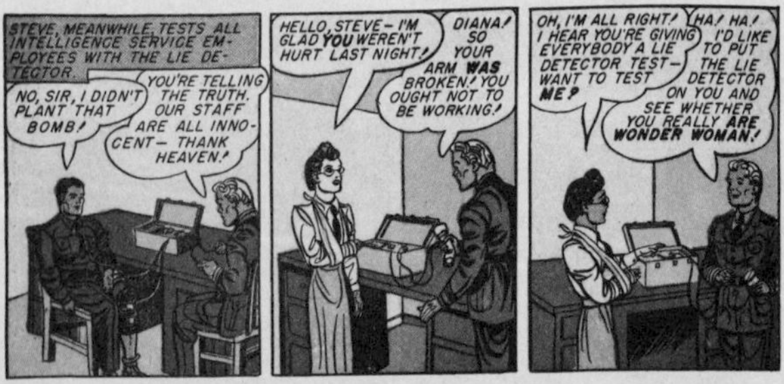


▲

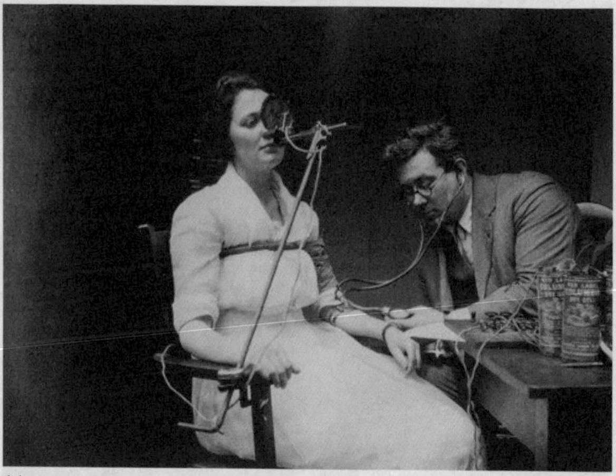

▲▲

## NARCO-ANALYSIS

In December 2003, after Abdul Karim Telgi's arrest for alleged involvement in the "6,000 crore stamp paper scam," he was subject to a narco-analysis test in Bangalore during which he named a few important politicians as part of the fraud. In a first of its kind, a number of news channels telecast the test live: people watched in fascination and horror as doctors grilled the semiconscious Telgi about the role of the various people involved. The broadcast of Telgi's narco-analysis test was the first, but many subsequent trials have seen the accused subjected to the same test. Since Telgi, the three technologies of truth-detection—the polygraph, narco-analysis, and brain mapping—have officially entered popular consciousness and introduced a new kind of "legal event" on television, which supplements the established forms of "live tri-

▲ William Moulton Marston, "Wonder Woman," in: *Sensation Comics, Vol. 2, No. 15,* New York 1943.

▲▲ William Moulton Marston, *Polygraph test,* administered to [Marston's] secretary, s.l. 1921.

als" and "trial by media." What we now see emerging is a form of forensic publicity in which the idea of legal truth emerges as an uncontested and self-apparent thing in itself, even before the commencement of a trial, and in which a regime of information and a regime of truth are indistinguishable.

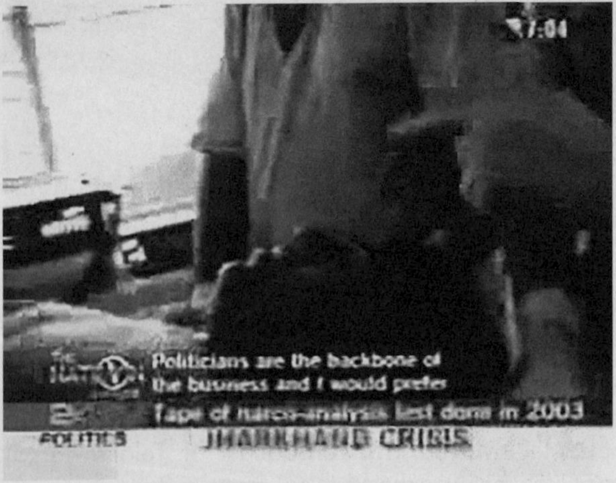


▲

▲ NDTV, *Narco test: Telgi names Pawar on tape*, 2003, 3.17 min.

## BRAIN MAPPING

Brain mapping consists of forensic investigation using the P300 test in which people's responses are measured through 32-channel EEG-ERP Neuroscan cording systems, carried out by placing 32-channel electrodes directly on the scalp. During the test, which is conducted twice and where each word is presented in three parts randomly, the suspect is instructed to relax and listen to the words presented in the auditory mode, but not expected to offer any oral response. After the test has concluded experts then analyze the data for indications as to whether the suspect is in possession of knowledge concerning the subject relevant to the investigation in order to collect evidence. Brain-based lie-detection abandons the body of polygraph and narco-analysis to focus exclusively on the "biological mind," but both depend on a mechanistic understanding of the body and its organs. Thus, while the polygraph saw a direct link between physiology and emotion, brain mapping treats the brain as a computer from which the data is retrievable and analyzable by experts.

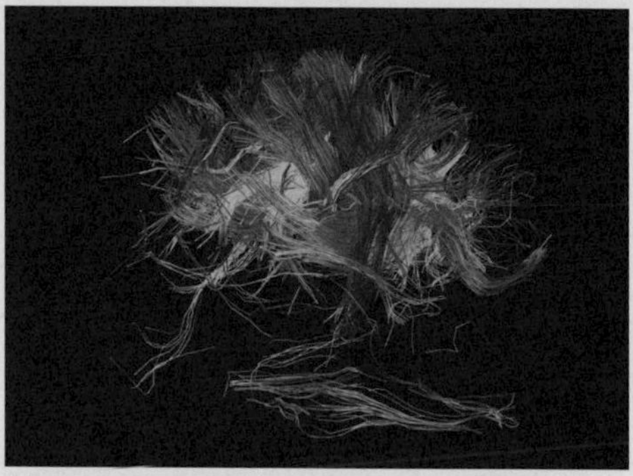

▲▲

▲▲ *White Matter Fibers, Parietal areas*, Los Angeles 2013.

## SHERLOCK HOLMES: THE SIGN OF FOUR

Detective fiction remains the largest archive of the nervous nation-state, containing all the anxieties of moral, political, and cultural decay. Sherlock Holmes is the exemplary figure of the detective novel, which, during the heights of the colonial period, inaugurated a set of anxieties about imperial order. Holmes often solved mysteries that deal with alien incursions and pollution from mysterious illnesses, often brought back by returnees from the colonies. He secures the national space through science and rationality. The continued popularity of Sherlock Holmes and the detective as a fictional figure alerts us to the persistence of moral and political decay in the context of safeguarding territories and borders, and to which the developing technologies of data collection serve as mystical aids. Holmes' enduring legacy lies in Franco Moretti's description of the detective genre as one that "resolves the deep anxiety of an expanding society" even as it reassures readers "that society is still a great organism: a unitary and knowable body."[3]

3 Franco Moretti, *Signs Taken for Wonders: On the Sociology of Literary Forms*, London 1983, 143.

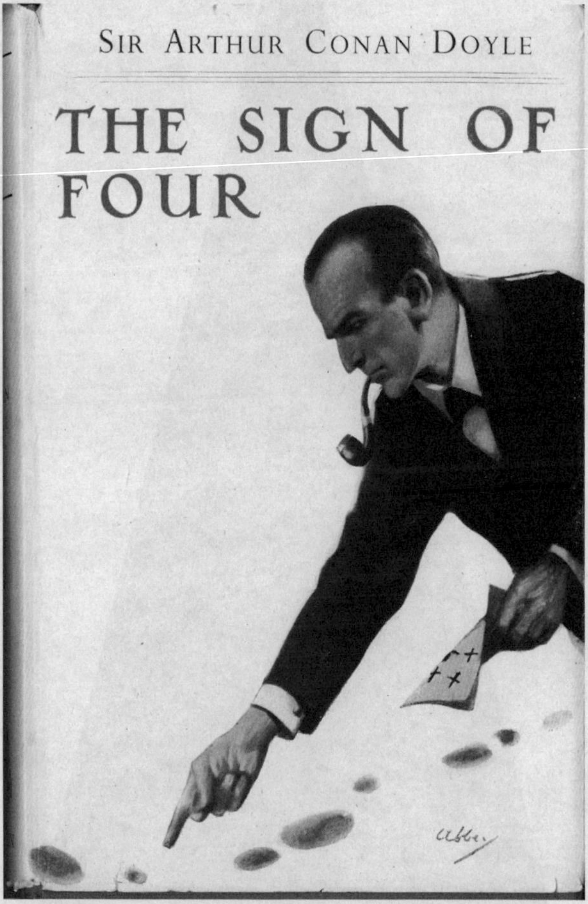


▲ Sir Arthur Conan Doyle, *The Sign of Four*, London 1890/1954.

NOORTJE MARRES

# *THE LABOR OF INTERPRETATION*

This contribution features three seemingly ordinary objects that support the technical, social, material, and personal work of digesting climate change through quantification. Each of the artifacts featured—teapot, seeds, car-engine circuit board, etc.—is in some respect mundane: we live in intimate proximity to them; they are part of the fabric of everyday life. But these objects also share an exceptional capacity: they contain traces of the vast, complex problem that is atmospheric pollution, and as such, they are able to provide insight into the "slow disaster" that is the degradation of the air, the environment, and the soil—and may help to problematize the part we all play in it.

It is often assumed that knowing climate change requires a vast machine, a complex techno-scientific system that includes Earth system simulation models, globally managed weather stations, integrated satellite networks, and large computational laboratories needed to process all the data, run the simulations, and then attempt to integrate the two. Few of us are immune to the fascination with this vast machine, but many recognize that something else is required too, if knowledge of climate change is to take hold—on a personal, institutional, and societal level. To really know climate change, we must become more intimately acquainted with it, we must grasp it as something that touches our lives, as something that is happening *inside* the air we breathe, the appliances and energy we use, and the plants growing everywhere. In other words, to achieve an interpretation of climate change, we must engage in "digestive work": the knowledge of climate change must somehow pass through our bodies. Each of the artifacts assembled here has the special, valuable capacity to support this "digestive" work.

The double quality of the artifacts—teapot, seeds, car part, etc.—the way they are both ordinary thing and archival datum (object), is critical to their ability to facilitate the labor of interpretation of climate change. As archival objects, they contain the traces of vastly distributed, problematic processes stretching across times and spaces, which are millions of times longer and bigger than they are themselves. As mundane objects, they remind us that everyday environments, habits, bodily movements are NOT removed from these processes, but are among the very settings in which they play out.

In this respect, it would be wrong to think that to understand climate change we must somehow "add" warm feeling to cold mathematic reasoning. Rather, as stated above, we must let knowledge pass through our bodies. These objects, then, do not merely support abstract knowledge of the changing atmosphere, soil, and climate; they also raise the social question: How do we live WITH global warming, with carcinogenic $NO_X$ emissions, with digitally enhanced, "semiautonomous" cars and power plants that change their behavior without telling us? Crucially, moreover, they suggest that this social question is not the opposite of a technical question: the technical labor of data interpretation is at the very same time the intimate labor of letting the world—tea, $NO_X$, seeds, etc.—pass through our (collective) bodies.

There is no routing around issues of measurement: we need to pass through technical matters to get to the social question. Equally, there is no routing around the intimate issue of how we digest knowledge as part of social life, that is, if we are to take on the scandal of the ongoing, routine, but life-threatening degradation of our environments.

## THE ENVIRONMENTALLY AWARE TEAPOT

The Tea Light is an experimental prototype that presents a way to realize "intelligent" energy-use both at home and at work. It foregrounds an everyday practice ("making tea"), and shows how it is possible to take into account "the environment" as part of such everyday activity.

The teapot's interface tells its user about the constantly changing composition of the current energy supply: when dirty energy sources—such as coal-fired power plants—are switched on across the grid, the tea light turns red ("now is a bad time to make tea"). When the orb glows green, there is less carbon-intensive energy available.

Known as a technology for "responsive energy demand," this tea light is special insofar as it includes an environmental signal in the user interface. An early prototype of this tea light technology was developed in 2009 in a place called the Hub, a community center in London. Today, virtually all large energy companies in the UK support some form of dynamic demand management, but they have largely rejected the idea of using so-called "smart" electricity meters to communicate emission-related data to users. The only responsive social mechanism their smart grids acknowledge remains that of the price of energy (£), upholding an old, highly un-innovative, consumptive model of society.

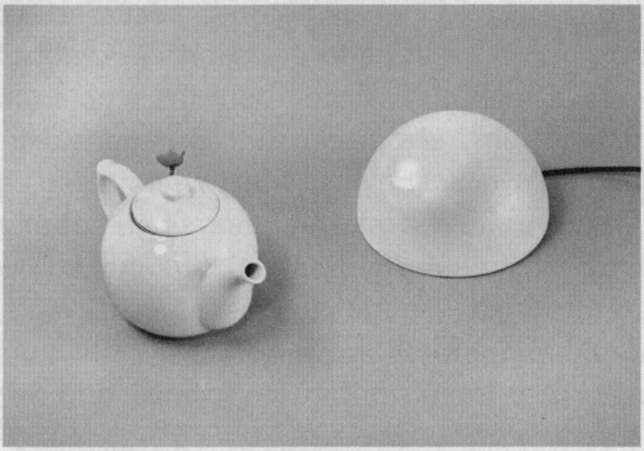

▲ Chris Adams and James Gardner, *The environmentally aware teapot*, London, 2009.

## PALEOBOTANICAL SEEDS AND FOSSIL LEAVES[1]

These seeds are small enough to hold in your hands, and indeed, you could almost step on them, but they are also millions of years old and, what's more, they contain intricate records of the changing climate.

Paleobotanists can deduce past climate states (weather patterns) from these fragments of plant matter. The Mastixia is a tree, the seeds from which were found in brown coal layers in East Germany, which means the region must have been warmer about ten or twenty million years ago as today Mastixia only grow in South East Asia.

And it is not just seeds that lead this double life as plant matter and geological record, so do other parts of plants, like leaves, such as these leaf fossils (*Credneria denticulate*) that were found in central Germany near the Harz Mountains. Large and round, these, too, suggest that the climate was warmer in this region about eighty million years ago than it is today.

Paleobotanists date these plant materials by analyzing the layer of the earth where they were found, looking in particular at the mineral and fossil content.

However, the seeds and leaves are not alone in leading a "second life" as historical records: so does the apparatus for the interpretation of Paleobotany. Drawers of index cards accompany these paleobotanical objects from the Museum für Naturkunde in Berlin, showing us layers of archival writing, reminding us that the apparatus for the interpretation of paleobotanical objects equally changes over time, offering a historical record of our knowledge cultures.

Indeed, plant fossils have not always been appreciated as instruments of climate science, and we may

1 With many thanks to Tahani Nadim for her invaluable suggestions, and to Barbara Mohr for sharing her knowledge.

measure changes in our knowledge cultures—our "epistemic climates"—by following the writing on these index cards from across the decades. They remind us that knowing is something we do with our hands, our bodies, and not just our brains.

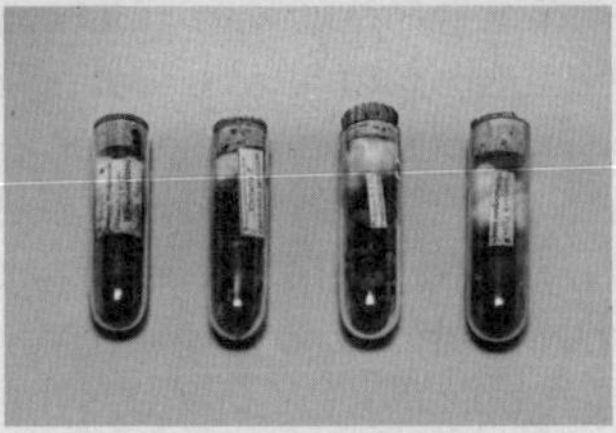

▲

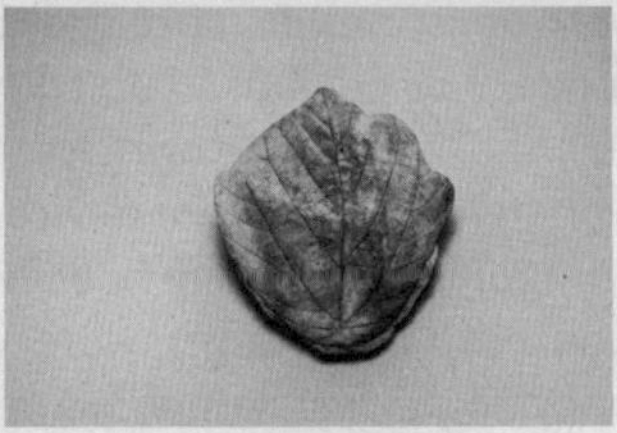

▲▲

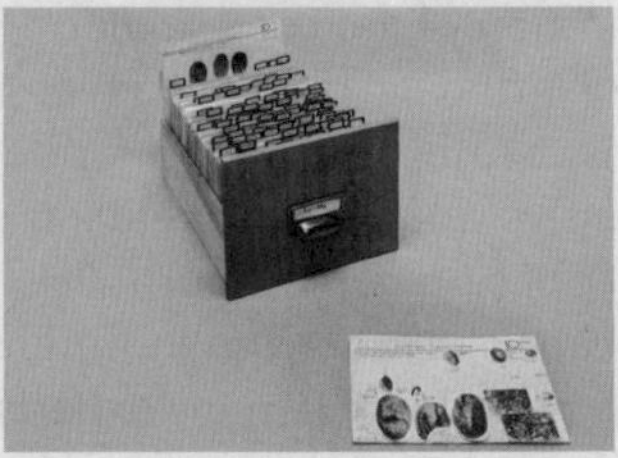

▲▲▲

▲ *Ganitrocera persicoides* – Miocene – Klettwitz, Germany; *Mastixicarpum crassum* – Miocene – Altenburg, Germany; *Mastixicarpum cacaoides* – Eocene/Oligocene – Haselbach, Germany; *Mastixicarpum cacaoides* – Miocene – Regis, Germany; *Credneria denticulate* – late Cretaceous – Quedlinburg, Germany.

▲▲ *Credneria denticulate* – late Cretaceous – Quedlinburg, Germany.

▲▲▲
Card index box A of the paleocarpological collection (Coll. D. Mai), Berlin.

## VOLKSWAGEN ENGINE CONTROL UNIT

An object sits at the heart of Dieselgate, the emissions violation scandal that engulfed car manufacturers in 2015: the Engine Control Unit (ECU). On it runs a piece of software publicly known now as a "defeat device."

Most cars are equipped with ECUs today, but this particular model is capable of cheating on emissions tests, and currently sits in an estimated eleven million cars. It is able to detect when the car in question is being driven under so-called "test conditions"—by monitoring things like speed and the position of the steering wheel—in which case the ECU adjusts the car's performance, dramatically reducing its emissions of $CO_2$ and carcinogenic $NO_X$. When these artificial test conditions no longer apply, emissions increase radically. This particular ECU model was purchased on eBay by two curious individuals, Felix Domke and Daniel Lange. To expose the workings of the defeat device, they used a method called "real-time logging": hooking up the ECU to his own car, Felix ran the firmware while driving around for many hours, first around his neighborhood, then on a so-called "dyno" in a garage.

On a more general level, the ECU offers an impressive demonstration of the complicated "work of interpretation" that is done in our economies and societies. The public exposure of the ECU's dodgy behavior required extensive work of interpretation by engineers, researchers, policy-makers, journalists, and media publics. Their societal labor was indispensable to producing the scandal. In fact, many experts were aware of the existence of defeat devices in diesel cars before the scandal. The "known" fact of emissions rigging could only be proven unacceptable—undigestible—on a societal level. If insights into our individual and collective misbehavior are to really take hold, this knowledge must pass through social channels. It is not just $NO_x$ and other carcinogenic particles that pass through the most intimate parts of life today—through our cars, our world (the air), and our bodies. So must our knowledge.

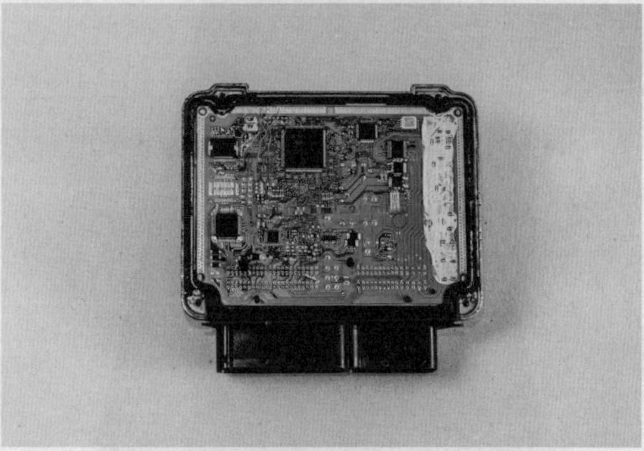

▲ Defeat Device, Lüneburg, 2011.

MATTEO PASQUINELLI

# *THE SPIKE: ON THE GROWTH AND FORM OF PATTERN POLICE*

*For science would go completely mad if left to its own devices. Look at mathematics: it's not a science, it's a monster slang, it's nomadic.*
—Gilles Deleuze and Félix Guattari, 1980[1]

*He spent a fair amount of time tapping on the keys and then studying coded responses on the data screen—a considerably longer time, it seemed to me, than he'd devoted to the people who'd preceded me in line. In fact I began to feel that others were watching me. I stood with my arms folded, trying to create a picture of an impassive man, someone in line at a hardware store waiting for the girl at the register to ring up his heavy-duty rope. It seemed the only way to neutralize events, to counteract the passage of computerized dots that registered my life and death. Look at no one, reveal nothing, remain still. The genius of the primitive mind is that it can render human helplessness in noble and beautiful ways. 'You're generating big numbers,' he said, peering at the screen.*
—Don DeLillo, 1985[2]

*If in these tests someone is still listening for a confession, it is evident that this confession is no longer the story of a crime by its author. This was completed notably by the mapping of heavy crime zones in urban planning systems, and beyond this by the 'criminostat' (computer-aided visualisation of statistical fields) currently being tested by the police. We could imagine that at this level the gaps and hazards inherent in the ordering of materials should disappear, since with computers they could make the accusing discourse perfectly coherent....*

1 Gilles Deleuze and Félix Guattari, *A Thousand Plateaus: Capitalism and Schizophrenia*, tr. Brian Massumi, London and Minneapolis, MN 1987, 24; original French version published 1980.
2 Don DeLillo, *White Noise*, New York 1985, 138.

*At that point, they could do totally without the confession of the accused, who would be less informed about his own crime than the computer, and who, no longer being the one who knows "the truth", would have nothing left to confess.*
—Paul Virilio, 1977[3]

*Even the most striated city gives rise to smooth spaces: to live in the city as a nomad, or as a cave dweller. Movements, speed and slowness, are sometimes enough to reconstruct a smooth space. Of course, smooth spaces are not in themselves liberatory. But the struggle is changed or displaced in them, and life reconstitutes its stakes, confronts new obstacles, invents new paces, switches adversaries. Never believe that a smooth space will suffice to save us.*
—Deleuze and Guattari, 1980[4]

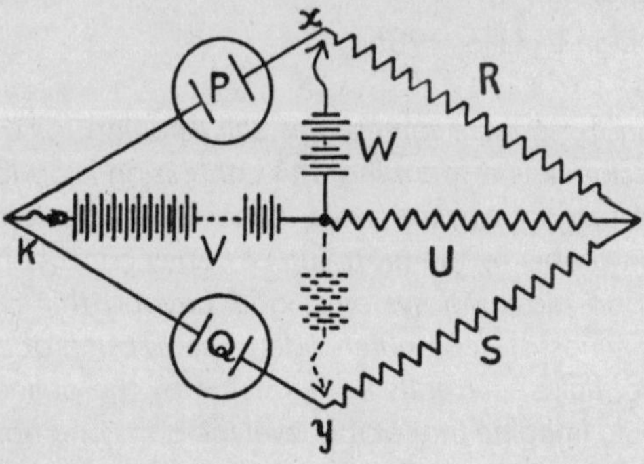


▲

▲ "Electrical Model illustrating a Mind having a Will but capable of only Two Ideas," from Lewis Fry Richardson, "The Analogy Between Mental Images and Sparks," *Psychological Review*, 37, 3 (1930): 222.

3 Paul Virilio, *Speed and Politics*, 2nd ed., New York 1986, 170.
4 Deleuze and Guattari, *A Thousand Plateaus*, 500.

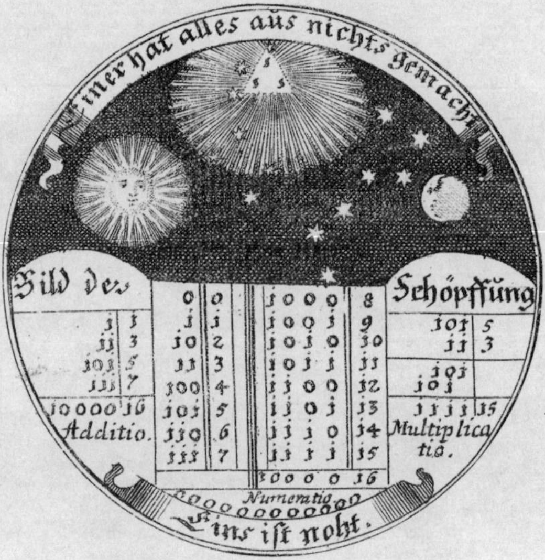


▲▲

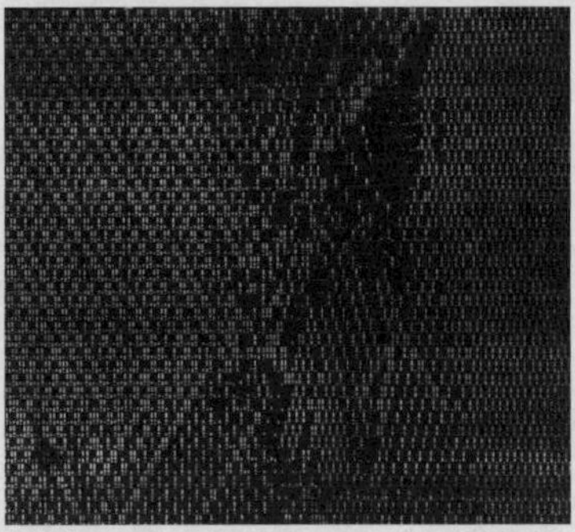

▲▲▲

▲▲ Gottfried Wilhelm Leibniz, "Einer hat alles aus nichts gemacht," in: Johann Christian Schulenburg, *Unvorgreifflicher Vorschlag zur Vereinigung der Festzeit: auf alle Ostern künfftiger Zeiten gerichtet*, Frankfurt am Main 1724.

▲▲▲
Nils Barricelli, "Baricelli's Universe blueprint 1c," New Jersey 1953.

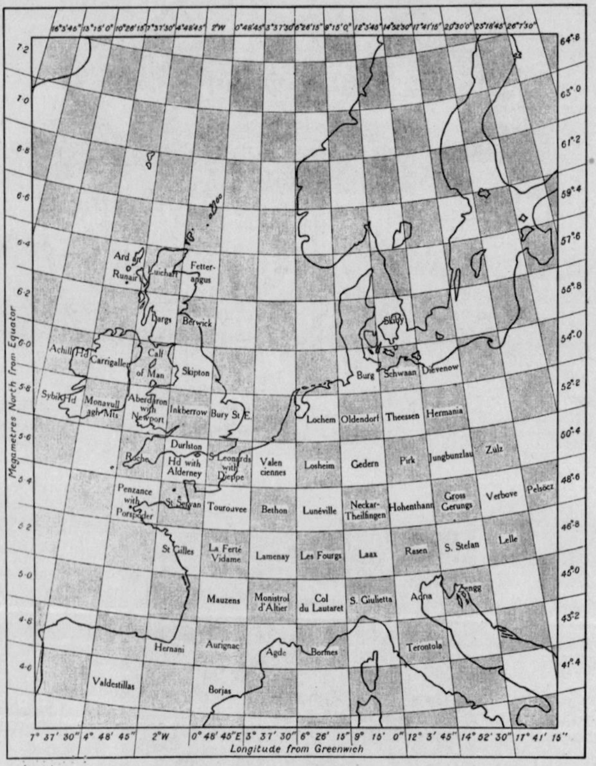


An arrangement of meteorological stations designed to fit with the chief mechanical properties of the atmosphere. Other considerations have been here disregarded. Pressure to be observed at the centre of each shaded chequer, velocity at the centre of each white chequer. The numerical coordinates refer to these centres as also do the names, although as to the latter there may be errors of 5 or 10 km. The word "with" in "St Leonards with Dieppe" etc. is intended to suggest an interpolation between observations made at the two places. See page 9, and Chapters 3 and 7. Contrast the existing arrangement shown on p. 184.

▲ Lewis Fry Richardson, "Computational grid over Northern Europe," in: *Weather Prediction by Numerical Process*, Cambridge 1922.

## THE GROWTH OF THE DATA LANDSCAPE

Data are not numbers but diagrams of surfaces, new landscapes of knowledge that inaugurated a vertiginous perspective over the world and society as a whole: the eye of the algorithm, or algorithmic vision. This is no longer the magic *second sight* of the Stochastic Man of the pre-digital age.[5] The accumulation of numbers by the Information Society has reached the point at which numbers themselves turn into space and create a new topology. The digital matrix is eventually morphing into a world of curves and waves rather than bits and quantities: vectors of tendencies, clusters of social patterns, dorsals of anomalies and spikes, concretions of intelligence. A new collective geography opens to colonization.

The magnitude of this epistemic revolution is comparable to previous paradigm shifts. As much as the Copernican, Darwinian, Newtonian, and Einsteinian revolutions each further displaced the centrality of the human; Turing's revolution has displaced the human from the hegemony of cognition in two ways: as an accumulation of information that exceeds the scale of human memory and as a growth in computing power that exceeds the scale of human thought.

Global data centers continuously concentrate knowledge about the world's climate, stock markets, logistic chains, and more importantly social networks of billions of individuals. Data centers convert information into the Gestalt of global intelligence. The science-fiction novelist William Gibson already described this landscape, as cyberspace, in 1984:

> *A graphic representation of data abstracted from the banks of every computer in the human system.*

5 Robert Silverberg, *The Stochastic Man*, New York 1975.

> *Unthinkable complexity. Lines of light ranged in the nonspace of the mind, clusters and constellations of data. Like city lights, receding.*[6]

These are the new lands (or the new skies) of information politics. Such a new data space emerges as an extension of previous institutions of knowledge and power, although now under the complex and heavy rule of mathematics. As a symbolic and political form, the database is the new archive of power. If the Michel Foucault of the twentieth century could speak the same language of the archives he was studying, the Foucault of the twenty-first century would need extensive technical training to access the archives contemporary to him. We live in the age of *data overlords* and, accordingly, the media theorist Lev Manovich identifies three "data classes":

> *The explosion of data and the emergence of computational data analysis as the key scientific and economic approach in contemporary societies create new kinds of divisions. Specifically, people and organizations are divided into three categories: those who create data (both consciously and by leaving digital footprints), those who have the means to collect it, and those who have the expertise to analyze it.*[7]

The scaffolding of this new episteme has been gradual and continuous, following the slow bifurcations of the *machinic phylum* since the Industrial Revolution. It has been a long process of technological bifurcations that has made data emerge out of the division of labor. The industrial engine, as the French philosopher Gilbert Simondon remarked, separated old manual

6 William Gibson, *Neuromancer*, New York 1984, 49.
7 Lev Manovich, "Trending: The Promises and the Challenges of Big Social Data," in Matthew K. Gold (ed.), *Debates in the Digital Humanities*, Minneapolis, MN 2011, 470.

labor into energy (nature) and information (worker).[8] The Turing machine separated information into data and metadata. The database separated metadata into patterns and vectors. Each new machine grounding new plateaus and growing a new bifurcation: the industrial society bifurcated into the information society; the information society bifurcated into the metadata society. A gradual process of germination of new technological forms; in fact, new divisions and multiplications of labor.

Deleuze registered this shift that marks the passage from Foucault's disciplinary society to the "societies of control" based on "data banks." In the liquid space of data, the modulation of flows replaces the discipline of bodies.[9] The norm (the standard of social behavior) is no longer constructed through the archives of institutional knowledge but mathematically computed from below. Turing machines are the "recording machine" of social patterns—the cybernetic machines that register and measure population and production, the machines "of the second synthesis" that continuously cut and codified the flows of the desired production—according to Gilles Deleuze and Félix Guattari.[10]

## THE CELLULAR AUTOMATA OF A NEW POWER

If we could visit Gibson's original cyberspace, its data skyline would not resemble the buildings of virtual reality, but the contours of new abstract institutions. The datascape is an alien "nonspace of the mind," which had to be translated into familiar

8 See: Matteo Pasquinelli, "Italian Operaismo and the Information Machine," *Theory, Culture & Society*, 32, 3 (2015): 49–68.

9 Gilles Deleuze, "Postscript on the Societies of Control," *October*, 59 (Winter 1992): 3–7, tr. Martin Joughin from the original French version published in *L'autre journal* (May 1990).

10 Gilles Deleuze and Félix Guattari, *Anti-Oedipus*, tr. Robert Hurley, 1977, 9.

metaphors in order to be accessible: patterns, clusters, constellations, nodal points, vectors, waves, tails, splines, spikes. Although data do not create dimensional space, they are rendered into human geometry in order to be navigable, therefore disclosing superhuman geometries.

Datascapes were born in the registers of the ancient archives as simple squared grids: horizontal lines detailing the person's name and vertical names carving out and ordering political data: age, gender, class, disease, crime, etc. The register's grids expanded their territories with the bureaucracy of the modern state. The encounter of statistics with the first mainframe computers generated the database as political form. The database depicts *mathematically* the formations of power that Foucault recorded *institutionally* in his visits to the archive. Today the securitarian category of "asocial behavior," for instance, is computed by a machine in real time: no longer is there the need for a stable taxonomy codified by the disciplines of psychology or criminology.

Databases escalated to planetary dimensions with the rise of the network society. But already in around 1998 the first Google database marked the beginning of the *metadata society*: a parasitic infrastructure of global data centers, growing in parallel to the better-known and supposedly horizontal network society, each new data center consolidating the verticalization and privatization of cognitive capital on a global scale—and then hidden, like Swiss vaults, in the most remote parts of the planet. No wonder, the first Google data center was called the Cage.[11]

The mathematical grid of the archive has also evolved from the relational database structure (SQL)

11 Angela Moscaritolo, "15 Years Later, Google Remembers Its First Data Center," *PC magazine*, February 6, 2014, online http://www.pcmag.com/article2/0,2817,2430421,00.asp (accessed 02/09/2016).

to the non-relational one (NoSQL), where connections between elements can open up infinite dimensions because they are no longer confined to a squared grid. In such an abstract space metadata can freely describe strings of individual and collective patterns. The multi-dimensional model of the universe (on which physics and string theory speculate) would be useful also to popularize the multi-dimensional political datascape that is growing parallel to our reality.

In 1980, Deleuze and Guattari described power according to the binary opposition of "smooth space and striated space—nomad space and sedentary space—the space in which the war machine develops and the space instituted by the State apparatus."[12] Ten years later, in the "Postscript on the Societies of Control," Deleuze will realize that the striated space of "data banks" will be able to generate itself a new smooth space. The grid of that binary code started to dissolve into waves. Its form of power would be *modulation* rather than discipline and its navigation technique *surfing* rather than numeration.[13]

Large datascapes, in fact, describe curved spaces —the curved spaces of the collective mind. Data are not numbers, but *Gestalten*, structures that become image: infinite points that draw the silhouette of a new Singularity emerging against the background of "apparently meaningless data," as everybody has learnt to say. Hills and undulations are the aggregation of social patterns; spikes and abysses the emergence of social anomalies. This is the smooth topology of a new power.

The first electronic matrix that was run on the first computer was not squared, but already corrupted by life. The universe of self-replicating automata, which was inoculated by the mathematician Nils Aall Barri-

12 Deleuze and Guattari, *A Thousand Plateaus*, 474.
13 Deleuze, "Postscript on the Societies of Control"; see: David Savat, "Deleuze's Objectile: From Discipline to Modulation," in: Mark Poster and David Savat (eds), *Deleuze and New Technology*, Edinburgh 2009.

celli into the IAS computer at Princeton University on March 3, 1953, was the imitation of the evolution of life by the digital.[14] Barricelli's universe was made up of only 512 cells: yet for the first time, the matrix bent. Looking back, maybe, today, we have all become cellular automata just of a larger social matrix.

Over the last few decades mathematicians and engineers have been working on translating and visualizing information that emerges from chaotic datasets for decision-making. Police departments already employ *predictive policing algorithms* (PredPol) to forecast crimes in major cities. This new discipline is sometimes called Social Analytics (especially for those in marketing), but it would be more correct to call it Pattern Police.

## A COMPUTATIONAL NORM: THE SPIKE

Anomaly Detection at Multiple Scales (ADAMS) is a thirty-five-million-dollar Defense Advanced Research Projects Agency (DARPA) project, designed to identify anomalous behaviors in the large datasets of big institutions like the US Army, and the threats from potential subjects such as: "a soldier in good mental health becoming homicidal or suicidal or an innocent insider becoming malicious."[15] ADAMS attempts to predict *anomalies* in the data flows of individuals and groups by monitoring email traffic, mobile phone geolocation, social media, bank activity, etc. The same approach, in fact, is applied today in all fields of Intelligence. As the French philosopher Grégoire Chamayou observes in the case of war drones:

14 George Dyson, *Darwin among the Machines: The Evolution of Global Intelligence*, New York 1998. See also: Alex Galloway, "Creative Evolution," *Cabinet*, 42 (Summer 2011): 45–50.

15 "Anomaly Detection at Multiple Scales (ADAMS) Broad Agency Announcement DARPA-BAA-11-04," US General Services Administration, October 22, 2010, online www.darpa.mil/program/anomaly-detection-at-multiple-scales (accessed 01/27/2016).

> *Any behavior that diverges from the web of habitual activities may indicate a threat. 'According to an Air Force intelligence analyst who spoke on condition of anonymity, analyzing imagery captured by drones is like a cross between police work and social science. The focus is on understanding* patterns *of life, and deviations from those patterns. For example, if a normally busy bridge suddenly empties, that might mean the local population knows a bomb is planted there.' ... Gregory sums this up as follows: 'Essentially, the task consists in distinguishing between* normal *and* abnormal *activity in a kind of militarized rhythm-analysis that takes on increasingly automatized forms.' Automatic detection of abnormal behavior operates by predicting the possible developments resulting from different types of behavior. Having noted the characteristic features of a familiar sequence in a particular situation, analysts claim to be able to make probable inferences about future developments, and intervene so as to prevent those developments from ever occurring. Thus recognition of particular scenarios can serve as the basis for early threat detection.*[16]

"The two epistemic poles of pattern and anomaly are the two sides of the same coin of algorithmic governance. An unexpected anomaly can be detected only against the ground of a pattern regularity. Conversely, a pattern emerges only through the median equalisation of diverse tendencies."[17] Also gender, race, and social class are all patterns that can emerge from datasets and are reinforced computationally.

16 Grégoire Chamayou, *A Theory of the Drone*, New York 2014, 43.

17 See also: Matteo Pasquinelli, "Anomaly Detection: The Mathematization of the Abnormal in the Metadata Society" (talk given at Transmediale, Berlin, 2015), online http://matteopasquinelli.com/anomaly-detection (accessed 01/27/2016).

Anomaly is the corresponding Foucauldian definition of the *abnormal* for the age of the metadata society. Here, the norm of behavior is not standardized by policing protocols and state institutions, but algorithmically computed from below. Machine learning algorithms, more recently, have started to operate as an automated bureaucracy that silently reinforces the more dominant patterns of behaviors. It is a norm that emerges as a computational pattern. It is a *computational norm* rather than an institutional one.

The social anomaly appears, then, as a spike, a peak on the datascape. The spike appears like a ruffle along the smooth data space of the intelligence of power. It is an obstinate peak that rebels against geometrical order, reassuring waves, and normalized patterns. The spike forms as an Event on the metadata horizon of the society, the topological translation of a kick to the collective body (or collective mind).

You can see the spike from both sides. From the point of view of power, as abnormal behavior to modulate and from the point of view of collective intelligence, as the birth of a new supernormal behavior, the mark of a new extra-social form of life. What French philosopher Georges Canguilhem once noted about the abnormal can be applied to anomaly detection: "the anomaly, while logically second in relation to a pattern, is existentially first."[18]

18 "The abnormal, while logically second, is existentially first." Georges Canguilhem, *The Normal and the Pathological*, New York 2007, 243.

## DO NOT SPIKE TO THE EYE OF THE ALGORITHM!

Anomaly detection is the new paranoia of power apparatuses that spasmodically attempt to extract meaningful patterns out of "apparently meaningless data." Such voracity produces frequent cases of *apophenia*, that is, the recognition of an image, a person's face, a pattern, where there is none. Drone strikes have hit wedding parties in Pakistan as they resemble (have the same data signature as) an "assembly of terrorists." Apophenia is a delirious mirage on the hot surface of the datascape.

The new domain of data, the scale of "big data," and the geography of social media are not just describing a new form of power, but a matrix where social actors come often to fulfill political roles and narratives that have been designed for them. Anomaly detection produces paranoia both ways: in power apparatuses as much as in the forms of resistance to power. If old techniques of surveillance engendered their own forms of counter-surveillance, these new techniques of social modulation are engendering their own forms of counter-modulation.

"Do not spike!" seems to be the imperative of a new generation growing up under the surveillance of machine learning algorithms that constantly record the patterns-of-life among the whole population. "Do not spike!" resounds in the villages of Afghanistan, in populations aware that any detour from a daily routine could be interpreted as a threat by the eye of algorithm watching from the drone. "Do not spike to the algorithm!" is the new instinct of a docile multitude that has assimilated counter-algorithmic behaviors: the fear of searching too often for a specific keyword on a search engine, for instance, as it may be interpreted as a psychological profile.

Algorithmic paranoia may also enter the structure of our philosophies and critical theories, when too often we ourselves have the sensation of looking like an algorithm. As Alex Galloway remarked:

> *Why, within the current renaissance of research in continental philosophy, is there a coincidence between the structure of ontological systems and the structure of the most highly evolved technologies of post-Fordist capitalism? … Why, in short, is there a coincidence between today's ontologies and the software of big business?*[19]

Maybe, when one gazes for a long time into the data abyss, the abyss also gazes into one. How much space is there for alternative architectures of knowledge, alternative pedagogies, and epistemologies? In Gibson's *Neuromancer* the cyberspace of data was an animistic universe and required shamanic skills, unconscious cunning of abstractions, plus methamphetamines, in order for the individual to navigate and fight within it.

How does one address a form of power that is absorbing social data like a cyclone sucks up the water of the oceans? How does one face the monopolies of planetary computation without access to computing power and data centers? Alternatively, how realistic are the tactics of obfuscation and dissimulation in the long term?[20] Is invisibility really necessarily the best strategy to embrace?[21] Can the datascape be subverted to claim a political autonomy of data, as data activism is starting to address today?[22]

19 Alexander Galloway, "The Poverty of Philosophy: Realism and Post-Fordism," *Critical Inquiry*, 39, 2 (2013): 34–66.

20 Finn Brunton and Helen Nissenbaum, *Obfuscation: A User's Guide for Privacy and Protest*, Cambridge, MA, and London 2015.

21 The Invisible Committee, *To Our Friends*, Cambridge, MA, and London 2015.

22 Stefania Milan and Miren Gutiérrez, "Citizens' Media Meets Big Data: The Emergence of Data Activism," *Mediaciones*, 14 (2015): 120–33.

Where is it possible to hide from the eye of the algorithm, an eye that is no longer patrolling individuals but *condividuals,* collective patterns made out of our digital footprints or *dividuals*?[23] "No one is reading your emails," reassures the US National Security Agency (NSA): a machine just crunches your metadata. Nevertheless it is becoming obvious that: "metadata represent the shift to a different and higher dimensional scale in relation to information: they disclose the collective and *political* nature that is intrinsic to all information."[24] This has led to people being killed on the strength of metadata.[25]

You can see the spike from two sides: from the point of view of power, as abnormal behavior to modulate, or from the perspective of collective intelligence, as the rise of a super-normative behavior, the mark of a superhuman form of life. In fact, data centers establish a revolutionary perspective on the collective mind that is extraordinary and whose political control must be contested. No one can withdraw from building more complex architectures of knowledge.

Do spike!

23 On the history of the "dividual," see: Gerald Raunig, *Dividuum: Machinic Capitalism and Molecular Revolution*, vol. 1, tr. Aileen Derieg, Los Angeles, CA, and New York 2016.

24 Pasquinelli, "Italian Operaismo and the Information Machine," 14.

25 David Cole, "We Kill People Based on Metadata," *The New York Review of Books*, May 10, 2014, online www.nybooks.com/blogs/nyrblog/2014/may/10 (accessed 02/08/2016).

NISHANT SHAH

*MECHANICAL LABOR*

Labor is human function. The capacity of a human body to perform work, measurement of its efficiency under duress, and the need to sustain interest and pleasure in repetitive actions are all tied closely to the technological condition. Technologies amplify the functions of the body. Technologies augment the capacities of the body. Technologies reduce the sovereignty of the body. Technologies make the body redundant or fragile. The human and the technological are combatively pitted against each other, produced as oppositional—the one bereft of agency and the other denuded of innocence.

Mechanical Labor that recognizes the machinistic redundancy of work from which the human worker needs rescuing, as well as the affective machinations that catalyze and inform machine tasks, produces some expected and prewired tropes to understanding the relationship between machines and humans. The body and the technology become measures of each other. Objective technologies provide a quantified self. The unpredictable body offers new standards to which technologies must measure up. Clean technologies help contain unclean bodies. The affective bodies resist the ledger-led normativization that technologies produce. Technology becomes the measure of human productivity, the tool of human monitoring, and the ruthless replacement of the human worker in the quest for automatization.

This confrontation between technology and body, where they are at first forcefully separated and then made to interact at specific moments, is characterized often as critical, anxious, and maybe nervous. However, the moment of conflict is fiercely contingent on perpetuating the notion of both the body and technology as having discrete presences and accidental interactions. It focuses on the body only in its predetermined matrices of access, adoption, penetration, and usage, reducing the messiness and the irrationality of the body to informatics of domination and control. Simultaneously, it contains the technology in reified surfaces, interfaces, and devices, denying it the pleasure of serendipity and the joy of the glitch, forcing it to enter into a system of enumeration and quantification.

The function of the body, in this context, is to make it legible, intelligible, and accessible to the logics and logistics of the mechanical systems within which it is installed. The measure of the body's work, and worth, is formed, informed, and formalized by the design and designation of the technosocial circuits into which it is integrated. Clearly defined functions, and promises of labor premised on a fragile body, produce new circulations of care and configurations of affect; one where the human takes care of the technologies that excel at performing care of human beings better than humans do themselves.

The triumvirate of objects in this collection argue that these imposed imaginations of the role of the body and technology in our understanding of mechanical labor needs reinstallation. The body and the technology need to be thought of not as separate, separable, or separating each other, but as co-emergent, embedded in shared contingent ontologies, where each forms and informs the formulation and information of the other. The body and technology are not in a state of random encounter or hostile contradiction, but work together to produce a new site of labor, which is not an exclusive either/or but an ironical and/also framework. The technological is not a tool, but a condition within which our bodies exist. It is an ontological moment that counts, accounts, discounts, and miscounts the constructs of the body with which it pulsates. The body is not an agential actor but is narrated, rehearsed, enacted, and produced by technologies of data mining and statistical predictions.

This is the quantified self. It is the product itself, the description, and the aspiration, which subjects the human body and the technological apparatus to processes of control, containment, and censorship. Each indexical item in this collection helps illustrate how the quantified self's role is to transform affect into efficiency, emotions into accuracy, and intentions into predictability.

In all of these examples of the quantified self, I am proposing a shift in our understanding of mechanical labor and the human–technological relationships it espouses. Discourse around mechanical labor has often been concentrated on the naturally present body; how to equip it, empower it, and amplify its capacity to deal with the machines and the technologies that surround it. I am suggesting that we need to understand the aspiration of mechanical labor as producing new forms and frameworks of being human. In the process, we stop thinking about the work that the body does, as if the technology merely helps in expanding the scope of this labor, and start looking at the work that technologies do to produce new bodies—materially, physically, affectively, and socially—for the integrated circuits of our future.

## CHART 6540

The quantified self has a history that predates the digital wave of self-counting. Melissa Gregg, a user-experience researcher at Intel and author, in her work "Getting Things Done," unearths an archive from the Baker Library at Harvard University that documents the ways by which the body of the female assembly-line operators at the Hawthorne Plant in Cicero, Illinois, in 1928, was monitored and trained in the service of producing efficient technologies. While design and ergonomics might have focused on the efficiency of the assembly-line system, basing it on frequency, ease of access, and relay of labor, the female operators themselves were in the process of being manipulated, monitored, framed, and produced, to be efficient. In the chart on display, is a data-mining project where the temperature, weight, mood, showering habits, and menstrual cycles of the female operators have been tabulated meticulously, reducing the female body to nothing more than an efficient typing machine. The idea of privacy, which is so ingrained in the academic- and rights-based discourse around the affective experiences of the body and its practices, suddenly becomes an information set that can be mined for patterns, trends, and predictions, inviting the body to surrender the affect of feeling private, to the conditions of being watched in the service of efficiency. This reformulation of her body as a set of private informatics, which can reassemble her as an efficient worker, marks the trend of contemporary quantified-self projects that work intimately with us and penetrate our deep informational selves in the service of producing a normative body that can work and be worked upon.

The following is Dr. Olmstead's report of examination of
#1 clock No. 167, Department 6329:

Summary of May 17, 1928

1. No illness since last examination. Feels very well.
2. Temperature 99.2. Throat red. Tonsils chronically infected.
3. Chest negative.
   Heart: Mitral regurgitation and aortic insufficiency.
4. Weight 113 pounds - a loss of three pounds since last examination. Does not know why she has lost weight.
5. General physical condition fair.

1. Blood pressure on reexamination: 114/60/54.

2. Data on skin stimulation in the morning:

   a. Shower or tub:
      Tub twice a week.
   b. Sponge bath:
      Almost every day.
   c. Cold water on face, throat and chest:
      Cold water.
   d. Vigorous all-over rub with rough towel.
      Dry - not vigorous.

3. Regularity and time of bowel movement:
   Daily in morning.

4. Menstrual History:

   a. Date of periods, etc.:
      Menstruating now. Last period April 12.
      Regular. No dysmenorrhea.

▲ Western Electric Company, Dr. Olmstead's report of examination, Illinois, 1928.

The following is Dr. Olmstead's report of examination of clock No. 500, Department 6329:

#2

Summary of May 17, 1928

1. Has been well since last visit. Temperature 99.4.

2. Weight 107 pounds - a gain of 1 pound.

3. Chest - rough breath sounds. Heart negative.

4. Throat - red.

5. General physical condition fair. Not improved since last time.

1. Blood pressure on reexamination:
   128/90/38

2. Data on skin stimulation in the morning:

   a. Shower or tub:
      Tub
   b. Sponge bath:
      No
   c. Cold water on face, throat, and chest:
      Lukewarm.
   d. Vigorous all-over rub with rough towel:
      Turkish towel - lightly.

3. Regularity and time of bowel movement:
   Irregular - sometimes morning or evening.
   Once daily.

4. Menstrual History:

   a. Date of Periods, etc.:
      Menstruating now.
      Last period four weeks ago.
      Regular.
      No dysmenorrhea.

▲ Western Electric Company, Dr. Olmstead's report of examination, Illinois 1928

## THE INVISIBLE BOYFRIEND

I am not positing the quantified self as a body in a condition of victimhood. This is not the story of how technologies are rendering us fragile and redundant. Instead, it is a way of thinking of the body as discursively and materially produced by these technologies of life, living, and loving. The advertisement for the companion app "Invisible Boyfriend," launched in the United States in 2014, is perhaps a telling example of the way in which the quantified-self computes affect. The application uses digital social media of connectivity and distribution, allowing subscribers to select a user-submitted selfie and a set of traits desirable in a boyfriend. An algorithm creates a profile, which, circulated among "microworkers" on the platform Crowdsource, helps one fake a relationship through text messages, voicemails, and other "evidences" of being in a functional relationship, and that one can produce to appease nosey parents or irritating friends who nag one about not "settling down."

The subscribers, who pay twenty-five dollars a month for this service, are aware that what they are dating is an algorithm, and a work-distribution protocol. They interact with real-life persons, but these are anonymous, and performing a role in the scripted desires of their apps. The app simulates a boyfriend based on one's own revelations, and the quantification of one's social-network activities, that both catalyzes and informs the discontinuous conversations and distributed affective investments. And yet, in an uncanny move, there have been reports of users who have fallen in love with their invisible boyfriends, chatting with a string of strangers about their quotidian acts and affects. How could one not, when one's invisible boyfriend shows concern when one fails to reply quickly, asks about one's day, and wants to know one's thoughts about the movie seen last night. There have been reports of microworkers who have dropped out of providing care performances, feeling unsettled by the continued investment of affect and interest in users who are only available at random distribution by a predictive algorithm. This sounds equally plausible, especially when the conversations often reveal not only accounts of people's desires but also the depths of their loneliness and the emotional upheavals of their daily lives. The payload of the algorithm is in ensuring that it matches users to enough people who are alike, so that the conversations are seamless and the interactions intimate—thus replacing emotional states with algorithmic accuracy. If the role of the quantified self in the case of the female typists was to codify her physical affective conditions into a matrix of efficiency, in the case of the Invisible Boyfriend, the quantified self infuses affective intimacies to technological protocols that simulate social orders, which are no longer either fathomable or fashioned by human intentions or accidents.

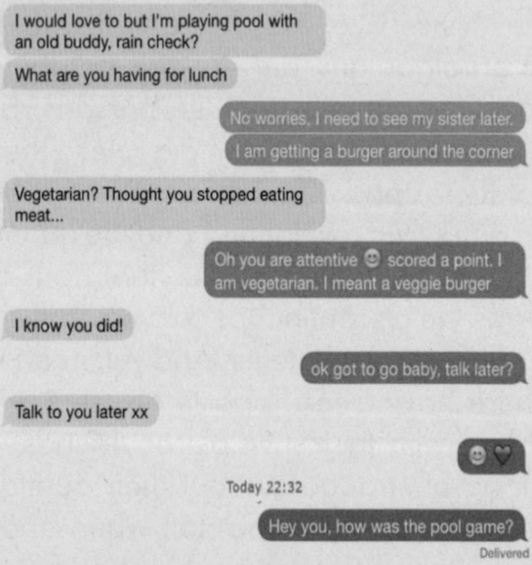


▲ Demo recording registration *Invisible Boyfriend* 2016.

## AADHAAR DOG IDENTITY CARD

The quantified self is also at the heart of foundational changes in governance of the self. With the introduction of new biometric databases of governance, where the citizen is constructed using multiple datasets that emerge out of governance practices, the quantified self has become the new unit of e-government. The information relationship, which depended on the individual narrating herself to the state that was embracing her in a condition of simultaneously recognizing her but not identifying her, interacting with her but not evaluating her, has moved into a politics of informatics. The new informatics self enters into a dialogue through processes of verification, authentication, and validation rather than identities, narratives, and interactions. The individual is presented in this structure only as the biological entity that bears the database markers in order to engage with the state. Even as the databases use extremely personal biometric datasets, like fingerprinting, iris scans, and even DNA sequences, the body of the individual and her material practices are redundant in the production of the quantified self.

In India, in the Aadhaar project which is poised to become the world's largest biometric database governance initiative, one of the enrollment agency supervisors Azam Khan in Umri, Haryana, created an identification card that bears the picture of a dog and which he officially issued through the system. The presence of an identification card that bears the picture of a dog becomes a telling example of the reduced importance of the human bodily presence in these new systems of governance. The dog ID card might be discarded easily as a glitch, as a machine error, as human forgery, as something that needs to be corrected so that our human sensibilities can be assuaged. However, for the network logic of Aadhaar, the appearance of the dog on the ID card is neither an anomaly nor a problem. The card is merely to provide the human recipient something tangible to hold on to. The metadata that is stored behind that card, associated with the number—the biometric information that claims to identify the individual in question—disregards the human readable data and only works with the human informatics associated with the Aadhaar number. Even without changing the card, the human bearer can perform transactions using the number. Similarly, even if the human does not have the card corrected, its different profile sets would soon populate and even auto-correct this association, eventually replacing the picture of the dog with a selfie that has more weight and importance in the digital footprints of the individual.

The foundational understanding of state–citizen relationships in informational systems has been about the capacity to narrate, to interpret, to negotiate, and to produce meanings of self/selves in a dialogue with the state. However, the quantified self not only makes the self incapable of knowing itself—the amount of data generated around the self can only be processed and be made meaningful by algorithms—but also reduces the subject's capacity to interpret and communicate with the state. The quantified self thus produces a subject who engages with the state through other proto-state entities that help in intelligent and strategic storing, sorting, sifting, retrieval, and protection of information sets, which necessitate a close working together with the digital technologies. The role of the quantified self is to produce a meta-self, much like the metadata in our opaque computational practices, which overrides and supersedes the individual, rendering it into a node that can be activated when the network requires it to perform functions of distribution and circulation.

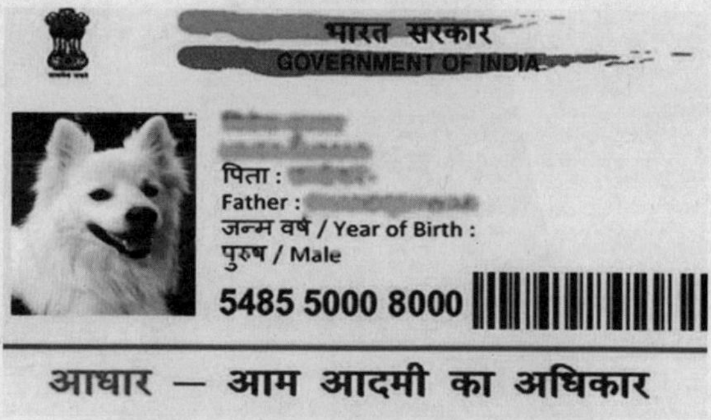


▲ Aadhaar Dog Identity Card, 2016.

MUSHON ZER-AVIV

# *TERRITORIAL AMBIGUITY*

Throughout most of human history, mapping the world was a failure-ridden poetic pursuit—an attempt to visualize that which is just too close to see. Cartographers collected discrete signals and attempted to put them together into the "big picture." But the question of context and distance kept arising, as one cannot successfully measure a discrete geographic location without first questioning one's own position in relation to it. Another term for a discrete global position is datum, or in plural data. We will attempt to navigate this history of data and follow its path across oceans and dry land, through four exhibits that chronicle the paradox of position, distance, reference, and documentation.

Centuries ago it was a piece of wood tied to a rope floating in the ocean that transformed the way we gather data. It required the captain to keep a log and analyze the data *en masse* to locate the ship and its movement in relation to the Earth. With the advent of sensing technology and digital automation, the role of ship's captain was outsourced to technology. We stopped representing our bodies as moving on a map, but rather the map started moving beneath our feet.

This shift of power can be tracked along the stretched rope of the chip log. If once it was us that counted the knots from our position of strength onboard the ship's deck, it seems that we've been unknowingly thrown off-board. Now we are the datum, dragging along behind the pirate ship as it quickly sails away steered by its quiet and ghostly algorithmic captain that can never get wet.

Inspired by Jorge Luis Borges' fable "On Exactitude in Science" the deconstructionist French philosopher Jean Baudrillard suggested we no longer inhabit the world but are instead living on the map, the simulacra. Rather than the map shreds being forgotten in the desert he suggested it was reality itself that was deserted and left behind.

The simulacra are subjected to the rules of digital data analysis. These rules are limited by the boundaries of binary systems and by their ability to disambiguate and successfully analyze the data. As artificial intelligence algorithms become more powerful and complex they rely more heavily on signals that they cannot understand and can only analyze statistically through machine learning. If we're positioned as teachers to these mechanic learners, we can also use this as an invitation to perform. Rather than serve these systems with reductive signals that are easy to disambiguate and do little to represent the richness of our lives, we could choose to re-ambiguate the signal instead, using poetry, obfuscation, noise, hacking, jamming, spoofing, trolling, sheer nonsense, and other wonderful traits of the bad data that makes human culture.

## CHIP LOG

Surrounded by water with no land in sight sailors navigating the oceans were always challenged with finding ways to measure their location and speed. The log technique was developed in around the fifteenth century: a sailor would throw a piece of wood overboard, set with metal weights to stabilize it; the log would float in the water as a rope, extended from it to the ship. The sailors would use an hourglass to measure the length of the rope, released for thirty seconds until the sand ran out. *Knots* and *half-knots* were placed in equal intervals along the rope and, to this day, the units for measuring speed used by both sailors and pilots are called knots.

The ship's captain would chronicle the speed of the boat and other measurements in what we've come to know as the *captain's log*, named after that very same chip log. Logging has traveled a long way since and is now an integral part of technology and culture, though most bloggers are unfamiliar with the history of wet wood that defined the origins of their practice.

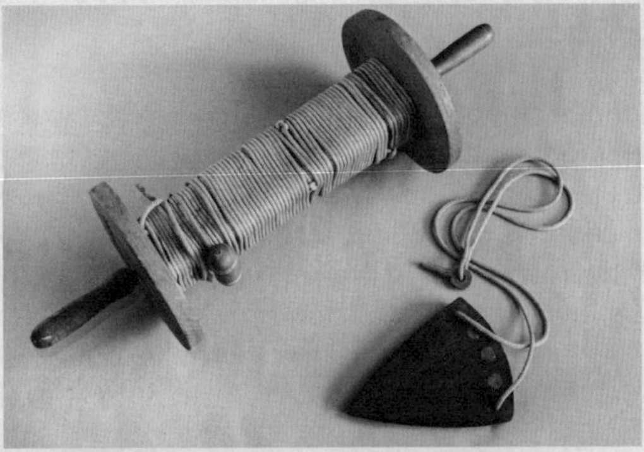

▲

## THE ETAK NAVIGATOR

Launched in 1985, the ETAK Navigator was the first commercial digital car navigation system. This revolutionary product reached the market more than fifteen years before GPS technology became available for public use. It used motion sensors, a digital compass, and many tapes of digital geographic data, mapping the streets of mid-1980s San Francisco. The two founders, both yacht-sailing enthusiasts, first got their hands wet in commercial GIS, when they developed one of the world's first digital marine navigation systems. Media analyst Tristan Thielmann writes:

> *The ETAK Navigator was also used in the First Gulf War (Desert Storm), which was primarily because the Navigator did not require any maps. That is a further*

▲ Chip log, s.l. 20th century.

*central distinction to today's GPS navigation systems. The ETAK Navigator is based on the principle of ship navigation: dead reckoning. Starting from a known location it is possible to determine the unknown locations. As a result this system can also be used to advance into uncharted territory.*

Yet another innovation of the ETAK Navigator was representing the traveler as a static marker at the center of a dynamic map. Now the map becomes the ever-changing, scrolling, zooming, irresistible force and the traveler, the immovable object, much like Narcissus, unable to move, staring at his own reflection on the screen in the form of a shiny blue dot.

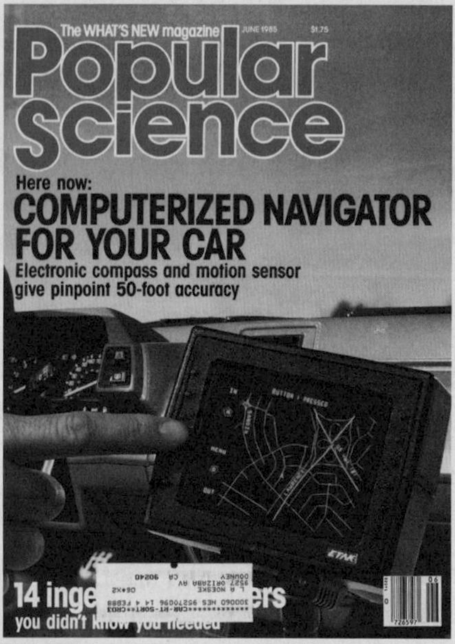


▲ *Popular Science* magazine 6, 6 (1985).

## ON EXACTITUDE IN SCIENCE

*In that Empire, the Art of Cartography attained such Perfection that the map of a single Province occupied the entirety of a City, and the map of the Empire, the entirety of a Province. In time, those Unconscionable Maps no longer satisfied, and the Cartographers Guilds struck a Map of the Empire whose size was that of the Empire, and which coincided point for point with it. The following Generations, who were not so fond of the Study of Cartography as their Forebears had been, saw that that vast map was Useless, and not without some Pitilessness was it, that they delivered it up to the Inclemencies of Sun and Winters. In the Deserts of the West, still today, there are Tattered Ruins of that Map, inhabited by Animals and Beggars; in all the Land there is no other Relic of the Disciplines of Geography*

— Jorge Luis Borges[1]

In Borges' famous fable, the modernist project of total knowledge reaches the level of the absurd, as the map grows so vast that it covers the entire territory. In the following generations, their disillusionment with the promise of cartography and science leads to a total rejection of all mapping and geography. Borges makes sure we read this short story as a fable by titling it "On Exactitude in Science." Today we're invited to use this cautionary tale to question the totalizing myth of big data, the scientific map that covers the territory to such a degree that the two become indistinguishable. Both the totalizing pursuit of exact representation and the extreme iconoclastic backlash against it are, suggests Borges, misguided. This contemporary reading of the fable calls for ridding ourselves of the myth

1 Jorge Luis Borges, *Collected Fictions*, tr. Andrew Hurley, New York 1999, 325.

of big data. Not by foregoing the practice altogether, but by balancing it against what often seems to be a rush to favor the map over the territory.

## WAVE BUBBLE

In 2004, the American electrical engineer Limor Fried designed a self-tuning, wide-bandwidth portable RF jammer. It provides up to two hours cell phone jamming or four hours GPS and Wi-Fi jamming. These types of devices are illegal in the United States. As Fried described it, it is illegal to sell or use one in the US, but it is not illegal to tell others how to build it. Which is why the Wave Bubble project is not so much an RF-jamming device, as the open source instructions for building one, a piece of speculative design, or as Fried calls it "Design Noir." As small as a pack of cigarettes, this humble device shoots radio noise in a twenty-degree diameter reducing the signal-to-noise ratio of the Radio Frequency waves, obfuscating wireless communication including GPS signals.

The Wave Bubble also inspired some more nuanced and even more subversive interventions like GPS Spoofing. In 2013, an eighty-million-dollar yacht was set off its course by a small device that generated strong GPS signals indistinguishable from genuine GPS. This time it was the work of University of Texas at Austin researchers, led by assistant professor Dr. Todd Humphreys, exploring the dangers of GPS spoofing.

RF jamming and spoofing are our generation's *ad hoc* wireless version of Borges' discarded empire map. They are the brute countermeasures that kick the blue dot off the center of the computerized navigator. They are the chip log, unknotted, lost at sea. These technologies are mostly regarded as dangerous threats and are even criminalized; they could also offer us temporary autonomous zones and a glimpse of the rapidly diminishing benefit of the doubt. Rather than discard the map completely, these technologies allow us to poke some holes in the map to watch the clear unclouded skies free of radio signals. There should still be room for ambiguity in today's disambiguated data culture. Exploring it is not a crime (yet).

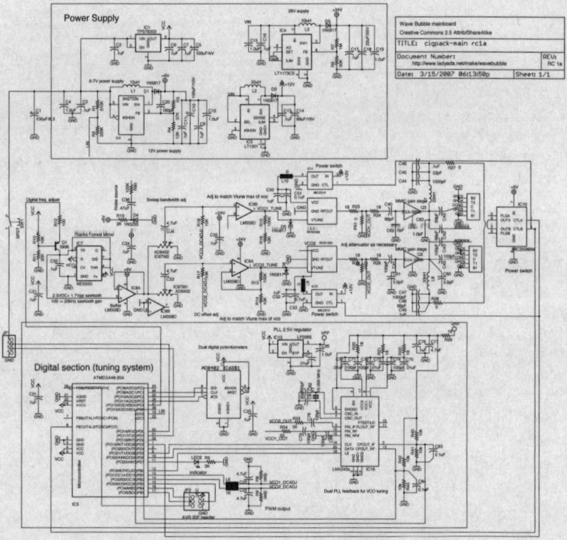


▲ Wave Bubble mainboard, cigpack main-RCLA, 2007.

# TACTICAL TECH AND THE WHITE ROOM

Maya Indira Ganesh, Stephanie Hankey, Marek Tuszynski

Playful, impassioned, sometimes radical and sometimes not, Tactical Tech's engagement with technology is like a one-armed embrace: warm, but wary. For Tactical Tech, technology provides a space for political play, experimentation, and action as much as for reflection and interrogation. After almost fifteen years working with thousands of activists worldwide as practitioners and educators, our discoveries have led us to ask yet more questions. *The White Room* is a place where some of our learning and questions come together.

*The White Room* combines selected artworks, digital products, investigations, and activist projects that seek out and create a vocabulary for the forms and practices of quantification. Positioned as critique from within, artists, engineers, and practitioners, familiar with the tools and practices of quantification itself, leverage this familiarity to fashion their critique.

The world as presented in *The White Room* is not one that belongs just to the people who know how to code. This world exists beyond a laptop or mobile phone; it permeates all the institutions, expectations, and popular cultures we experience everyday. *The White Room* is an animated space, where the artifacts are more for exploration than consumption. The Bar workers, or, 'Ingenious-es' are there, not to assist with sales or fixes but to offer reflection, experimentation and play. They lead visitors through The "App Center," so this could continue beyond the exhibition."

*The White Room* moves beyond the familiar framings of "internet freedom," "privacy," and "surveillance" and raises questions of knowledge, power, and wealth instead. It asks about what kinds of quantified societies we wish to live in and how we should go about the task of valuing, deconstructing, and understanding them.

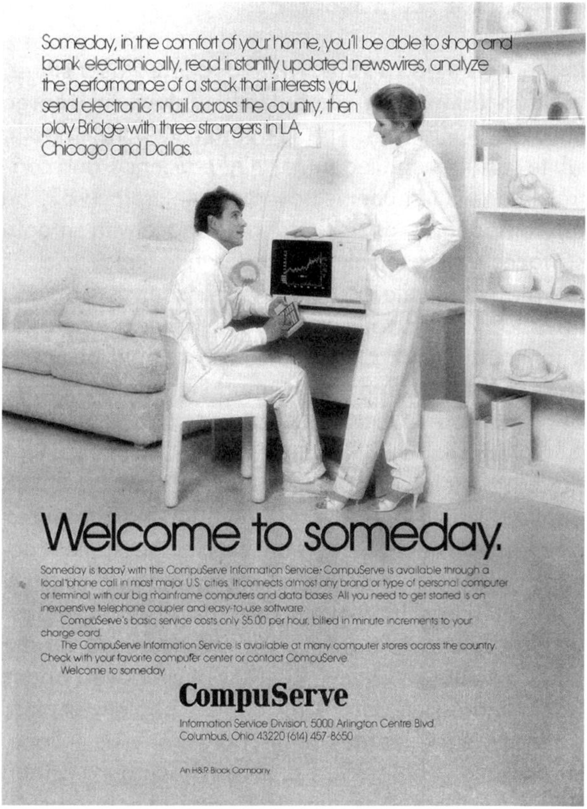


▲ "Welcome To Someday" is an advertisement for CompuServe from 1982. CompuServe is now part of AOL. Scanned from *Omni* magazine, 4, 11 (August 1982), 115.

## THE WHITE ROOM

*Time present and time past*
*Are both perhaps present in time future*
*And time future contained in time past.*
–T.S. Eliot, "Burnt Norton, I"[1]

In the 1970s and 1980s, white appeared as a strong motif in visions of a computerized future. In George Lucas' dystopian first film *THX 1138* (1971) the smooth, white surfaces implied uniformity, efficiency, and control. In one CompuServe advertisement from 1982, the future appeared as a clean, white space with smooth surfaces where nicely dressed, white, middle-class people with white objects on their shelves wouldn't have to do any work, because computers would do it for them. Work and leisure; both would be taken care of by the computer. Human life would *improve*, become more *efficient*, *better*.

Advertising history was made in January 1984 during the telecast of the American Super Bowl with another, significant advertisement for the computerized future. The advertisement was for the Apple Macintosh computer, with Ridley Scott, who had recently completed the film *Blade Runner*, its producer. A pastiche of Michael Radford's film *1984*, based on the book by George Orwell, the Macintosh advert opens with a depressing view of the future. A phalanx of men, dressed in sack-like grey outfits, part-drone, part-clone, shuffle into a hall where a ghostly face on a screen addresses them. A monotonous voice-over booms: "a garden of pure ideology, where each worker would bloom secure from the pests of contradictory and confusing truths." Their eyes glazed, mouths slightly open, the serfs receive their dose of indoctrination. Suddenly,

1 T.S. Eliot, "Burnt Norton, I" (1935), *Four Quartets*, London 2001.

a different figure emerges running down a corridor: a young woman with short, blonde hair, dressed like an athlete in a white T-shirt and bright red shorts, and carrying a hammer. The scene cuts away to close-ups of police wearing visors, marching: they have already been alerted to the disturbance caused by this unique individual. The woman outruns them and makes it to the hall. She spins around with the hammer in her hands to gain momentum, and hurls the hammer at the screen; the police are approaching swiftly now. The screen explodes and floods the grey men with light and the strapline unfurls across the screen: "On January 24, 1984, you'll see why 1984 won't be like '1984.'"

The advertisement does not feature a product; it ends before the viewer can tell what happens when the police finally arrive. The grey men in the Macintosh advertisement reference the dominant, industry leader, IBM, as the Old World Order, and the athletic young individual that breaks the mold represents Apple, which is also distinct for its use of white. At that time, the individual referred to the personal computer, and not literally the individual-as-celebrity, or as "producer-consumer," which is a key feature of web 2.0. The past can seem like a foreign country—they do things differently there—and equally so does the future. Through digital technologies the past appears to us now as *deja raconte*, the experience of things already recounted or told. The advertisements are haunting, because they are inexact, and yet coded with some uncanny knowledge of what has already happened, less prediction than self-fulfilling prophecy.

Welcome to *The White Room*. Here, past dreams and assumptions of an efficient, better future, are refracted through the realities of the present and served up anew. *The White Room* explores the social life of that future in which we now live, with its smooth interfaces and efficient systems, playing out constructions of individual identities, in concert with the state and corporations. What are the parallel and multiple selves, industries, communities, and ministries that have developed around and because of this dream of a certain future? *The White Room* asks how societies organize themselves (ourselves) around the digital now, now that it has become core infrastructure *and* scaffolding, content *and* form, vehicle *and* destination. The converse is perhaps a more difficult question: Was the dream of the future only a dream?

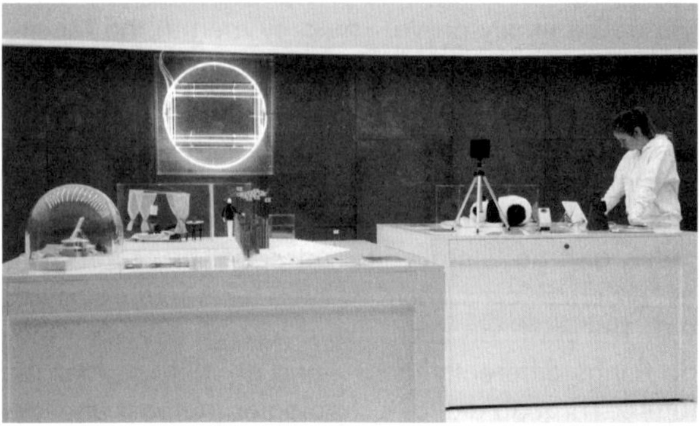

▲

▲ *The White Room* is a live installation space by Tactical Tech, it includes the *Bar* where workers interact with visitors to the exhibition. Through workshops, demos, and hands-on sessions, the *Bar* workers introduce visitors to what lies behind the screens of *The White Room*.

## THE BAR

> *Information has become wealth to be extracted and accumulated, transforming capitalism.*
> —Tiqqun[2]

*The White Room* is built upon the success of the fundamental micro-act of the economic-political system we inhabit: the sale. The smoother, less tense, the more *friction-less* the sale, the more money made and time saved. Michael Sandel reflects on this, and in particular the shift from market *economies* to market *societies*; what he describes as "a way of life in which everything is for sale." This affects norms and values he says: "when market thinking and values enters some social goods and practices, they may change the meaning of some practices worth caring about."[3] In a quantified environment every action or experience, literally, becomes data that are company assets, which are then saleable. Very little is known about the data-brokering industry, why it is so valuable and how it works. Tactical Tech's *Confessions of a Data Broker* anonymously collects the stories of the few data brokers that have talked, thereby providing some insight into an otherwise closed jargon-saturated world. The sale of invisible, intangible, but real assets we all produce merely by using social media, or participating in the "sharing economy," is hard for us to understand in terms of value until we look at the balance sheets of Uber, Airbnb, LinkedIn, or Facebook. All of the intimate moral economies of care, relationships, family, self-expression, and creativity, quantified and monetized, are such that they escape

2 Originally published in French by *Tiqqun II*, 2001, online http://www.archive.org/details/Tiqqun2; translated into English in 2010, online http://cybernet.jottit.com/ (both accessed 02/10/2016).

3 Michael Sandel, "Why We Shouldn't Trust Markets With Our Civic Life," *TED Talks*, June 2013, online https://www.ted.com (accessed 02/10/2016), and see also: Michael Sandel, *What Money Can't Buy: The Moral Limits of Markets*, New York 2013.

the view of the data-producer (you). The value of Spotify lies neither in providing us with music (as it seems to us), nor in paying musicians (the best of whom could not even make a minimum wage from those deals), but in knowing what music we make love to. The value of LinkedIn is not in helping us to find a job, and not even in identifying United States Intelligence Agency personnel as Transparency Toolkit's Intelligence Community *IC Watch* does; analysis of LinkedIn user-data provides governments advice on how best to invest in education. The point of sale has turned into a trade where moments of actual transaction are not always possible to pinpoint. Are we the users the products: as the adage goes, "if you are not paying you are the product," or; are we the workers, unwittingly signing up as data laborers, creating knowledge of the world by just being ourselves?

Working backwards from the sale (of data) as a singular indicator of success it is possible to identify various industries and subcultures devoted to it: window dressing, object fetishes, customer relations, and the help desk. In that vein, the *Bar* is both a commentary on, and a vantage point from which to understand how the quantified society really works. Like a keyhole in a door, the artifacts in the *Bar* allow a specific view of the practical, straightforward, material, and immaterial realities of quantification. There are no metaphors here: data is data. The *Bar* narrates experiences of the self and constructions of state power and corporate power in a quantified society. This is what it means to carry a mobile phone; this is what it means to connect to a shared Wi-Fi router; and this is what it means to read a news website, an act constantly documented by trackers in the browser, as Tactical Tech's *Trackography* shows. The customer-relations-help-desk-problem-solving aspect of these transactions is sometimes the only human interface with the corporate and business entities behind what dances on our screens. This doesn't mean that corporations and technology industries are not human, or humanized; they are some of the warmer and fuzzier companies to be a part of. Yet, as a user, you often have no perception of what it actually takes to maintain the business of invisible products like those advertised by Apple in 1984.

Hamid Ekbia and Bonnie Nardi distinguish between three kinds of work: automation, augmentation, and heteromation. According to them, when machines take center stage this is automation; when machines "come to the rescue" this is augmentation; and the third, heteromation, is when "the machine calls for help." Through the case studies of Mechanical Turk, citizen-science projects such as *Foldit*, and video games, Ekbia and Nardi describe how heteromation works. In the gaming industry, players sit on tribunals to police other players' behaviors and respond to complaints. This is because for the gaming company to respond to every email about players' toxic behavior is just not possible at scale. Amazon's Mechanical Turk is a clearinghouse for the tasks that need doing in order to keep digital services working: people work to tag images, transcribe audio snippets, and other such "data janitorial" tasks for online services.[4] As tech entrepreneur Jeff Bezos' infamous line describing Mechanical Turk goes, "you've heard of software-as-a-service; this is humans-as-a-service."

You and me, we, users, provide the impetus for Turking, *Foldit*, and many others. Users keep the machines we built humming. Politicians Balthasar Glättli and Malte Spitz discover themselves as data points. In *The Monitored Life of National Councillor Balthasar Glättli*, Glättli, a Swiss Green Party member, voluntarily

4 See: Hamid Ekbia and Bonnie Nardi, "Heteromation and its (Dis)Contents: The Invisible Division of Labor Between Humans and Machines," *First Monday*, 19, 6 (2014), online http://dx.doi.org/10.5210/fm.v19i6.5331 (accessed 02/10/2016).

revealed six months' worth of his personal smartphone data retained under Swiss law. It is possible to learn a great deal about Glättli's routine, habits, and networks. Starting in 2009 with a Freedom of Information request to Deutsche Telekom, Malte Spitz, the German Green Party politician, author, and privacy activist, retrieved detailed information about his movements and whereabouts as recorded by his legacy phone. His curiosity piqued by this vision of self, Spitz approached in total forty insurance companies, medical services, databases, and data centers of various state and private institutions with which the average person interacts. Spitz discovered himself as endless logs of mundane details: travel histories, medical details, geolocations, phone numbers, and Amazon purchases for friends and family. In one instance, the police confirmed his identity and stated that they had checked the Missing Persons and Deceased Persons databases for his name.

Such artifacts serve to re-frame the individual, not in terms of what they knowingly exchange, but in terms of the new currency of quantification: metadata. Perhaps the second most infamous line ever uttered by a high-ranking official of the United States Military industrial complex, in this case ex-National Security Agency (NSA) and ex-Central Intelligence Agency (CIA) director, Michael Hayden, was "we kill people based on metadata." Metadata is data about data: when, how, and where a data point was created. In a large mass of data about billions of online flight bookings and searches, texts and phone logs, metadata is, seemingly, meaningless. A kind of safety-in-numbers mentality sets in. However, it is because of this mass of (meta)data that anomalies and outliers are most apparent: a change in routine or a difference in behavior become immediately visible. What we find is the reverse logic to that we have become familiar with: now the haystack helps us find the needle. What starts out as a list—data points about data points—becomes, in aggregate, patterns, like grooves in the sand made by the waves. Quantitative data becomes qualitative data, laying out a narrative about behaviors, habits, and routines: when we go to bed every night, and therefore when we had a late night; the times when we are at home, and therefore when we stay out; who we spend our time with, and therefore who we don't meet. A strange anxiety is borne out of not knowing exactly which detail will reveal your true self.

The implications of this have been discussed in the mainstream media in the context of the surveillance revelations of 2013. *"If we had eyes to see what Snowden has given us"* is a mind-map made by Alan Rusbridger, the former editor-in-chief at *the Guardian* newspaper responsible for breaking the story of the leaks in the United Kingdom. It presents a set of notes from one of the few people who had been through almost all of the leaks, mapping out what they tell us, far beyond the realm of technologies and going into international relations, patriotism, and law. Looking deeper into the industry that feeds this surveillance, *The Wiretappers' Ball*, by Eric King and Matthew Rice at Privacy International, reveals the companies that develop, market, and sell these technologies. Hundreds of brochures collected at surveillance technology trade-shows are evidence of the products and rationale of this multi-million-dollar digital arms trade. One such company from Italy, Hacking Team, trades in surveillance technology, with the governments of Kazakhstan, Sudan, Bahrain, Saudi Arabia, and the like, to monitor criminals and terrorists, but also journalists and activists. Ironically, Hacking Team was hacked in 2015, and 400 gigabytes of their internal emails and documents were placed on WikiLeaks for public scrutiny. *Inside Hacking Team* by Share Lab is a series of analyses and visualizations of metadata from the emails in the cache. These create a vivid picture of communications both within and outside the organization. Based only on metadata, it could be speculated that "l.guerra@hackingteam.com" worked in an administrative role, since 1.guerra received few emails internally, but had to send out many externally, to Yellow Taxi and Eurostar, and the electricity company and DHL.

Just as the digital services offered by this quantified life run on human labor, the digital itself comes from tangible, real, materials, and with it, all the heavy imbrications of history, politics, place, and economics. There are objects that reveal the true, material manifestations of quantification: logs records, reports, sketches, brochures. Data also has a body. Spitz's own records are actual printouts. Richard Vijgen's *Architecture of Radio* is an iPad application that reveals the invisible landscape of wired and wireless signals in the environment—radio frequency waves, cell-towers, satellites, Wi-Fi signals, and more. James Bridle's *Citizen Ex*, a browser extension, looks up the location of where websites visited are registered and collects and analyses this data; based on this, it assigns an "algorithmic citizenship" to a user. *Citizen Ex* shows that websites have a material reality—they exist in data centers, housed in buildings in specific countries, governed by certain laws.

In presenting how quantification is enabled, the obvious question arises as to how to respond to it. It is not that the gaze of the unblinking data machine is something one can unequivocally escape from, or that "opting out" is still an option. However, there may be ways to flip, evade, confuse it, or at the least test its limits. One of the ways to do this is through use of the anonymous browser Tor, or *The Onion Router*. Tor invites the possibility of considering that autonomy within such a system may be as limited as that—a fragile free space. The *Bar* offers this, and more, in a suite of obfuscation, evasion, and masking techniques through tools and tricks compiled as the "*App Center*."

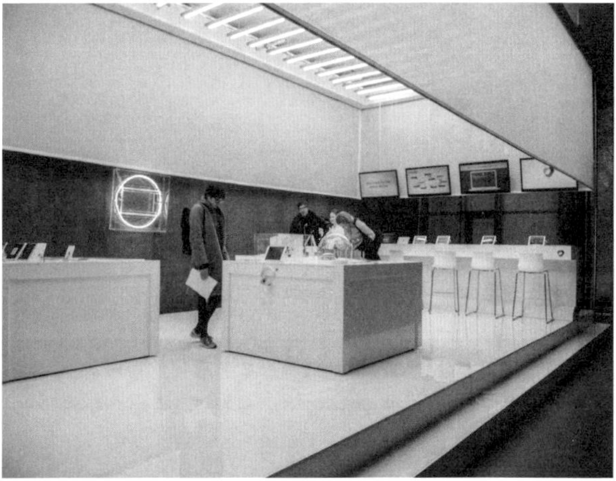

▲

▲ *The White Room* is a live installation space by Tactical Tech, it includes the *Bar* where workers interact with visitors to the exhibition. Through workshops, demos, and hands-on sessions, the *Bar* workers introduce visitors to what lies behind the screens of *The White Room*.

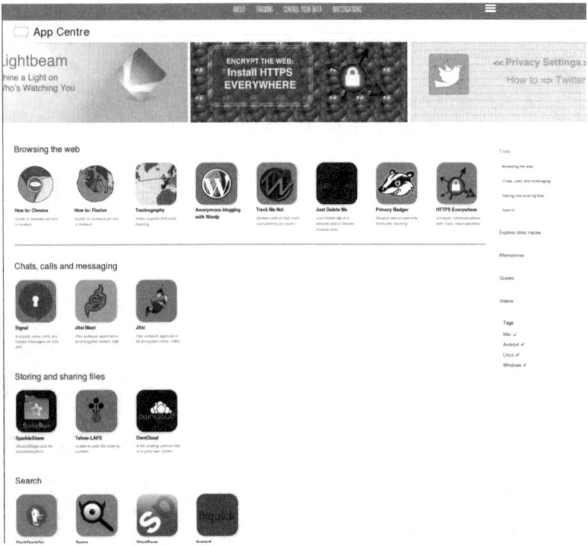


▲

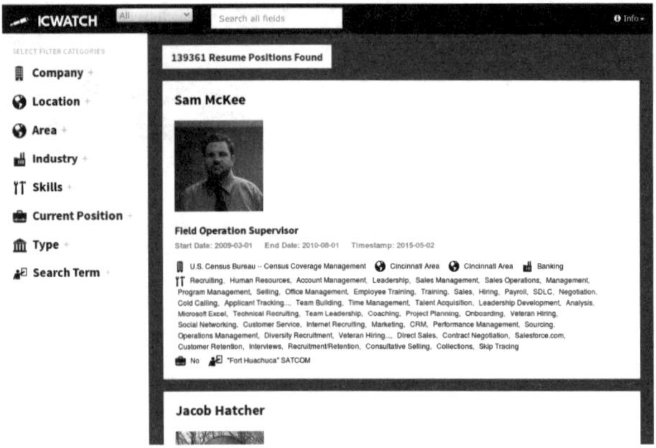


▲▲

▲ The *"App Center"* is a collection of *The White Room*'s recommended tools, plugins, and software with which to explore data traces and increase privacy online.

▲▲ *IC Watch* aggregates LinkedIn profiles to identify NSA employees working on its various surveillance programs. The profiles directly mention technical skills sets and the names of NSA surveillance programs.

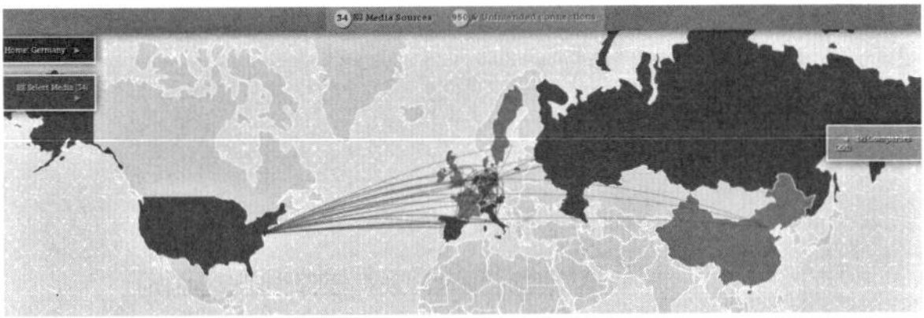


▲▲▲

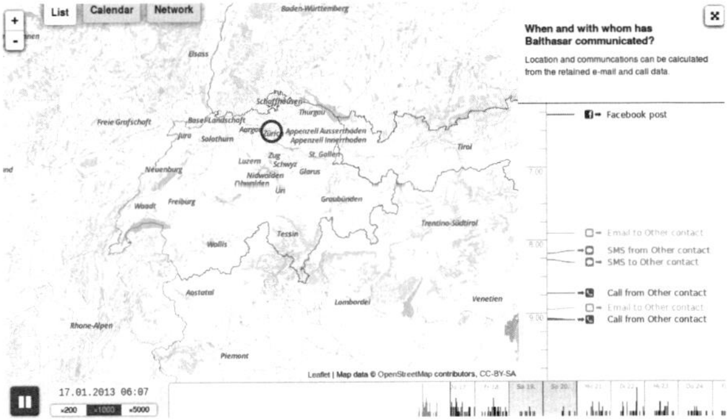


▲▲▲▲

▲▲▲
*Trackography* visualizes the data traces of anyone who reads news websites and the third-party trackers who trade in this data. It is based on data from close to two thousand news websites and blogs in thirty-eight countries.

▲▲▲▲
*The Monitored Life of National Councillor Balthasar Glättli* visualizes a six-month record of the personal and professional online and offline life of Swiss Green Party member Balthasar Glättli as recorded by his smartphone. Glättli used a Freedom of Information request to access his personal data in possession of telecommunications companies.

**Malte Spitz**

**#1**

```
X---ENDOFPNR---
LQ0732/1A MUC1A RM 04MAY
1.1SPITZ/MALTEMR
5 UA1793W 14JUN EZEIAD HK1   830P  609A^       TU/WE   E
EZE/0710CT/OFF   910A12.24L ARPT
IAD/1512CT/ETA   636P12.27L ARPT
6 UA 952M 17JUN IADFRA HK1   707P  910A^       FR/SA   E
IAD/0648CT/DPTS  707P        OT
FRA/0648CT/ARVS  910A        OT
7 LH 178H 18JUN FRATXL HK1  1015A 1120A          SA    E
8 CO  52Y 14JUN EZEIAH HK1   935P  615A^       TU/WE
SEAT DATA EXISTS       9D
FREQUENT FLYER DATA EXISTS       MP
FONE-MEMO  ETKT EVEN EXCHGD DUE TO IRROPS  DTWTC/12JUN/P5
2 NOTS/EMAIL:MALTESPITZ
3 NOTI/EMAIL:MALTESPITZ
TKTG-T/HDQ 13JUN1346Z R6 TS    ELECTRONIC TICKET
GFAX-OSIYY CTCT BER              b(6) & b(7)(C)
2 SSROTHSUA LHRTXL4843Q18JUN.NO ASR FLT/CLASS
3 SSROTHS1ANO1 PNR SUBJECT TO CANCEL DUE TO INVALID SFPD DATA
4 SSRADTK 1A TICKET UA SPACE BY 07MAY TO AVOID CANCEL
5 SSRDOCSUAHK1/////14APR84/M//SPITZ/MALTE/JOHANNES
6 OSIYY REAC CXLD UA0846 EZEIAD 13JUN 1802Z12JUN
7 OSIUA RECORD LOCATOR AC IS (b) (4)
8 SSRNSSACONN01 EZEIAH 0052Y 14JUN
9 SSROTHS1AKK1           ATTN LH
10 SSROTHS1AKK1 THE FLIGHT UA 846 ON 13 JUN FROM EZE-IAD
11 SSROTHS1AKK1 HAS BEEN XXLED DUE TO AIRPORT CONDITIONS.
12 SSROTHS1AKK1 IT DID NOT FLY FOR SURE.
13 SSROTHS1AKK1 DUE TO THE IRREGULAR OPRATIONS ITS OK TO
14 SSROTHS1AKK1 BOOK THE IAD-FRA IN B OR M CLASS.
15 SSROTHS1AKK1            UA/14JUN
16 OSIYY INVOL RERTD IADFRATXL DUE CANX UA 846 AUTHO FOR RERTG
/UPSELL
17 OSIYY BY UA IN PNR BERLH
18 SSRDOCSUAHK01 ALLFLT 0001        -1SPITZ/MALTEMR.P/DEU/
ZNZG/DEU/14APR84/M/05APR20/SPITZ/MALTE/
RMKS-1001 ROBOT AUTO-PROCESS 2359/07MAY2011 - SET 05/04/11 0219
2 A/ITN EMAIL-MALTESPITZ
3 A/ITN EMAIL-MALTESPITZ
4 A/ITN EMAIL-MALTESPITZ
5 A/ITN EMAIL-MALTESPITZ
6 XSELL 004 EPLUS: ACCEPTED
7 EPLUS RECEIPT FOR MALTESPITZ           PROCESSED/14JUN0852P
Z
8 XSELL 002 HERTZ: DECLINED
ACKN-UA/BD H76JC     04MAY 0746
2 UA/BD H76JC     10MAY 0330
3 CO AX1TPY    13JUN 1343
4 CO AX1TPY    14JUN 2232
---HISTORY---
RCVD-040746//1803A44C/
REC LOC-MUC1AZMTQFI/BERLH0808/2349012/BER/LH/A/DE//SU
```

▲

▲ *What are you doing with my Data?* evidences a process of how Malte Spitz, the German Green Party politician, author, and privacy activist, requested information from forty governmental institutions and commercial organizations—from police to airline records and from health information to credit ratings—to find out what information was held on him and how such data is collected and generated in Germany. Here, two documents from that collection are shown: PNRs of flights Spitz had taken and a letter from the police department stating that they had checked the Missing Persons and Deceased Persons databases.

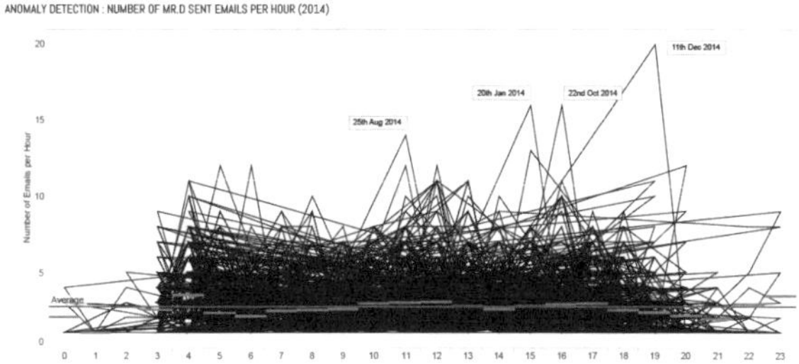


▲▲

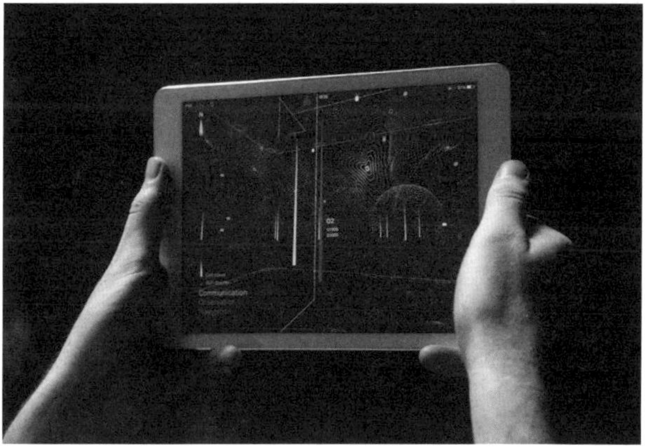

▲▲▲

▲▲ *Metadata Investigation: Inside Hacking Team* shows a detailed picture of the Italian surveillance technology company Hacking Team, who were hacked in 2015. Based only on email metadata, the visualization reveals the organization's dealings, social networks, internal communications, and relationships.

▲▲▲ *Architecture of Radio* is an iPad application that reveals an invisible landscape of Wi-Fi, satellite, and electromagnetic spectrum waves.

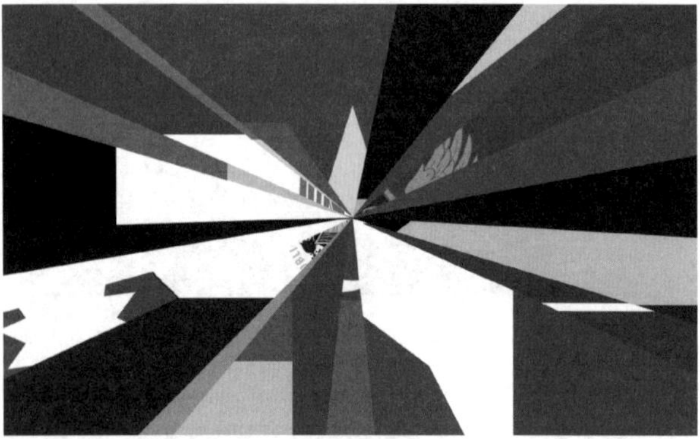

▲

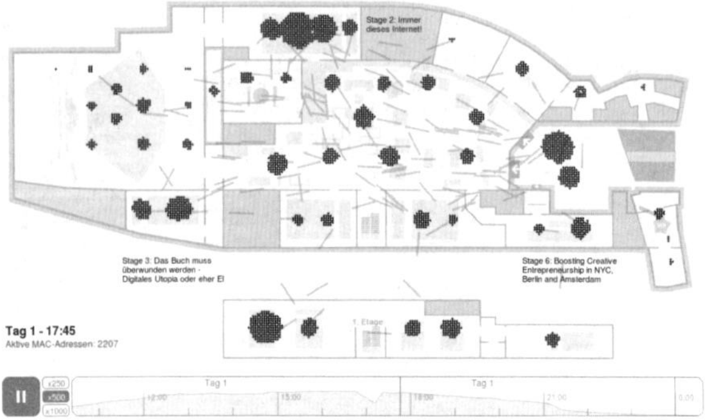


▲▲

▲ *Citizen Ex* is a browser extension that detects where the websites are that people have visited; and based on these results, computes a user's "algorithmic citizenship"—based on where a user "lives" online.

▲▲ *RE:LOG* is a visualization of flows of users connecting to public Wi-Fi and then moving around the re:publica conference held in Berlin in 2013.

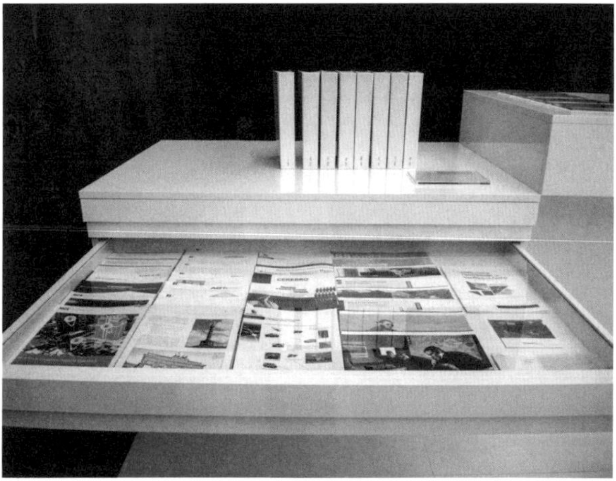

▲▲▲

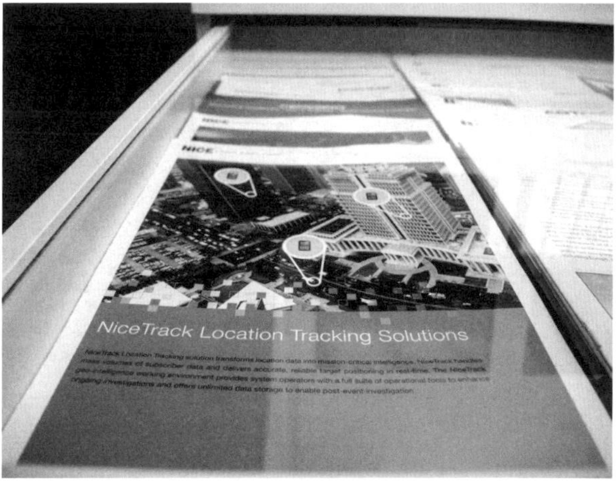


▲▲▲

▲▲▲
*The Wiretappers' Ball* contains some of the 287 brochures and promotional material collected by a network of investigators attending surveillance technology trade shows in Europe and North America. Here, a selection of these are seen installed in *The White Room*.

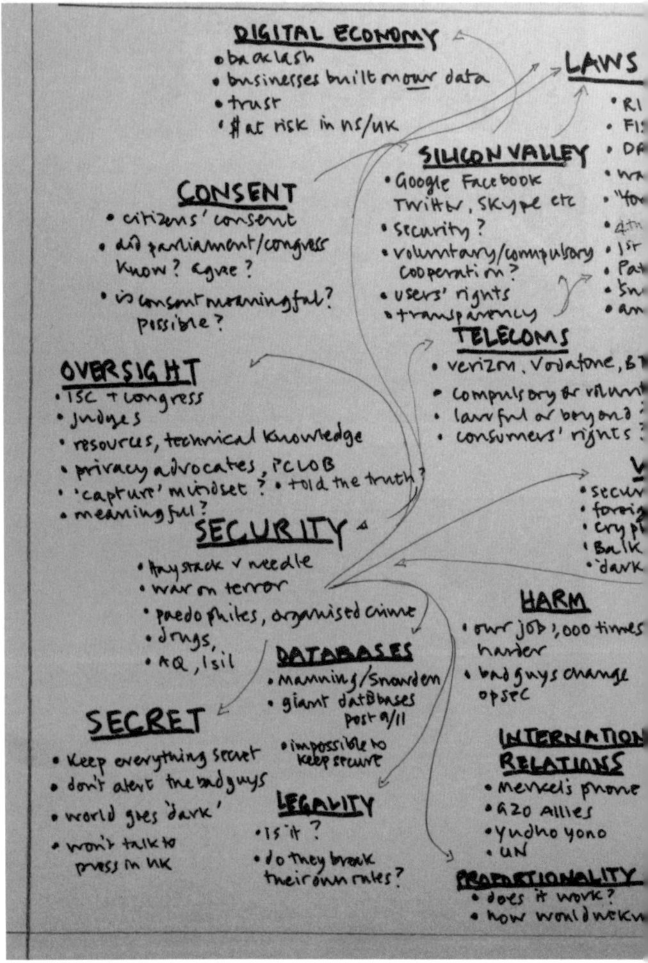


▲ *"If we had eyes to see what Snowden has given us"* is a mind-map created by *the Guardian* newspaper's former editor-in-chief Alan Rusbridger, showing the breadth and depth of the questions the Snowden documents reveal.

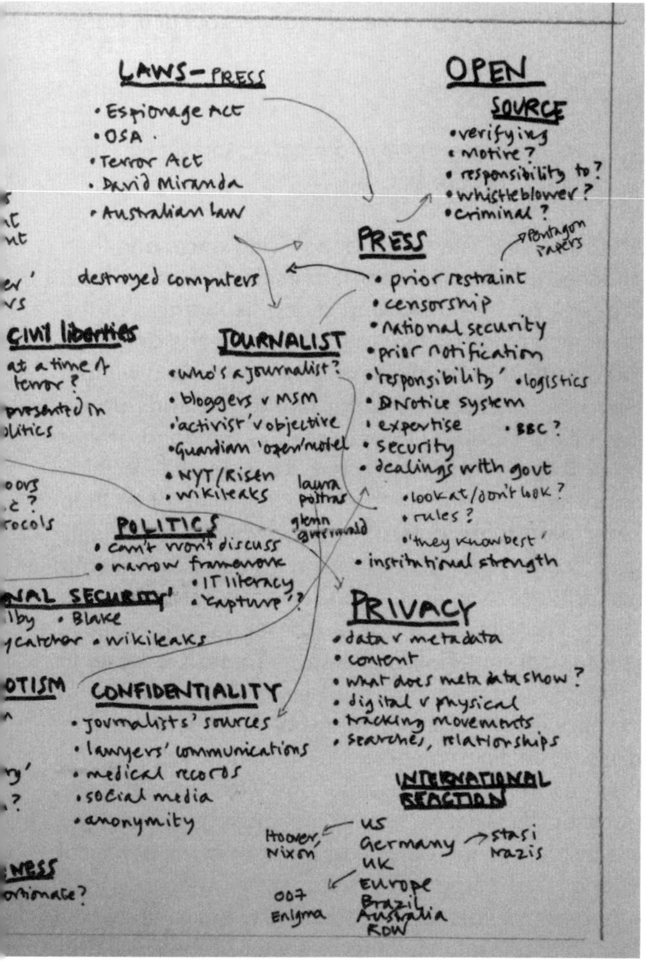
LAWS-PRESS
• Espionage Act
• OSA
• Terror Act
• David Miranda
• Australian law
destroyed computers
OPEN SOURCE
• verifying
• motive?
• responsibility to?
• whistleblower?
• criminal?
PRESS
Pentagon papers
• prior restraint
• censorship
• national security
• prior notification
• 'responsibility'
• logistics
• D Notice system
• expertise
• BBC?
• security
• dealings with govt
• look at/don't look?
• rules?
• 'they know best'
• institutional strength
civil liberties
JOURNALIST
• who's a journalist?
• bloggers v MSM
• 'activist' v objective
• Guardian 'open' model
• NYT/Risen
• wikileaks
laura poitras
glenn greenwald
POLITICS
• can't won't discuss
• narrow framework
• IT literacy
• 'capture'?
• Blake
• wikileaks
PRIVACY
• data v metadata
• content
• what does metadata show?
• digital v physical
• tracking movements
• searches, relationships
CONFIDENTIALITY
• journalists' sources
• lawyers' communications
• medical records
• social media
• anonymity
INTERNATIONAL REACTION
US
Germany
UK
Europe
Brazil
Australia
ROW
Hoover, Nixon
stasi
nazis
007
Enigma

## SOMETHING TO HIDE

> *The human skin is an artificial boundary; the world wanders into it, and the self wanders out of it, traffic is two-way and constant.*
> —Bernard Wolfe[5]

> *… we are drowning in information. And yet we know nothing. For sure.*[6]

A Möbius strip is a flat ribbon twisted once, and then attached end-to-end to form a circular twisted surface. Imagine an insect walking along its surface; at the beginning of the circular journey the insect is clearly on the outside, but it traverses the twisted ribbon without ever lifting its legs from the plane and ends up on the inside. Elizabeth Grosz uses this metaphor in her book *Volatile Bodies* to explore if it is possible to think about sexuality and the body in something other than binary terms. She presents the body and its materiality as a "conceptual blind spot" in contemporary feminist and philosophical theory: it is more than a just a "thing," but at the same time, it never quite rises above its physical materiality, she says. There is a need to resist reductionism and dualities and yet not give in to theories of holism or monism. There is a need to dissolve limiting categories of the body, yet ignoring them entirely is not possible. She wrestles with these questions in order to "rethink the relationship between the inside and the outside of the subject, its psychical interior and corporeal exterior by showing not their fundamental identity or reducibility, but to show the torsion of one into the other … the uncontrollable drift

5 Bernard Wolfe, *Limbo*, New York 1952, cited online http://faculty.georgetown.edu/irvinem/theory/Clark-Natural-Born-Cyborgs-Intro.pdf (accessed 02/16/2016).

6 Excerpt from an internal US NSA op-ed, "(U) Op-ed: Leave Bright Pebbles, Not I You," September 24, 2010, online https://fveydocs.org/document/leave-bright-pebbles/, archived May 28, 2015 (retrieved 05/28/2015, last accessed 02/12/2016).

of the inside into the outside and the outside into the inside."[7] The self, according to Grosz that is both—and neither—visible and invisible, gay and straight, this and that, is actually constructed by this in-between-ness, and "uncontrollable drift" from one pole to the other.

*Something to hide* explores two particular dimensions to this commonly heard response "nothing to hide"—in discussions about privacy and data protection: what the *self*, which is curiously both *something* and *nothing*, has come to mean in a *quantified society*. This is enabled by a series of works by creative, critical practitioners who use the very apparatuses of quantification as a means of exploring the relationship between the twin poles of quantification, and nothing-ness, the state of *nothing to hide*, which is assumed to exist despite the generation of data. Between self and nothing, what exists? Why is it so difficult to have something [to hide]? Avatars, profiles, and handles are phantom placeholders for online selves in a quantified world; as are the geolocations, phone-call metadata, and the billions of other data points generated online. The volume of data generated by a single person on their various quantified journeys is also not static; it is expanding and morphing so that it is impossible really, ever, to know it completely. At once both anonymous and identifiable, being, and not being, *just* a data point, what is the value of the citizen, consumer, and resident of the quantified society? Most likely: *something,* which is supposed to amount to *nothing*.

One of the features of the quantified society is the project of self-improvement through technical fixes, means, and services: "an atomic and anomic dream of self-mastery that elsewhere we call the "neoliberal subject," according to Benjamin H. Bratton in his text

7 Elisabeth Grosz, *Volatile Bodies: Toward a Corporeal Feminism*, Bloomington, IN 1994, 116.

"The Black-Stack."[8] This can range from enhancing the physical body to improving the perception and presentation of the self. If you don't really like the self you have, you can appear differently online under another name and some other appearance. You can frame your photograph around your very pretty face and have that "liked" by hundreds of people; the unhappy reality of everything below the neck conveniently ignored. In *Life Is Too Short*, Veridiana Zurita re-enacts self-help videos on YouTube. Unhappiness, depression, panic attacks, and fear of failure, all presented as limitations of the self that "experts" help overcome through "narratives of victory." Zurita asks what exactly it means to improve the self, who is so mimicable. *UnFitbits* follows in that vein; by hacking self-quantification devices, like the physiological activity monitor Fitbit, this series of objects reveals that the personal data used to determine insurance premiums, for example, could actually be rubbish. At the same time, *UnFitbits* introduces the possibility of the user-gone-rogue; "data dissent" in itself is an act of grace.

The paradox of the self emerges when self-knowledge derived from quantification is marketed as making you more efficient, attractive, or successful; however, when the quality of the knowledge or the means of quantification are exposed they are shown to be banal, meaningless, or even risky. In 2014 at Berlin's annual re:publica media and technology event, the culture jammers, Peng! Collective, masqueraded as Google executives and presented fictitious new products like *Bee* (a personal drone) and *Hug* (using geolocation to identify people close by who advertise they want to give and receive hugs). The jammers mimicked the casual, informal style of tech start-ups and the

8 Benjamin H. Bratton, "The Black Stack," *e-flux*, 2014, online http://www.e-flux.com/journal/the-black-stack/ (accessed 02/10/2016).

showmanship of tech-industry leaders, so that it took the audience a little while to understand that these were neither real products nor Silicon Valley executives. Peng! Collective's fictitious products seemed almost real: *Hug* in fact foreshadowed Cuddlr, which is like Tinder, but for people who want to hug strangers in a platonic manner. They played on the paradox of the self where there is an increase in personalization of devices and objects—from mobile phones to personal drones—and yet the data generated through these, while personal, are neither necessarily private nor belong to the individual. The weaknesses of the self, who feels lonely and needs a hug, is exploited to create unpaid labor, which powers a data-driven industry wrapped up in the fiction of personal empowerment.

*Buttons* by Sascha Pohflepp and *Descriptive Camera* by Matt Richardson are two works that tackle the idea of the self that has *nothing to hide* through an activity by which self is commonly produced in the quantified society: taking photographs. *Descriptive Camera* generates photographs that are not images but *descriptions* of images. When an image is taken and sent to Mechanical Turk, "Turkers" are tasked with writing a description of the image-content and returning it as a printout, much as a Polaroid camera returns an image. *Buttons* is a camera without a lens and only a shutter that records the exact time and location the shutter was released. This information is used to perform an online search, which returns a photograph with either the exact location metadata or the time of creation. *Buttons* suggests that your photograph, taken with a unique sense of individual place, expectation, and emotion, in fact, links to someone else's. According to Pohflepp:

> *In this project, we focus on the data about the time that a photo was taken, since we consider the notion*

> *of the moment of great importance. For almost any given moment since early 2004, it is possible to find a photo on the web which was taken in the exact same second. For every one of my photos that I myself have a memory of and an emotional connection to, I can see someone else's moment. I can see what happened in another part of the world while I was doing what I remember when I see it.*

Pohflepp's hacking of the infrastructure of self-knowledge suggests that the bright, white-room future may not be as robust as advertised. It is eventually, built on some *things*, and these things are potentially manipulable. Julian Oliver and Danja Vasiliev built *Newstweek* as a device for manipulating news read by other people on wireless hotspots. Built into a small and innocuous wall plug, it attacks the local wireless network such that all traffic is routed through itself, a "man-in-the-middle" exploit difficult to detect. The owner of the device can then remotely edit the news on that network, from anywhere on the internet, without the awareness of users at the compromised site. In one instance, the "BBC" "reported" that the United States wanted Julian Assange as its Secretary of Defense.[9] Aram Bartholl's *Forgot Your Password* is a series of printed books of LinkedIn passwords released in a leak. The books are a reminder that while on the one hand smooth, clean machines are actually messy, with leaks, holes, and unlocked back doors, on the other, they are an invitation to find ourselves in the data trove-turned-book, hiding behind our fig-leaf-like passwords. *Panda to Panda* by Jacob Appelbaum and Ai Weiwei also references the reality of vast amounts of data: what it does or

9 See: Julian Oliver, Gordan Savičić, and Danja Vasiliev, "Critical Engineering Manifesto," *The Critical Engineering Working Group*, 2011, online https://criticalengineering.org/ (accessed 02/10/2016).

does not mean when everyday panda soft toys are stuffed with the shredded printouts of the documents released by Edward Snowden. The piece asks why these documents are considered special and dangerous—three people have been exiled and jailed because of them—and shredding them, symbolically dismantles the aura of power assigned to data.

Self-knowledge through personal informatics is the starting point for change, a process Europeans have engaged with since the 1800s. To improve the self is to know the self and to know the self is to discipline and regulate the self. Michel Foucault's work on biopolitics traces shifts in the relationship between people and institutions of power and sovereign control from the top down, to formulate a model of discipline through distributed systems of control.[10] In the nineteenth century, as European governance and civic life started to alter with the demand for a reliable workforce for new industrial developments, citizens needed managing more carefully. There was a need for healthy, able-bodied workers to work the new engines of social development, and thus the state developed mechanisms to measure, record, and evaluate citizens. Through this, it was also possible to identify social "deviants": the poor, illegitimate children, the disabled, and the mad.[11]

This project to identify, name, and categorize people was made knifepoint sharp through colonialism. Portrait photography and biometric measurements —"*objective*" measurements—were used to document the physical features of people of color, to create

10 See: Michel Foucault, *Discipline and Punish: The Birth of the Prison*, tr. Alan Sheridan, 2nd ed., New York 1995; and Michel Foucault, *The History of Sexuality Volume 1: An Introduction*, tr. Robert Hurley, reissue ed., New York 1990.

11 See: Hamish Robertson and Joanne Travaglia, "Big data problems we face today can be traced to the social ordering practices of the 19th century," *The Impact Blog: The London School of Economics and Political Science*, October 13, 2015, online http://blogs.lse.ac.uk/impactofsocialsciences/2015/10/13/ideological-inheritances-in-the-data-revolution/ (accessed 02/10/2016).

eventually a rationale for colonialism, owing to the *scientific* superiority of white people. Apartheid erased black and mixed-race people from South Africa in a similar fashion. Apartheid was maintained through the bureaucratic applications of technology, such as biometric identifiers, elaborate racial categories, the identity passbooks referred to colloquially as *Dompas* ("stupid pass"), the forced removals of communities from their homes, and architectural and geographical segregation. Paul Edwards and Gabrielle Hecht write that, "The apartheid state aimed to manage its race-based identity registration—the hated passbooks and their related fingerprint databases—with computer technology, thereby muting the system's oppressive character beneath a quest for *bureaucratic efficiency through automation*."[12] There was, thus, an odd cancelling-out effect of any black or mixed-race citizens: making invisible through hyper-visibility, and using bureaucratic procedures for counting and monitoring people of color in order to manage and control them.

David Graeber uses the idea of structural violence to describe how bureaucracies and their technologies perpetuate violence, and further, that the threat of real, physical violence is what makes them successful as structures of violence too:

> *[F]orms of pervasive social inequality that are ultimately backed up by the threat of physical harm invariably tend to create the kinds of willful blindness we normally associate with bureaucratic procedures. To put it crudely: it is not so much that bureaucratic procedures are inherently stupid, or even that they tend to produce behavior that they themselves define as stupid, but rather, that they are invariably ways of*

12 The emphasis is our own, see: Paul N. Edwards and Gabrielle Hecht, "History and the Technopolitics of Identity: The Case of Apartheid South Africa," *Journal of South African Studies*, 36, 3 (2010): 619–39, here 620.

> *managing social situations that are already stupid because they are founded on structural violence.*[13]

Over time, what was "species-level" ordering through taxonomic systems of the nineteenth century became distributed systems of management through bureaucracies, technocratic management systems, theories of self, and computer networks. The process of self-knowledge and self-regulation continues now from the discipline society to the control society, seamlessly automated through a suite of online products and services, which can directly harvest data from personal movements and the one-account-for-everything. Increasingly we use technology, not only to self-regulate, but also to know ourselves through its regulation. Based on one's job, income, interests, education, aptitudes, and personality, dating websites promise to find one the most compatible mate; they offer custom-made algorithmic tweaks to achieve the best possible success at finding love, based on an analysis of a number of rational data points. Both Fitbits and dating websites present the self as a "black box," a creation of one's own, which we do not understand; one that technology can help understand and "fix." This is an idea played out to its nightmare conclusion in Charlie Brooker's dark series of televised short stories set in the not-to-distant-future, *Black Mirror* (2011). The quantified self, in this context, appears as a series of nested black boxes, indistinguishable from one another, and holding nothing entirely special.

13 David Graeber, "Dead zones of the imagination: On violence, bureaucracy, and interpretive labor. The 2006 Malinowski Memorial Lecture," *HAU: Journal of Ethnographic Theory*, 2, 2 (2012): 105–28, here 112, online http://eprints.lse.ac.uk/53222/1/Graeber_Dead_zones_imagination_2012.pdf (accessed 11/02/16).

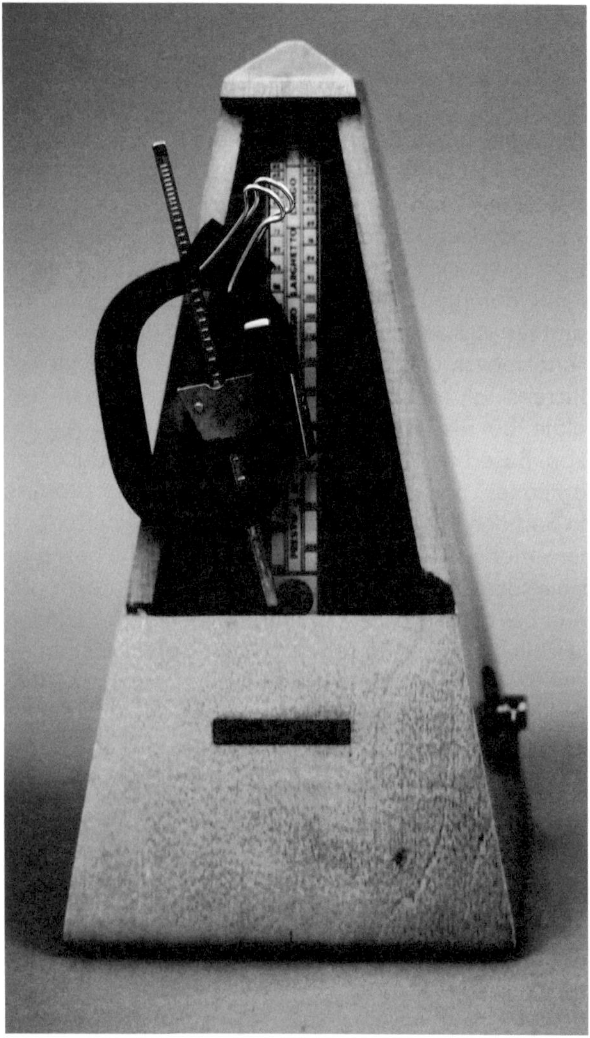

▲ *Metronome* is one of several devices from the *UnFitbits* series, provocations that generate fake physical-activity data for personal-activity trackers, such as that produced by the company FitBit.

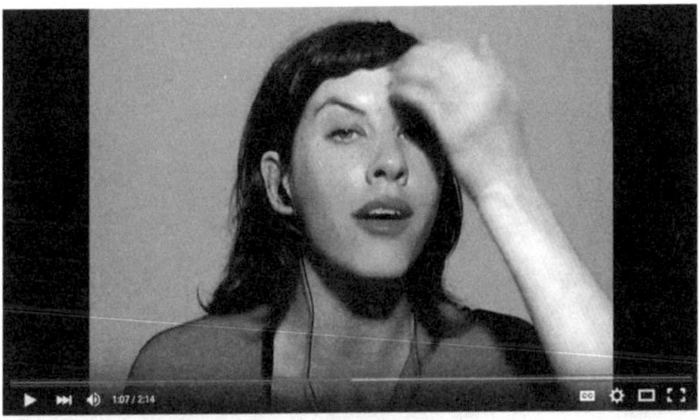

See how "Love" emotion affects your blood

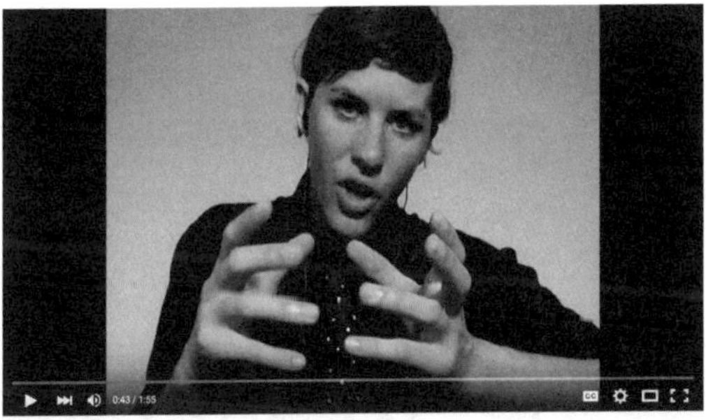

Strong Words From a Great Mind

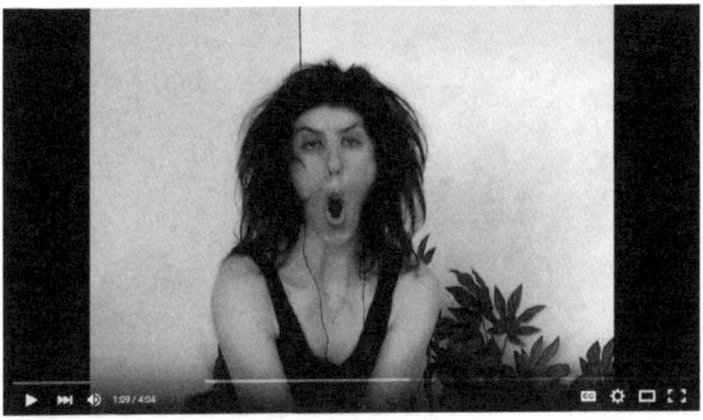

Facial Fitness System by Skyler Moore

▲▲

▲▲ *Life Is Too Short* is a series of video re-enactments of self-help YouTube videos that question the notion of individuality and self-made celebrity.

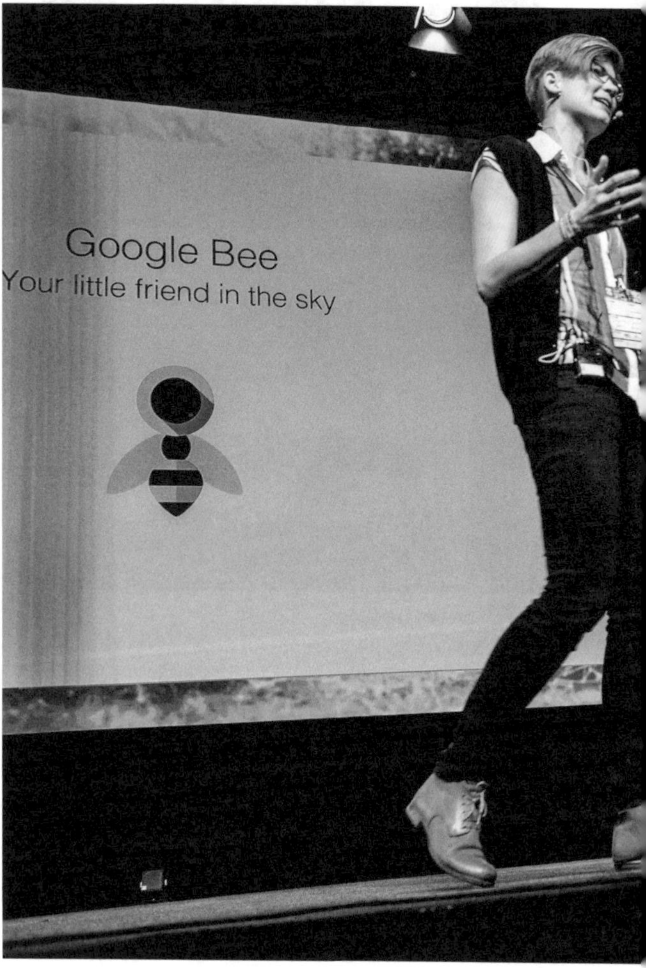


▲ *Bee* and *Hug* were hoax interventions presented at the technology and society conference re:publica in Berlin, 2013. Activists from the culture-jamming group Peng! Collective posed as Google executives marketing fictitious new products.

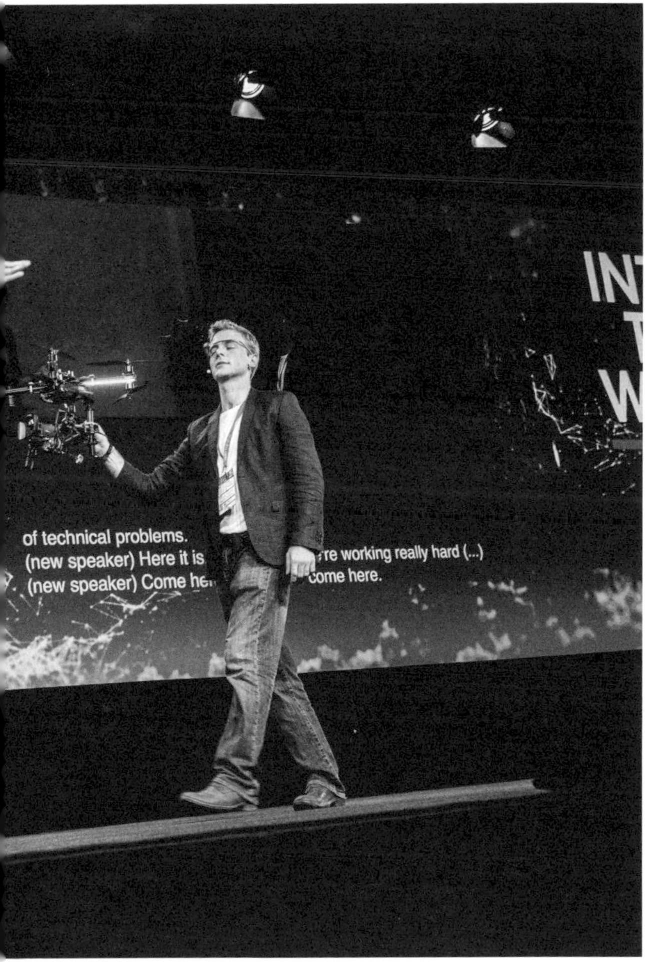
of technical problems.
(new speaker) Here it is
(new speaker) Come he
re working really hard (...)
come here.

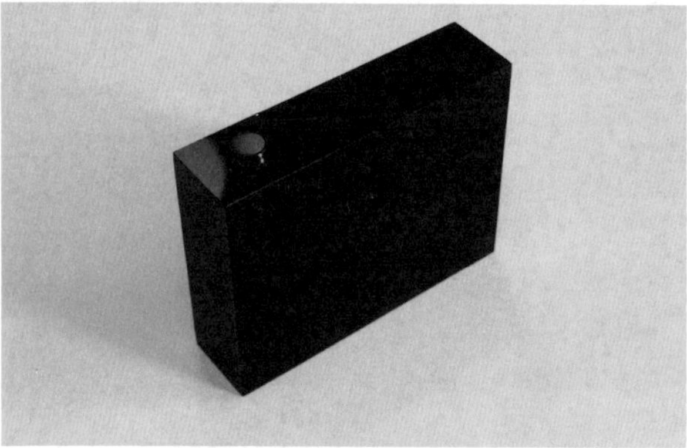

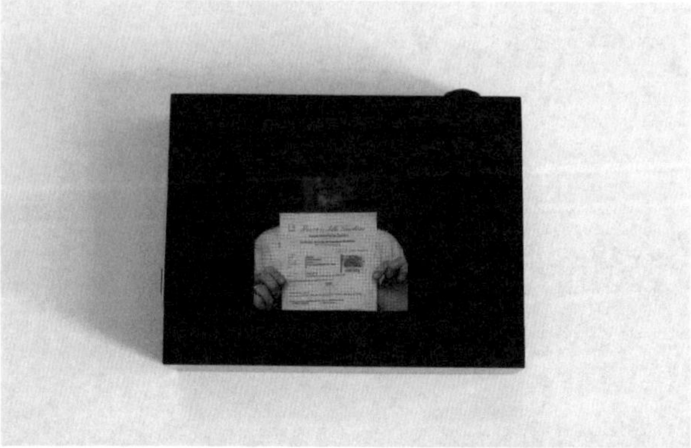

▲ *Buttons* is a camera without a lens and only a shutter that records the exact time and location the shutter was released. This information is used to perform an online search, which returns a photograph that was created either at the same location or at the exact same time.

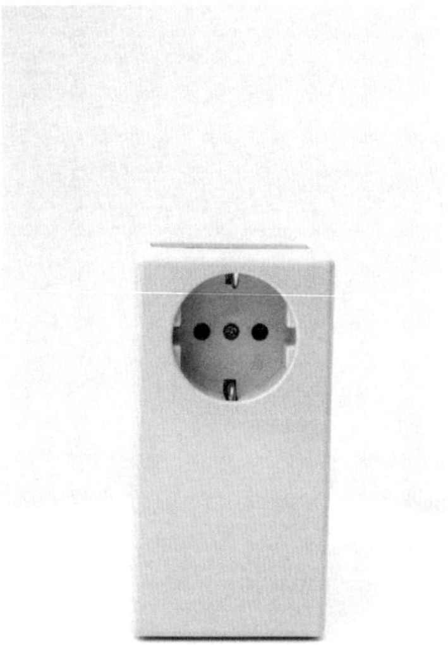

▲▲

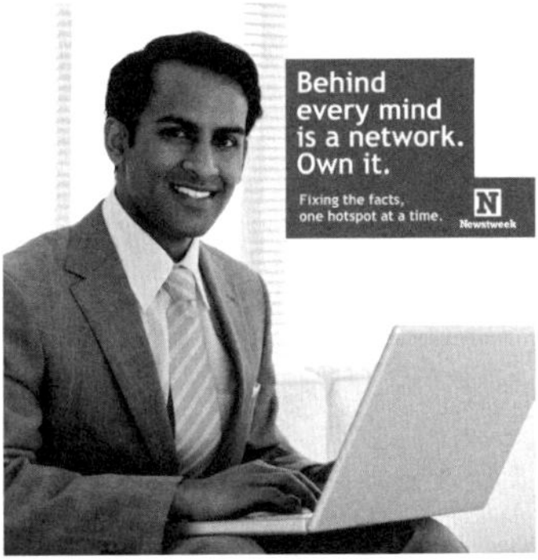


▲▲

▲▲ *Newstweek* is a small, innocuous wall plug that appears as part of the local Wi-Fi infrastructure. It allows writers to edit remotely news items read on wireless devices without users being aware, thus subverting the top-down model of news production as well as exposing the vulnerability of the wireless architecture.

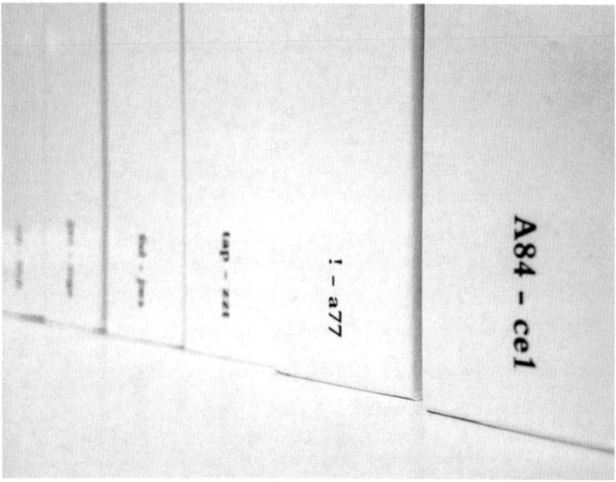


▲

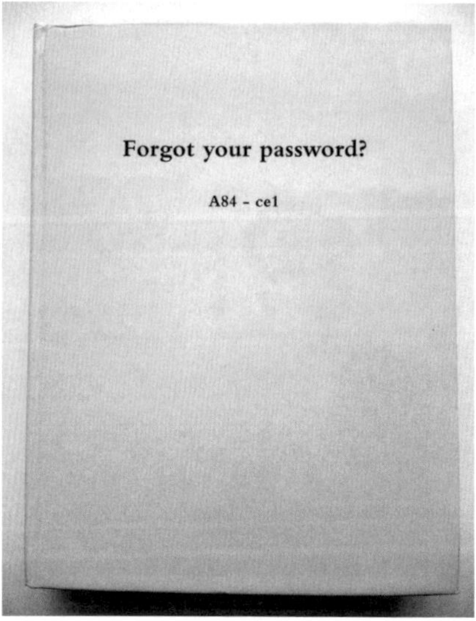


▲

▲ *Forgot Your Password* is a set of eight hardcover volumes of 4.7 million hacked and leaked LinkedIn passwords that invites viewers to browse through, perhaps even finding their own.

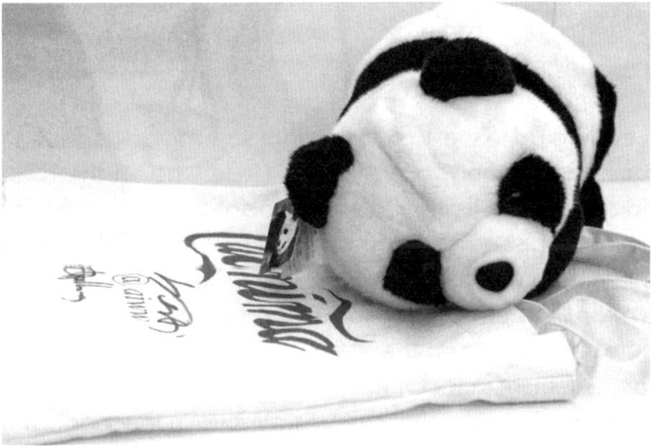

▲▲

▲▲ *Panda to Panda* is one of twenty toy pandas (in China, "panda" is a word used to refer to the secret police) stuffed with shredded paper copies of the documents released by the ex-NSA contractor and whistle-blower Edward Snowden; it also contains documents on an SD card.

## BIG MAMA

*The Cloud's fiction of infinite storage capacity for history ... is a misunderstanding that hinges on a weird, sad, very human hope that history might actually end, or at least reach some kind of perfect equipoise in which nothing terrible could ever happen again. As though if we could only collate and collect and process and store enough data points, the world's infinite vaporware of real-time data dashboards would align into some kind of ultimate sand mandala of total world knowledge, a proprietary data nirvana without terror or heartbreak or bankruptcy or death.*
—Ingrid Burrington[14]

Leading up to the 1973 coup that saw the assassination of President Salvador Allende, Chile was on the road to developing the world's first "socialist internet." British technologist and management guru, Stafford Beer, was developing with the Chilean government a communications system that collected and processed detailed information about the everyday lives of people, from absenteeism in factories to the outputs of factories, and various other economic issues. Writing in the magazine *Jacobin*, Eden Medina says of the project:

*The system would provide daily access to factory production data and a set of computer-based tools that the government could use to predict future economic behavior. It also included a futuristic operations room that would facilitate government decision-making through conversation and better comprehension of data. Beer named the system Cybersyn in recognition of cybernetics, the scientific principles guiding its*

14 Ingrid Burrington, "Why Amazon's Data Centers are Hidden in Spy Country," *The Atlantic*, January 8, 2016, online http://www.theatlantic.com/technology/archive/2016/01/amazon-web-services-data-center/423147/ (accessed 02/10/2016).

> *development, and* synergy, *the idea that the whole of the system was more than the sum of its technological parts.*[15]

The Cybersyn data, then shared with government agencies as tables, charts, and information graphics, was used to help decide on a course of action or relevant policies. The infographics, sent to the back room for immediate make-up by graphic designers and transferred to slide format, were then placed in a projector carousel wheel for viewing in the central control or "Opsroom." The arms of the chairs there had built-in cupped ashtrays, and buttons that simply changed the slides. Beer's son also developed opinion meters for workers to record their feelings about working conditions, but unfortunately, these never were implemented fully. Data collected from across the country was relayed back to factory workers, both to help them understand the context of the country and reflect on their own output, and in order to adapt their own practices. Cybersyn was never intended to be about government surveillance of people, it was seen as a genuine effort to understand and manage society through the collection of useful data.

There was, however, a distance between Cybersyn's vision and the technology of the day, so that the effort remained somewhat incomplete. Nevertheless, roughly thirty years later, Cybersyn achieved a sort of reincarnation halfway across the world in a different geopolitical context and with some radically updated technologies. In the months after 9/11, Peter Ho, Singapore's permanent secretary of defense, visited Rear Admiral John Poindexter at the United States Defense Advanced Research Projects Agency (DARPA),

15 See: Eden Medina, "The Cybersyn Revolution: Five Lessons from a Socialist Computing Project in Salvador Allende's Chile," *Jacobin, 17: Ours to Master* (Spring 2015), online https://www.jacobinmag.com/2015/04/allende-chile-beer-medina-cybersyn/ (accessed 02/10/2016).

responsible for supporting early development of some of the useful, innovative technologies of the day: the internet, Google Maps, GPS, Siri, and video conferencing, to name a few. Ho was there to talk about a new system that Poindexter had developed to harness enormous amounts of electronic information and analyze it for patterns of suspicious activity—mainly potential terrorist attacks. Poindexter's Total Information Awareness (TIA) program proposed to collect all electronic messages—emails, call logs, hotel and plane bookings, credit card transactions, medical reports—and use these to detect traces left behind by terrorists planning future attacks. While this program never received formal approval in the United States, because it was believed to contravene the country's laws around personal privacy and liberty, it was quietly exported to Singapore where it is now a thriving program known as *Risk Assessment and Horizon Scanning (RAHS)*. The program collects data about various aspects of current and future scenarios facing the small island-city state, which informs government policy. Current projects under RAHS include "Developing Strategies for Building Student-Centric Meritocracy" and "Examining the Attitudes of Young Singaporeans towards Emigration." What is in fact a system of total top-down surveillance has transformed into a system of collaboration and care. Unlike most other surveillance regimes, the Singapore government has implemented this system in an open and participatory way, closely monitoring citizens' actions and feelings by operationalizing it under the umbrella of the nation's well-being.

Top-down state surveillance by the "Five Eyes" has taken over discussions of technology since the Snowden revelations, but seen through the perspective of the Chilean and Singaporean examples, more than Big Brother, there is a sense of Big *Mother*. The artifacts in the section of *The White Room* called *Big*

*Mama* demonstrate the idea that the state's reinvention of itself as either e-government or digital agency, and its use of data and the development of industries and infrastructure for this, is dressed up as *care*. If the Hollywood-inspired vision of surveillance includes sleek spies scaling buildings and dangling off helicopters, and gifted, if slightly unhinged, hackers wearing black, the reality is more banal: it is your mother with all her quirks, strong instincts for protection, and perhaps a flower-print dress.

This notion of care and protection is evident in the development of applications like Healthy Day or *Sickweather*, both of which encourage users to report their own symptoms, and signs of flu and disease (coughing, sneezing, fever, etc.) in others. What emerges from the screen in *Sickweather* are hundreds of bubbles pinpointing coughs, fevers, and sneezes identified by others, a sort of topography of hypochondria. By encouraging the volunteering of personal data and the tracking of other people's symptoms—now marketed as "disease surveillance"—these apps build a database that aims to predict the future likelihood of disease outbreaks. The phrase "disease surveillance" has long been used in Public Health without irony. The United Nations Global Pulse Program is conceptualized along similar lines, to track a range of different kinds of data from social media to census data, but with a global perspective and a mandate to apprehend the fallouts of human-made and natural disasters and disease epidemics.

The institutionalization of observation, tracking, and pattern recognition, changes when enfolded within a discourse of care and community. For example, *Churchix* is "facial recognition software [designed] for Church administrators and event managers who want to save the pain of manually tracking their members' attendance to their events." Schools monitor children's computer usage to keep them safe from harmful online content; the state uses predictive policing to prevent crime in an effort to "keep communities safe." From CyberSyn to *Churchix* there is a discourse of lateral surveillance among communities of care to maintain safety and security. To surveil another is to contribute valuable information toward the greater good. In China, *Sesame Credit* refers to vast troves of personal user-data to rate consumer's credit worthiness. The buying habits, interests, social graph, and comments of a user are exploited to evaluate creditworthiness. For markets in developing countries, micro-credit companies are rolling out a credit-ratings design that analyzes data from Facebook profiles, how often and by how much you top-up your mobile phone credit, and, as in Indonesia, based on the type of roof on your house—concrete or tiled—as identified through aerial photographs. There is a trickle-down effect here, resulting in what is known as data-veillance, surveillance through data, not for concerns of national security, but for corporate and state bureaucracy. Bruce Schneier states, "surveillance is the business model of the internet," one that seeps into different institutional and interpersonal relationships.[16]

Combining financial services with data-veillance fosters what Josh Lauer refers to as a mechanism of social control through "moral accounting." Looking at the history of the financial system, Lauer notes that there was a time when calculation of creditworthiness was in terms of personal characteristics, such as one's position in the social hierarchy.[17] With the evolution of the financial industries and the banking system, this then shifted to more specific data points based on income, financial assets, and one's ability to meet debt. With

16 Bruce Schneier, *Data and Goliath: The Hidden Battles to Collect Your Data and Control Your World*, London 2015.

17 Josh Lauer, "The Good Consumer: Credit Reporting and the Invention of Financial Identity in the United States, 1840–1940," *Enterprise & Society*, 11, 4 (2010), 686–94, online https://muse.jhu.edu/login?auth=0&type=summary&url=/journals/enterprise_and_society/v011/11.4.lauer.pdf (accessed 02/13/2016).

data-veillance, there has been a subtle, real shift back to character-based evaluations of creditworthiness based on identity, as evidenced through digital footprints: place of residence, social networks, personal and leisure habits, all of which is easily tracked and analyzed now, to make predications and enforce regulations. Philosopher Antoinette Rouvroy uses the term "data behaviorism" to refer to this practice:

> *The implicit belief accompanying the growth of "big data" is that, provided one has access to massive amounts of raw data (and the world is actually submersed by astronomical amounts of digital data), one might become able to anticipate most phenomena (including human behaviours) of the physical and the digital worlds, thanks to relatively simple algorithms allowing, on a purely inductive statistic basis, to build models of behaviours or patterns, without having to consider either causes or intentions. I will call "data behaviourism" this new way of producing knowledge about future preferences attitudes, behaviours or events without considering the subject's psychological motivations, speeches or narratives, but rather relying on data.*[18]

Other projects adopted by governments in partnership with corporations raise questions about how state power is being reshaped in a quantified society, leading to new views of the ever-increasing trend for outsourcing. The *Nigerian National Identity Card* project, which combines biometrics, voting, residency, movement, and spending data, is in the process of implementation in partnership with MasterCard, a financial services company. A Freedom of Information request from Paradigm Initiative

18 Antoinette Rouvroy, "The End(s) of Critique: Data-behaviourism vs. Due-process," in: Mireille Hildebrandt and Ekatarina de Vries (eds), *Privacy, Due Process and the Computational Turn: The philosophy of law meets the philosophy of technology*, Abingdon, Oxon, and New York 2012, 1.

Nigeria (PIN) to the Nigerian Identity Management Commission asking for details of the contract awarded to MasterCard was ignored on a technicality, and workers at PIN were harassed. This promoted the need to send "reminder letters" to the Identity Management Commission, asking them to reply to the Freedom of Information request. The United Nations High Commission for Refugees (UNHCR) has set up a cash-delivery system to Syrian refugees with the Cairo-based Amman Bank, which scans the irises of would-be beneficiaries to verify their identities. The iris scanners are made by IrisGuard, a company that has the former head of MI6 and the homeland security advisor to the US president as two of their three advisory board members. Lockheed Martin, one of the world's most notorious defense contractors and weapons manufacturers, implemented the US census in 2000 and 2010, the UK census in 2001 and 2011, and the Canadian census in 2006 and 2011. Why?

In the *Big Mama* world, low-grade surveillance has been pushed into institutional infrastructures, into self-regulation and lateral surveillance. This is also a world of the weakened social contract between individuals and the state, one in which corporations have carved out a stronger role for themselves. While governments have been instrumental in funding technology developments that have brought us to this state of data ubiquity, they are increasingly taking up a facilitative role. They do not build or own the infrastructure, but instead outsource to private companies, helping themselves to the systems they have seeded but no longer need to finance or fuel. In this sense, states become somewhat parasitic: they feed off the scale of the data industry and citizens' self-motivated efforts to create continuously more data. As old and new industries—governments, weapons manufacturers, online dating services—jump into the data business, the system picks up a new rhythm and scale.

NGOs and international aid and development actors are similarly excited at the prospect of data infrastructures to predict, manage, and improve social and civic problems. While Karen Levy states "rape is not a data problem," Hollywood stars support data hackathons to "end sexual violence in conflict" in the Congo. A slew of "innovation projects" have been initiated to tackle complex issues such as illegal political detention, child protection legislation, medicine distribution tracking, gender inequalities, water supply monitoring, and more such, across Africa and Asia: there is no problem too big that it cannot be fixed with the application of data.

New personal tracking tools such as "ethical apps" monitor personal consumption and generate data geared at reducing environmental footprints, and creating efficient transport and smart housing. Between the "quantified self" and the "smart city" falls the shadow of the benevolently surveilled: "It's for your own good." The city-state of Andorra has sold all its data to various companies in order to raise capital for itself and its smart city future. Somewhere there is a belief—among NGOs and civil society, both in the global North and South—that the chaos of rogue *tuk-tuk* drivers, crony capitalist-infested government bureaucracies, histories of ethnic violence, and endemic social inequalities can all be bureaucratically managed by data, such as open government data. Both the Clinton and Gates foundations have contributed to an initiative called "No Ceilings: The Full Participation Project," to accumulate all available statistics about girls and women worldwide in order to inform initiatives for gender equality; the problem of gender inequality can only be addressed if there are no more *knowledge gaps*. The system is no longer a management flowchart or a rapidly sketched infographic slide, as in *Project Cybersyn*. The system has been animated.

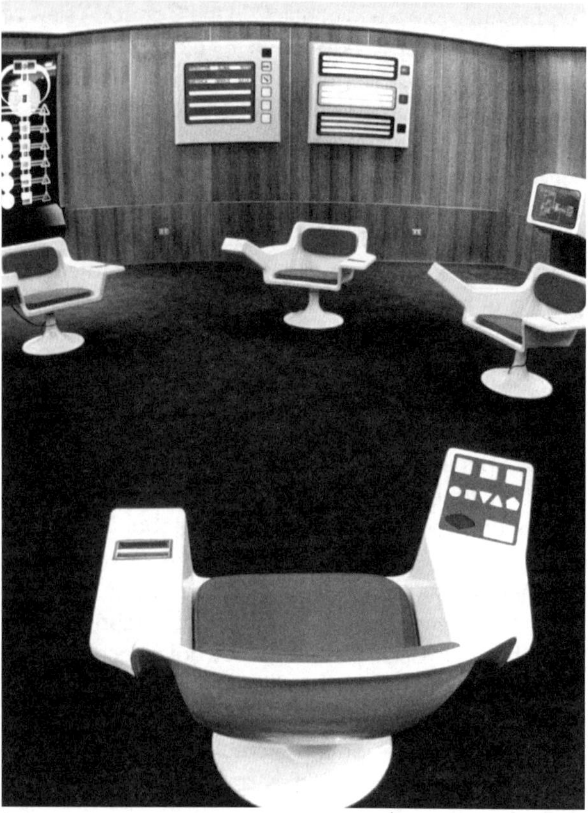

▲

▲ The control room, "Opsroom," of *Project Cybersyn*, the cybernetic governance project of the former Chilean president Salvador Allende in collaboration with Stafford Beer, a British engineer.

PARADIGM INITIATIVE NIGERIA

**Paradigm Initiative Nigeria**

LAGOS: 2nd Floor, 385 Herbert Macaulay Way
Yaba, Lagos, Nigeria
+234 1 342 62 45

eMail: info@pinigeria.org
Website: www.pinigeria.org

ABUJA: 2nd Floor (Rock & Rule Suite)
Valley Mall, 215 Ademola Adetokunbo Crescent
Wuse II, Abuja, Nigeria
+234 9 291 63 01

September 4, 2014

The Director General/Chief Executive
National Identity Management Commission
11 Sokode Crescent
Off Dalaba Street
Zone 5, Wuse

NATIONAL IDENTITY MANAGEMENT COMMISSION
OFFICE OF ... RECEIVED
11 SEP 2014
RECEIVED

Dear Sir,

**Freedom of Information Request: Procurement and Contract Records for the Provision of Payment Solution by MasterCard for General Multi-Purpose Card**

On behalf of the Paradigm Initiative Nigeria and the Public and Private Development Centre, and in accordance with the Freedom of Information Act 2011, I write to request for copies of the procurement and contract documents for the above referred contracting process.

I hereby specifically request for contracting records including:

1. Copies of all documents showing the contract details, including the contract sum, the contract currency, the effective (start) date of the contract and the end date of the contract, the terms and conditions of the contract, payment schedule, the payment terms, etc;
2. Signed copies of letter of award and final contract award documents for the award of this contract;
3. A NEEDS assessment document justifying this project;
4. A procurement and project plan clearly showing timelines for implementation of various phases of the project;
5. Documentation showing expected impact of the project;
6. Copies of documents containing the specification and scope of services to be provided by MasterCard;
7. Copies of documents showing the specification and scope of services to be provided by Access Bank;



▲▲

▲▲ The *Nigerian National Identity Card* is in the process of implementation in partnership with MasterCard. Paradigm Initiative Nigeria (PIN) and the Public Private Development Centre (PPDC) put in Freedom of Information requests to learn more about the procurement process by which MasterCard won the contract from the Nigerian government. The card acts both as a biometric identification card and provides "financial solutions" for so-called "unbanked" citizens.

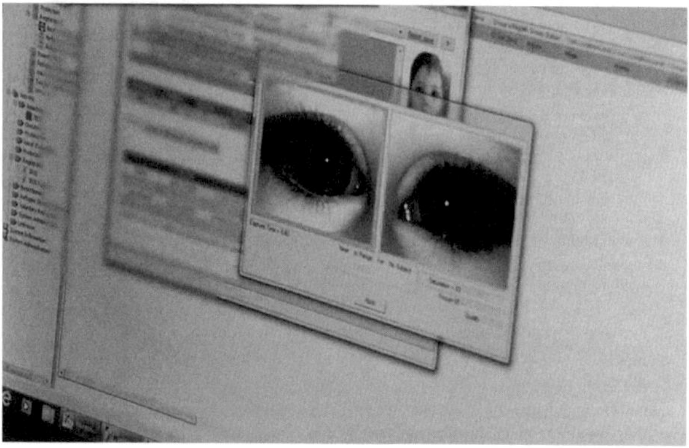

▲

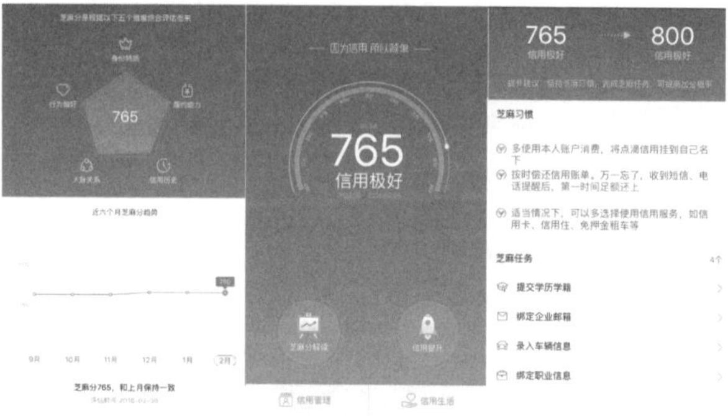


▲▲

▲ *The United Nations High Commissioner for Refugees (UNHCR)* uses IrisGuard's technology to scan the irises of customers to validate their identity. This is considered a secure and reliable way to disburse cash to Syrian refugees via ATMs. Here, screen shots from a promotional video by UNHCR depicts how it works; over 1.6 million refugees were on the database by 2016.

▲▲ *Sesame Credit* is a credit-rating system that creates scores based on spending behavior, habits, patterns, interests, and affiliations. It is created by Ant Financial Services, the financial arm of the world's largest online shopping platform: Chinese technology company Alibaba.

## NORMAL IS BORING

*We know where you are, we know where you've been, we more or less know what you are thinking about.*
—Eric Schmidt[19]

*Any sufficiently advanced technology is indistinguishable from magic.*
—Arthur C. Clarke[20]

The US-American state of California has been at the epicenter of disruption through technology since 1872. In that year, Edward James Muybridge photographed a galloping horse named Occident, owned by one Leland Stanford, who founded and generously funded the American university of the same name in memory of his son. Muybridge's early photographs were the first time an image of high-speed motion had been captured, such that it was possible to see that a galloping horse, at some point, has all four hooves off the ground. Rebecca Solnit refers to these early photographs as "[the] bridge to a new art that would transform the world."[21] Moving images were an invention of slightly after and in parallel with the railroad, and both were transforming ideas of time and space. Railroads were connecting people from different places, resulting in a refreshing sense of both liberation and alienation, in equal measure. Moving images could conjure up the past, and convey ideas, people, and occurrences happening in faraway places. There was no need to be bound to the immediate or the local. These

19 Eric Schmidt, former Google CEO, May 23, 2013, quoted in: Derek Thompson, "The laws are written by lobbyists," *The Atlantic*, October 1, 2010, online http://perma.cc/A3PN-3XFT (accessed 02/13/2016).

20 Arthur C. Clarke, the "Third Law," in: *Profiles of the Future: An Inquiry Into the Limits of the Possible*, New York 1962, rev. 1973, 73 note.

21 Rebecca Solnit, *River of Shadows: Edward Muybridge and the Technological Wild West*, New York 2003, 3.

changes completely undid the beliefs and perceptions of everyday people. Solnit continues, that "annihilating time and space is what most new technologies aspire to do: technology regards the very terms of our bodily existence as burdensome."[22]

In the late 1950s, California saw another radical departure, this time in how the business of science and technology was organized. The "Traitorous Eight" were a group of eight scientists who, under the leadership of a scientist called Robert Noyce, left the Nobel Prize-winning, leading developer of semiconductors at the time, William Shockley. They were unhappy with the controlling work environment at Shockley Semiconductors and wanted a different kind of workplace where they didn't have to be suits. They just wanted to build semiconductors. Noyce and his group relocated to California, where, with the money from entrepreneur Sherman Fairchild, they set up a technology business called Fairchild Semiconductors. Robert Noyce and Jack Kilbey are credited with assembling the first integrated circuit, the founding of Intel, and thereby, Silicon Valley as it is known today.

This legacy of dissent and disruption persists. "Disruption" is a sought-after commodity, with disruptive technologies like Uber and Airbnb being wildly successful, and fundamentally altering the core infrastructure and working of an economy. Evgeny Morozov notes that where once a taxi company transported passengers, now, they connect drivers to passengers. None of this is actually about transporting people, on which traditional taxi companies tended to focus: "Most platforms are parasitic: feeding off existing social and economic relations. They don't produce anything on their own—they only rearrange bits and

22 Idem., 11.

pieces developed by someone else."[23] The internet was a space for radical shifts in communities of knowledge-production for fifteen years, according to the Israeli-American Yochai Benklar, Professor of Entrepreneurial Legal Studies at Harvard Law School, but has shifted to the wholesale commercialization and digitization of this as a service industry in the past five years. There has been an externalization of risk onto customers, and the erasure of the social and communitarian solidarity with service providers such as Uber drivers and Turk-ers. Thus, when Uber drivers turn away disabled passengers, or rape customers in cabs, and drivers themselves can be fired via SMS, Uber itself is not held responsible for any of this: they aren't a company, see, they're just a platform.

The success of the "Un-companies" powering the new sharing economies is attributable in part to start-up culture, a distinctive organizational, lexical and design aesthetic that celebrates "disruption" and "anarchy." According to Kate Losse, part of the ethos taught to young employees at Facebook is how to "break things": "If you're not breaking things in Palo Alto, you're not doing your job." Losse notes that being a young, white man is license to "break things"; people of color who "trespass" into University Avenue in Palo Alto are more likely to be "Stopped & Frisked."[24] The belief in the power of breaking things is now available off the shelf, like something Andy Warhol promised we could buy. *Radimparency* (Vooza, 2012) is a short film that aptly captures the canned disruption that technology entrepreneurs believe is fundamental to the creation of their products.

23 Evgeny Morozov, "Where Uber and Amazon rule: Welcome to the world of the platform," *the Guardian*, Sunday June 7, 2015, online http://www.theguardian.com/technology/2015/jun/07/facebook-uber-amazon-platform-economy (accessed 02/13/2016).

24 Kate Losse, "The Unbearable Whiteness of Breaking Things," *Medium*, 2013, online https://medium.com/@katelosse/the-unbearable-whiteness-of-breaking-things-521cb394fda2#.xqk9dfche (accessed 02/10/2016).

Start-up culture is as much myth as how-to guide. It is believed there are ways to replicate the mythology of Steve Jobs and Steve Wozniak cooking up the future in a grungy garage. This signature style now finds itself iterated worldwide, through open-plan offices with table tennis tables and cappuccino machines, from Silicon Allee in Berlin to Silicon Savannah in Nairobi and Chilecon Valley in Santiago, each gambling on the new oil-rush of data. As they hit the ground in other contexts, they take on new forms, mushrooming into giants with new scope and reaching across entire regions, such as China's internet giants Alibaba, Baidu, and Tencent.

Back in California, the aesthetic continues to evolve beyond technology production to values and social commentary. The reception area in GitHub's head office in San Francisco is a replica of the Oval Office; however, the carpet in the foyer reads "In Meritocracy We Trust." Swearing allegiance to hard work and success, the text has no disclaimers about this switch in faith. The head office of Palantir (the data-mining company whose main client is the CIA), named *The Shire*, evokes J. R. R. Tolkien's fantasy trilogy, *Lord of the Rings*. Maybe it's just fun and games or maybe it's a certain worldview that informs the views of Peter Thiel, venture capitalist and co-founder of PayPal and Palantir. In his book *Zero to One: Notes on Startups, or How to Build the Future* (2014), he advocates running start-ups as cults: "The startup uniform encapsulates a simple but essential principle: Everyone at your company should be different in the same way—a tribe of like-minded people fiercely devoted to the company's mission."[25]

The roots of the disruptive sentiment are grounded on the libertarian design of the technologies on which

25 Idem.

these tools and services run. Most of these technologies and services have grown out of the decentralized and open principles of the internet and from the philosophy of free and open source technologies. While these ideas were nurtured for many years by hobbyists and geeks who thought they could change the world in one way, these technologies have now been subsumed into large corporations that think they can change the world in some other way. Lord Richard Allan, Facebook's Head of Policy, frequently speaks at civil society conferences describing Facebook as "a load of hackers and hippies" trying to realize the "democratizing force" of the internet. On the surface, this is California meets cybernetics, birthplace of the *Whole Earth Catalog* and the internet. Underneath, it is business: the radical ideas of ingenious mathematicians and engineers have now become the designs of marketing departments, Washington, D.C. migrants, and Wall Street analysts. There is now a sad irony that Facebook is located at a "vanity address": 1 Hacker Way, Menlo Park, CA, 94025.

To others, the idea that big business has corrupted utopic ideals is the wrong reading: for Alexander Galloway, for example:

> *[T]he founding principle of the Net is control, not freedom. Control has existed since the beginning. Perhaps it is a different type of control than we are used to seeing. It is a type of control based on openness, inclusion, universalism, and flexibility. It is control borne from high degrees of technical organization (protocol), not this or that limitation on individual freedom or decision making (fascism)....*[26]

26 Alexander Galloway, *Protocol: How Control Exists After Decentralization*, Cambridge, MA 2004, 142.

Is it possible that we bought into the idea that a distributed network was an equal one, that control was impossible when power became diffuse, and in doing so, overlooked a more technocratic way of thinking?

From the outside, what we notice most among the various Silicon spaces are the primary colors of the offices, the youthful genius founders, the nerdy coders. This serious economy still does not have a serious image. Additionally, we as consumers do not yet treat our participation in the accumulation of their power seriously. *The Google Empire* is the third largest company on Earth, making a bankable net profit of fifteen billion dollars annually. In 2015, Google's parent company, Alphabet, owned more than 270 other companies and invested in many more. Google thinks in terms of "moonshots," in its case literally, as the company will award thirty million dollars to winners of the XPrize Foundation challenge who manage to land their robots on the surface of the moon, travel 500 meters over the lunar surface, and send images and data back to Earth. The moon is perhaps all that remains, since Google has digitized hundreds of millions of books, entered our homes through the temperature-regulating Nest, and our cars, with Android Auto, and mastered machine learning across their suite of services. Google makes robots for the US Military through the subsidiary company Boston Dynamics; can recreate the US census based on mining Gmail data; and owns a patent: 8,996,429; a robot with a feature called "Be Mom," which changes personalities based on user-information mined from location, events, photographs, audio, and social media information.

Fred Wilson, the Silicon Valley venture capitalist, states that tech companies have moved from creating "laughable toys to becoming dominant monopolies in a decade." The anonymity of the individual becomes increasingly impossible, while the opacity of institutions and those in power increases, in what Frank Pasquale refers to as the "Black Box Society." There is "the one-way mirror" he says, where "[important] corporate actors have unprecedented knowledge of the minutiae of our daily lives, while we know little to nothing about how they use this knowledge to influence the important decisions that we—and they—make."[27] Google has not only an army of engineers and scientists with doctorates, but also lobbyists, a revolving door with government, and, on their payroll, most of the scholars leading critical debate, notably in areas such as information ethics. Jared Cohen, Google's "Director of Ideas," came from the State Department, working as an advisor to both Condoleezza Rice and Hillary Clinton. The book he wrote with the then-CEO of Google, Eric Schmidt, titled *The New Digital Age: Reshaping the Future of People, Nations and Business* (2013), he lectures on worldwide in order to dissipate Google's insights into International Relations.

*Scientia potentia est*, or, Knowledge is power, was the motto over the door of the Information Awareness Office run by John Poindexter, the National Security Advisor to the Reagan administration. The question is to whom should we entrust this power?

The question seems to have been answered: the "tech-oligarchs." Zuckerberg doubled his personal wealth by a 100 percent in just one year, a gain of fifteen billion dollars. Bill Gates is the richest man in America, for the sixteenth year running, and is now worth over eighty billion dollars. In his book *The Internet is NOT the Answer*, Andrew Keen asks, how can a network designed to have no center or—the internet—a network designed to have "neither a heart, a

27 Frank Pasquale, *The Black Box Society: The Secret Algorithms that Control Money and Information*, Cambridge, MA 2015, 9.

hierarchy, nor a central dot" have such a "top down winner take all economy?"[28]

These one percent-ers have now assumed the position of second-generation social cyberneticians believing they can solve the problems of "the next billion" through their inventions, foundations, and companies. It is believed that the infrastructure and capital that enables the sharing economy and social media will offer solutions for infrastructural gaps in the developing world, as if they were literal, physical, gaps and not complex social, economic, and political issues. Mixing philanthropy with can-do capitalism, there is no accountability framework—such as human rights—that informs the cybernetic fixes promised to the developing world. Humanitarian aid and development interventions usually have to reconcile with effects at a local level. In the design and engineering of technology, however, things just need to work in a lab, or in the Silicon Valley bubble, not *in situ*. How are local power struggles, corruption, social inequalities, and resource and income disparities reckoned with in rolling out Wi-Fi generating air balloons? The messy political, social, and ethical questions are pushed down the line to marketing departments and in-house lawyers, something Facebook's Free Basics program has had to learn in relocating from Hacker Way to the streets of India.

Not all the tech-oligarchs are investing in the emerging market of the global South though; some spend their money on trying to help us get away from our earthly realities. Elon Musk of PayPal has invested in colonizing Mars; others, such Musk's colleague, PayPal co-founder Peter Thiel, experimented with "seasteading," a project that aims to establish "permanent, autonomous ocean communities to enable

28 Andrew Keen, *The Internet is NOT the Answer*, London 2015.

experimentation and innovation with diverse social, political, and legal systems."[29] Thiel, like Google, now dabbles in "radical life extension," or, "longevity" technologies; Bill Gates is working in a different direction, seeking to control not death, but birth. In 2018, a Gates-funded lab in Boston, Microchips Biotech Inc., will roll out a slow-release contraceptive chip that can be implanted in a woman's body for up to sixteen years to remotely control of her fertility: *the Fertility Chip* is seen as a technical solution with "great potential for the developing world."

Each of these acts of faith and innovation—eradicating poverty, prolonging life and preventing it, exploring and colonizing new territories—show that what was traditionally the work of governments, is now in new hands. It is testament to the rapid and acute accumulation of power, knowledge, and wealth that we now see centered around Silicon Valley and its emulators, and to ongoing participation in its rapid evolution. In this sense, the information revolution may have more in common with the Industrial Revolution than we imagined. If we could capture an image of high-speed motion now, it may perhaps not be the horse whose hooves we see simultaneously lifted off the ground. Edward Muybridge may not have pictured any of this.

29 See the Seasteading Institute, online http://www.webcitation.org/5aLaQdMrS (accessed 02/10/2016).

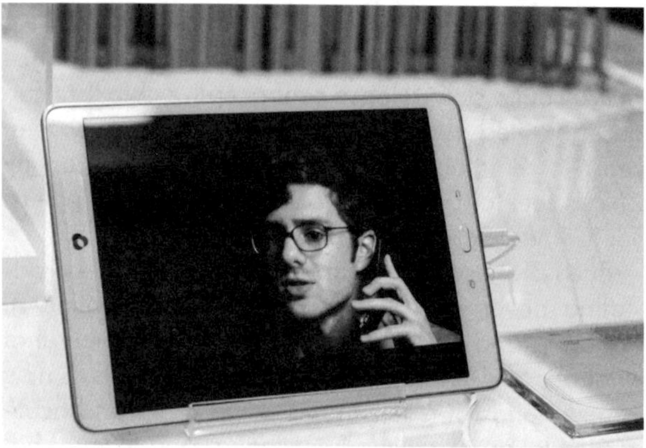

▲

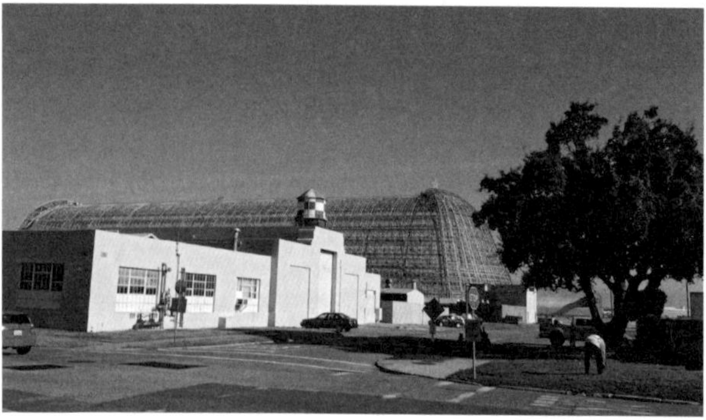

▲▲

▲ *Radimparency* is a parody of a promotional video for a fictitious digital product with a "pitch" feel. Replete with tech start-up buzzwords and clichés, Vooza takes the ideology and terminology of the "Un-company" to the extreme.

▲▲ "Moonshot" projects in Silicon Valley are ambitious in terms of scale: sometimes they are literally about the moon. Google has invested thirty million US dollars in the start-up Moon Express, which is developing technology to extract resources from the moon.

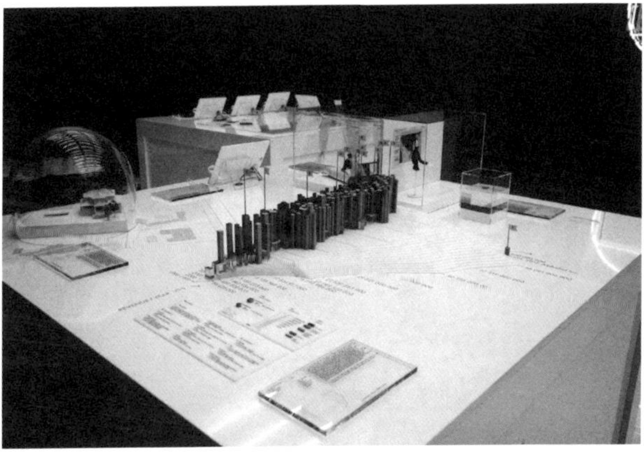

▲▲▲

▲▲▲
Installation shot of *Normal is Boring*.

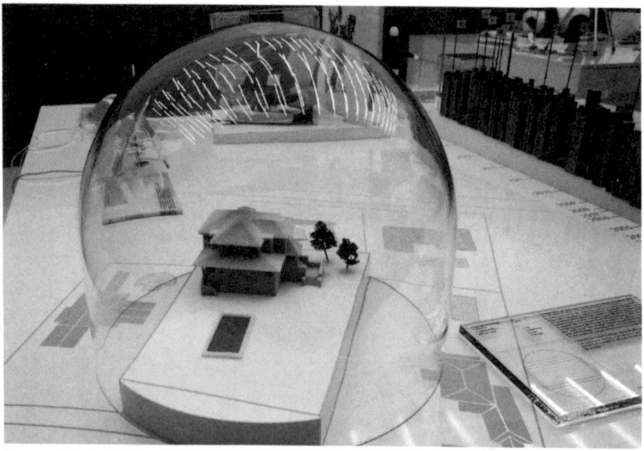

▲

▲ *The Zuckerberg House* is inspired by reports that between 2012 and 2013 Mark Zuckerberg, the founder of Facebook, paid over forty million US dollars to buy the four houses surrounding his own home in Palo Alto, California. This is in contrast to a talk he gave in 2010, where he stated that "social norms" had changed around privacy, and he was widely quoted in the news media as stating that the age of privacy is over.

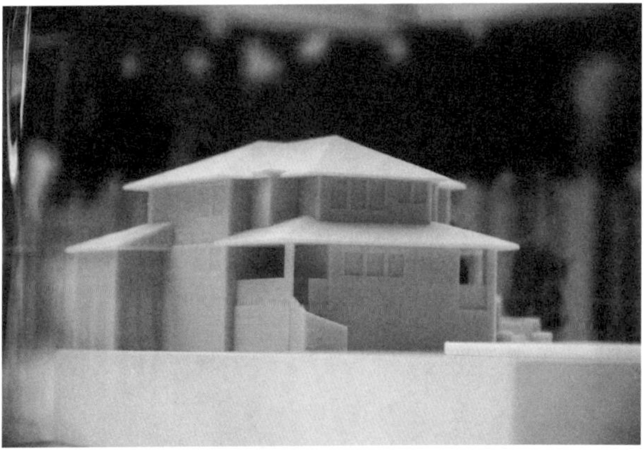

▲

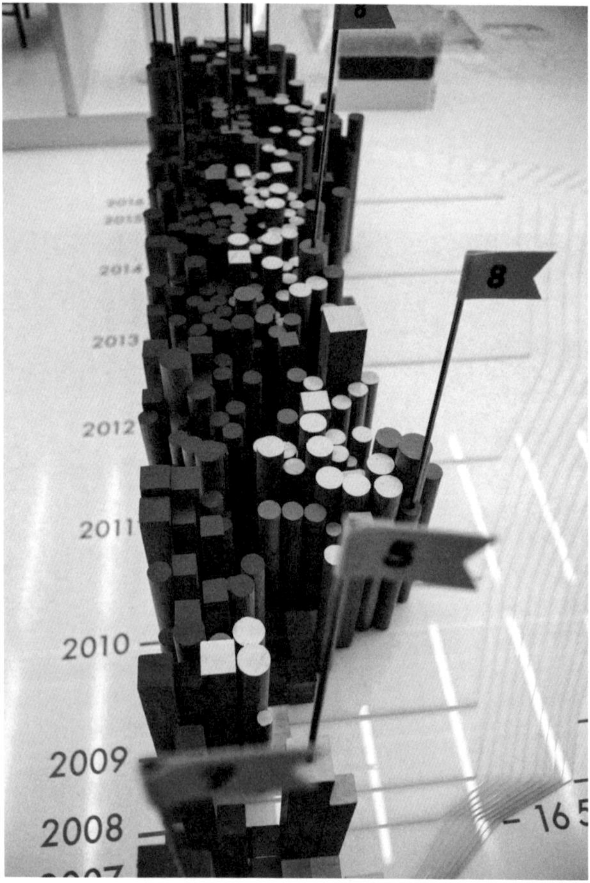


▲

▲ The *Google Empire* is a three-dimensional infographic showing the 180 companies Google has acquired, and the more than 400 companies it has invested in since it was founded in 1998. Now re-branded as Alphabet, the infographic shows the company's rapid growth to different markets, from home security to self-driving cars and from DNA databases to robotics.

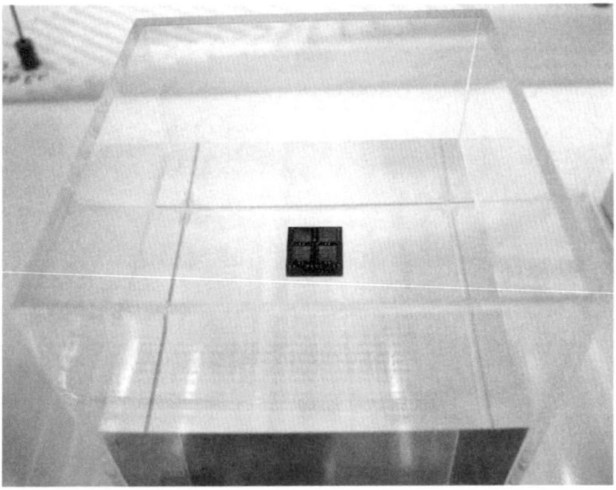

▲▲

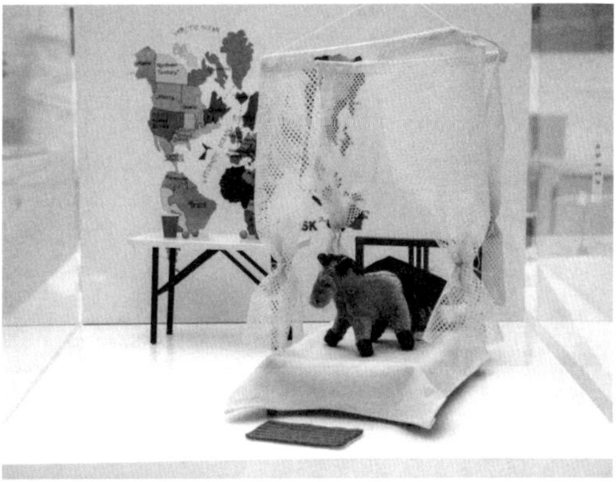

▲▲▲

▲▲ *The Fertility Chip* is inspired by widely available images of a chip funded by the Bill and Melinda Gates Foundation, being developed by a US-based company Microchips Biotech Inc. The chip can be implanted in a woman's body for up to sixteen years to remotely control her fertility, with a particular focus on women in "developing countries." The chip is currently under development and is set to be trialed in 2018.

▲▲▲
*The Shire* is a model inspired by photographs of Palantir's office taken by Peter DaSilva for *The New York Times* in May 2014. The data-analysis company, founded by PayPal founder Peter Thiel, has contracts with twelve US Government Groups including the CIA, NSA, and FBI, the Marine Corps and the Air Force. The world map on the wall of a meeting room is based on the strategy board game "Risk: The Game of Global Domination." In the world of venture capital a "Unicorn" is a start-up worth a billion dollars or more.

# APPENDIX

# THE ARTISTS

Lawrence Abu Hamdan is an artist, "private ear," and currently a fellow at the Vera List Center for Art and Politics at the New School, New York City. The artist's forensic audio investigations are conducted as part of his research for Forensic Architecture at Goldsmiths, University of London, where he is also a PhD candidate. His solo exhibitions include *Earshot* at Portikus Frankfurt (2016); *(Taqiyya)* at Kunsthalle St Gallen (2015); *Tape Echo* (2013) in Beirut, Cairo, and at Van Abbemuseum, Eindhoven; *The Freedom of Speech Itself* (2012) at The Showroom, London; and *The Whole Truth* (2012) at Casco, Utrecht. In addition, his works have been exhibited and performed at the New Museum Triennial (2015), Shanghai Biennial (2014), and at the Whitechapel Gallery and Tate Modern, London, the Museu d'Art Contemporani de Barcelona (MACBA), and the Museum of Modern Art Antwerp (MuHKA).

Vito Acconci, based in New York, has been a vital presence in contemporary art since the late 1960s. His confrontational, ultimately political works have evolved from writing through Conceptual art, bodyworks, performance, film, video, multimedia installation and architectural sculpture. Implicating the viewer as witness, Acconci assumes a manipulative stance in aggressive or seductive encounters with the spectator. Solo exhibitions include those at the Sonnabend Gallery, New York; Museum of Contemporary Art, Chicago; Kölnischer Kunstverein, Cologne; and Brooklyn Museum, Whitney Museum of American Art, and MoMA, all in New York, among others.

Timo Arnall is the co-founder of Ottica, working with design, product invention, filmmaking, photography, and strategy to develop and explain emerging technologies through visual experiments, films, visualizations, speculative products, and interfaces. Over fifteen years he has directed commercials, animated films, designed exhibitions and urban screens, and built web and mobile applications. Recent exhibitions include those at MoMA, New York, and the Victoria and Albert Museum and Design Museum in London. Arnall is part of the visiting faculty at several institutions and gives regular talks about design, media, and technology at international conferences. He has a PhD in interaction design.

Mari Bastashevski is based between Lausanne, Berlin, and Kiev. Her work, spread across the disciplines of investigative research, journalism, and art, deliberately crosses the boundaries between them in an attempt to challenge existing information-delivery modes and bridge the spaces between these practices. Bastashevski's work has been featured in *Medium*, *Prix Pictet*, *Time* magazine, *The New York Times*, *Courrier International*, *Le Monde*, and *Vice*, and has been exhibited at Musée de l'Élysée (nominee Prix Elysée), Lausanne; Art Souterrain, Montréal; Noorderlicht Photofestival, the Netherlands; the Open Society Foundation, London; and Galerie Polaris, Paris, among others. In 2010, she spent a year as artist in residency at Cité Internationale des Arts, Paris. She studied Art History and Political Science in Copenhagen.

Emma Charles is a London-based artist. Working with photography and video/film, her practice stems from an inquiry into temporality. Drawn to the boundary as a physical and conceptual notion, she uses the photographic medium as a tool to address wider social and political systems of time and space. Charles has been particularly concerned with the financial sector and the perceived alteration of time, productivity, and labor through technology. More recently, she has directed her practice toward exploring the materiality of the internet, seeking to uncover the hidden, physical infrastructures that support our technology-driven lives.

Mike Crane is an artist based in New York. He is a graduate of the Cooper Union School of Art. His work has been exhibited at the Bass Museum of Art, Miami; Manifest Gallery; Ohio; Centre for Contemporary Art, Derry, Northern Ireland; Friday Exit, Austria; Dublin City Gallery The Hugh Lane; Chashama Gallery, Harlem; and the Banff Centre in Alberta, Canada, among others. Most recently, his work has been exhibited at the Bronx Museum Biennial and the Berlinale Forum Expanded. In 2015, Crane was an artist in residence at the Triangle Arts Association, Brooklyn, and at the Rupert Centre, Lithuania. He was awarded an apexart Award in 2014 and a Creative Capital visual arts grant in 2015. Mike Crane will be a recipient of a 2016–17 New York Community Trust Van Lier Fellowship as part of his Smack Mellon Studio Program residency.

Stéphane Degoutin is an artist who lives and works in Paris. He creates film, video, and sound installations, theoretical texts, and places, such as *Mute*, *Empty*, and *Cyborgs in the Mist*, or the photoblog *Lost in Créteil*. He co-founded the collective project "Nogo Voyages." He is author of the essay "Voluntary Prisoners of the American Dream" (2006); and teaches at École nationale supérieure des arts décoratifs, Paris. Gwenola Wagon is an artist and a professor in the Art Department of the Université de Paris 8. She has produced numerous video, sound, and interactive installations in France and abroad, including *Blackpool Manchester*, *Globodrome*, *Hypnorama*, *le Musée du terrorisme*, *Discothèque sauvage*, and *Mute*.

Arthur M. Eisenson is a screenwriter based in Los Angeles. While he was a student at Stanford University he co-produced with Gary Feldman *Ellis D. Kropotechev and Zeus, A Marvelous Time-Sharing Device*—a parody of the trials and tribulations of a college hacker. His credits include the long-running series *Kojak: Mouse* (1978) and the TV movie *Beggarman, Thief* (1979).

Harun Farocki (1944–2014) lived and worked in Berlin as a filmmaker, artist, and writer. His essay and observational films question the production and perception of images, decoding film as a medium and examining how audiovisual culture is related to history, politics, technology, and war. His projects have been shown at festivals and in solo, group, and retrospective exhibitions worldwide, at important events and international institutions, including the 2010 São Paulo Biennial; Documenta X and XXII,

Kassel; Tate Modern, London; Museu d'Art Contemporani de Barcelona (MACBA); Museum Ludwig, Cologne; and Galerie nationale du Jeu de Paume, Paris. Between 2011 and 2014, Harun Farocki realized the long-term project *Labour in a Single Shot*, together with Antje Ehmann.

Charles Gaines is a Los Angeles-based artist celebrated for his photographs, drawings, and works on paper, which investigate how rules-based procedures construct order and meaning. In 2015, he presented a critically acclaimed retrospective exhibition at the Hammer Museum, Los Angeles, which had traveled from the Studio Museum, Harlem. Recently, his work has been featured in major group exhibitions at the Museum of Contemporary Art, Chicago; the 56th Biennale, Venice (2015); the Contemporary Arts Center, New Orleans (2014); and the Montréal Biennale (2014).

Melanie Gilligan, based in New York, works in video, performance, installation, and music. She studied Fine Art at Central Saint Martins, London, and was a fellow at the Whitney Independent Study Program, Manhattan. She regularly contributes to publications, such as *Artforum*, *Texte zur Kunst*, *Mute*, and *Grey Room*. Selected solo exhibitions include those at Künstlerhaus KM, Graz (2016), de Appel, Amsterdam (2015), Museum De Hallen, Haarlem (2014), Casco, Utrecht (2014), Chisenhale Gallery, London, and Kölnischer Kunstverein, Cologne (2010). Upcoming and recent exhibitions include Trondheim Kunstmuseum, Jumex Foundation, Mexico City (2016), British Art Show 8, Leeds (2015), Dojima River Biennial, Osaka (2015), Fridericianum, Kassel (2015), and MoMA PS1, New York (2014).

Goldin+Senneby define themselves as a "collaborative framework exploring juridical, financial and spatial constructs." The elusiveness of this description is somewhat apt. Since 2004, when Simon Goldin and Jakob Senneby started working as a duo, they have speculated around the layerings of contemporary economics, analyzing and employing different dimensions of financial markets. Their collaborative strategies have shaped a withdrawn approach wherein the artists are akin to puppeteers: "their production mostly comprises choreographing the labour of others" (João Laia, *Frieze*).

Laurent Grasso lives and works between Paris and New York. His work has been presented in solo exhibitions including the Hermès Foundation, Tokyo; Musée d'Art Contemporain de Montréal; Kunsthaus Baselland, Muttenz, Switzerland; Jeu de Paume, Paris; Hirschhorn Museum and Sculpture Garden, Washington; Bass Museum of Art, Miami; Palais de Tokyo; Centre Pompidou, Paris; and the MIT List Visual Arts Center, Cambridge, USA. He has participated in the Gwangju Biennal, Manifesta, Sharjah Biennale, Moscow Biennale, and Busan Biennale. He has conceived a number of public installations.

Douglas Huebler (1924–1997) established himself as a minimal artist in the early 1960s. He was part of the seminal show *Primary Structures* at the Jewish Museum in 1966. During the late 1960s, Huebler focused on Conceptual work, using diverse systems of documentation to chronicle rule-based but unscripted events and encounters in his "Duration Pieces," "Variable Pieces," and "Location Pieces." His solo shows include retrospectives at the Palais des Beaux-Arts, Brussels (1994), Camden Arts Centre, London (2002), the Musée d'art moderne et contemporain (Mamco), Geneva (2006), and Paula Cooper Gallery, New York (2012). Selected group exhibitions include Documenta 5, Kassel (1972) and *A Minimal Future? Art as Object 1958–1968*, Museum of Contemporary Art, Los Angeles (2004). He is currently represented by Paula Cooper Gallery.

On Kawara (1933–2014) was a Japanese Conceptual artist based in New York, where he was an intermittent resident until his death. Stripping art of aesthetics and reducing it to pure information, On Kawara gave special prominence to language as did Lawrence Weiner, Joseph Kosuth, and Hanne Darboven. His exhibitions comprise, among others, a retrospective at the Solomon R. Guggenheim Museum, New York, an exhibition at the Museum für Moderne Kunst (MMK), Frankfurt, and participation a number of times in Documenta exhibitions, and the Venice Biennale.

Paul Klee (1879–1940), one of the most important figures for the formation of modern art, started his artistic career as part of the German pre-war avant-garde group *Der Blaue Reiter*, at which time he affiliated with Wassily Kandinsky and August Macke. In 1920 he was appointed to the Bauhaus, the school of art founded by Walter Gropius. He taught there until his call to the Kunstakademie, Düsseldorf, in 1931. After Hitler's rise to power, he immigrated to Switzerland where he died.

Korpys/Löffler, based in Bremen, is an artist duo concerned with the question of technological mediation and the power structures related to this mediation. Starting as filmmakers in the early 1990s, they have collaborated ever since. Recent exhibitions include those at the Zentrum für Kunst und Medientechnologie (ZKM) Karlsruhe; Kunst-Werke Institute for Contemporary Art, Berlin; Kunsthalle Düsseldorf; Galerie Meyer Riegger, Karlsruhe; Marta Herford; Museion, Bolzano; K21 Kunstsammlung Nordrhein-Westfalen, Düsseldorf; and Manifesta 7 in Trento. In addition, they are lecturers at the Hochschule für Künste Bremen.

Audrey Maurion studied philosophy at the Sorbonne in Paris, where she lives and works as a director and film editor. She was head of the editing team on a number of documentaries and features. *I Love you all* (2004), Maurion's second cooperation with Eyal Sivan as co-director, was awarded the Special Jury Award of the Taiwan International Documentary Festival (TIDF) in 2005, and the Jury Award of the Festival Internazionale FILMMAKER Doc 9, Milan, in 2004.

!Mediengruppe Bitnik, based in Zurich and London, and founded in 2003, work on and with the internet. Consisting of Carmen Weisskopf and Domagoj Smoljo, their practice expands from the digital to affect physical spaces. Their works have been shown internationally including at the M21: 21st Century Minsheng Art Museum, Shanghai; Kunsthaus Zürich; The Netherlands Media Art Institute, Amsterdam; Space Gallery, London; Cabaret Voltaire, Zurich; Beton7, Athens; Museum Folkwang, Essen; the Contemporary Art Center, Vilnius; and the Roaming Biennale of Tehran. In addition, the practice has received a number of awards, including the Swiss Art Award, Migros New Media Jubilee Award, and Honorary Mention at Prix Ars Electronica.

Henrik Olesen discusses questions about identity, language, the body, and their construction, to describe relations of power and social norms. Recent solo exhibitions include: Museum Ludwig/Wolfgang-Hahn-Price, Cologne (2012), MoMA – Projects 94, New York (2011), Museum für Gegenwartskunst, Basel (2011), Malmö Konsthall, (2010), Portikus, Frankfurt (with Judith Hopf, 2007), and Migros Museum für Gegenwartskunst, Zurich (2007). Recent group exhibitions include those at La Ferme du Buisson, Noisiel (2015), Punta della Dogana, Venice (2015), Venice Biennale (2013), New Museum, New York (2012), Generali Foundation, Vienna (2012), Gwangju Biennale, South Korea (2010), and Berlin Biennale for Contemporary Art (2010).

Julien Prévieux, a Paris-based artist, intervenes with his works in the field of social practices by displaying forms of normalized behavior. He is the winner of the Marcel Duchamp Prize 2014. He has presented a number of solo exhibitions, among others at the Centre Georges Pompidou (2015–16), at the Fonds régional d'art contemporain (FRAC Basse-Normandie, 2012), and at Galerie Jousse entreprise in Paris. His participation in numerous group exhibitions include The Grand Duke Jean Museum of Modern Art (MUDAM, Luxembourg, 2015–16), Yerba Buena Center for the Arts, San Francisco (2015–16), Witte de With (2014), Musée d'art moderne de la Ville de Paris (2013), Museum of Contemporary Art, Santa Barbara, and at the Los Angeles Municipal Art Gallery (2012).

Jon Rafman is an artist living and working in Montréal. In 2015, he had a major solo exhibition at the Musée d'art contemporain de Montréal. He has previously had solo exhibitions at the Contemporary Art Museum, St. Louis (2014), Palais de Tokyo, Paris, and the Saatchi Gallery, London. His works have featured in numerous group exhibitions worldwide, and notably, in 2015, at the Biennale de Lyon and Moscow Biennial, as well as recent exhibitions examining the interface of digital culture and subjectivity at: Kunstverein Hannover; Kunsthalle Vienna; the Museum of Contemporary Art, North Miami; Museum of Modern Art, Warsaw; and Museum Fridericianum, Kassel.

Miljohn Ruperto, a Los Angeles-based artist, received his Master of Fine Arts from Yale University in 2002, and his Bachelor of Arts degree in Studio Art from the University of California, Berkeley, in 1999. Recent exhibitions featuring his work include: *Afterwork*, Para-Site, Hong Kong; *The As-if Principle*, Magazin4, Bregenzer Kunstverein, Austria; Whitney Biennial, Whitney Museum of American Art, New York; *Janus*, Dunlop Art Gallery; Regina Public Library, Saskatchewan, Canada; *Ulrik Heltoft and Miljohn Ruperto, Voynich Botanical Studies*, Thomas Solomon Gallery, Los Angeles; *Made in L.A.*, the Hammer Museum, Los Angeles; and *Picture Industry (Goodbye to All That)*, organized by Walead Beshty, Regen Projects, Los Angeles.

RYBN.ORG is an extra-disciplinary artistic research platform, founded in 1999, and disseminated on several servers on the internet. RYBN.ORG operates through interactive and networked installations, digital/analogue visual cross-performances, and pervasive computing. Their work has been shown in numerous contemporary art exhibitions and media art festivals, such as Ars Electronica, Transmediale, ISEA International, Elektra, and Cellsbutton, and museums and institutions such as the Zentrum für Kunst und Medientechnologie (ZKM) Karlsruhe, Laboral Centro de Arte y Creación Industrial, Gijón, and Centre Georges Pompidou and La Gaîté Lyrique, Paris.

Dierk Schmidt is an artist and author based in Berlin. His paintings pursue questions of everyday politics and their historical origins by creating a series of images that explore a critical revision of painting. His work *The Division of the Earth* focuses on the relation of (colonial) international law, abstraction, and a recent case of restitution. Another work relates to the production of dyestuffs produced by the early chemical industry. He has taught at the Royal Danish Academy of Fine Arts Schools, Copenhagen.

Eyal Sivan is a documentary filmmaker, theoretician, and scholar. After working as a professional photographer in Tel Aviv, he left Israel in 1985 and settled in Paris. Known for his controversial films, Sivan has directed more than ten award-winning political documentaries including *Common State* (2012) and *The Specialist* (1999) and has produced many others. Besides worldwide theatrical releases and television broadcasts, Sivan's films are exhibited regularly at major art exhibitions. He publishes and lectures on the Israeli–Palestinian conflict, documentary filmmaking and ethics, political crimes and representation, the political use of memory, and genocide and representation.

Deborah Stratman makes work that investigates power, control, and belief, considering how places, ideas, and society intertwine. Recent projects have addressed freedom, surveillance, sinkholes, comets, exodus, and faith. She is based in Chicago where she teaches at the University of Illinois at Urbana-Champaign.

Alex Verhaest lives and works in Brussels. During the year spent studying for her Masters of Fine Arts, Verhaest traveled to China where she discovered the Asian-hacker subculture. After a six-month residency at the island6 Arts Center, Shanghai, she joined the former artist collective Platform for Urban Investigations. In

2009, she decided to focus more on her own practice and left the collective, which resulted in participation in several group exhibitions. Her debut solo show *Temps Mort / Idle Times* opened at the Grimm Gallery, Amsterdam (2003). Verhaest recently won the prestigious Japanese Media Arts New Face Award and the Golden Nica at Prix Ars Electronica. She is currently represented by Dauwens & Beernaert Gallery in Brussels.

Stephen Willats has situated his pioneering work—from the 1960s to the present day—at the intersection between art and disciplines such as cybernetics, systems research, learning theory, communications theory, and computer technology, developing an interactive practice grounded in the variables of social relationships and settings. He has recently staged solo exhibitions at venues including Museo Tamayo Arte Contemporáneo, Mexico City (2014–15); the Whitechapel Gallery and Raven Row (both London, 2014); Modern Art Oxford (2013); and the South London Gallery (2012). In the 1960s, Willats founded the magazine *Control*, which is still in publication.

# THE EDITORS

Anselm Franke is the head of the Visual Arts department at the Haus der Kulturen der Welt in Berlin, where he was part of the curatorial team of the *Anthropocene Project* and organized exhibitions such as *Animism* (2012); co-curated with Diedrich Diederichsen *The Whole Earth* (2013); with Eyal Weizman *Forensis* (2014); and with Hila Peleg *Ape Culture* (2015). He was chief curator of the Taipei Biennale 2012 and the Shanghai Biennale 2014. He completed his PhD at Goldsmiths, University of London in 2015.

Stephanie Hankey has worked worldwide to bring together design and technology with activism for the past twenty years. She is the executive director of the Tactical Technology Collective, an organization she co-founded in 2003, and the co-director of the politically focused creative agency Tactical Studios. Hankey has a Masters from the Royal College of Art in London and she was awarded an Ashoka Fellowship in 2013 for her work as a social entrepreneur.

Marek Tuszynski is a producer, filmmaker, technology designer, and social interventionist. He co-founded Tactical Technology Collective in 2003 and co-directs Tactical Studios.

# THE CONTRIBUTORS

Grégoire Chamayou is a research scholar in philosophy at the Centre national de la recherche scientifique (CNRS – ENS Lyon). He is the author of *A Theory of the Drone (The New Press, 2015 / Ferngesteuerte Gewalt Eine Theorie der Drohne, Passagen Verlag, Vienna, 2014)* and *Manhunts: A Philosophical History* (Princeton University Press, 2012).

Maya Indira Ganesh is the director of applied research at Tactical Tech. She has spent more than ten years working with and writing about media and digital technologies. Maya Indira Ganesh has also worked with feminist and queer movements and organizations, and has published widely on these topics. She holds two Masters degrees and is a PhD candidate at Leuphana Universität Lüneburg, looking at ethics, machine learning, and shared autonomy between humans and machines.

Avery F. Gordon is a professor of Sociology at the University of California, Santa Barbara, and a visiting professor in the Department of Law at Birkbeck, University of London (2015–18). She is the author of *Keeping Good Time: Reflections on Knowledge, Power and People* (Paradigm, 2004) and *Ghostly Matters: Haunting and the Sociological Imagination* (University of Minnesota Press, 2nd ed., 2008) among others. She serves on the editorial committee of the journal *Race & Class*, and is the co-host of *No Alibis*, a weekly public affairs radio program on KCSB FM Santa Barbara.

Orit Halpern is an associate professor in Interactive Design and Theory in the Department of Sociology and Anthropology at Concordia University, Montréal. Her work bridges the histories of science, computing, and cybernetics with design and art practice. Her most recent book *Beautiful Data: A History of Vision and Reason since 1945* (Duke Press, 2015) is a genealogy of interactivity and our contemporary obsessions with "big" data and data visualization.

Ben Hayes worked with the London-based civil liberties organization Statewatch (1996–2014). His work includes groundbreaking research into the proliferation and impact of terrorist "blacklists" (e.g. on human rights and conflict resolution) and the impact of counter-terrorism laws on charities, development, and "civil society" organizations. He is a fellow of the Transnational Institute, an Amsterdam-based "think tank" comprised of "scholar activists," an associate of the Human Security Collective in The Hague, and a researcher at the Peace Research Institute, Oslo.

Tung-Hui Hu studied at Princeton University, Michigan, and obtained his PhD at Berkeley, California. He is the author of *A Prehistory of the Cloud* (MIT Press, 2015) and three books of poetry all published by University of Georgia Press: *The Book of Motion* (2003); *Mine* (2007); *Greenhouses, Lighthouses* (2013). He has received awards from the National Endowment for the Arts, Yaddo, MacDowell Colony, Peterborough, New Hampshire, and the San Francisco Foundation, among others. He is an assistant professor of English at the University of Michigan.

Lawrence Liang is a lawyer and independent researcher based in Bangalore. A co-founder of Alternative Law Forum, a collective of lawyers, Liang works on the intersection of law, culture, and technology. In addition, he is involved with a number of other organizations such as Sarai (New Delhi). Along with Camp and 0xDB, he has initiated numerous other web resources including Pad.ma, indiancine.ma, and OML. Liang has published widely on intellectual property, law and cinema, and freedom of speech and expression, and contributes regularly to the journal *e-flux*.

Noortje Marres is an associate professor at the Centre for Interdisciplinary Methodologies (CIM) at the University of Warwick, Coventry, England. She studied Science, Technology and Society at the University of Amsterdam and at École des Mines, Paris, and much of her research focuses on problems of participation in technological societies. Her first book, *Material Participation* (Palgrave Macmillan, 2012) came out in paperback in 2015, and she is currently completing a second on Digital Sociology (Polity).

Matteo Pasquinelli is a philosopher and an assistant professor in Media Studies at the Pratt Institute, New York. He wrote the book *Animal Spirits: A Bestiary of the Commons* (NAi, 2008) and edited the anthology *Alleys of Your Mind: Augmented Intelligence and Its Traumas* (Meson, 2015) among others. With Wietske Mass, he co-authored *The Manifesto of Urban Cannibalism* (2012).

Nishant Shah is the co-founder and former director of the research and policy think tank Centre for Internet and Society, Bangalore, India. He is a professor at the Institute of Culture and Aesthetics of Digital Media at Leuphana Universität Lüneburg where he is also academic director of the Digital School, as well as a knowledge partner with HIVOS, producing frameworks for understanding changes in practices in the future. His interests lie at the intersections of technology, identity, activism, and social justice.

Mushon Zer-Aviv is a designer, educator, and a media activist based in Tel Aviv. His work and writing explore the boundaries of the interface and the biases of technoculture. Co-founder of the Shual.com design studio, Zer-Aviv is involved in multiple collaborations mixing media art, network-politics, government transparency, and civic engagement. He is an alumnus of Eyebeam in New York and a senior faculty member at Shenkar School of Engineering and Design, Tel Aviv.

## COVER

Mari Bastashevski
*Shreds Of Accountability*, 2014; detail
Courtesy the artist

## ARTWORKS

p. 30 Courtesy the artist and mor charpentier
Photos Kunst Halle Sankt Gallen,
© Stefan Jäggi
p. 34 Courtesy Electronic Arts Intermix (EAI)
p. 36 Courtesy the artist
p. 40 Courtesy the artist
p. 42 Courtesy the artist
p. 46 Courtesy the artist
p. 50 Production: IRREVERENCE FILMS
Courtesy the artists
p. 52 Courtesy Stanford University, Department of Computer Science Films (F0110). Department of Special Collections and University Archives, Stanford University Libraries, Stanford California
p. 56 Courtesy Harun Farocki Filmproduktion
p. 60 "Numbers and Trees V, Landscape, #3", 1989, Courtesy the artist and Susanne Vielmetter. Los Angeles Projects
Photo: Robert Wedemeyer
p. 62-3 Courtesy the artist and Susanne Vielmetter. Los Angeles Projects
p. 64 Courtesy the artist and Galerie Max Mayer
p. 68 Courtesy the artists
p. 72 Courtesy the artist and Galerie Perrotin
© Laurent Grasso / ADAGP, Paris, 2016
p. 76 Printed Matter Inc., New York
© 2016, Estate of Douglas Huebler / Artists Rights Society (ARS), New York / VG Bild-Kunst, Bonn
Image courtesy the Museum of Modern Art, New York, and Paula Cooper Gallery; Courtesy Central Library Technische Universität, Berlin
p. 78 Private Collection, Courtesy Campagne Première
p. 80 Courtesy Galerie Meyer Riegger
p. 84 Courtesy !Mediengruppe Bitnik
Photos: Laura Fiorio
p. 88 Courtesy Galerie Buchholz
p. 92 Courtesy Galerie Jousse Enterprise
p. 96 Courtesy the artist and Future Gallery
Additional support by the Haus der Kulturen der Welt
p. 100 Courtesy the artist and Koenig & Clinton; Photo: Miljohn Ruperto
p. 104 Courtesy RYBN.ORG in co-production with ZKM Zentrum für Kunst und Medientechnologie
Vitrine Design: Stadelmann Schmutz Wössner Architekten, Berlin
Photos: MissXmx and Anatole Serexhe, © RYBN.ORG
p. 106 © VG Bild-Kunst, Bonn; Courtesy KOW, Berlin
p. 110 Courtesy zero one film
p. 114 Schwabe & Co. Verlag, Basel
p. 116 Courtesy the artist
p. 120 Courtesy Dauwens & Beernaert Gallery
p. 124 Courtesy the artist and Victoria Miro
© Stephen Willats

## INSTALLATION SHOTS

Photos: Laura Fiorio

## TRIANGULATIONS

Grégoire Chamayou

p. 198 Courtesy Collège de France – Archives
p. 198 (below) Courtesy The Perlinger Archive
p. 200 (above)
Courtesy Fondation National de Sciences Politiques
Copyright Presses Universitaires de France
p. 202 (below)
Copyright McGill University, Canada

Avery F. Gordon

p. 209 Courtesy Photograph by Waldon Fawcett, Library of Congress, Prints & Photographs Division [Repro. No.] LC-USZ62-45687
p. 211 Courtesy LSE Library Collections, BOOTH/E/1/1–12
p. 213–4
Courtesy University of Pennsylvania Press
p. 217 Courtesy Charité–Universitätsmedizin Berlin, Institute for the History of Medicine and Ethics in Medicine
p. 220 (below)
Courtesy Library of Congress, Prints & Photographs Division [Repro. No.] LC-DIG-ggbain-09570

Orit Halpern

p. 224 (below) Copyright The Free Press, a Division of Simon & Schuster, Inc.
p. 226 With permission of Springer
p. 233 Copyright SCALA, Florence
p. 234 Courtesy of The Jewish Museum, New York
p. 236 Copyright Defense Advanced Research Agency, Principal Investigator Nichols Negroponte, Project Director Andrew Lippman

Ben Hayes

p. 249 Courtesy Ben Hayes
p. 250 (below)
Courtesy Paul-Emile Dupret

Tung-Hui Hu

p. 253–6
Courtesy The Trustees of the Mass Observation Archive, University of Sussex
Reproduced with permission of Curtis Brown Group Ltd, London, on behalf of The Trustees of the Mass Observation Archive
p.258 Courtesy Jon Healy, Co-Founder of Techno-Patriots

Lawrence Liang

p. 262 Copyright DC Comics
p. 263 Courtesy Moulton Marston and The Dibner Library

p. 264 Copyright New Delhi Television
p. 265 Courtesy Laboratory of Neuro Imaging and the Athinoula A. Martinos Center for Biomedical Imaging, Consortium of the Human Connectome Project

Noortje Marres

p. 271 Photo: Laura Fiorio
p. 273 Courtesy Museum für Naturkunde – Leibniz-Institut für Evolutions- und Biodiversitätsforschung
Photos: Laura Fiorio
p. 275 Courtesy Felix Domke
Photo: Laura Fiorio

Matteo Pasquinelli

p. 279 (above) Courtesy Gottfried Wilhelm Leibniz Bibliothek–Niedersächsische Landesbibliothek: F-A 125, Ausschnitt, Titelblatt
(below) Courtesy Records of the Electronic Computer Project. From the Shelby White and Leon Levy Archives Center, Institute for Advanced Study, Princeton, NJ, USA.
p. 280 Courtesy University of California Libraries

Nishant Shah

p. 297–8
Courtesy The Western Electric Company Hawthorne Studies Collection, Baker Library
p. 300 Copyright Invisible Industries https://invisibleboyfriend.com/
p. 303 Copyright Unique Identification Authority of India (UIDAI)

Mushon Zer-Aviv

p. 307 Courtesy Deutsches Schiffahrtsmuseum, Leibniz-Institut für deutsche Schifffahrtsgeschichte Inventory No. I/03365/85N
Photo: Laura Fiorio
p. 308 Copyright Bonnier Coperation, USA
p. 311 Creative Commons 2.5 Attribution / Share-Alike http://www.ladyada.net/make/wavebubble

# THE WHITE ROOM

*The White Room* is a live installation space by Tactical Tech, which has a *Bar* with workers who interact with visitors to the exhibition. Through workshops, demos and hands-on sessions, *Bar* workers introduce visitors to what lies behind the screens of *The White Room*.

p. 315 Compuserve in *OMNI* magazine, August 1982
p. 318 Photo: Andrea Figari
p. 325 Photo: Andrea Figari
p. 326 (above) Tactical Technology Collective, 2016
(below) M.C. McGrath, 2015
p. 327 (above) Tactical Technology Collective, 2015
(below) Open Data City, 2014
p. 328 Malte Spitz, 2011
p. 329 (above) Share Lab, 2015
(below) Richard Vijgen, 2015
p. 330 (above) James Bridle, 2015
(below) Open Data City, 2013
p. 331 Eric King and Matthew Rice, 2013
Photos: Andrea Figari
p. 332–3
Alan Rusbridger, 2014
p. 342 Tega Brain and Surya Mattu, 2015
p. 343 Veridiana Zurita, 2010
p. 344–5
Peng! Collective, 2014
p. 346 Sascha Pohflepp, 2006
p. 347 Julian Oliver and Danja Vasiliev, 2011
p. 348 Aram Bartholl, 2013
Photos: Andrea Figari
p. 349 Jacob Appelbaum and Ai Weiwei, 2015
Photo: Andrea Figari
p. 358 Design: Industrial Design Group Intec, Chile,1973; Copyright: Gui Bonsiepe
p. 359 Paradigm Initiative Nigeria, 2013–14
p. 360 (above) Sesame Credit, Online account user, 2016
(below) Jordan: Iris scanning in action, screenshot from United Nations High Commissioner for Refugees (UNHCR), promotional video online
p. 370 Vooza, 2012
Photo: Andrea Figari
p. 370 Photo: Stephanie Hankey, 2015
p. 371–3
The Tactical Technology Collective in collaboration with La Loma, 2016
Photo: La Loma
p. 374–5
The Tactical Technology Collective in collaboration with La Loma, 2016
Photos: Andrea Figari

## EXHIBITION

This book was published in association with the exhibition *Nervous Systems: Quantified Life and the Social Question* held from March 11 to May 9, 2016 at the Haus der Kulturen der Welt.

Curators
Anselm Franke, Stephanie Hankey, Marek Tuszynski

Exhibition architecture
Kris Kimpe

Graphic design
Joris & Terry Kritis

Project and research coordination
Eylem Sengezer
Production coordination
Elsa de Seynes
Trainee
Adrian Waschmann
Internship
Pujan Karambeigi, Dominik Mayer, Johanna Nuber, Alma Seiberth, Brandon O. Scott

## TACTICAL TECHNOLOGY COLLECTIVE

White Room concept and research
Stephanie Hankey, Marek Tuszynski

White Room producer and co-initiator
Diana McCarty
White Room design
Malgorzata Gurowska
White Room production
Sophie Macpherson
Animations and films
Klaas Diersmann, Leil-Zahra Mortada
"Normal is Boring" table co-production
La Loma

Research and development
Maya Indira Ganesh, Fieke Jansen
Research support
Jeff Deutch,Lisa Gutermuth, Gabi Sobliye, Maria Xynou
Technology and website
Alistair Alexander, Christo Buschek, Niko Para, Allan Stanley
Communication and website
Caroline Kent, Helen Kilbey
Production support
Daniela O'Halloran, Caroline Kent, Franziska Kursawe
Events
Andrea Figari, Ling Luther
*The White Room* sessions
Claudio Agosti, Evelyne Austin, Crille, Dan Ó Clunaigh, Clara Friedrich, Maya Indira Ganesh, Lisa Gutermuth, Alex Hache, Fieke Jansen, Hadi Al Khatib, Helen Kilbey, Franziska Kursawe, Ling Luther, Leil-Zahra Mortada, Vanessa Rizk, Hannah Smith, Gabi Sobliye, Bobby Soriano, Ulrich Schlenker, Kaustubh Srikanth, Maria Xynou

And support from all the Tactical Tech Team members who have not been named above.

## HAUS DER KULTUREN DER WELT

Director
Bernd Scherer

Visual Arts and Film department
Head
Anselm Franke
Program coordination
Sonja Oehler
Program assistance
Janina Prossek
Processing
Franziska Janetzky, Cornelia Pilgram

Technical department
Technical director
Mathias Helfer
General coordination exhibition set-up
Gernot Ernst & Team
Architectonic coordination
Paul Beaury, museeon GbR
Video-editing
Matthias Hardenberger, Isabelle Lonitz, Nurio Takasugi
Building facilities
Frank Jahn, Benjamin Brandt & Team

Communications and Educational department
Head
Silvia Fehrmann
Editorial office
Franziska Wegener, Laida Hadel
Press office
Anne Maier, Nabila El-Khatib
Internet
Eva Stein, Jan Koehler, Fabian Hartjes, Laura Mühlbauer
Public relations and marketing
Christiane Sonntag, Sabine Westemeier
Education program
Maria Fountoukis, Leila Haghighat, Eva Stein

# COLOPHON

Editors
Anselm Franke, Stephanie Hankey, Marek Tuszynski

Managing Editors
Martin Hager, Eylem Sengezer

Text on Artworks
Michael Baers, Anselm Franke, Stephanie Hankey, Marek Tuszynski

Translation of Preface
Colin Shepherd

Copy-editing
Mandi Gomez

Graphic Design
Joris & Terry Kritis

Image editing
Ruksaldruck GmbH + Co. KG Repro plus Offset

Typeface
Bitstream Futura Book & Medium
Paper
Munken Pure, Arctic Volume, Sirio Color Celeste, Munken Polar

Printing and Binding
Ruksaldruck GmbH + Co. KG Repro plus Offset

First edition
Printed in Germany

ISBN 978-3-95905-093-7



Published by
Spector Books
Harkortstraße 10
04107 Leipzig
www.spectorbooks.com

Distribution
Germany, Austria: GVA, Gemeinsame Verlagsauslieferung Göttingen GmbH&Co. KG
www.gva-verlage.de
Switzerland: AVA Verlagsauslieferung AG, www.ava.ch
France, Belgium: Interart Paris, www.interart.fr
UK: Central Books Ltd, www.centralbooks.com
USA, Canada: RAM Publications + Distribution Inc., www.rampub.com
Australia, New Zealand: Perimeter Distribution, www.perimeterdistribution.com
Other Countries: Motto Distribution, www.mottodistribution.com

Haus der Kulturen der Welt
John-Foster-Dulles-Allee 10
10557 Berlin
www.hkw.de

An exhibition by the Haus der Kulturen der Welt in collaboration with the Tactical Technology Collective. *Nervous Systems* takes place as part of "100 Years of Now."

HKW Haus der Kulturen der Welt

TACTICAL TECHNOLOGY COLLECTIVE

Supported by
Open Society Foundations, Omidyar Network, and Pro Helvetia, Swiss Arts Council

Haus der Kulturen der Welt is a division of Kulturveranstaltungen des Bundes in Berlin GmbH (KBB).



Haus der Kulturen der Welt is funded by

Federal Government Commissioner for Culture and the Media

Federal Foreign Office

# THANK YOU

*Nervous Systems* has been made possible thanks to the support and generosity of many individuals and organizations. The Haus der Kulturen der Welt and Tactical Technology Collective would like to thank all participating artists, authors, and lenders who contributed to the *Grid, The White Room,* the Triangulations and this publication as well as our funders and supporters.